The Biker Trials

The Biker Trials

Bringing Down
the Hells Angels

PAUL CHERRY

ECW Press

Published by ECW PRESS
2120 Queen Street East, Suite 200, Toronto, Ontario, Canada M4E 1E2

LIBRARY AND ARCHIVES CANADA CATALOGUING IN PUBLICATION

Cherry, Paul, 1968–
The biker trials : bringing down the Hell Angels / Paul Cherry.

ISBN-13 : 978-1-55022-638-6
ISBN-10 : 1-55022-638-X

1. Hell's Angels. 2. Trials (Narcotic laws) — Québec (Province) — Montréal.
3. Drug traffic — Québec (Province). 4. Motorcycle gangs — Québec (Province).
5. Organized crime — Québec (Province). I. Title.

HV6491.C32Q4 2005A   345.71'0277'0971428   C2005-904372-5

Editor: Emily Schultz
Production: Mary Bowness
Cover Photo: Photonica
Printing: Transcontinental

This book is set in Minion and Scratch

With the publication of *The Biker Trials* ECW PRESS acknowledges the generous financial support of
the Government of Canada through the Book Publishing Industry Development Program (BPIDP),
the Canada Council for the Arts, and the Ontario Arts Council, for our publishing activities.

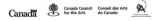

DISTRIBUTION

CANADA: Jaguar Book Group, 100 Armstrong Ave., Georgetown, ON L7G 5S4
UNITED STATES: Independent Publishers Group, 814 North Franklin Street,
Chicago, IL, USA 60610

PRINTED AND BOUND IN CANADA

ECW PRESS
ecwpress.com

To S and C

Table of Contents

Acknowledgements ix

Introduction 1

1   The Peak 23

2   Mom 47

3   Arrests en Masse 101

4   The Hits 117

5   An Ocean of Cash 140

6   Santa Claus aka Gerald Matticks 169

7   Project Rush: Guilty Pleas and Surprises 188

8 Stéphane Sirois: A Man Inside 211

9 Stéphane Gagné: Trigger Man 232

10 Serge Boutin: Nowhere to Go But Out 283

11 The Colombian Connection 312

12 The View From the Other Side 329

13 A Jury Decides 356

Conclusion 382

Cast of Characters 389

Acknowledgements

Seeing as how this book is about crime and the courts it is fitting that this begin with a confession. I was not able to attend all of the court procedures covered in this book. The three main trials mentioned in this book stretched out over a period of months and in one case more than a year, all while I covered crime on a daily basis for *The Gazette*. Writing about some key parts required a thorough listening of digital recordings after the hearings took place.

Keeping informed of what was significant and interesting would not have been possible without help from several people, including the journalists who followed the trials on a daily basis like Isabelle Richer of Radio Canada, Marc Pigeon of the *Journal de Montréal*, Charles André Marchand and especially André Cédilot of *La Presse* who, along with Michel Auger of the *Journal de Montréal*, gave much support through their encouragement.

Writing this also would never have been possible without the support of author Lee Lamothe. Antonio Nicaso, author of several books on organized crime, also lent support through his advice.

I also want to thank everyone at ECW Press who helped, especially Jack David, David Caron, Mary Bowness, Crissy Boylan, Emily Schultz and Emma McKay.

It goes without saying that writing a book requires time and I wouldn't have had that valuable commodity without Ross Teague and George Kalogerakis, the current and former city editors at *The Gazette*, who both juggled complicated schedules while allowing me to dedicate time towards this book.

The other valuable commodity that was always in supply while writing this was advice and information and for this I would like to thank Guy Ouellette, a retired Sûreté de Québec sergeant and the province's foremost expert on biker gangs, Gary Francoeur, Rita Legault of the *Sherbrooke Record*, Peter Edwards of the *Toronto Star* and Adrian Humphries at the *National Post*.

Researching this material required the patient help of many clerks at courthouses across Quebec.

There are several other people I would like to thank including several friends and family members who would rather not see their names appear in such a book.

Most disputes over criminal matters like drug turf appear nebulous to the average, law-abiding citizen. "Who were the people behind this explosion?" or "What could have motivated someone to gun down that young man on my street?" are questions often left hanging as two criminal organizations battle it out in a metropolitan area like Montreal. It took a while, but eventually the war between the Hells Angels and a group of criminal organizations called the Alliance, which started in 1994, held little mystery for the average person.

Not Garbagemen

By August 1995, after a series of explosions and murders, and in particular the death of an innocent boy, many people in Quebec were aware of what the war was about and who the two sides were. Unlike most shadowy criminal organizations the Hells Angels and a rival gang called the Rock Machine advertised who they were with patches on the backs of their leather jackets. Like politicians or corporations eager to generate name recognition, both sides handed out T-shirts and baseball caps to drug dealers who sided with them.

Operation Springtime 2001 signaled the beginning of the end of what came to be known as the biker gang war. On March 28, 2001, more than 2,000 police officers across Quebec were dispatched to carry out more than 130 arrest warrants and seize gang assets, including 20 buildings, 70 firearms and $8.6 million Canadian and $2.7 million U.S.

The massive police roundup was the result of two police

investigations, "Project Rush" and "Project Ocean." Project Rush was put together using what was, at that point, recently adopted federal anti-gang legislation. Investigators and prosecutors built a case geared toward charging gang members with the murder of their rivals, even if they had a limited role the gang's affairs.

The primary target of Project Rush was the Hells Angels whose members were the leaders in the war. The lengthy police investigation involved years of gathering evidence like wiretaps, countless hours of police surveillance and working informants. It began in 1998 with the police zeroing in on people who were members of the Montreal-based organization and its underling gang, the Rockers. For the latter part of the investigation the officers involved were part of Regional Integrated Squad, which grouped together Montreal-area investigators from the RCMP, La Sûreté du Québec and the Montreal Urban Community police. The squad was based on an earlier model called the Wolverine Squad, an elite investigation unit focusing on the biker gang war.

Project Rush spawned another investigation, Project Ocean, during which the police learned how incredibly organized the Hells Angels had become. It was through Project Ocean that police discovered how the gang managed its drug money. Though Project Ocean was an almost accidental offshoot of Project Rush, it produced evidence that led to the arrests of more Hells Angels than any other police operation in Canada in more than a decade.

The end result of these investigations was dubbed "Operation Springtime 2001." It created a brief void in Montreal's drug trade that year. But the gangsters who were part of the battered and bruised Alliance would regroup and join the Bandidos, an international biker gang similar to the Hells Angels. Sporting new patches, the Bandidos would mount an effort to take over the drug turf abandoned by the jailed Hells Angels. These efforts would be short-lived since anyone in Quebec associated with the Bandidos was arrested on June 1, 2002, in "Operation Amigo." This police investigation produced 62 arrest warrants and resulted in charges of drug trafficking and conspiracy to commit murder.

While most Quebecers knew what the biker war was all about, the details that spilled out in the subsequent trials from Project Rush and Project Ocean would raise eyebrows as they revealed just how much money was involved and how fully the Hells Angels assumed they were immune to prosecution. The tough question to answer is how did it all get started, what chain of events could have precipitated a conflict that would end up taking more than 160 lives, including those of several innocent victims? To that end, this book benefits from the notes on a person who was there when it began. More specifically, they are the notes of Dany Kane's handlers in the Royal Canadian Mounted Police. The RCMP began to use Kane as a window into a world to which the police had very little access when the conflict between drug dealers erupted in 1994.

Predictably, Kane's reports to his police handlers clearly included self-serving lies. For example, he tried to pin a murder he himself had committed on someone else through the "tips" he was supplying to the police in 1995. Though they later realized his duplicity, the police were still willing to use Kane as a way to infiltrate the Hells Angels. If one can accept Kane as a partially reliable narrator of the start of the biker war — and there is corroborating evidence to indicate that he was — then his dispatches serve as the most accurate version of what was going on with the Hells Angels in Montreal in 1994.

Kane also offered insight into the men who were assembling the Nomads chapter with two goals in mind: to win the war against the Alliance and to expand "business" into those areas of Canada not already dominated by other Hells Angels.

Needing help with this westward expansion the Nomads

chapter was interested in using Kane. That is what the Hells Angels were preparing him for when he first contacted the Interpol office in Ottawa during the autumn of 1994. He asked to speak to someone knowledgeable about biker gangs. He was put in contact with RCMP Sgt. Jean-Pierre Lévesque, an analyst for Criminal Intelligence Service Canada (CISC). As part of the Ottawa-based bureau, Lévesque was sent intelligence reports on biker gangs collected by police forces in cities and towns across Canada. Lévesque seized the opportunity and set up a meeting with Kane. He then contacted Corporal Pierre Verdon, an RCMP investigator in Montreal.

At that point, Kane had had about seven years' experience as a criminal working inside and outside the biker gang world. He had been a member of a gang called the Concordes, based in Saint-Hubert, a town in Montreal's South Shore region. The Concordes was later fused into a Hells Angels' underling gang called the Evil Ones, also based in the South Shore.

Instead of becoming part of the Hells Angels' growing criminal enterprise, Kane decided to go out on his own, concentrating on his own activities, like drug trafficking, contraband cigarettes and weapons. He kept good ties with the Evil Ones but began to notice that without gang ties, he lacked influence. During the summer of 1993, he accepted an offer from two members of the Hells Angels' Montreal chapter to preside over a new affiliated gang in Ontario. The project didn't go well and Kane ended up behind bars, later blaming the debacle on "the imbeciles" he was asked to work with. But when he was released, he had no trouble making contact with the Hells Angels again.

Kane told Lévesque and Verdon that he was willing to work with the RCMP for a long time. His ultimate goal was to become a member of the Hells Angels, which he estimated would take between three to five years, while supplying the police with information. In Verdon's notes from the first meeting, the only motive mentioned was that Kane expected to be paid well for his information. Lévesque and Verdon knew that having someone like Kane working for the police was a once-in-a-lifetime opportunity, and they decided he should be kept as a paid informant. Kane was code-named "C2994" to protect his identity.

On November 4, 1994, Kane made his first mention of Maurice (Mom) Boucher. He had serious concerns about working for the police and betraying such a powerful head of a criminal organization. Verdon noted the concern at the end of 20 pages of notes generated from that November meeting. He wrote: "The source is worried about the possibility of leaks coming from our department. The source is worried about the fact that a police officer who makes $55,000 per year can be bought by the other side. According to the source, a member of the Hells Angels, like Maurice (Mom) Boucher, one of the richest and most influential of the group, is ready to pay double a police officer's salary for those who provide them with information."

At that point, Boucher was far from being the household name in Quebec he would eventually become. But any police detective involved in organized crime in the province knew his name. By 1994, he was an elusive figure to some frustrated investigators. He appeared to be involved in the Hells Angels' large-scale drug deals, but never in a way that generated enough evidence to implicate him in a major offense. As 1994 neared its end, Boucher, who was then 41 years old, had been head of the Hells Angels' Montreal chapter, which was actually based in Sorel, a city 60 kilometres northeast of Montreal. He had joined the Hells Angels seven years earlier.

The Montreal chapter was chartered on December 5, 1977, becoming the first Canadian chapter of the Hells Angels, joining several others already established in Australia, England and the U.S. at that point. The first chapter had been founded in San Bernardino, California, on March 17, 1948. Even before the Hells

Angels opened shop in Quebec, the province already had its share of biker violence thanks to gangs that plagued Montreal and smaller cities or towns. The Hells Angels in New York were friendly with a gang called the Popeyes in Montreal. The Popeyes had already garnered headlines in Quebec with their violence long before becoming Hells Angels. They were engaged in a bloody war with a gang called the Devil's Disciples. And about a year before they became Hells Angels, several members of the Popeyes were arrested in a small town northwest of Montreal after trashing a hotel and taking three women hostage inside. The Popeyes were friendly with similar Quebec-based biker gangs with names like the Missiles in the Saguenay region and the Sex Fox in Chibougamau (the gang actually used the Looney Toons' character Wile E. Coyote for its patch, instead of a fox). Originally, 17 members of the Popeyes were chosen to be part of the first Hells Angels' chapter in Canada and they later recruited members from other gangs.

One of the Popeyes who joined the Hells Angels was Yves (Le Boss) Buteau, an influential biker who maintained good ties with other gangs in the province. According to news reports after his death, Buteau was a charismatic man and a natural leader, traits that helped him spread the Hells Angels' dogma to other parts of Canada. Buteau would be killed in 1983 while he was the Hells Angels' Canadian national president. The shooter, a 22-year-old drug dealer named Gino Goudreau who had ties to a rival biker gang, went into hiding but was arrested months later. He said he had been dealing hashish in various Sorel parks and in a bar called Le Petit Bourg, the place where he shot Buteau and another biker named Guy Gilbert on September 8, 1983. He testified during a coroner's inquiry that the Hells Angels threatened him on several occasions in the four months before the murder.

Goudreau said he had been shooting pool in Le Petit Bourg when Buteau threatened him yet again and told him to leave the bar. As Goudreau exited the bar, three bikers followed him outside, confronting Goudreau as he and his girlfriend were preparing to leave on a motorcycle. Goudreau said Buteau threatened him again, saying it was his last night in Sorel as he unzipped his jacket and reached for a revolver tucked under the front of his belt to make his point. Like some cowboy in a Hollywood western, Goudreau claimed he merely beat Buteau to the draw. He pulled a revolver out of a storage box on his motorcycle and opened fire, shooting Buteau, who was the closest. Earlier that summer Goudreau had traded a large quantity of hashish for the gun with one of his customers. Buteau was struck four times, the bullets entering his heart, a lung and a major artery. Buteau and Gilbert were killed. Another Hells Angel was wounded in the shooting. Goudreau was charged with two counts of second-degree murder but was acquitted after claiming self-defense.

The day after Buteau's funeral, a young boy found a bomb, equipped with a remote control detonator, placed along the route where the funeral procession, made up of many bikers, had passed. As the police investigated the bomb, composed of dynamite and 50 pounds of nails and gravel, they theorized that it had been placed on the side of the road and camouflaged the night before the funeral. At the time of his death, Buteau was considered a key player in the plan to bring the Hells Angels' name and ideology to Quebec and then expand into other provinces in Canada.

Buteau was replaced by Michel (Sky) Langlois, another influential Hells Angel who helped the gang gain notoriety in the years to come. But by then, with the violent people he had selected to wear the Hells Angels' patch, Buteau had already laid the foundation for the gang's take-no-prisoners philosophy.

Luc Michaud was among the members of Missiles selected to join the Hells Angels. The Missiles were based in the Saguenay village of Saint-Gedeon, where they terrorized the 1,750 residents.

They openly trafficked in drugs, and used firearms for target practice in residential neighborhoods. During the late 1970s, Michaud ran a stripper agency for the Hells Angels before becoming a "full-patch" (or full-fledged) member in 1980. He would become part of the gang's second chapter in Quebec, based in Laval, an island city north of Montreal. But two years later, he asked to return to the Montreal chapter as he and other Hells Angels began to realize some members of the Laval chapter were unwilling to discipline themselves into a well-tuned, organized gang. Michaud would later be described as a zealot of the Hells Angels' doctrine and he was believed to be a driving force behind the March 24, 1985, slaughter of five members of the Laval chapter, dubbed the Lennoxville Purge. He was convicted on five counts of first-degree murder for his role in the murders and sentenced to life with no chance of parole until he had served 25 years.

In 1993, however, while he was serving his sentence, Michaud wanted nothing to do with the Hells Angels and was expelled from the gang. He was apparently a changed man. In 2001, he used section 745.6 of the Criminal Code, the judicial review provision, better known as Canada's "faint hope clause," to convince a jury that he deserved a break on his sentence and was given a chance at parole after having served 20 years. He described his role in the slaughter, saying he had merely pointed a firearm at one of the victims and told him not to move, just before the five Hells Angels were shot dead.

Michaud was released on day parole in May 2003 and impressed parole officials with his rehabilitation. He spent two years in a halfway house, being gradually reintegrated into free society and becoming a family man. He admitted to the National Parole Board that he had been morally blind to what the Hells Angels were doing when he was a member and that he joined them out of an immature need to belong to something, no matter how criminal. He was released on full parole in June 2005.

Among the five Hells Angels murdered in the Sherbrooke chapter's clubhouse in 1985 was Michel (Willie) Mayrand, a former member of the Marauders, a gang based in the Eastern Townships mining town of Asbestos. The Marauders was another of the smaller gangs the Hells Angels used to select its members from during their early years in Quebec. Mayrand's brother Richard joined the Hells Angels' Montreal chapter a year before his brother was murdered. After the slaughter, Richard Mayrand chose the gang over sibling loyalties and decided to stay with the Hells Angels. He even did time for refusing to talk at a coroner's inquest about what happened in Sherbrooke. He would later take on an important role in the Nomads chapter and be a key player in the Hells Angels' expansion into Ontario. He would also be among the people arrested in Operation Springtime 2001.

The Hells Angels' ability to purge five of their own members in such a violent way in 1985 brought them notoriety in Quebec and would influence future developments. The gang's Montreal chapter was left scattered after the purge as many of its members were rounded up as suspects or went into hiding. The chapter needed new blood, younger members who were willing to join an organization with a reputation for killing its own.

Boucher was made a member of the Montreal chapter in 1987, joining Walter (Nurget) Stadnick, who had earned his patch in 1982. Both men would play important roles in the gang's future, not only in Quebec but in the rest of Canada as well.

Stadnick had been a member of the Wild Ones, a gang based in Hamilton, before joining the Hells Angels. Like Boucher and most other members of the Nomads chapter, Stadnick grew up in a working-class neighborhood, but in his case it was in Ontario. Between 1971 and 1988, he had been convicted at least four times for crimes committed in Hamilton and Toronto. The longest sentence he had served was six months for a weapons offence. He eventually became the Hells Angels' national president, despite the fact he does not fit the profile of a typical biker gang member. He stands only 5 foot 4 inches tall and is thin. When appearing in court he is soft-spoken, polite and quick to smile. But he is also a survivor.

On September 8, 1984, the first anniversary of Yves Buteau's death, Stadnick and a group of about 20 other bikers were riding their motorcycles in a close formation along Highway 143 in Saint-Pie-de-Guire, a small town outside of Drummondville. Buteau was from Drummondville and had been buried in a cemetery there. Riding with Stadnick that day were other important members of the Hells Angels from both the Montreal chapter and what would become the Sherbrooke chapter. They were on their way to the cemetery to pay their respects. Denis Houle, a future member of the Nomads chapter was among the group, riding his red 1984 Harley. Michel (Sky) Langlois, who had just replaced Buteau as president of the Montreal chapter, was there too. Ronald Lauchlin MacDonald, the future president of the Halifax chapter, was also along for the ride.

At the same time, a 57-year-old priest driving his car down Rural Road 13 was heading to an event planned as part of the pope's visit to Quebec that year. The priest was apparently late. His car went through a stop sign and barreled into the Hells Angels and their motorcycles. The close formation the bikers were riding in caused a chain reaction as the priest's car plowed through them. Thirteen motorcycles were involved in the accident and four of them caught fire. A Hells Angels' prospect named Daniel Mathieu died shortly afterward in a Sherbrooke hospital. Stadnick was burned badly in the accident and ended up losing several fingers. He also suffered severe burns to his face that were still visible 20 years later.

In 1996, while Boucher was busy with the war in Montreal, Stadnick spent time traveling across Canada making and maintaining important contacts for the gang as it prepared to spread westward. Stéphane Sirois, a member of the Rockers, traveled that year with Stadnick to Winnipeg where the Hells Angels planned to set up a Rockers chapter whose members would sell drugs supplied from Montreal. Stadnick had no way of knowing Sirois would later leave the Hells Angels' organization on bad terms and agree to work for the police. Stadnick told Sirois that he already had drug dealers working for him in Manitoba so that setting up a puppet club in Winnipeg only made sense. It's hard to know how good business was in Manitoba, but four years earlier, a bag the police suspected was Stadnick's was seized at a Winnipeg airport. Inside it, they found $80,000. Stadnick was charged with possession of the proceeds of crime, but his criminal case ended with the Crown dropping the charges, possibly due to a lack of evidence. Sirois was also with Stadnick as they prepared to travel to Saskatchewan to visit members of the Rebels, a gang celebrating their anniversary. Stadnick talked of how his dream was to see the Hells Angels become the only biker gang in Canada. Two years later, the Rebels were made prospect members in the Hells Angels.

On July 21, 2000, another part of Stadnick's dream was fulfilled. The police in Winnipeg had been monitoring a clubhouse that belonged to a gang called Los Bravos. They were aware of what was about to happen. Every member of the gang was present that day and could be seen wearing their Los Bravos colors outside the clubhouse before they all walked inside. Stadnick arrived at the clubhouse carrying a large white bag that appeared to be full. Minutes after he walked in, the police could hear a loud cheer emerge from within. As they filed out of the clubhouse, the gangsters were sporting new patches on their backs revealing that they had become prospects in the Hells Angels.

The following day, the Winnipeg police spotted Stadnick in a local strip bar, partying with members of the Satan's Choice, a gang from Ontario, the next province on the Hells Angels' wish list. Although they resided in Ontario, Stadnick and fellow Hells Angel Donald (Pup) Stockford were frequently in Montreal during the biker gang war. The police initially assumed that they and David (Wolf) Carroll, the only other anglophone in the Nomads chapter, ultimately planned to set up their own chapter in Ontario.

Despite being ten years apart in age, Stadnick and Stockford appeared to be good friends according to underlings who would later turn informant. They were rarely seen apart when in Quebec. Sirois later testified that Stadnick and Stockford often slept at the Rockers' fortified bunker in Montreal on Gilford Street as a security measure during the biker war. The Ontario pair faithfully attended the Hells Angels' monthly meetings in Montreal even though they did not speak French. After they were arrested in Operation Springtime 2001, the Ontario pair asked for a separate trial in English. They asked that 500,000 documents the Crown had as evidence against the Hells Angels be translated into English, a process estimated to cost $23 million. Their request was turned down by a judge who said they would have to be content with a summary of the evidence in English.

The request was a further sign that, despite being longtime members of the Hells Angels in Quebec, neither Stadnick nor Stockford had made a serious effort to learn French. Wiretap evidence gathered during Project Rush revealed that the francophone members of the group had to switch to English when talking on the phone to Stadnick or Stockford. One informant, who would testify at their trial, said the pair required a translater, a Hells Angels' prospect, when he explained to them how to cut down the PCP he had supplied to them. Although they lived outside the boundaries of the biker war, Stadnick and Stockford were on high alert. In 1995, Kane told the RCMP that both men had complained of strange visits from people claiming to deliver pizzas they had not ordered. Kane also said Stadnick talked of nearly being abducted in Hamilton while he was out riding his Harley-

Davidson. Kane said Stadnick believed members of the Outlaws, a long-established Ontario gang, were behind the incident. He told Kane that a pickup truck pulled up beside him at a red light and someone tried to grab him. He managed to fight off the would-be abductor and sped off on his motorcycle. At the time, Stadnick was under investigation for what appeared to be preparations for a drug pipeline between Thunder Bay, Ontario, and Winnipeg, Manitoba.

As early as December of 1994, with the war only five months old, Kane was able to tell RCMP officer Verdon that it looked like Boucher was giving the orders behind the attacks on the Rock Machine, a gang partially composed of men Boucher had been friends with before. As well, the Hells Angels had put out an ultimatum to street-level drug dealers in Montreal's east end. They had to buy their drugs exclusively from the Hells Angels, or else.

Long before the war began, the Rock Machine was formed by Salvatore and Giovanni Cazzetta, brothers who had gained influence in Montreal's drug trafficking circles. That influence quickly made them targets for the police. But as the Cazzetta brothers would point out later, they were behind bars for almost the duration of the war.

Despite using the same hierarchy system as the Hells Angels, the Rock Machine was actually not a biker gang until it officially constituted itself as one in June 1999, as its members prepared to join with the Bandidos. But when the war started, the Rock Machine was just a part of a group of criminal organizations called the Alliance whose members refused to back down before the Hells Angels. Its members were issued rings with an A surrounded by a circle of diamonds. Because it resembled the Hells Angels in many ways, the Rock Machine was the most visible part of the Alliance. Like the Hells Angels, members of the Rock Machine wore leather jackets with patches on their backs proclaiming their identity. Dealers sympathetic to their side were

A newly minted member of the Hells Angels shows off his new colors after leaving the Hells Angels' bunker in Sorel, Quebec. The photo was taken by police monitoring a party where dozens of members of smaller biker gangs were "patched over" to become Hells Angels on December 29, 2000.

given Rock Machine paraphernalia like T-shirts and baseball caps.

The Rock Machine also adopted a hierarchy system similar to that which the Hells Angels had used internationally for years. This system served as a form of probationary period meant to weed out undesirables, especially potential informants. In this hierarchy, the official entry-level position is that of a "hang-around" and the probationary period normally lasts eight months. The second level is that of a "prospect," where the potential member is allowed to wear a bottom rocker, or the lowest-ranking emblem, on the back of his leather jacket identifying which chapter he is from. The "prospect" level generally lasts a year. Only those who graduate to being a full-fledged, or "full-patch," member can wear the Hells Angels' legally registered logo, a winged skull, nicknamed "the Death Head." Another introductory level is that of "friend." It is sometimes used by the Hells

Angels to label people who work for the gang but have no intention of joining them.

In fact, the Hells Angels used underling gangs to carry out their dirty work during the gang war. One of those groups, the Rockers, used a similar hierarchical system, but in their case, a "prospect" was called a "striker."

Another gang to join the Alliance was the Dark Circle, a group partially composed of successful drug traffickers who had managed to invest millions of their drug money in real estate and other legitimate businesses before the biker war started. The Dark Circle was supposed to be like silent partners in the Alliance, financing murders, arson and extortion. At the beginning of the war, the Dark Circle had roughly 18 members who, according to former members, decided by July 1994 that they were willing to wage war with the Hells Angels. Their plan was to hit the gang hard without making it obvious the Dark Circle was involved. Members would not wear leather jackets with patches on their backs. Instead, each member was issued a ring bearing the leg of an eagle and a diamond. The Dark Circle had no president, as other gangs did, but was run by an executive committee whose four members were considered to be intelligent, influential men in Quebec's underworld. Members of the Dark Circle actually had good relations with the Hells Angels' chapter in Sherbrooke prior to joining the Alliance, but they grew unwilling to tolerate Boucher and his ambitions to dominate Montreal's drug trade. Among the four was Michel Duclos, a former teacher, described as a cultivated and intelligent man, who had owned a bar for six years before the war started. He would later claim he joined the Dark Circle in the interests of protecting his business from the Hells Angels. While serving a sentence for attempted murder, Duclos apparently decided to quit his gang; he stopped associating with Alliance members as well while behind bars.

Another member of the Dark Circle's executive committee

was Salvatore Brunnetti, a man who would eventually defect to the Hells Angels after waging war with them for years. He was arrested in Operation Springtime 2001, despite being a member of the group for only a matter of months. The two other members of the committee survived the biker war, despite contracts on their lives for helping to finance plots to murder various Hells Angels. One of these men would tell the National Parole Board he had no interest in being released from his federal penitentiary because he feared for his life on the outside. The other broke the unwritten rule of the underworld and cooperated with the police in 1998 to help arrest two Hells Angels' associates who were planning to kill him.

Also under the umbrella of the Alliance was the Pelletier Clan, a gang led by brothers who had controlled drug trafficking in large parts of eastern Montreal until the Hells Angels gave them an ultimatum — to start selling drugs for them. When the Pelletier Clan's leader, Sylvain Pelletier, was killed in a bomb blast on October 28, 1994, most drug dealers in Montreal were left with no doubt that war had been declared in the streets, parks and bars where they sold drugs.

By January 1995, the RCMP was paying Kane $1,000 each time he met with them to deliver information. His reports became more detailed, particularly about Boucher's plans for the new Nomads chapter. Kane's reports at that point indicated there was a rift in the Hells Angels since some members of the Montreal chapter were not fully on board with Boucher's war with the Alliance. Kane learned that the Montreal chapter was closed to new members because some of its older members were not impressed with its most recent recruits. "Future members would have to prove themselves in a way that was very evident to be accepted," Verdon wrote after talking with Kane early in 1995.

On that same day, Kane said the new Nomads chapter would be ready to roll on June 24, 1995 — it turned out to be the day it was officially chartered. The term "Nomads" is used by the Hells Angels worldwide to identify special elite chapters whose members are not limited by territorial boundaries, as others are. Its membership was to be composed mostly of senior members of the Montreal chapter who were active in the war.

"According to the information received, the 'Nomads' will be more 'rock and roll' and take territory all over Canada. The leadership will be maintained by Maurice (Mom) Boucher and the Rockers will be their affiliates," Verdon wrote one day in what proved to be a very accurate description of what was to come. The note was followed by others that were equally accurate predictions:

• "That (Mom) Boucher said that the next members to join the H.A. Nomads would not be garbagemen."

• "That the Nomads will pick their future prospects from the Rockers."

With only one exception, this was indeed how Boucher would recruit members for the Nomads as the biker war dragged on.

René Charlebois and Normand Robitaille were among the first to become Hells Angels through this route. Charlebois and Robitaille began their careers in the Hells Angels' vast network as members of the Rockers, the gang Boucher himself created in 1992. It was a collection of drug dealers and "muscle" who moved cocaine and hashish for the Hells Angels in eastern Montreal. Before he joined the Rockers in April 1997, Charlebois was, according to one informant, a penniless criminal delivering drugs and contraband cigarettes out of a submarine sandwich restaurant in eastern Montreal. Previous to that, Charlebois' expertise appeared to be limited to credit card fraud. But he often got caught. Being in the Rockers, and later the Hells Angels, brought Charlebois status he had likely never dreamed of as an independent dealer, moving his product along with greasy sandwiches. While he was with the Rockers, he was estimated to be making $12,000 a month from drug trafficking. One informant also told the police that

Charlebois and two other Rockers were able to finance a $1.7 million drug deal with a dealer in British Columbia. Charlebois boasted of making a $45,000 profit on the deal; but on his 1996 taxes he only claimed $18,000.

Things appear to have got much better when he was made a Hells Angel in 2000. Charlebois was often seen driving a Cadillac Seville — which he rented through a numbered company. When his luxury home was raided during Operation Springtime 2001, the police found that the biker had acquired expensive tastes. They found bottles of expensive wines including a bottle of 1989 Château Haut-Brion, worth an estimated $1,325, and a 1990 Château Lafite. Charlebois also had more than $7,000 in cash lying around as well as five $1,000 gambling chips from the Casino de Montréal. While he was a Hells Angel, Charlebois had a bodyguard from the Rockers constantly by his side, even when he tended to his legitimate businesses, which included a car wash. Charlebois' lavish wedding on August 5, 2000, caused controversy across Quebec after photos were published in the crime tabloid *Allô Police*. Singers Ginette Reno and Jean-Pierre Ferland had been hired to perform at the reception.

A few months before the wedding, the police listened in on a phone conversation as Charlebois reserved 14 rooms at a motel for his wedding guests, telling the clerk taking the reservations that he was a Hells Angel and they should be expecting several Hells Angels to arrive the weekend of the wedding.

Dany Kane had been invited to the wedding as well. Just two years earlier, Kane had managed to walk out of a Nova Scotia court after a judge declared a mistrial in the murder case against him. While he was still awaiting that trial, the RCMP had to drop him as their informant, though he had worked for them from 1994 to 1997, collecting a total of $250,000. The Hells Angels had begun to suspect that he was a police snitch. But somehow, Kane managed to regain the trust of both the police and the bikers.

René Charlebois (standing to the right of the man wearing the Hells Angels' patch) admires his wedding gift from his fellow bikers, a Harley-Davidson.

On August 23, 1999, Kane was approached by Benôit Roberge, a detective with the Montreal Urban Community police and a member of the Regional Integrated Squad. Roberge had worked intelligence since 1990, specifically focusing on biker gangs. Within a matter of months, Kane would sign on as an *agent source*, a French term that meant Kane was more than just a paid tipster — he was now under contract with the Sûreté du Québec, expected to detail everything he did with the Hells Angels and testify about it in court. He and Roberge would communicate a few times a week and meet in person once a week.

The Rockers, for their part, had also welcomed him back into their fold, giving Kane access to people like Boucher. It also gave the police an opportunity they had never had before. Up until then, deciphering where the Rockers might hold their secret monthly meetings had been impossible. The gang had developed clever tricks to avoid being monitored. One was to carry the business cards of restaurants or hotels on them. Each business card was marked with a number. The day before a meeting, referred to as "church" or "Mass" (*messe* in French), someone in the gang would page each member with a coded message that gave the time and date of the meeting. The location would only appear as a number, so even if the police could intercept the page, they could not decipher the location. But with Kane working undercover for them, the police were given several hours advance notice of where and when meetings would be held. Armed with the information the anti–biker gang squad were able to videotape Rockers' meetings held in hotel conference rooms in and around Montreal.

To help protect his "cover," the police agreed to supply Kane with money. That included giving him $1,000 so he could bring a gift to Charlebois' wedding. Days after the wedding, Kane's body was found in his home in St-Luc along with a confusing suicide note, full of questions concerning morality, his sexual identity and the conflict inherent in being both a biker and an informant.

Months prior to his death, Kane had been taken on by Normand Robitaille to work as his chauffeur. He would drive Robitaille all over Montreal and the surrounding area, taking him to meetings with other members of the Hells Angels and occasionally, members of Montreal's Mafia. He also took Robitaille to his squash games with other members of the Hells Angels. One day while he chauffeured Robitaille around, Kane was told of plans to apply the Hells Angels' corporate strategy to a different type of business. The plan was to start linking all of Quebec's pawn shops through a Web site where their products could be sold over the internet. Robitaille was going to be partners with Maurice (Mom) Boucher and Robert Savard, a notorious loan shark at the time. It sounded like a good idea as other online stores were attempting E-business around the same time. But the Hells Angels did not see themselves as the next Amazon.com. Instead, their plans, as Robitaille explained them to Kane, were to burn down the pawn shops of any owner who did not want to get on board with them. A few weeks later, Robitaille told Kane the Hells Angels were serious about their plan and intended to send Kane and another man into Quebec's pawn shops to test the waters. If anyone disagreed, others would be sent in to intimidate the owners.

Robitaille had joined the Hells Angels organization as a Rocker in 1994. Four years later, at the age of 30, he became the youngest member of the Nomads chapter, joining members of the Hells Angels who were showing a lot of grey hair. He was about 20 years younger than members like Boucher and Stadnick and represented the future of the gang in Quebec. In the latter years of the biker war, Robitaille was often seen at Boucher's side. He was also a constant presence at any important meeting the Hells Angels held with other criminal organizations during 2000. The new generation of Hells Angels was, for the most part, clean-cut men who took good care of themselves and worked out constantly. Gone was the beer gut associated with the image of a debauched biker who rides his Harley-Davidson for hours on end. In fact, some of the younger Hells Angels looked pretty awkward on the massive motorcycles which they were occasionally required to ride to abide by the gang's international rules.

Normand Robitaille appeared to be a quick learner. In 1995, during his time as a Rocker, he had taken part in an ill-planned extortion attempt that landed him in a federal penitentiary for a couple of years. A few years later, he joined a team of Rockers, along with Charlebois, who controlled drug traffic in the Hells Angels' most profitable areas in Montreal. While Robitaille was under investigation in Project Rush, the police found documents in his suitcase that outlined a business plan to gather significant chunks of real estate. For this reason, the pawn shop idea likely made perfect sense to Robitaille. The Hells Angels had used the same strategy to take over significant areas of Quebec's drug turf. Why couldn't it be applied to another line of business, one already filled with shady characters who were unlikely to call the police for help?

It was the way the Hells Angels did things. And by the end of 2000, it all seemed to be working well.

1

The Peak

They probably never saw it coming.

The Hells Angels in Quebec had reached the peak of criminal arrogance by the freezing cold afternoon of December 29, 2000. As police watched, more than 300 men sporting leather jackets with gang patches were converging at a relaxed pace on an imposing, white, three-storey building on Prince Street in Sorel, a city less than a hour's drive from Montreal. The building had served for years as a hangout and secure bunker for the first chapter of the already notorious gang, chartered in Canada on December 5, 1977.

Inside the building, members of the Hells Angels from all over Quebec were enjoying one of the biggest parties they had ever thrown. The gang that had developed a remarkable ability to dodge the police while it conducted million-dollar drug deals was doing nothing to camouflage this gathering. Anyone looking at the building from the street could tell it was no ordinary club-house. A flag bearing the gang's menacing insignia of a bare skull with wings flapped in the frigid air. Surveillance cameras were visible on several parts of the building and on the land surrounding it. The one thing about the party that resembled any other that might have been going during that holiday week in Canada was that someone had taken advantage of the cold weather and stacked several cases of beer outdoors on a balcony to keep them cool.

But this was no ordinary party. It was the beginning of an

unprecedented initiation that months earlier could not have been foreseen, if only because its purpose broke entirely with the Hells Angels' longstanding traditions. The gang was using their fortified bunker in Sorel for a mass, overnight conversion of new members. Dozens of members of biker gangs from Ontario with names like Satan's Choice and ParaDice Riders, were ready to participate in a ceremony that would see them pledge allegiance to the most powerful outlaw motorcycle gang in the world.

For years, the Hells Angels had toyed with the idea of setting up a chapter in Ontario but had held back for various reasons, including an inability to find members they felt stacked up to the level of criminal organization and discipline the Hells Angels had achieved in Quebec. It was apparent to police that influential Hells Angels from Quebec had long been calling the shots on possible expansion into Ontario. Minutes from a Hells Angels' meeting seized in 1994 indicated the gang had already begun courting the ParaDice Riders. But minutes from another meeting held in 1997 instructed Hells Angels' members to maintain a calm approach toward eventually setting up a chapter in Ontario. The Montreal chapter was the gang's beachhead in Canada. As it grew in influence and notoriety, its members spearheaded expansion in parts of British Colombia, Nova Scotia and Manitoba.

The members of the Nomads chapter in particular appeared keen on expansion. It was put together in the mid-1990s, near the start of the biker war, by Maurice (Mom) Boucher, who by then, at the age of 41, had been a Hells Angel for seven years. Through informants, the police learned that Boucher had grown frustrated with the passive attitude many of his fellow members in the Montreal chapter were taking during his violent conflict with other drug dealers in the east end of Montreal. Dispatches from informant Dany Kane made it clear to police that Boucher only wanted gang members for his Nomads chapter who were willing to participate in the war. He later planned to use a gang of underlings called the Rockers, which he had created years earlier, as a proving ground, like a sort of minor league "farm team," for anyone else who wanted into the Nomads chapter.

The Patchover

In an extremely rare move, the Hells Angels allowed members of the long-established Ontario outlaw gangs to join them without having to go through the traditional initiation process. Normally, those eager to join would go through distinct and often lengthy stages before earning the coveted status of the full-patch member. This "prospect" system set up by the gang in the United States was a decades-old tradition that determined a potential member's loyalty and dependability. In some cases, it could take years to earn the right to wear a Death Head patch. But now, in a move showcasing their arrogance and criminal influence, the Hells Angels in Quebec obtained the blessing from other chapters around the world to allow more than 160 people to join the gang in one day. Before the sun set that day, a truck carrying two industrial-sized sewing machines pulled up to the Sorel bunker. Some of the gang's underlings hoisted them up a stairway into the bunker, away from prying eyes.

Outside, members of the Sûreté du Québec and the Ontario Provincial Police (OPP) watched, many cursing the cold and the fact they had had to cut their holidays short to monitor the party. Confirmation that the massive "patchover" was going to take place had come days earlier in a box searched at the Canadian border. It contained dozens of patches ordered from Austria, where they are made exclusively for the gang. The police had also listened in on wiretaps as longtime Hells Angels like Donald (Pup) Stockford and Richard (Dick) Mayrand prepared for the expansion throughout most of December. Now, police videotaped as gang members drove up to the bunker's gates in flashy sport-utility vehicles and minivans. The police took careful note of every biker member who showed up for the party, but they were also keen to record who among the Hells Angels' underlings were working guard duty. The young men who stood at the gate that afternoon were likely unaware that what they were doing could be used against them later in court. Because of changes to Canada's anti-gang legislation, prosecutors could now argue that by doing guard duty the underlings were facilitating the loftier objectives of a criminal gang.

To those police investigators who had probed the Hells Angels in Quebec for years, the "patchover" of Ontario gangs was not a surprise, although the scale and the rapidity of the event was. Only weeks earlier, the gang's main rival in the bloody biker war, the Rock Machine, had been informed that it had been accepted into the fold of the Bandidos, the only outlaw motorcycle gang with an international membership comparable to that of the Hells Angels. Six years of war had taken a huge toll on the members of the Rock Machine, and on the Alliance, a collection of gangs and influential drug dealers who battled with the Hells Angels. But now they had the Bandidos as allies in Quebec and the new chapters they had created over the previous summer in Ontario. The Hells Angels in Quebec were forced to react, especially to the fact the Bandidos would be in Ontario, and react in a way that would reflect their *modus operandi* — unambiguous intimidation backed by huge numbers.

In a typical show of the gang's force, dozens of men who were part of the Hells Angels' now vast underling network worked security outside the Sorel bunker. Boxes of brand-new walkie-talkies were distributed to those working guard duty, or "the watch," while one prospect lectured his colleagues on how to operate them. At a small Sorel hotel a few kilometres from the bunker, full-fledged (or full-patch) members of the Hells Angels from chapters all over Canada were being escorted to the party in minivans under heavy guard. Despite the party atmosphere, the war with the Rock Machine and the Alliance was still on, a drug-turf war that had, to that point, seen 150 people killed over claims to lucrative areas in cities like Montreal and Quebec City, where street-level drug dealers peddled drugs like cocaine and hashish. The Quebec Hells Angels knew their rivals might be looking for targets.

Standing outside the Sorel hotel was 29-year-old Paul (Schtroumpf) Brisebois, a prospective member of Boucher's Montreal-based Nomads chapter. A squat, chubby man who slightly resembled his nickname (Schtroumpf is French for Smurf), Brisebois appeared nervous as he arranged for the guarded transport of his superiors. The aggressive underling, who had quickly climbed the ladder to prospect, had only seven months earlier taken part in the murder of a drug dealer who was selling for the Rock Machine. On May 1, 2000, 25-year-old Patrick Turcotte was shot dead after leaving a video store in Verdun, a working-class suburb of Montreal. Weeks after the murder, Brisebois graduated from the level of "striker" in the Rockers to full-fledged membership. It was yet another sign to the police that the quickest way to graduate in the network was through murder. Seven months later, Brisebois took yet another step by graduating from the Rockers and was made a prospect in the Nomads chapter. By comparison, some former Rockers had been members of the Hells Angels' underling gang for more than five years without yet being promoted. Being a Hells Angel was a far cry from how Brisebois had started his career as a drug dealer. At the age of 18, he had sold tiny bags of cocaine and marijuana out of rented apartments. Now, at 29, he appeared headed for full membership in the Nomads, making him a partner in a multi-million dollar drug network.

Brisebois was not supposed to be at this party. There was a court order forbidding him from associating with known criminals, and yet here he was, arranging for several of them to be

Paul Brisebois is arrested
on December 29, 2000.

(Marcos Townsend,
The Montreal Gazette)

chauffeured to the party. The local police grabbed Brisebois, spread him out on a car, searched him for weapons and hand-cuffed him. It was perhaps the only hitch for the Hells Angels that day. Even though their leader Maurice (Mom) Boucher, the architect of the Nomads chapter, was behind bars awaiting his second trial on charges that he had ordered the murders of two prison guards, other members of the Nomads like Denis Houle, Walter Stadnick and René Charlebois partied inside with their new Ontario brothers. They had even invited a photographer from the crime tabloid *Allô Police*, to take pictures and get the word out that the Hells Angels had once again expanded. All the while, a seamstress busily sewed the winged-skull patches onto the jackets of the new members.

As day became night, the members of the Nomads chapter likely felt they were unstoppable. Even with Boucher in prison, the gang was clearly dominating the war. It was a conflict like no other in Quebec, with one side so fixated on supremacy over a major metropolitan city that murder was epidemic. By that point, the Hells Angels had more than 100 members spread across Quebec in six chapters, including the elite Nomads chapter based in Montreal. What would soon become public knowledge was that the Nomads very nearly achieved their desired monopoly on the cocaine market in Montreal. Now, through the contacts they had established over several years and the eight new Ontario chapters they had created overnight, the members of the aggressive Hells Angels' chapter were planning to increase their share of markets in cities like Toronto, Hamilton and Oshawa. Everything seemed to be going as the Hells Angels willed it.

Scott Robertson, a member of one of the now-defunct Ontario gangs, walked out of the Sorel bunker sporting his new Hells Angels' patch, and when police asked him to pose for a picture with his leather jacket, he obliged. Mayrand, who only months earlier had moved from the relative peace and quiet of the Hells Angels' Montreal chapter apparently to replace Boucher and assist the Nomads when it came to diplomatic issues, walked out of the bunker looking bushed. Guy Ouellette, a Sûreté du Québec sergeant who had probed the Hells Angels for more than a decade, managed to talk to him. Mayrand said he had had a long day. Sergeant Ouellette replied that his was going to be longer — he had to record how many new members the gang had. Mayrand shrugged his shoulders and informed Ouellette there were 168 new Hells Angels for the police to deal with.

The day after the party, Maurice (Mom) Boucher searched for news on what had transpired in Sorel. From his cell in a special wing of a women's provincial detention center, where he had been placed for security reasons, Boucher called Pierre Provencher, a trusted member of the Rockers. As the police listened in, Provencher gushed about the party. He told Boucher about being amazed by the enormity of it all. Then their thoughts turned westward, toward Ontario and the possibilities that came with creating 168 new brothers.

"Hey that's some province," Provencher said of the Hells Angels' newly acquired territory.

"Oh yeah, it's a big province," Boucher replied.

What Boucher and Provencher didn't know was that the final preparation of years of work was underway in a special office for prosecutors at the Montreal courthouse. Their recorded conversation was going to be one small part of the evidence. Transcripts of hours of wiretaps were already being carefully read and reread. Secretly recorded videotapes of meetings the Rockers had held were being scrutinized carefully. It was all in preparation for a well-kept secret; the network Boucher and the rest of the Nomads had built over the years was about to crumble.

Only three months later, before the sun emerged on March 28, 2001, more than 2,000 cops from all over Quebec began pounding on doors and arresting dozens of people, including any members of the Nomads chapter who could be found. The roundup was dubbed "*Opération Printemps* (or Springtime) *2001*."

All of those arrested were named in warrants on charges that ranged from drug trafficking to first-degree murder. Of those charged, 42 were singled out for an indictment accusing them of 23 of the most serious crimes, including a failed plot to level an entire building in Verdun with a bomb, and 13 specific counts of first-degree murder. Those charges stemmed from the Project Rush investigation. Another 49 were named in another warrant, generated by the Project Ocean investigation, accusing them of either supplying or dealing the drugs that fueled the network.

Paul (Schtroumpf) Brisebois

Brisebois, the short man who had worked security at the Sorel party only weeks before, was among the 42 gang members included in the Project Rush indictment, including the Turcotte murder in Verdun. By now Brisebois knew the drill. During the spring of 1990, when he was 18, the RCMP had received a complaint from someone living on the same street where Brisebois was selling. Too many people were coming and going to the apartment. The Mounties asked an undercover officer from the Montreal Urban Community Police to buy drugs from Brisebois. The officer knocked on a door and was greeted by Brisebois. He only asked who had referred him to his illicit pharmacy. Then he walked through the apartment to a living room table where the officer watched as he pulled out a little bag of cocaine from a margarine container that had been shoved inside an empty beer pitcher.

With the purchase made, the RCMP got a warrant to search the apartment. Inside, they found several more of the little bags along with a small quantity of hashish. Brisebois was arrested, charged and released on bail to await a possible trial. But while his case was still at the preliminary stage, Brisebois was caught again, selling quarter-gram bags of cocaine, just a few doors down from where the RCMP had nabbed him a year earlier. He eventually served a combined 13 months in prison for the two busts.

Ten years later, Brisebois was rising quickly through the Hells Angels' ranks. But to the investigators who had spent years targeting the biker gangs, the real coup that day were the arrests of almost all the full-patch members of the Nomads, including some who had been Hells Angels for more than a decade.

Denis Houle

At 47 years old, Denis Houle, whose nickname was once Pas Fiable (Not Reliable), had 20 years as a Hells Angel under his belt and had already done serious jail time while wearing the gang's patch. Years before the March 2001 roundup, Houle made it clear to authorities he was committed to the gang.

"With the Hells, I have found a family," Houle once told a prison psychologist while serving a nine-year sentence for being an accomplice after the fact in the 1985 murders of five fellow Hells Angels' members. The sordid event became known as the

"Lennoxville Purge" or the "Lennoxville Slaughter," as the five members were invited to the Hells Angels' Sherbrooke chapter bunker on March 24, 1985, where they were gunned down. After the bloodbath, the bodies were stuffed into sleeping bags, weighed down with barbells and dumped in a river. The Hells Angels had purged their own members in part for consuming cocaine the gang intended to sell for profit. Houle had a small role in this purge, an event that awoke Canada to the violent potential of the Hells Angels. The same psychologist told the National Parole Board that Houle, while serving his sentence, found a source of personal value in the gang, and described him as a well-structured individual "in his delinquency." Life in his adopted family would permit Houle to live a lifestyle that, by 2001, according to court documents, was clearly incompatible with his declared revenue. He allegedly managed to hide $4.5 million in the Antilles and was believed to own $800,000 in real estate in Nova Scotia. During the early part of his sentence, Houle was caught selling drugs in a federal penitentiary and intimidating other inmates, so he was transferred from a minimum-security institution to Donnacona, a maximum-security penitentiary near Quebec City. The parole board held back on granting Houle full parole during the early 1990s because he refused to discuss the details of his role in the Lennoxville murders. In 1993, he told the board he would not discuss the slayings because other Hells Angels found guilty of taking part were still appealing their sentences. The parole board reports filed during Houle's sentence revealed a fierce gang loyalty that belied his nickname. In 1994 that loyalty would be paid off as he was picked to be one of the founding members of the Nomads chapter despite having spent the past several years in prison.

The police half-jokingly referred to the Nomads chapter members as the "elite" of the five other Hells Angels' chapters chartered by the gang in Quebec by 2001. The newly created

Nomads represented some of the gang's most influential members in eastern Canada. At the helm was Boucher, a man who had become so influential as a drug dealer in Montreal's east end that a short stint behind bars during the mid-1990s caused panic, uncertainty and shortages among his many drug dealers in the Rockers. Like some of the other founding members of the Nomads, Boucher had held prominent positions within the gang including president of the Hells Angels' Montreal chapter. Because of details Dany Kane, a Hells Angels' underling who turned informant in 1994, was feeding them, the police were already aware of the existence of the Nomads well before it was chartered on June 24, 1995. Also, just months before it was chartered, Houle's parole had been revoked because it was clear he had been involved in setting it up.

Houle had been arrested for drunk driving, possession of drugs and uttering threats to the police officers who had arrested him. Inside his car, the police had found the brand-new Nomads patches. Now they knew what those patches were for.

One parole report revealed that even though Houle had dropped out of school by the age of 15, while he was in grade 8, tests he agreed to undergo in prison indicated he had a superior intellect. Behind bars, he worked to complete high school and took accounting courses. While on parole, he told the board that he was working as a sales representative for a company with a salary of $30,000. He also was involved in a small recycling company, owned by other Hells Angels' members, that the police believed was actually selling recycled products to small municipalities in Quebec's Eastern Townships. Houle made it clear that when his sentence ended and he was no longer subject to parole conditions he would rejoin the Hells Angels.

Near the end of his sentence, Houle returned to the minimum-security penitentiary closer to Montreal, where members of the Alliance tried to eliminate him. He and a fellow Hells Angel were hanging out in the prison yard while men positioned outside the prison fence fired 11 shots from a semi-automatic rifle in their direction. The assassination attempt failed. One month later, four men tied to the Alliance were arrested and charged with attempted murder. All four eventually pleaded guilty and were sentenced to prison terms of less than three years. Two of the men arrested turned informant and alleged that members of the Dark Circle, leaders in the Alliance, had given the green light on Houle's murder and had provided support.

Testimony the informants gave in court opened a very public door on the biker war. If the Hells Angels didn't already know who was pulling the strings in the Alliance, they did now. Those members of the Dark Circle, a collection of the province's more influential drug traffickers who opposed the Hells Angels and their monopolistic attitudes, were arrested a month after the botched attempt on Houle. They were charged with conspiring to commit murder. The names of the Dark Circle members charged in the conspiracies would become a Hells Angels' hit list. At least 6 of the 17 men charged in a series of conspiracies and attempted murders would later be targets themselves.

Within a two-year period, two would be killed, three would be wounded by gunfire and another would escape death only because the hit men shot the wrong person (Serge Hervieux, 38-year-old father of two and one of several innocent victims of the biker war). One Dark Circle member ended up asking the National Parole Board if he could fully serve his seven-year sentence because he feared for his life if he got out while the biker war was still being waged.

The first of the two successful hits would take place the night of September 25, 1998. Jean Rosa, 32, was gunned down in front of his home in Laval, a Montreal suburb. He was found lying near his Pontiac Grand Prix covered in blood and barely alive, but was declared dead at a nearby hospital where a doctor found seven entry and exit wounds, the fatal ones to his head. Less than a month later, on October 22, 1998, Pierre Bastien, a hot-tempered bar owner and member of the Dark Circle, was shot, also outside his home in Laval. Just after 8 p.m., he parked his car and was still behind the wheel when someone shot him several times. All the while his eight-year-old daughter crouched in the back seat, fearing for her life. One bullet lacerated Bastien's heart and he died quickly. Only a few months earlier he had completed his 30-month prison sentence for the conspiracy to kill a Hells Angel.

Houle was not arrested at home during Operation Springtime 2001. He learned of the charges he faced while behind bars, just like Gilles (Trooper) Mathieu, who at 50, was also a longtime member of the Hells Angels. Mathieu had gone more than a decade without being charged with a crime. Until February 15, 2001, just weeks after the Sorel party, Mathieu and Houle, along with six other men who were members of the Nomads or the Rockers, were arrested as they held a meeting in a downtown Montreal hotel suite. They had been looking over photos of their enemies in the Bandidos.

"We can assume they were not exchanging hockey cards," Commander André Durocher of the Montreal Urban Community Police said at a press conference after the arrests. One photo found on a table in the hotel suite was that of Alain Brunette, president of a Bandidos chapter, who just days earlier, had been wounded by gunfire while riding in a car along a highway north of Montreal.

Alain Brunette, president of a Bandidos chapter

While members of the Nomads chapter held their meeting, underlings in the Rockers stood guard at various strategic points in the hotel. When the police arrested the eight, they found that each was carrying a loaded handgun and about $10,000 cash.

Mathieu and the others quickly pleaded guilty to the weapons charge and were sentenced to a year in prison. In exchange for their plea, Crown prosecutor André Vincent agreed not to charge the eight with new federal anti-gang laws created specifically to target Quebec's violent biker gangs. Vincent remained tight-lipped about why he had accepted the guilty pleas. But at the time, Vincent was one of a handful of people who knew that Operation Springtime 2001 was about to be launched. Pursuing potential three-year prison terms for gang members like Houle and Mathieu would have been a waste of time for a prosecutor who knew what was going to happen to the Nomads in a matter of weeks.

Gilles (Trooper) Mathieu

While Boucher was under constant police surveillance during the late 1990s, Mathieu always seemed to have the ear of the president of the Nomads chapter. To some, he appeared to be one of Boucher's most trusted advisors.

During the investigations that led to the Operation Springtime 2001 arrests, the police used double agents to infiltrate the lower ranks of the gang. Betrayal by double agents was nothing new to Mathieu. More than twenty years earlier, the RCMP had used one such agent to catch Mathieu and a few other people who were part of an LSD trafficking ring. The double agent arranged to buy 5,000 blotters of the drug at $1.45 per unit from a Montreal drug dealer. Mathieu appeared to be working as protection for a man who delivered the LSD to Montreal from a town about an hour's drive west of the city. The double agent was told to go the drug dealer's house. Once there, he was told by the dealer's wife he would have to wait because the drugs were in transit. Eventually, a gray Pontiac pulled up to the house and a man got out. He carried the LSD blotters with him. A small group of RCMP officers moved in and arrested him. Mathieu and another man were waiting in the grey Pontiac when they saw the RCMP apprehend the delivery man. But before they could flee, they too were arrested.

When the case went to court, Mathieu pleaded ignorance. Backed by testimony from the delivery man and the driver of the Pontiac, he told the judge he was merely a 31-year-old maritime inspector, from a small town in western Quebec, who happened to be in the wrong place at the wrong time. In reality, Mathieu had joined the Hells Angels on December 5, 1980. While testifying in his own defense, Mathieu told Judge Patrick Falardeau that, in the hours before the drug deal, he and his wife traveled to a friend's house for a visit, where he happened to find one of the men he would end up getting arrested with. Mathieu claimed he piled into the Pontiac with the others because they were heading to Montreal where he wanted to visit a friend about having car parts painted. While inside the car, the delivery man never mentioned anything about a drug deal, Mathieu told the judge.

"He denies any participation in this affair. Plus he has no criminal record," Falardeau wrote in his June 26, 1981, judgement of the LSD case, but he made it clear he was not impressed with Mathieu's testimony.

"The explanations he supplied lack logic and plausibility," Falardeau wrote, noting there were several holes in Mathieu's story, namely that before making the long trip to Montreal, Mathieu never called the man who was supposed to paint his car parts to make sure he would be home. Mathieu would claim he ended up with a one-year prison sentence and two years probation for bumming a ride into Montreal.

Mathieu is likely to have stashed away millions while he was a Hells Angel. During the preliminary hearing in Operation Springtime, evidence presented indicated that he owned a company worth $2.3 million based out of the West Edmonton Mall. A source had also told the police that Mathieu had hidden $1 million in a tax haven.

In the years that followed his drug conviction, Mathieu managed to avoid prison. He was among the few Hells Angels who got off on the Lennoxville Purge murder charges — he was able to prove he had shown up at the bunker sometime after the slaughter.

But Mathieu and other Nomads members like Houle and Boucher were accused of having a role in all 13 of the murders the Hells Angels were charged with in Operation Springtime 2001. The Crown's theory was that the gang members were like pirates on a ship, all sharing the same goal and aware of what was happening to achieve those goals.

Normand Robitaille

Another pirate on the Nomads ship was Normand Robitaille, who was at that point only 32 years old but already a full-patch Hells Angel in the Nomads chapter. Robitaille had risen to the top ranks of the gang at a rate that raised some eyebrows. When he was 27, while out on bail in a 1995 drug trafficking case, Robitaille was arrested for extortion, forcible confinement and possession of a weapon. By the time Robitaille appeared before a parole board he had been a member of the Rockers for only a year. He was placed in a minimum-security penitentiary on May 23, 1995, and by November was alleged to have been running a small drug network inside it.

While in prison, Robitaille told the parole board that his decision to join a biker gang was influenced by his desire to expand his clientele and make more money. He told a prison psychologist that he realized if he didn't quit the Rockers, he would end up dead. After getting out of prison, Robitaille obviously decided the risk of being a Hells Angel was still worth taking. He quickly ascended the ranks of the Hells Angels' network and was a Nomad by October 5, 1998. On June 9, 1999, his own prediction to the parole board almost came true. As Robitaille dined at a

Montreal restaurant that night someone fired two shots at him, striking him in the right shoulder and the lower back. He was taken to a hospital where he was treated, but he refused to tell the police anything.

Jean-Guy Bourgoin

Jean-Guy Bourgoin was an accomplice in the same extortion case Robitaille had served time for. A member of the Rockers, Bourgoin was involved in the biker war from the very start, according to informants.

Like Robitaille, Bourgoin would tell the National Parole Board he blamed his criminal life on heavy drug consumption. A psychologist who met with Bourgoin during his sentence filed an assessment to the parole board and wrote the following: "He behaves like an immature individual whose masculine identity has not been assured. On a base of aggression towards an absent father, he made certain compromises with his proper image of the good father of a family." The psychologist recommended Bourgoin reinforce his family life if he wanted to avoid the criminal life. But almost as soon as his two-year sentence had ended, it became obvious that Bourgoin, a high school dropout, considered the Rockers his family. To him, the other members of the gang were brothers while he and other members of the underling gang referred to their superiors as *mon oncles*, my uncles.

It was a 1998 incident involving Bourgoin that brought the Rockers considerable public attention. On September 15 of that year, Bourgoin and other members of the gang were partying at a trendy bar on Saint-Laurent Blvd. when an argument broke out on the dance floor. Stephen Reid, a six-foot-two linebacker for the Montreal Alouettes, was exchanging words with the bikers when Anthony Calvillo, the team's quarterback, and another Alouettes teammate joined in. Everyone involved was tossed out of the bar, but the dispute continued on the street and became violent. Bourgoin struck Reid with a metal post used to line up customers outside the bar, and Reid suffered cuts to the back of his head, neck and elbows.

"Take a good look at my face my man," Bourgoin said. "You file a complaint and I'll never forget your face." But Reid did file a complaint and Bourgoin pleaded guilty to assault causing injury and was fined $2,000 for the incident.

Two years after the scuffle with the Alouettes, Bourgoin, who controlled much of the distribution of large quantities of drugs in Montreal's trendy Plateau district, would be secretly recorded by a man he considered his brother. Stéphane Sirois had quit the Rockers, but he rejoined them after being convinced to work as a police double agent. He was wearing a hidden recorder as the pair dined on sushi at a Montreal restaurant on February 2, 2000. Sirois was pretending to want back into the Rockers. He asked Bourgoin what it took to rise through the organization quickly.

During the dinner, Bourgoin began listing what the Hells Angels would pay for successful hits on their enemies. He rattled off the prices in a matter-of-fact way, but in doing so, he revealed how far the Hells Angels were now willing to go in their efforts to eliminate their rivals. A full-fledged member of the Rock Machine could net the killer $100,000. Lower-level members had price tags of $50,000 and $25,000, depending on their rank. While working as a double agent, Sirois would inform the police that Bourgoin was making what he estimated to be $7,000 a month for his role in the Nomads' drug network.

During the first case to go to trial based on information from Project Rush, Sirois would tell a jury of his reasons for leaving the Rockers. He said he had orders from Boucher himself to choose between a woman he was seeing and the gang. The woman's previous boyfriend had been murdered and was rumored to have been a police informant. Sirois chose the woman, setting off a chain of events that the Hells Angels would regret.

Daniel Lanthier

Bourgoin ran the Rockers by committee, and one of the other two on the committee was Daniel (Boteau) Lanthier, a man who had no visible means of employment though he lived in a $150,000 home in a suburb across from the south shore of the Montreal Island. Before he was arrested, he was routinely seen driving around in luxury cars. As a Crown witness, Stéphane Sirois would tell investigators Lanthier made about $12,000 a month dealing drugs for the network. Sirois' estimates were based on what the Rockers members were able to contribute to the gang's ten percent fund, a collection of criminal profits used to cover things like lawyers' fees and, witnesses like Sirois would allege, to purchase weapons.

A convicted drug dealer named Ronnie Harbour, also a police informant, told investigators that, like Bourgoin, Lanthier was involved in the biker war from the beginning. The dealer told the police both men were involved with the Hells Angels as early as October 28, 1994, when 32-year-old Sylvain Pelletier, part of the Pelletier Clan, a gang of brothers who chose to join the Alliance and oppose the Hells Angels early in the biker war, was killed when his Jeep was blown up. Pelletier's murder, allegedly on orders from Boucher, served as an announcement that the Hells Angels considered it open season on anyone not willing to sell their drugs, at their prices.

Lanthier officially joined the Rockers on April 15, 1994, and during that same spring was already reaping the benefits. Montreal Urban Community Police officers on routine patrol arrested him and two other men in a park in Montreal's east end. Lanthier and the others appeared to be surprised when they saw the uniformed officers riding through the park on bicycles, one officer recalled in court. The trio quickly headed for two white cars parked nearby. The patrol officers followed them. When they reached the cars, one noticed a firearm inside one of the vehicles. Another officer noticed that the passenger in Lanthier's car was trying hard to close the glove compartment. The officer assumed that the man was trying to hide a gun. The situation grew tense as the patrol officers and colleagues who had arrived as backup drew their weapons and ordered Lanthier and his friends to get out of the cars.

Inside the two cars, the police found a 9-mm pistol with chrome plating and a black cross on the handle. They also found a smaller calibre handgun under a back seat. Both weapons were loaded. Three bulletproof vests were in one of the trunks. The passenger in Lanthier's car pleaded guilty to possessing all the weapons and received a four-month prison sentence. Lanthier was acquitted shortly after his friend was sentenced. The incident fit a pattern police would see in the coming years where Rockers underlings were expected to "take the fall" for full-patch members. The Hells Angels expected the same loyalty from the Rockers.

Gregory Wooley

Gregory Wooley was another member of the Rockers who was targeted in Project Rush. Wooley had grown up in a tough section of northern Montreal and gravitated to a street gang composed of the children of Haitian immigrants who had developed a distinct community in Montreal North and the city's St. Michel district. Despite being black, Wooley rose quickly through the ranks of the lily-white Rockers. Though he knew he had little chance of ever becoming a Hells Angel because of the gang's racist exclusionary rule, he did not seem deterred.

Like Houle and Mathieu, Gregory Wooley was behind bars when Operation Springtime 2001 was carried out. When the charges were filed, he was still recovering from a serious head injury he had suffered while in a maximum-security penitentiary. On January 31, 2001, Wooley was pushed during a fight in the penitentiary's weight room, and when he fell, his head struck the metal bar of a bench press. The man suspected of nearly killing Wooley was in prison for homicide but had no ties to the biker war. He was never charged with the assault, but Wooley's parole officer, aware of the biker's reputation, would later call the attack "a suicidal act" on the part of the other inmate.

Some police detectives in the Montreal police force wondered if Wooley had run out of luck on April 5, 2000. The full-patch member of the Rockers was preparing to board a flight to Haiti when security checking one of his suitcases found a .44 Smith & Wesson handgun inside. Wooley was arrested and quickly pleaded guilty to possession of the weapon, which earned him his first significant sentence.

Investigators in the Montreal police were puzzled by Wooley's apparent miscue, and some speculated that he might have believed he was untouchable at that point. They also couldn't help but notice that Wooley was leaving Canada just after two members of an underling gang he ran, called the Syndicate, had been murdered outside a Montreal strip club.

Mere months earlier, a judge had tossed out evidence in a trial against Wooley on a weapons charge; he had been acquitted. A gun had been recovered on a sidewalk near where Wooley had been stopped for what the police claimed was a routine traffic stop. That summer night in 1999, Wooley had been driving through downtown Montreal on a motorcycle. According to the official police version, he was pulled over because he was speeding and the muffler on his motorcycle was making a lot of noise. He was stopped at a downtown intersection by Constable Michel Bureau, a Montreal police constable who would later testify that he immediately recognized Wooley and noticed he was wearing his gang colors. The cop found out that Wooley only held an apprenticeship licence and was supposed to be accompanied by another motorcyclist. After Officer Bureau returned to his car and began processing the traffic violations, he said he noticed

Wooley make a sudden movement and seemed to be adjusting something under his jacket.

"I knew at that moment that Mr. Wooley had already been implicated in murders. He was a violent individual, and he was the only black to be admitted into a biker gang. There were certainly reasons to assume that he was violent," Bureau later said in court. Bureau called for backup and, within minutes, five police officers were involved in what was supposed to be a traffic violation. Bureau would testify that he feared for his safety and even tried to compromise with Wooley.

"I can make you a deal, for my security. Show me what you have in your jacket and we can forget the towing," Bureau said he told Wooley. The biker replied: "You have no business." Bureau said he then increased the immunity offer by telling Wooley he would look the other way if he found drugs. Again, Wooley refused. Bureau asked a third time, ordering Wooley to "show me what you have" under the jacket. Wooley said no and reminded the officers that he wasn't under arrest. They informed Wooley he was indeed under arrest for the traffic violations, and they searched him while he sat on his motorcycle. They found no weapon on him, but a semiautomatic Springfield Armory .45-calibre pistol was spotted lying on the sidewalk nearby.

When the case went to court, a judge analyzing the evidence refused to believe the pull-over was routine and theorized that it was part of a police surveillance operation where the officers involved used the traffic violation as an excuse to check in on Wooley. The judge ruled that the biker's constitutional rights had been violated and the evidence the police had filed in the case was tossed out. The biker was acquitted of possession of an illegal firearm a month later.

By the time of that bungled arrest, Wooley had already developed a reputation with the Montreal police. They suspected him of several murders, and while he had been awaiting trials in previous cases, he was involved in at least three fights with other inmates. The reports on the fights suggested he used "excessive and extremely violent force" in each case. As well, in the days leading up to the weight room fight, Wooley had been caught attempting to smuggle PCP into the penitentiary. The parole board learned the attempt to smuggle the drugs was part of a plan with other inmates who hoped the PCP would provoke violence, disorder and mutiny in the prison.

"The information also indicates that you were the head of the conspiracy," the board noted when it refused Wooley parole — for several reasons. One was that a prison-security report filed to the board alleged that Wooley was also the head of a crack ring early on in his sentence and that he had successfully smuggled drugs into a penitentiary. It was also early in his sentence that a psychologist determined Wooley's central problem was his temper, a rage he could not control. The psychologist who filed an evaluation to the board also determined that Wooley had weak judgement, low self-esteem and, at the age of 16, had attempted suicide.

In April 2001, Wooley refused to undergo any more psychological evaluations. The nine murder charges he now faced through the evidence collected in Project Rush were not his first. Wooley was charged in the March 28, 1997, slaying of a 25-year-old Rock Machine member named Jean-Marc Caissy who was about to play floor hockey with some friends when he was shot outside a recreation center in Montreal. Less than three weeks later, the Montreal police arrested the gunman, a Hells Angels' associate named Aimé Simard. The hit man decided to turn informant and fingered members of the Rockers, including Wooley, as taking part in the conspiracy to commit murder. Wooley was arrested and charged, along with the other members of the Rockers, but a jury ultimately acquitted all of them in a case that left police and other authorities in Quebec questioning the value of informants.

But informants and double agents would provide much of the evidence that led to the Operation Springtime 2001 arrests. Their information would be used by the Crown to paint a portrait of a drug trafficking network intent on having sole control over Montreal's drug market.

"We are talking about a war. We must not forget that," Vincent said on October 21, 2002, at one of the so-called megatrials that were the result of Operation Springtime 2001. One year after catching five Nomads with guns, hit money and photos of their enemies and after looking the other way, the Crown attorney could now prosecute almost all of them for orchestrating a massive, murderous conflict.

2

"The ideology of expanding and totally con-
trolling the traffic of drugs in Montreal came
from Maurice Boucher."

— Stéphane Sirois, ex-member of the Rockers, who wore a
wire for the police as they probed the Hells Angels.

At the center of the conflict that became the war between the
Hells Angels and the Alliance, a collection of drug traffickers in
gangs like the Pelletier Clan and the Rock Machine, was a man
called Mom.

Maurice "Mom" Boucher could not tolerate competition, so
he relentlessly plotted to eliminate it. He expected full loyalty
from his drug dealers, and he asked them to adhere to the same
structure and rules expected of him as a member of the Hells
Angels when he created his own gang in 1992, calling them the
Rockers. And when he felt other members of the Hells Angels'
Montreal chapter were not bloodthirsty enough for his war, he
created his own chapter in 1995.

But years before the biker war ever started, the police already
knew Boucher was a major player in Canada's drug trafficking
scene. During an RCMP operation dubbed Project Jaggy, an investigation that began in September 1992, Boucher was drawing
attention that indicated to the police how closely the Hells Angels
were associated to other forms of organized crime. Project Jaggy
began as an investigation into a conspiracy to bring 3.2 tons of
cocaine into Canada from Jamaica. The police were tipped off that

members of the Hells Angels' Quebec City chapter were meeting with people from eastern Canada to plot smuggling routes.

All Aboard!

André Imbeault, a founding member of the Quebec City chapter, and Richard Hudon, convinced a man named Fennie Bungay to accept $1.5 million for his work in preparing a boat that would be used to smuggle drugs. The Hells Angels also gave Bungay $240,000 to buy them a boat. As they continued to monitor this partnership, the RCMP noticed other Hells Angels were coming on board as well, including Daniel Beaulieu and Marius Perron.

Bungay bought a boat called the *Arctic Trader* and spent $75,000 trying to make it seaworthy between April and May of 1993. But at the end of June, Perron had to give Hudon the bad news that the *Arctic Trader* couldn't be used. To offset their losses, the Hells Angels called in a specialist from Edmundston, New Brunswick, to strip their investment of anything worth money. Within a month, the Hells Angels apparently recovered from the setback because the new boat, called the *Fortune Endeavor*, left Marystown, Nova Scotia. As the police would learn, the illegal venture was crawling with Hells Angels. They would be charged eventually in connection with Project Jaggy, but Boucher was not one of them. However, his name kept popping up in surveillance reports as RCMP investigators followed the key players.

Raynald Desjardins and the Montreal Mafia

One of the first instances of police surveillance came on May 25, 1993, when Imbeault held a meeting with a man named Raynald Desjardins, who, the police would later learn, was financing the smuggling operation. Accompanying Desjardins that day was Boucher, sporting his Hells Angels' colors. That Boucher was with Desjardins was a noteworthy fact to investigators. Desjardins was well known to the police as being the right-hand man of Vito

Rizzuto, the reputed godfather of the Mafia in Montreal. What Desjardins brought to the Hells Angels was access to the Montreal Mafia's financial support and his personal experience in drug smuggling, which dated back at least to 1980. As early as 1986, Desjardins was already being referred to in police intelligence reports as "the supplier" of drugs for Montreal's Mafia.

Desjardins would get one of the stiffest sentences to come out of Project Jaggy, 15 years, but he used the time to either solidify his contacts or make new ones. While he served his sentence he was the subject of at least two major investigations by corrections officials for crimes including an attempted murder, a failed hit he allegedly ordered from prison. By the time of his statutory release date on June 2, 2004, having served two-thirds of his sentence, Desjardins was still considered an influential man despite spending more than a decade behind bars. While serving his sentence, he associated with both mob figures and Hells Angels. A February 2004 parole board report alleged that he frequently broke penitentiary rules.

"You have acquired over the years an important status at the head of structured, criminal organizations and maintained those associations inside the penitentiary," the parole board wrote in a report. Nonetheless, they were required by law to release him. All the parole board could do was warn Desjardins that if he maintained those links while serving what remained of his sentence outside, he would be sent right back to a penitentiary. He was also required to supply a summary of his revenues and spending on a monthly basis.

But Correctional Service Canada was likely glad to see Desjardins go. During his time behind bars he had allegedly ordered two inmates to kill another, named William Fisher, in April 1995. According to a final report of a CSC investigation of the incident, the conflict was over Desjardins not wanting drugs to enter the wing of the penitentiary where he was staying. He was also suspected of trying to poison another inmate while at the Leclerc Institution, and was thought to have been the mastermind behind several violent incidents that occurred while he was serving his sentence.

In 2001, in an unsuccessful bid to get out on parole, he claimed to have left the organized crime world, saying, "At the level I am at I don't need authorization (to leave)." But while out on a day pass on September 25, 2002, Desjardins was spotted meeting with Francesco Cotroni, the son of Frank Cotroni, an influential underboss in the same Mafia organization that bore his family name. (Frank Cotroni died of brain cancer during the summer of 2004.) Both Desjardins and Cotroni's son claimed the meeting was of little significance, an unplanned crossing of paths, between an inmate out on a day pass and another out on parole. But it landed both men in hot water with the parole board.

Maurice (Mom) Boucher and the *Fortune Endeavor*

Back in 1993, Desjardins had risen to such prominence in the underworld that some police began referring to a Rizzuto-Desjardins organization. Desjardins drove around in an expensive Mercedes-Benz, spent his leisure time on a 40-foot pleasure boat and had amassed an impressive collection of rare and antique cars. Besides accompanying Desjardins for the meeting in May 1993 with Imbeault — his fellow Hells Angel from Quebec City — Boucher was seen meeting with Rizzuto's right-hand man a second time, weeks later in Longueuil.

During the summer of 1993, Boucher was also overheard on wiretaps making a series of calls to Desjardins and the latter's business partner Julio Cesari. It was around this time that Imbeault had told an RCMP informant that Desjardins was financing the *Fortune Endeavor* smuggling operation. The police also noticed that Desjardins and Rizzuto were talking to each other on a regular basis. A particularly interesting day in Project

Maurice (Mom) Boucher
(left) and Luc (Bordel)
Bordeleau

Jaggy was August 17, 1993. A surveillance team watched as Boucher walked out of Desjardins' company, Amusements Deluxe, and into a car. The Hells Angel was obviously concerned about being monitored by the police because he had shown up for the meeting driving a car registered in the name of the mother of Luc (Bordel) Bordeleau, who was a member of the Rockers at the time.

Just days prior to this meeting, the *Fortune Endeavor* had penetrated Canadian waters on its return from Jamaica but had run into trouble. It reported problems to the authorities at the Halifax port. Worried that they would go through an official inspection, those on board dumped 750 kilograms of cocaine packed into plastic pipes weighed down with lead and chains. While dumping the cocaine overboard appeared to be part of the Hells Angels' ultimate plan, they had apparently planned to do it in shallower waters. On August 17, the same day Boucher held a meeting with Desjardins, Imbeault set off from Shippagan, New Brunswick, in a pleasure boat. He planned to locate the cocaine using sonar. On board with him was Bordeleau, who besides being a founding member of the Rockers and a close friend of Boucher, was also a professionally trained scuba diver. After eight days of diving attempts in the Gulf of the Saint Lawrence, the men were unable to find the cocaine and they quit. Whenever Bordeleau and the others would came back to shore without their sunken illicit treasure they were closely followed by the RCMP. Surveillance teams noticed that Bordeleau did little to hide the fact that he was always armed. To the police, it appeared Boucher had personally recruited Bordeleau for the cocaine recovery operation. The subject would come up later at Bordeleau's parole board hearings while he was serving five years for his failed scuba diving expeditions. Despite having apparently little to do with the larger smuggling plan, Bordeleau was charged, shortly after giving up the search for the cocaine, along with the other major players, like Imbeault and Desjardins. The cocaine was located about a year later by the Canadian Armed Forces.

Boucher wasn't even arrested. His telephone conversations with Desjardins provided little of actual interest to investigators. But by now, it was clear he had become a major player in Quebec's lucrative illicit drug scene. It had been a long and messy road.

Maurice (Mom) Boucher — The Man Himself

Boucher was born on June 21, 1953, in Causapscal, a village in the Gaspé peninsula located where the Matapedia and Causapscal rivers meet. The village's name is a Mi'kmaq word meaning "pebbly point."

When he was two years old, his family moved from the peace of the remote village to one of Montreal's rougher neighborhoods, where Boucher's father worked in construction as an iron worker. His mother stayed home to look after Boucher and his seven siblings, three brothers and four sisters. The details of his early life are contained in a presentencing report filed when Boucher was 21 and, by then, a petty criminal with a serious drug problem, by his own admission. The report was filed to a judge in February 1975 by criminologist Guy Pellerin who interviewed

Boucher, his mother, a friend and an investigator with the Montreal police.

At the time of Pellerin's assessment, Boucher was charged with breaking and entering. He had been nabbed in connection with three different break-ins during the fall of 1974. The first arrest came on November 5, just after midnight. Boucher smashed the front door window of a neighborhood grocery store in Hochelaga Maisonneuve, the low-income Montreal district where he had grown up. He grabbed 23 cartons of cigarettes and headed out. But his actions had set off an alarm heard by two cops in a nearby patrol car. When they pulled up to the front of the store, the officers saw Boucher standing in front of it. A green plastic bag filled with cigarette cartons lay at his feet.

Boucher was charged with breaking and entering and was released on a promise he'd stop breaking the law long enough to have his case heard. But a little over three weeks later, he broke into a woman's apartment on Hochelaga Street and stole her Fleetwood brand television, a luxury model worth nearly $400 at the time. Boucher had simply forced open the woman's door, grabbed the color television and made off with it. In October, the police found it and a bunch of electronic goods stolen from a stereo store in Boucher's apartment. Boucher claimed to have been high on drugs at the time of the break-ins and barely aware of what he was doing.

In his interview for Pellerin's report, Boucher told the criminologist he had quit hard drugs altogether. He said that while he enjoyed getting high he was also fully aware what damage the drugs could do to him. His girlfriend Diane Leblanc was eight months pregnant and Boucher said he realized that a huge responsibility was about to be placed on his shoulders.

At that point in his young life, Boucher had tried LSD, cocaine and heroin. He claimed to have quit hard drugs two months before his arrest, but admitted to still drinking alcohol and doing soft drugs like marijuana. He told Pellerin that he had created a habit and needed the softer drugs to compensate. He claimed he had stopped taking amphetamines because they were making him paranoid — he had become fearful of everything and often slept with a firearm.

Growing up, Boucher got along well with his mother but had developed a difficult relationship with his father, an abusive man with a drinking problem, according to Pellerin's report. Boucher's father was also a strict man who would not tolerate foolishness from his children. Boucher and his siblings distanced themselves from their father and Boucher, in particular, developed an attitude of indifference. If his father started yelling, he would simply leave the room, Pellerin was told. Boucher's mother told the criminologist that her husband's iron discipline with their children would often cause her to side with them.

Boucher dropped out of school while in grade 9 at the age of either 17 or 18. His performance in school was mediocre and he never developed an interest in his studies. He left home shortly thereafter. It was a time when he and his father were clashing constantly, but that didn't prevent Boucher from keeping in close contact with his mother. He even arranged to find an apartment near his family's home. Boucher took up a series of jobs, but for very short periods of time. He found them to be poor paying jobs that offered little in terms of a future. He also admitted that his drug use affected his focus.

Just before his arrest in 1974, Boucher had earned a competence card in construction. He told the criminologist he was eager to work in the same industry as his father because he had heard it paid well. But at the time, the construction industry in Montreal was dead. There were strikes and work stoppages. Boucher had found work on a construction site, but only for a week which discouraged him.

Pellerin, who went over Boucher's case, acknowledged that

the three months he spent in a detention center awaiting the outcome of his case had been difficult for him. He suffered from insomnia and was going through withdrawal. Boucher told the criminologist that the only drugs he could get in prison were from a doctor who was giving him something for the insomnia. Pellerin wrote that he believed the three months had been a lesson for Boucher, but he had doubts the lesson would stick. For example, he cautioned that Boucher's claims that he wanted to keep away from drugs were possibly the words of a man desperate to get out of jail.

"He has come to the moment of choice," Pellerin wrote in summarizing his report, adding he was concerned that if Boucher continued to take drugs, his life of crime would also continue. "Only time and experience will let us know if his motivation is real and if he has the energy to change his life," he wrote. On April 11, 1975, Boucher's girlfriend gave birth to a son, Françis. But fatherhood would not be the turning point the criminologist had hoped it would be. Five months after becoming a father, Boucher was incarcerated again. The judge who had received Pellerin's report ignored his suggestion that the jail time Boucher had already served would work as a deterrent — he sentenced Boucher to two months and fifteen days. And when he got out, Boucher continued his life of crime. Years later, he also would welcome his son Françis into the Rockers, his underling gang of drug dealers, thugs and hit men. Time would reveal that at the "moment of choice" Pellerin referred to in his report, Boucher had opted for the life of a criminal.

On November 5, 1975, only months after Pellerin filed his report, Boucher graduated to the big time. At 5:40 p.m., he burst into a butcher's shop on Ontario Street East with an accomplice named Laurent David and they threatened the 71-year-old owner with a rifle and a butcher's knife. All they managed to steal was $138.39. There were three other witnesses to the robbery, and

Boucher and David were quickly arrested. They each received a 40-month prison sentence, giving Boucher his first federal prison term. Up to that point, his criminal record showed only minor things like theft and mischief. David also had only served relatively light sentences, as well, for things like theft and being in possession of counterfeit money. Boucher ended up serving most of the 40 months of his sentence behind bars.

Like Boucher, Laurent David would continue a life of crime. But unlike Boucher, the rest of David's career would be influenced by a drug and alcohol problem. In 1995, when Boucher was putting together the Nomads, assembling a group of Hells Angels who were millionaires willing to kill to obtain a monopoly on their market, David was serving a sentence for the same type of crime he and Boucher did 20 years earlier. At the age of 47, David was still committing hold-ups with a firearm, including one in 1993 where he used a 9-mm handgun. He had spent most of his time in the interim hanging out in bars and trying to hold down jobs as either a nurse or an insurance salesman, with little success. A psychologist who examined David in 1994 determined that he had an immature and narcissistic personality. Although he was intelligent, David's career as a criminal was heavily influenced by alcohol.

The next time Boucher would be caught committing a crime was in 1978, soon after his 40-month sentence. This time around, his accomplice would be a lot closer to him. Boucher and his slightly younger brother Christian Boucher were charged with two break-ins committed at the same home in December 1978. According to the police reports, during the first break-in, the brothers stole a television, tools and library books from the victim. Less than two weeks later, and a few days after Christmas, they went back to the same home on Pie-ix Blvd. accompanied by a third man. According to the police report, this time, the Boucher brothers were looking for the victim's .22-calibre rifle.

They punched the victim in the face and forced him to sign a document saying he had sold them the rifle. They then used the rifle to rob $222 from the victim's friend, who was visiting. As the Boucher brothers were leaving, Christian told them that if they called the police he would kill them. The police were called, but the charges against them were eventually dropped.

Like his brother Maurice, Christian had done time for a few minor offences before being arrested in the holdup. He had served sentences for stealing cars and breaking and entering. After the 1978 arrest, Christian followed a different path from his brother. He would continue to be picked up for relatively minor crimes while living at the address on Leclaire Street that he shared with Maurice Boucher during the early 1980s. In 1986, Christian pleaded guilty to conspiring with another of the Boucher brothers after they were arrested for a break-in. For his part in the conspiracy Patrick Boucher was sentenced to two years in prison. In 1990, Christian Boucher would serve four months for assaulting a woman. In 1992, while his brother Maurice was growing in influence within the Hells Angels and creating the Rockers, Christian was busy stealing cars, and did five months for stealing a Mazda 626.

Patrick Boucher, three years younger than Maurice, would also end up spending most of his adult life in and out of prison. During the early 1990s, he was turned down for day parole while serving a sentence for breaking and entering into a home on Saint-Catherine Street East. He was later released after serving two-thirds of his two-year sentence. But even his statutory release was revoked because the Montreal Urban Community Police picked him up for breaking into his own home after a night of heavy drinking. In 1988, Patrick Boucher was sentenced to two years for the armed robbery of a woman. Three years later he would get another 18 months for breaking and entering on Leclaire Street. He ended the 1990s serving a sentence of two years probation after being caught in another break-in where he assaulted the arresting officer.

During the early 1980s, Maurice Boucher appeared to be headed down the same petty criminal path as his brothers. He was arrested late in December 1981 for breaking into a home in Montreal's east end, but in order to get bail, Boucher told the authorities that he was holding down a job at a manufacturing plant on Notre Dame Street East and living with Diane Leblanc. He had been hired at the appliance factory on July 9, 1979. He worked with plastics, earning a little over $10 an hour. According to letters filed in court, it was a job he would keep for at least four years. Boucher and an accomplice were accused of breaking into the home by smashing a window. They stole a radio, cassette player and some tools. But the charges against him were thrown out several months later after the victim somehow decided not to show up in court to testify against Boucher.

It was after a 1982 arrest that Boucher's criminal record began to indicate he was more than just a thief capable of smash-and-grab jobs. He was arrested for trying to extort money from a man working in a café. The victim accused Boucher of trying to force him to commit a robbery so he could pay back a debt. The charge was eventually dismissed, but by now the police appeared to have taken serious notice of Boucher. There was a note in the police report indicating the police had an intelligence file on Boucher. It noted that he appeared to operate out of a brasserie in Montreal's Hochelaga Maisonneuve district. The next time Boucher would be picked up was about a year later, in June 1983, for a stolen Visa credit card. He was fined $250. A few months later, he would be arrested again, this time for a minor theft, and fined $300 with a sentence of two years' probation.

Boucher and the SS

It was around this time that Boucher joined the SS, a motorcycle gang based in Pointe aux Trembles, on the eastern tip of the Montreal Island. Normand (Biff) Hamel, a man Boucher would later choose to become a founding member of the Nomads, had been part of the ss since 1981. Another member in the gang at the time was Salvatore Cazzetta, a man who would play a significant role in Boucher's life in the years to come. Cazzetta and his brother Giovanni later formed the Rock Machine, a gang that would eventually stand in opposition to the monopolistic attitude the Hells Angels and in particular, Maurice (Mom) Boucher took toward eastern Montreal in the early 1990s.

The Cazzetta Brothers

Like Boucher, Salvatore Cazzetta started out as a petty criminal who put little thought into what he was doing. He was arrested in 1975 for stealing a Ford Mustang over the Thanksgiving weekend and then scrapping the car for parts. Cazzetta made solving the crime a snap by leaving the skeleton of the stripped vehicle behind his home. Two years later, Cazzetta earned himself his first federal sentence when he broke into a bar with his brother Giovanni to steal a measly $300 in coins from cigarette machines. One reason he got two years for the minor crime was that Cazzetta rushed a cop who found him hiding in the basement.

By 1980, he was apparently interested in becoming a biker. He was caught prowling around the back of a woman's house at night, preparing to steal her Harley-Davidson. Years later, while recording information from another arrest, police would notice Cazzetta had the image of a Harley-Davidson motorcycle tattooed onto his arm along with the word "Brothers."

In 1981, Cazzetta was involved in what appeared to be gang-like activity at the Bordeaux detention center. An inmate, Wayne Story, was playing cards when other inmates stormed into the room and beat him with metal bars, killing him. But the case against Cazzetta and the four other inmates accused of killing

Story was weak. A jury acquitted them all on December 17, 1981.

By 1982, Cazzetta had developed a cavalier attitude toward the law. Just before dawn on November 26, he simply smashed in the window of a clothing store on Centre Street and grabbed whatever he could. A tenant in the building saw Cazzetta — who sported the same ponytail and beard he would keep for years — step out of the broken window with 26 leather coats draped on his shoulder. Cazzetta's dog followed behind him, making him even more recognizable. Another witness, a woman who was coming home from work, would later tell the police she saw Cazzetta standing outside the clothing store just minutes before the break-in. She couldn't help but notice him because he was urinating on a wall nearby while his dog faithfully waited beside him. She told the cops Cazzetta appeared to be drunk. Hours later, when the tenant told the store's owner what had happened, he jumped into a car and drove around looking for the mysterious bandit with the telltale ponytail. Within minutes, he located Cazzetta just a few streets away, walking the same dog he had been seen with during the break-in. Cazzetta served two years less a day for stealing the leather jackets. Shortly after completing that sentence, Cazzetta was involved in moving drugs. He served two months for possession of 56 grams of PCP.

A decade later, the police had intelligence that the Cazzetta brothers, Salvatore and Giovanni, were the heads of the Rock Machine and that the gang had its hands in drugs, prostitution and loan-sharking. Although Salvatore was one of the leaders in the biker war, he was actually behind bars for practically all of it. Arrested in 1994 for attempting to smuggle 200 kilos of cocaine into Canada through the U.S., Cazzetta was extradited to Florida and convicted. He spent three years in the U.S. penal system, earning a high school degree, and then was transferred back to Canada to serve out the remainder of his sentence. After serving two-thirds of his sentence, he was paroled and released from a medium-security penitentiary in Sainte-Anne-des-Plaines in June 2004. Salvatore Cazzetta smiled broadly when he learned the National Parole Board would not require him to live in a halfway house for the rest of his sentence. He told the panel of three commissioners that he ultimately planned to move to Ontario. "I am less known there," he said adding that the violence of the biker war was "not my style." He blamed the biker war on other members of the Rock Machine who took over after his arrest in 1994. He described his vision of the Rock Machine as "an association of businessmen" who merely planned to sell clothing through boutiques.

Like his brother, Giovanni Cazzetta denied involvement in the biker gang war. When he was up for parole in May 2005, Giovanni said the Rock Machine was formed years before the war started, and he pointed out that he too was behind bars when it began. He added that when the Rock Machine was formed, its members already had a sizeable share of Montreal's drug turf, at least enough to keep them satisfied, he said. Appearing before the parole board, Giovanni Cazzetta said the Hells Angels started the war and that if he hadn't been behind bars at the time, things might have turned out differently.

The 48-year-old Giovanni Cazzetta, who was greying at the temples but had managed to stay trim while serving a lengthy sentence for drug trafficking and possession of the proceeds of crime, said he planned to move to Calgary and start his life over in the construction industry.

"It was my choice. It was mine," Cazzetta said when asked about how he had become an influential drug dealer after spending his younger years "basically raising myself." Now he wanted to disassociate himself from members of the Rock Machine who by then had joined the Bandidos. He told Correctional Service Canada the same thing in 2004 when he was transferred from a maximum-security penitentiary to a medium-security one in Laval.

In 1997, while he was out on statutory release for a drug trafficking sentence, Cazzetta was arrested for the same offence
again. He told the parole board in May 2005 that his original plan
was to leave Montreal because he wanted no part of the war. He
claimed his arrest in 1997 was the result of him feeling obligated
to help out his old friends who needed his influence to score
large quantities of cocaine. "I had the contacts. I had the good
contacts," he said, adding he also stayed close to the Rock
Machine for his own protection.

Giovanni Cazzetta argued that he had had little to do with the
violence of the war, but he was asked, by parole board commissioner Paul Mercier, whether he had ever considered the other
victims of the war, like all the junkies both gangs had helped to
create. "There must have been many," Giovanni Cazzetta
acknowledged, but added later, "I made a decision. Crime is finished for me." The parole board turned him down.

Despite the fact that it would produce some of the major players in what would eventually become the biker gang war, the ss
amounted to little and disbanded sometime during the mid 1980s.

Maurice Boucher — Full-Patch

Maurice Boucher's criminal career was about to take a violent
turn. During the summer of 1984, he sexually assaulted a 16-year-
old girl while threatening her with a gun. He was arrested shortly
after and pleaded guilty within days. He was sentenced to 23
months in prison. After spending only a few days in a Joliette,
Quebec, detention center, he was transferred to Montreal where
he served most of his sentence behind bars and was released sometime in January 1986. But being behind bars didn't prevent Boucher
from committing crime. While incarcerated, Boucher managed to
receive unemployment payments on a biweekly basis. His little
scheme was discovered around the time he was released.

On May 1, 1987, Boucher's days of petty schemes, like cheating the unemployment office, were over. He received his full-patch as a member of the Hells Angels' Montreal chapter. The Montreal chapter was the first one ever established in Canada, and by the time Boucher joined it was a decade old. In the aftermath of the Lennoxville Purge, several members from the Montreal chapter were either fugitives or behind bars. A heavy recruitment process was on in Quebec. Boucher's buddy from the ss, Normand (Biff) Hamel had joined the Montreal chapter only months earlier. The police would later find it curious that Boucher received his patch just three days before 23-year-old Martin Huneault, the young leader of a biker gang called the Death Riders, was gunned down in a Laval brasserie on Cartier Blvd. At that point, the Death Riders were considered rivals of the Hells Angels.

In the minutes before he was gunned down, Huneault had been drinking a beer with his girlfriend and watching a hockey game on television. There were about six people in the brasserie at the time and a waitress was at the cash register. Someone walked in through the front door, strolled about twelve feet, stood facing Huneault from no more than three feet and opened fire. Three bullets struck Huneault — one square in the face, another went through his right arm and ricocheted through his upper body. Huneault fell to the floor and bled to death. What caught the attention of the police was that, within days of Huneault's death, members of the Death Riders were suddenly seen hanging out with Boucher and Hamel.

By then Boucher and Hamel were close friends. Hamel would ultimately be described by at least one of their associates as being more of a businessman than Boucher. But Hamel also had a

Normand (Biff) Hamel and Gilles Mathieu, members of the Nomads chapter.

violent streak. In 1986, as he was just about to become a Hells Angel, Hamel was detained at the Parthenais holding center, which used to be part of the Sûreté du Québec headquarters. Hamel was in the holding cell with about a dozen other inmates when one started to shout that he wanted to undergo a lie detector test. The inmate was soundly beaten by Hamel, who didn't appreciate the shouting.

If their criminal records are any indication, Hamel was involved in high-volume drug dealing long before Boucher was. During the summer of 1978, the Montreal Urban Community Police were investigating a major drug network operating in the city. It had taken them a long time to penetrate the network and their investigation took them to a Montreal bar called El Cid, where an informant had told an undercover officer he could buy some PCP. The undercover cop was able to buy 46 capsules from Hamel for $115. All the officer had to do was walk into El Cid where he was told he could find Hamel, who was easy to spot, thanks to the thick beard he would keep throughout most of his adult life. Hamel was seated under a television hung on the brasserie wall when the informant made the introduction. Hamel and the undercover cop went outside and made the deal in the investigator's rented car.

Hamel wasn't arrested right away. He was picked up later as the police busted the network. He was charged with the PCP sale. While he was awaiting trial, Hamel was arrested a second time. In this case, the police found almost the same amount of PCP as he had sold the undercover cop just months earlier. The drug was hidden in a closet in an apartment where Hamel lived with a girlfriend. The couple also kept a very precise scale in their bedroom. In October 1979, Hamel pleaded guilty to all the drug offences and was sentenced to a year in prison.

According to Ronnie Harbour, an informant for investigators in Project Rush, Hamel was already a major drug dealer when he joined the ss gang. Harbour admitted that he himself worked out of El Cid, the same brasserie where Hamel once sold. Harbour was able to move 20 grams of cocaine a night for Hamel. Harbour also told the investigators that by the early 1990s, Boucher, Hamel and Gaetan Comeau, another Hells Angel from the Montreal chapter, had graduated to major drug trafficking and were working as a unit.

Boucher's criminal record after he joined the Hells Angels began to reflect his involvement with the violent gang. In 1988, he was arrested by the Peel Regional Police after attempting to hijack a truck in Mississauga, Ontario, using nothing more than a board with a nail hammered through it. Boucher had the case transferred to Montreal in exchange for a guarantee he would plead guilty. When the case was transferred, Hamel posted a $10,000 bond to secure Boucher's release. Boucher arranged for the bond through his own company, Irazu Inc., which was involved in importing. According to court records, the company was involved in shipping legitimate products from Costa Rica. However, one of its sales representatives in 1991 was Richard Muselle, a senior citizen. Years later, Muselle would try to help the Hells Angels hide millions of dollars in his home when the Nomads learned the police were aware of the apartments they were using to store the millions in cash from drug sales. On the surface, at least, Irazu Inc. was run like a legitimate business and even took a company to court over a dispute concerning coffee beans from Costa Rica. Irazu had sold a large quantity of coffee beans on consignment to another Montreal company and felt it had been cheated $3,300. Boucher's company actually won its case, and a judge awarded the money they were seeking.

Boucher kept his promise to the Ontario court and was sentenced to five months for trying to hijack the truck in Mississauga. He was also placed on two years' probation. A year later, he was arrested for lying to a police officer in Sorel, where the Montreal chapter kept its bunker. Boucher quickly pleaded guilty to the offence and was given the choice of paying a $200 fine or spending a few months in jail. For some reason, Boucher chose jail and on New Year's Eve, he welcomed a new decade while in the Bordeaux detention center in Montreal. He was released in March 1990. Seven months later he was arrested while carrying a .38-calibre revolver. Again he pleaded guilty. But this time he chose to pay a $900 fine over doing another five months in a provincial detention center. Shortly after his arrest, Boucher claimed to be residing in Halifax. But he later changed the address he provided to the courts to the location of the Hells Angels' bunker in Sorel.

For his 39th birthday, on June 21, 1992, Boucher decided to treat himself and some friends to a ride on his boat. The pleasure craft was stopped by police patrolling the Saint Lawrence River in Sorel, and Boucher was fined $200 for not having a permit for the boat and because some of his passengers were not wearing life jackets. It would be Boucher's only run-in with the law that year, which was remarkable considering he had created the Rockers only months before, a gang of drug dealers who would take his orders and sell his drugs, an indication that his drug trafficking business was flourishing in Montreal.

Two of the first members of the Rockers were Richard and Patrick Lock, a father-and-son team of drug traffickers. Even before they were members of the Rockers, the Locks had reputations as big-time drug dealers in Montreal, and, according to a man named Jean Dubé who turned informant, they were even able to move large quantities of drugs to dealers in Ontario.

Months after forming the Rockers, Boucher was picked up again for a weapons violation. In May 1993, he was pulled over in Anjou, a Montreal suburb, and when the police searched his car they found a prohibited martial arts weapon, a telescopic bar. Again he pleaded guilty before the case went to trial and agreed to pay a $500 fine. During this time in the 1990s, Boucher frequently listed his address as being at or near the Hells Angels' Sorel bunker. If this was true, Boucher's son, Françis, spent his formative years living either in or next door to the Hells Angels' bunker. In 1994, days before his 19th birthday he proved he could be just like his old man and committed an armed robbery while breaking into a home with two other adolescents. In August 1994, Françis Boucher pleaded guilty and was fined $500 plus 100 hours of community service. Boucher's son, his accomplice Martin Brizard and an unnamed minor got off easy considering they were initially charged with armed robbery and confining the man they were robbing.

But in 1994, Boucher, the father, had a lot more on his mind than his son's petty crimes.

Lines Are Drawn

As informants would later spell out in court or in statements, 1994 was the year very clear lines were drawn in what would become the biker gang war. The Hells Angels and in particular Boucher were giving drug dealers an ultimatum: either buy drugs exclusively from us or face dire consequences.

For some, who would later shed light on the early years of the war, a key date was October 19, 1994. Maurice Lavoie had been shot dead in Repentigny just after he made a decision to begin buying his drugs from the Hells Angels instead of the Pelletier Clan. It appeared that the Pelletier Clan was sending a message to the Hells Angels. A 22-year-old woman who was seated in his vehicle next to him survived the attack despite being struck three times by bullets. Just months earlier, Pierre Daoust, a member of the Death Riders and close ally to the Hells Angels, had met with a similar fate. On July 13, 1994, around 10:30 a.m., he was working alone in the motorcycle repair garage he co-owned. He was inside the garage when three people walked in wearing masks and motorcycle helmets. Two of them walked toward Daoust and, after they made sure it was him, opened fire. He was taken to a hospital where he died about an hour later. At least eight bullets from one gun entered Daoust's body between the shoulder blades, ripping through his lungs and heart. Another six bullets from a different gun went through his stomach and part of his chest. Shots fired from a third gun went through his scrotum and his left thigh. He quickly went into cardiac arrest and bled to death.

Daoust's death is considered by many to have been the first in the biker war. When Lavoie's death followed, it meant two dealers who had chosen to side with the Hells Angels were dead and the conflict was about to boil over. The generally accepted version of events in the underworld is that things really heated up after Lavoie was killed. Some alleged that Boucher retaliated by ordering Sylvain Pelletier dead. Pelletier's friend Patrick Call had been arrested a day after the Lavoie murder, and the Pelletier Clan's fingerprints were all over the homicide scene. Nine days after Lavoie's murder, Pelletier was killed by an explosion from a bomb that had been planted in his Jeep. His girlfriend, who was seven months pregnant at the time, had just stepped out of the SUV before it was destroyed.

Several months later, informant Dany Kane would tell his handlers in the RCMP that he had heard members of a Hells Angels' puppet gang called the Rowdy Crew, structured along the same lines as the Rockers, had killed Pelletier. The police were already looking at the gang's members as possible suspects. A member of the Rowdy Crew had rented an apartment in front of Pelletier's home and then quickly canceled the lease the day after Pelletier was killed. The Rowdy Crew was a biker gang based in a small city east of Montreal and controlled by various members of the Hells Angels. Exactly who had actually carried out the bombing was an irrelevant point to street dealers in Montreal's east end. Pelletier's death signaled that, after months of rumors about a possible war, it was now a reality.

Within weeks of Pelletier's death, members of the Alliance called a meeting in a Montreal bar in November and hatched a plot to kill Boucher. The plan was to park a truck full of explosives in front of a restaurant where Boucher was known to hang out and detonate the explosives the moment he got close. Sylvain Pelletier's brother Harold was part of the Alliance meeting along with about a dozen drug dealers interested in seeing Boucher eliminated. Martin Pellerin, a member of the Alliance, was left in charge of placing the dynamite in the truck and making sure the bomb went off when Boucher arrived at the restaurant. Martin Simard, another Alliance member, was willing to finance the operation by paying for the dynamite. Also involved in the conspiracy were Alliance members René Pelletier, Bruno Lévesque, Hubert Lanteigne and a man named Normand Tremblay. The truck was parked in front of the restaurant and the Alliance members waited for Boucher to show up. But he never did. Or at least not before someone working for the city noticed the truck was parked illegally and towed it to a municipal lot. The dynamite was detonated in the lot by someone in the Alliance when no one was around.

By this time Dany Kane had been feeding information to the RCMP for a few months. He had been hanging out with Scott Steinert, an aggressive American who appeared to be willing to do anything to be a Hells Angel. Even before the Pelletier bombing, Kane had informed the RCMP that Steinert was gathering C4 explosives for the Hells Angels. He also told the RCMP that the Hells Angels believed the failed truck-bomb attempt was an effort to kill Boucher and Steinert together as they often met to discuss business at the exact spot where the truck had been parked.

Dany Kane (center, bottom row) hanging out with fellow members of
the Rockers. Also in the photo are René Charlebois (right, bottom row),
Jean-Guy Bourgoin (left, bottom row).

Informant Dany Kane

During his first meeting, in which he decided to turn informant,
Kane told his RCMP handlers that he had been recruited by David
(Wolf) Carroll and Walter (Nurget) Stadnick to preside over three
chapters of an Ontario puppet gang called the Demons Keepers.
The plan failed miserably. Kane said Carroll had a serious drinking problem and was constantly broke, so the Demons Keepers
didn't have the support they needed to intimidate drug dealers in
cities like Ottawa, Cornwall and Toronto. Kane also described the
men recruited to be Demons Keepers as "imbeciles."

The plans were shelved during the spring of 1994, and shortly
after that, Kane was introduced to Steinert who, by then, was a
prospect in the Hells Angels' Montreal chapter. Steinert told
Kane about plans he had to expand into places in Ontario like
Belleville and Kingston. It was during Kane's second meeting
with the RCMP, held in the parking lot of a hotel in Ottawa, that
he started to talk of what the other Hells Angels thought of
Steinert. The American, who apparently had the backing of

Robert (Tiny) Richard, the Hells Angels' national president, and Boucher, was considered greedy and impulsive by the others.

On November 7, 1994, Kane phoned Corporal Verdon and warned him that the Hells Angels were looking to kill a man because he might testify against Steinert in a drug trial. Verdon learned that the man was about to be transferred to the Longueuil courthouse and warned the Sûreté du Québec.

In January 1995, Kane was approached by Steinert about joining the Rockers. Steinert told him it was Boucher himself who was interested in seeing Kane become part of his gang. During that same month, Kane told the RCMP that Steinert and Gaetan Comeau, a longtime member of the Hells Angels, had gone out looking for Paul (Sasquatch) Porter, a leader in the Rock Machine. A few days later, Kane said Boucher and Steinert chased André (Frisé, or "Curly") Sauvageau, another member of

Paul (Sasquatch) Porter, seen here when he was a member of the Rock Machine. (John Mahoney, *The Montreal Gazette*)

the Rock Machine, along Highway 40 until they spotted two Sûreté du Québec vehicles. With these bravado acts, Steinert appeared to be gaining Boucher's respect.

Kane described Boucher as a shrewd criminal who went to bed early and woke up very early every morning. Kane said Boucher told him it was easier to do business this way because he felt it was tougher for the police to follow him during daytime hours. Kane said Boucher also appeared to be getting information from inside the Montreal Urban Community Police, which was not surprising since Kane had known for some time that the

Hells Angels were willing to pay dearly for inside information from the police. In particular, Boucher was willing to pay double a cop's salary for information on what the police knew about his organization. In March 1995, Boucher told Kane that he had a source inside the police who advised him to keep things cool for about a month because the police were now focusing closely on him. Kane's handlers felt it was no coincidence that Boucher learned this at around the same time the Montreal Urban Community Police formed a special unit within its anti-gang squad. Its assignment was to focus specifically on the activities of Boucher and his henchman André (Toots) Tousignant.

Kane described a strange incident that occurred after he, Boucher and other Hells Angels' underlings had eaten at a greasy spoon in Montreal's Hochelaga Maisonneuve district. As they were leaving the restaurant, a man driving a Mustang pulled up and spoke briefly to Boucher. It was obvious they were friends because the pair shook hands and Boucher stuck his head in the car to talk to the man. After the man drove away, Kane took note of the car's licence plate. Boucher turned to Kane and the two other men they were with and said, "He's my pig. He's on surveillance today."

Kane's RCMP handlers were concerned that Boucher had actually created an elaborate setup, hoping to use a possibly genuine police source to see if Montreal investigators verified the Mustang's licence plate number through police databases. If this was the case, Boucher would know that one of the men who dined with him that day was an informant. A discreet check was done days later and the car was found to be registered to a former employee of a security company. The man's girlfriend lived next door to one of Boucher's residences. By all appearances, Boucher had indeed been trying to sniff out an informant among the trio he had eaten with that day.

Kane's detailed reports gave the RCMP unprecedented insight

into the Hells Angels' inner workings. For instance, Kane told his RCMP handlers that the botched truck bombing attempt wasn't the first time Boucher had learned someone wanted him dead. Kane informed them that in November 1994, Boucher had put out a contract on a guy named Éric Morgan who had bragged that he was going to kill the Hells Angel. The police later deduced Kane was referring to Stéphane Éric Morgan. Kane had heard that Morgan once dealt drugs for Boucher but eventually decided to go to the other side and join the Rock Machine. Morgan would later be one of the victims among the 13 murder charges filed against Boucher and other members of the Nomads in connection with the Project Rush investigation.

As the war was beginning to heat up in 1994, Kane told the RCMP that the Hells Angels were aware that the Alliance was a serious group of well-financed drug traffickers. He also revealed that Boucher's plans to form the Nomads chapter were underway.

Informant Harold Pelletier

Months after the truck bombing attempt, Kane told the RCMP that some of the people involved in the conspiracy had turned against the Alliance and told Boucher who was behind the plot. Details on the conspiracy would only come to the police much later from someone else involved in it. A year after the plan failed miserably, Sylvain Pelletier's brother Harold turned himself in to the police, and, out of the blue, admitted to the murder of a man named Michel Beaulieu, a homicide that dated back to 1983. Rather than face the prospect of being hunted down by the Hells Angels, Pelletier, who was then 37, decided he would be safer behind bars, and became an informant, a decision that meant he would have to detail all of his past crimes.

He recounted how he used a .38-calibre Smith & Wesson revolver to kill Beaulieu, firing three shots in the man's face and neck from close range. Two of the bullets bounced around inside

Beaulieu's skull causing fatal damage. Pelletier had caught Beaulieu off guard as he lay in bed just before 6 a.m. on August 7, 1983. Pelletier had cut through a screen door at the back of Beaulieu's home using a knife. It was a hot day and the other door to the back entrance had been left open. Pelletier left the weapon behind as Beaulieu's girlfriend pretended to sleep through the shooting, hoping to keep alive. She had been awoken by the shots but kept her eyes shut, immediately realizing what had happened when Beaulieu's blood splattered on her. When Pelletier left, she hid in the living room and called the police.

Within hours of the shooting, homicide detectives were building a case that pointed to the Pelletier Clan. Beaulieu's mother told them he was involved in a mortgage with one of the Pelletier brothers. A friend of Beaulieu's told the police that he had been dealing hashish for a gang, while trying to eke out a living by staging phony car accidents, and he had gotten into trouble paying his bills. But after tracing the murder to the Pelletier Clan, the cops were unable to gather enough evidence to file charges. The case remained cold until Pelletier, apparently looking to protect himself from what was developing in the biker war, decided to become an informant.

After his arrest, Pelletier gave the police several statements between October 17, 1995, and June 18, 1996. In exchange for full disclosure, Pelletier could plead to second-degree murder in Beaulieu's death, despite the extremely cold-blooded way it had been carried out. And cold-blooded it was. Pelletier had met Beaulieu at a bar hours before killing him. The two men had a drink, and Pelletier even clinked glasses with the man he was about to kill. The guilty plea would come with a sentencing recommendation of life with a chance at parole after ten years. The contract called for Pelletier to be paid $140 a month in exchange for information while behind bars. He would also be paid $450 a week for three years once he got out of prison.

Harold Pelletier admitted that he killed Beaulieu for the Pelletier Clan because he had cheated the gang out of money. Pelletier admitted to taking part in 17 murders between 1983 and 1996. Despite the failed attempt on Boucher, he had developed a reputation as a reliable hit man for the Pelletier Clan. At the height of his tenure in the Clan, he was making $20,000 a week. What the Crown got in the deal was described as a "mine of information" on the Pelletier Clan and the biker gang world.

But Pelletier ended up violating two parts of his informant contract, one stipulating that he not commit another crime while under contract and the other that he behave himself while in prison. He nullified the contract when prison officials learned Pelletier was suspected of conspiring to kill another inmate. Because of this, he was denied day parole in September 2002. Just a year earlier, while carrying out their raids in Operation Springtime 2001, the police found a copy of Pelletier's informant contract at one of Luc (Bordel) Bordeleau's residences. It was among other papers Bordeleau had gathered on rival gangsters.

In interviews with police back in 1995 and 1996, Pelletier gave investigators several names of people who had attended the meeting in which the plot to kill Boucher was discussed. A little over a year after Pelletier's arrest, the police rounded up 14 people suspected of being in on the plot. At least four would end up convicted and serving federal prison sentences. But several were released for lack of evidence. Some would go on to play major roles in the biker war, including Yvon (Mon Mon) Roy, Serge (Merlin) Cyr and Gilles Lambert. All three were also quickly targeted for elimination by the Hells Angels.

Another man charged in the conspiracy and released was Tony Jalbert. In the months leading up to the failed plot to kill Boucher, Jalbert had gone from the Hells Angels to the Alliance. He would stay loyal to the Alliance throughout the biker war and, apparently, after it ended. While he was still with the Hells

Serge (Merlin) Cyr, a member of the Rock Machine who later joined the Bandidos.

Angels, he would unwittingly introduce Boucher to someone who would ultimately help convict the Hells Angel of murder. Shortly after it became public knowledge that Pelletier had become an informant, Jalbert asked to be placed in solitary confinement at the federal penitentiary where he was serving time for his part in a plot to steal a large quantity of dynamite. He told authorities he feared for his life and preferred doing hard time in a lonely cell to living among people who might be seeking revenge.

Jalbert was a member of the Rock Machine when the gang decided to join the Bandidos. In 2005, Correctional Service Canada hauled him back to a penitentiary after he violated the conditions of his statutory release. He was not supposed to associate with other criminals for the duration of his sentence for drug and weapons offences. But he was spotted working out at a gym run by the Hells Angels. He told the parole board he'd thought it would be therapeutic. His release was revoked primarily because there was evidence he had threatened to kill a woman he was seeing.

Serge Boutin and Jean-Richard Larivière were also let off for a lack of evidence in the 1994 plot to kill Boucher. Both were independent drug dealers who would eventually choose sides in the biker war. By the time they were charged in the plot to kill Boucher, they were already members of the Rockers, and he was their boss. It is very possible that one of the two were Boucher's mole at the meeting where the Alliance plotted to kill him.

The attempted truck bombing was not the first botched attempt to kill Boucher. Months earlier, the police caught Jean

(Le Français) Duquaire and Michel Boyer driving in a stolen car, crossing the Jacques Cartier Bridge. Inside the car was a .357 Magnum and two Cobray semiautomatic weapons, the weapon of choice during the biker war. It later became widely known in the underworld that Duquaire and Boyer were on their way to kill Boucher on that day in the summer of 1994.

Retribution from the Hells Angels was apparently swift. Boyer, a drug dealer for the Pelletier Clan, was shot to death as he arrived at his home in Repentigny on October 17, 1995. For years, Duquaire would remain a high priority on the Hells Angels' hit list. Another man high on that list was Normand Baker, a member of the Rock Machine. He was shot to death in Mexico on January 4, 1995. Kane told the RCMP the Hells Angels targeted Baker because they had information that he had killed Pierre Daoust, one of the first murders in the biker war. The Hells Angels also suspected Baker was behind a failed attempt to kill Normand Robitaille. On July 14, 1994, an unknown shooter opened fire on Robitaille at a garage on Rouen Street in Montreal. Robitaille survived the attempt, suffering only minor wounds. François Hinse, who would go on to become a member of the Hells Angels' Trois Rivières chapter, was arrested in Mexico shortly after Baker's murder, and the gun used in the murder was seized.

It appeared to be a clear-cut case. Witnesses had helped apprehend Hinse at the scene, and the police had the murder weapon. But Kane told the RCMP the Hells Angels were very confident Hinse would not only get off on the charges but that he would spend very little time behind bars awaiting trial. The police in Mexico, well known for their corruption, were believed to have been bought off by the Hells Angels. Kane told the RCMP that Boucher in particular appeared to have many connections in Mexico. The informant would also later tell the police of rumors he had heard that members of the Trois Rivières chapter complained that buying off the Mexican authorities to free Hinse had cost too much.

By early 1995, Boucher was rarely seen traveling without someone from the Rockers working as his bodyguard. He was also being followed frequently by the police. On March 24, 1995, he was riding in a car with André (Toots) Tousignant, a member of the Rockers, when they were pulled over by the Sûreté du Québec. Boucher was charged with carrying a loaded 9-mm Walther pistol with the serial number filed off. Kane would later tell the RCMP that Marc Sigman, a man who was then tied to the Rockers, told him that while the Sûreté du Québec were interrogating Boucher about the pistol, they let him know there was an informant in his organization.

Kane heard that Boucher reflected on this information and started putting together a list of suspects. Sigman was worried because he'd heard he was on the list and because he was the least well known to Boucher. Sigman told Kane that Boucher also considered him, Tousignant, Paul (Fon Fon) Fontaine, Steinert and a sixth person not closely tied to the gang, as possible informants.

A few days later, Steinert would tell Kane to relax and that talk of an informant wasn't serious. But it was. The RCMP did some digging and learned that while Boucher's case was before the courts, an investigator had been forced to admit that certain information the police had on Boucher had come from a coded source. Tousignant was in the courtroom following Boucher's case when this was said. Kane noticed that the Hells Angels began clamming up and were not saying much to each other. By now, according to Kane, tensions were beginning to develop within the Hells Angels' Montreal and Nomads chapters. Although he had become close to Boucher, who by then was the president of the Nomads chapter, Steinert was still a prospect of the Montreal chapter from which Boucher had separated himself at that point. Kane told the RCMP that Steinert was looking to take over control of the drug trade in Manitoba for the Hells Angels. But Walter (Nurget) Stadnick, a longtime Montreal chapter member who had jumped ship to the

Nomads along with Boucher, did not appreciate this because expansion westward was part of the chapter's ultimate plan. Internally, trouble was brewing, Kane told the RCMP.

This time around, Boucher wasn't given the choice of paying a fine on the weapons conviction. He was sentenced to six months in prison and three years probation. The sentence would set off an interesting chain of events Boucher would later regret.

Maurice Boucher and Stéphane (Godasse) Gagné

Boucher didn't know it yet but he was about to reestablish a contact during this prison sentence. On March 27, 1995, Boucher was transferred from a Montreal detention center to one in Sorel. As a now eight-year veteran of the Hells Angels, a gang that maintained a bunker in Sorel, Boucher had considerable influence over the other Sorel inmates. As a demonstration of that power, Boucher began ordering other inmates to do his bidding. One of those inmates would turn out to be Stéphane (Godasse) Gagné, a drug dealer Boucher already knew and a man he would regret ever meeting. Tony Jalbert had set up the previous introduction. Years later, Gagné would testify against the Hells Angels and more significantly, against Boucher.

Gagné would testify that he first met Boucher during the summer of 1993, shortly after being robbed by the Rockers of 15 or 20 quarter-grams of cocaine. He had been running a drug den in Montreal's east end. Boucher was impressed with Gagné and agreed to let him buy cocaine from him. Part of the deal involved cash up front. Another part was transacted "sur la bras," an expression used in Quebec's underworld meaning the dealer could purchase on credit.

Shortly afterward, Gagné was caught trying to sell drugs to a double agent and was sent to the Bordeaux detention center where Jean (Le Français) Duquaire, Michel Boyer and Stéphane Morgan tried to determine which side of the war he was on.

Duquaire placed a photo of Boucher on the floor and told Gagné to urinate on it. Gagné refused and was beaten for it. Shortly after the incident, Gagné was transferred to the detention center in Sorel where he got to know Boucher a little better. They would talk during Alcoholics Anonymous and Narcotics Anonymous meetings. Gagné requested a transfer to the same wing as Boucher but was refused. But they often ate together. At one meal, Boucher complained about the fact they were being served shepherd's pie two or three times a week. Boucher said he and other inmates were fed up with it and that something had to be done. Gagné took this to mean he had to take care of the problem, so he tried to organize a protest in which other inmates would refuse to eat shepherd's pie. One inmate scoffed at the plan so Gagné arranged to have him beaten in his sleep.

Jean Dubé, a man who eventually turned informant on members of the Rockers, told the police that in July 1995, Boucher's wing of the Sorel prison was denied access to leisure activities. Dubé said Boucher asked him to vandalize the pool in retaliation. Instead of doing the job himself, Dubé contracted it out, but he was still rewarded with a carton of cigarettes for arranging to have someone damage the pool's tiles with a razor blade.

But the most chilling tale to come out of Boucher's eventful stay at Sorel came from Nicole Quesnel, the detention center's warden. Her house was set on fire on June 9, 1995. She would later tell the police she was certain it was set ablaze on orders from Mom Boucher. In the weeks leading up to the arson, Boucher had made seven requests for temporary leaves. She turned him down every time because he was a Hells Angel and because he refused to change his ways while behind bars. Four days before the fire was set, Quesnel had turned Boucher down again. Days after the fire, when Boucher was refused leave yet again, he made a remark that suggested he wanted her to know he was behind the torching of her home.

Boucher was never charged with the arson but the police were now seeing how much influence the Hells Angel had, and the degree of Boucher's arrogance. Shortly afterward, Boucher was transferred, on July 14, 1995, to a prison in Cowansville where he finished out the final two weeks of his sentence.

While Boucher spent five months behind bars causing mischief and allegedly terrorizing prison officials, his network of drug dealers was in trouble. Boucher had apparently developed such a good reputation among Montreal's drug suppliers that the Rockers could purchase drugs on credit using his good name. But by May 1995, only a matter of weeks into Boucher's sentence, the Rockers were experiencing serious shortages in cocaine and hashish, Kane told the RCMP. Rival gang, the Rock Machine, appeared to gather steam and began taking over some of the territory the Rockers had controlled since 1992. Kane said Montreal's Gay Village in particular had become a hotly contested area. According to Kane, Paul (Fon Fon) Fontaine, a Rocker, was growing frustrated with the lack of supply and complained about having to pay $35,000 cash up front for a kilogram of cocaine, something he'd never had to do when Boucher was around. By June, the Rockers had developed a conspiracy theory that the Mafia was behind their shortages and were grumbling that it appeared the Mob would only deal with Boucher.

That same summer Steinert began causing serious problems for the Hells Angels. According to Kane, Steinert controlled a bar on Montreal's Crescent Street, a popular destination for thirsty tourists and young Montrealers. Steinert had a run-in with the bouncer of the bar beneath his and ignored the consequences. Kane said Steinert waited until closing time and then he beat the man severely. The problem was that the bouncer worked for another Hells Angel. This huge mistake only seemed to make Steinert more cocky. He told Kane that he was preparing to sell drugs in Winnipeg whether Stadnick and the other Hells Angels liked it or not.

By July 25, Boucher was out of prison. Steinert's apparent sup-porter in the Hells Angels was a free man again, but things were about to change.

A Rude Awakening

On August 9, 1995, something happened that woke up most Quebecers to the fact a war among biker gangs was going on in their streets. The wake-up call came in the form of a bomb that went off on Adam Street in Montreal, not far from the Olympic Stadium. The blast instantly killed 26-year-old Marc Dubé as he sat in his Jeep waiting for a friend. Eleven-year-old Daniel Desrochers was playing with a friend nearby and was struck in the head by a piece of the Jeep that had been propelled by the explosion. The boy suffered severe brain damage and died days later. His death would spark a widespread public outcry for the federal government to do something that would help the police take on the Hells Angels and the Alliance and put an end to their increasingly violent war.

Dubé had ties to drug dealers but one theory that eventually emerged was that the bomb was much more likely intended for Normand Tremblay, a member of the Alliance who had a suv similar to Dubé's. In fact, in the days leading up to the bombing, Tremblay had sold Dubé the wheels from his sports utility vehi-cle. Shortly after Dubé and Daniel Desrochers died, Tremblay was himself arrested for an attempted murder and for being in possession of explosive materials. He decided to become a police informant. His sworn statements would later end up in the Hells Angels' hands.

What was largely ignored by the media in the aftermath of Desrochers's death is that Tremblay managed to quietly plead guilty to being part of the 1994 conspiracy to kill Boucher with the truck bomb. The guilty plea came in January 1997, more than two years after the 11 year old was killed, but it provided a clear motive for the Hells Angels to have been behind the botched bombing that ended the boy's life. Nearly ten years after Daniel's death, his mother Josée Anne Desrochers died of pneumonia in a hospital over the 2005 Easter weekend. Despite a brave campaign in which she publicly criticized the biker gangs and pushed for tougher anti-gang legislation, Desrochers' mother never saw his killers charged with the crime.

More than a week after Daniel Desrochers died, Kane told the RCMP about Steinert's odd behavior both before and after the explosion. He said that in the days leading up to it, Steinert had ordered three bomb kits from a man with ties to the Hells Angels. Kane claimed the Hells Angels had been buying explosives from the man for months. According to Kane, Steinert was very eager for the kits and wanted them right away. He told Kane that things were about to "rock and roll." But after the death of an innocent boy, Steinert never spoke of the bomb kits again. Kane said Steinert started asking other gang members what they thought should happen to the person responsible for Desrochers' death. When they replied the culprit should be liquidated, Steinert grew more quiet. Kane said that in general the Hells Angels condemned the bomb because a child had been killed and the tragedy placed heavier police surveillance on them.

The gang's underlings had been warned before. In an earlier briefing to the RCMP more than two weeks prior to the bomb that killed Desrochers, Kane said that David (Wolf) Carroll warned the Rockers and other people associated with the Hells Angels about using bombs. Earlier that summer, on July 14, a bomb planted at a house in a small town north of Montreal had nearly killed two children. The police later found small quantities of drugs like cocaine in the house and said they believed the actual target was the homeowner's brother, a man with ties to the Alliance.

Daniel Desrochers' death would bring a more intense police focus on the biker war. Several members of both the Hells Angels and the Rock Machine were placed under constant police surveillance. A few months after his stint for carrying a firearm Boucher found himself under arrest again. He had been overheard on a police wiretap counseling Steven (Bull) Bertrand, a friend and fellow drug trafficker, on how to solve a problem with a baseball bat. Boucher's bail hearing on October 27, 1995, would reveal just how far he had come as a Hells Angel. Because of Desrochers' death and the fact the police quickly attributed it to the biker war, the bail hearing, even though it was for a relatively minor crime not related to the bombing, was widely covered by the media.

Sgt. Guy Ouellette, a longtime veteran investigator with the Sûreté du Québec, testified on the Crown's behalf in an attempt to have Boucher held on the minor charge. Ouellette had several years under his belt investigating the Hells Angels, and on September 6, 1994, he was made part of a multidisciplinary squad within the Sûreté that focused on the biker gangs. On October 5, 1995, he was part of a fusion of investigators from the Sûreté, the Montreal Urban Community Police and the RCMP. The special squad, dubbed Carcajou or Wolverine, was a response to the public outcry after Desrochers' death.

Part of Ouellette's role in the squad was to be prepared for such court hearings. He possessed a computer-like memory with the extraordinary ability to instantly recall the tiniest detail about a biker. Ouellette was asked to describe what the Hells Angels in Montreal were involved in at that point. "They have several sectors of activity," he said. "Everything that is economically profitable, that is to say drugs, trafficking in all its forms, importation in terms of drugs, prostitution, strippers in licensed establishments, money laundering, every activity where they could make money."

Boucher's lawyer Leo-Rene Maranda was opposed to this depiction. He acknowledged that Boucher was "a soldier," but questioned whether he should be blamed for all of the army's crimes. The judge ignored the objection and Ouellette was asked where the Hells Angels ranked in terms of drugs in Quebec. "They are on top of the pyramid when it comes to importation. They control dealing on the streets. They control the dealers inside bars," Ouellette testified, adding it was already clear to police that the Hells Angels were eliminating drug dealers in eastern Montreal and using murder, bombs and assault to get the job done.

With the war only about a year old, the police already estimated that between 25 and 30 homicides could be attributed to the conflict. Ouellette pointed out that when the war started, the Hells Angels had four chapters in Quebec. "Since the beginning of March 1995 a fifth chapter was formed and was called Nomads. According to the information we have, Mr. Boucher is the president of the Nomads, the Hells Angels," Ouellette said. "It is a chapter like the ten others that we have in Canada. But particularly, according to the information that we have, the Nomads do not have to observe the territorial limits of distribution, dealing of drugs or control over criminal activities. They can exercise their activities all over the province as well as in other provinces in Canada. What we are observing right now is that it is happening. . . . The information that we have in our possession at this stage is that the war going on now originated from the Nomads, originated from individuals who, in March [1995], regrouped under the name of the Nomads."

Ouellette also brought up the trouble Boucher caused while serving his most recent sentence. He said Boucher had actually asked to not be taken to the Bordeaux detention centre because he found it too violent at the time and had specifically requested the transfer to Sorel. Ouellette revealed that besides the fire at Quesnel's home, an assistant-warden's home had also been the target of a recent arson fire.

Then he began detailing the evidence the cops had on Boucher in the case he was charged in. Ouellette bluntly described Steven

(Bull) Bertrand as a man who was close to Boucher and operating a drug trafficking network for him. It was on September 23, 1995, around 3 a.m. that Bertrand's problems began. Bertrand was in a bar on Saint Laurent Blvd., discussing who had the right to sell drugs there with a few men. During the discussion, one of the men punched Bertrand in the face. He fell to the ground and two other thugs proceeded to kick him. In the hours that followed, Bertrand made several calls and paged Boucher twice. Boucher called him back at 5:33 p.m. that same day. Bertrand said he had been beaten badly and was sporting a black eye.

"Mr. Boucher said to not let it end there, to take revenge," Ouellette testified adding that Boucher told Bertrand to use a baseball bat to solve his problem. But then Bertrand advised Boucher that during his flurry of phone calls he had learned one of his assailants was friendly with members of the Hells Angels' chapter in Trois Rivières. Three days later, the police listened in as Boucher and Bertrand had another conversation. Boucher had done some asking around and determined that Bertrand had been given the green light to get revenge — but he added that a prospect in the Trois Rivières chapter named Mario Brouillette had advised that Bertrand let it go.

This was something for Bertrand to consider but Boucher advised him that he shouldn't accept what had happened to him at all. Boucher told Bertrand that if he wanted to be respected he had to take care of it. At one point in the conversation, Boucher told Bertrand "Don't patch that," meaning he shouldn't patch it up and forget about the beating he had received. By this point, the police knew about Boucher's home on a large real estate lot on Marie Victorin Street in Contrecouer, complete with a horse stable. His son Françis lived next door in a house mortgaged, according to a police affidavit filed during the Project Rush investigation, by the head of a Bank of Montreal branch who was under investigation for fraud at the time. The police were also investigating whether the same bank manager had whipped up a phony mortgage for René Charlebois, a member of the Nomads chapter. Months before Operation Springtime 2001 was carried out, the bank manager was charged with fraud amounting to several million dollars between 1996 and 1999, all of it related to mortgaging houses through his Bank of Montreal branch. As soon as he got out of prison for his scuba diving expedition in 1993, Bordeleau moved into a Contrecoeur house near Boucher's.

"Mr. Boucher is the head, or the instigator of the present biker war in Quebec. He is the godfather of an affiliated group that is called the Rockers of Montreal," Ouellette said during the bail hearing. Maranda decided to challenge Ouellette on this statement and asked him what he had personally witnessed about the Hells Angels or Maurice Boucher. He asked him what he knew about the biker war and what he knew of Boucher's implication in it. Maranda was an experienced and crafty lawyer. He likely knew he was about to open a floodgate, even if it might hurt his client's chances at bail. Ouellette revealed that Boucher was under investigation for several of the murders and bombings that had taken place in the war at that point. Ouellette said that, in particular, Boucher was suspected of having a contract out on Yvon (Mon Mon) Roy, a member of the Alliance.

When it came time for the defense to make its arguments, a used car dealer testified that Boucher worked for him, selling cars on a commission basis. The car dealer said he had known Boucher for two years. He said that Boucher worked mostly on the road and had made $70,000 in the past twelve months selling new and used cars. If it were true, it would have meant Boucher was a remarkable car salesman, considering he had spent five months of that year in prison. Boucher ended up making bail. As part of the conditions of his bail, he was forbidden to associate with anyone related to the Hells Angels. But other people appeared on the list who were not members of the gang, including Vito Rizzuto, the reputed head of the Mafia in Montreal. Also on the list was Gaetan Rivet, a former Sûreté du Québec officer who left the provincial police force and was on a very public campaign to try to discredit it during the 1990s. He would later be convicted of loan-sharking. Robert Savard, one of Montreal's more notorious loan sharks, was also on the list of people Boucher could not associate with.

By now, however, Boucher was already being more careful about who he was seen with. Kane told the RCMP that Boucher had selected André Chouinard, a member of the Rockers, as his right-hand man and drug courier. Kane said Chouinard was chosen because he was clean-cut and didn't yet have a criminal record. On January 31, 1996, Boucher pleaded guilty to the charge of counseling Bertrand to commit bodily harm and paid a $2000 fine.

Almost two weeks earlier his son Françis was arrested while carrying a .38-calibre Smith & Wesson revolver for which he did not have a permit. A few months later Mom's son would be acquitted on the weapons charge but plead guilty to lying to a police officer while he was in the Laurentians on September 9, 1995, and in doing so violating a probationary sentence he had received in 1994 for the break-in. He was fined a total of $250. Although he wouldn't become a member of the Rockers for another few years, sometime in early 1995, Boucher's son was, according to what Kane told the RCMP, granted a territory on which he could deal drugs for the gang. It was one of the first indications that Mom Boucher wanted his son to follow in his footsteps.

At some point in his life Françis Boucher had the word "warrior" tattooed onto his left pectoral, but to the other members of the Rockers he was known as Le Fils — French for "the son." Like his dad, he claimed to sell cars on his tax returns, pretending to earn more than $80,000 a year legitimately. In reality, the dealership where Françis Boucher claimed to work listed its business address at 2101 Bennett, the Nomads chapter's hangout. The police checked with the provincial car registration bureau and found that no cars were ever registered to the company. Mom Boucher had also set himself up in various registered companies while he operated as a Hells Angel. One was Les Produits Recycle Action which listed him as an administrator. It was the same company Denis Houle claimed to work for when he was before the parole board in 1994. During the years that Boucher was involved with the biker war he declared making a salary off commissions of no more than $53,000 annually. He was married to Diane Leblanc, Françis's mother, and lived with her on his farm in Contrecoeur. Meanwhile, the police noticed that he frequently visited his girlfriend Louise Mongeau at a house in Boucherville, a suburb of Montreal. In 1995, Mongeau was charged with possession of enough hashish to be considered a dealer.

Plans to Expand

By 1996, Boucher was apparently tiring of the war, and, according to informants who testified in court later, was plotting to kill as many members of the Rock Machine as possible in one fell swoop. Boucher now realized the police were constantly monitoring him. To counter this he took to holding meetings with gang members at the Montreal courthouse. Doing so would give the appearance his underlings or fellow Hells Angels weren't violating any court orders by associating with known criminals. Kane said the Hells Angels' leader was also doing business by coded faxes only and keeping a small circle of insiders who knew the intimate details of his drug trafficking. Boucher also kept up his early morning rituals, holding meetings before 9:30 a.m. at a brasserie in Montreal's east end.

By January 1996, the Hells Angels' plans for expansion across Canada appeared to be in full gear. Kane told the RCMP that Steinert and his drug-dealing partner Donald Magnussen had just shipped off a large quantity of drugs to Thunder Bay. The shipment contained 69 pounds of marijuana, 200 ecstasy pills and a few pounds of hashish. According to Kane, the delivery man was an employee from a stripper agency Steinert ran. But Kane added that Steinert was no longer the carefree Hells Angel he had been before 11-year-old Daniel Desrochers was killed. He was becoming increasingly worried about being deported back to the U.S. He talked of moving to Brazil or even Mexico where, according to Kane, Boucher had told him he could become a millionaire within a year working for the Quebec Hells Angels. But Kane said other Hells Angels were losing their faith in Steinert and his sidekick Magnussen. David (Wolf) Carroll in particular believed Magnussen to be a police informant, and he disliked Steinert's reckless methods.

Kane was also having his share of problems. In February 1996, Rocker Daniel Lanthier confronted Kane with a statement he had once given to the police in writing. The statement had nothing to do with Kane's work as an informant but it caused enough alarm that he was ordered to hand over his patches as a striker in the Rockers. Lanthier informed him the Hells Angels could not tolerate someone who talked to the cops, especially someone who put things in writing. But Kane was allowed to stick with the gang, and within two weeks learned that Boucher had his hands on a confidential police intelligence report. It was over a year old and had been shelved by the investigators who were using it. But Kane said Boucher called a meeting during which he highlighted the fact that Robert Johnson, a man with ties to the Rockers, was considered a suspect in a murder where there had been no witnesses, except the killer and the victim.

Despite the fact some Hells Angels did not trust Magnussen and Steinert, the latter received his full-patch as a member of the Hells Angels' Montreal chapter in March 1996. Kane told the RCMP that Steinert had also received a "Filthy Few" patch, a symbol believed to be awarded only to members who have killed for the benefit of the gang. He was also given a gold memento worn by a Hells Angel who had died months earlier of a heart attack.

While Steinert was apparently in the good books of the Montreal chapter, Donald Magnussen was still the subject of speculation that he was an undercover cop. Within weeks of Kane telling police this, Magnussen became the focus of speculation by other members of the Hells Angels that he had been behind the murder of David Boyko, a member of a Winnipeg-based gang called Los Bravos. Boyko had been shot to death while in Halifax to attend a Hells Angels' party there. The Los Bravos were part of the Hells Angels' plans for expansion, but now the gang believed Magnussen's temper had blown it. Members of the Winnipeg gang simply stopped talking to the Quebec Hells Angels. Kane told the police that the Hells Angels were ready to kill Magnussen and alleged that David (Wolf) Carroll was willing to do it himself.

In October 1996, Kane told the RCMP that Steinert had grown impatient with the Nomads chapter's criticisms that the Montreal chapter, the one Boucher had split off from, was doing nothing about winning the war. Steinert decided to form a splinter cell within the Montreal chapter that would become more involved. According to Kane, it was to include Michel Lajoie Smith and Normand Labelle, both members of the Hells Angels, as well as Magnussen and Marc Sigman. Kane said he was offered a chance to join the group but balked at their demand for $100,000 up front. Membership was costly because Steinert was preparing to buy the infamous Lavigueur mansion, a 17-room house on Laval's toney island Ile aux Pruches. It was previously owned by a family of ill-fated lottery winners who had become somewhat famous in Quebec. In order to purchase the mansion and make it look like it was owned by a numbered company, Kane said Steinert and Magnussen had paid a visit to an accountant the Hells Angels used often.

At around the same time, André (Toots) Tousignant,

Boucher's former chauffeur and a close associate, was assigned to kill Magnussen and had begun monitoring his movements. Kane was later offered $10,000 himself to get rid of Magnussen because Tousignant was having trouble doing the job. As the headaches continued for the Hells Angels in November 1996, Kane said Boucher determined that it would have to be a full-patch Hells Angel to kill Magnussen. Boucher felt Steinert and Richard (Dick) Mayrand, an influential member of the Montreal chapter, would never accept seeing an underling kill someone so close to the Montreal chapter. Kane alleged that Stadnick was selected as a possible candidate to carry out the murder because he had the most to gain from it with his plans for westward expansion.

To make matters worse, as the Nomads chapter was planning to kill Magnussen, they were approached by the Hells Angels' Montreal chapter to see if it was okay for Magnussen to become a "hangaround," the first step in becoming a member of their gang. Kane said the Nomads members told their Montreal brothers they had no problem with it. But immediately after the meeting, the Nomads members held their own meeting and discussed how it definitely must be a full-patch member who would eliminate Magnussen.

By February 1997, Kane said there were rumors that Magnussen had beaten up a relative of Vito Rizzuto, the alleged godfather of the Montreal Mafia, in a bar on St-Laurent Blvd., and that now, even the Mob was looking for Magnussen. Kane said that Magnussen would not leave home alone.

Steinert was also in serious trouble. He had received a deportation order in November 1996 and was trying to appeal the decision. Sometime later in 1997, both Steinert and Magnussen disappeared. Their bodies would turn up floating in the St. Lawrence River near Quebec City. They had been severely beaten before they were killed.

The year 1997 was a busy one in the biker war. Twenty-eight

murders in Quebec were attributed to the biker war that year, more than during the three years previous. There were another 30 attempted murders in 1997 that the police also suspected were tied to the conflict. But what drew the most public attention was the murders of two prison guards, killed on Boucher's orders in an effort to destabilize the justice system. Stéphane (Godasse) Gagné, whom Boucher had met during his 1995 detention in Sorel, turned informant against him and provided evidence that would help convict Boucher for the murders.

Gagné was the key witness during the first trial and, as Justice Jean Guy Boilard gave his final instructions to the jury, he said that the case essentially boiled down to Gagné's testimony. If the jury believed a former killer turned informant, then they should weigh the evidence that supported what he said. If they didn't believe him, they should all go home. The jury chose not to believe Gagné. After three days of deliberation, they acquitted Boucher on November 27, 1998. He mouthed a "Merci" toward the jury and walked out of the courthouse a free man, sur-rounded by several members of the Rockers. Normand Robitaille, who had been made a member of the Nomads just weeks before, threw his arm around Boucher and they both smiled as they walked away.

That night, Boucher took in a Friday night boxing card in Verdun and some people in the audience cheered as he was greeted by his fellow Hells Angels — Boucher had become a pub-lic figure in Montreal. His wire-rimmed glasses and broad smile made him easily recognizable, especially with all of the media coverage of his trial. Police investigators who monitored the Hells Angels after the trial were stunned to see he had gained a kind of folk-hero status in the Hochelaga Maisonneuve district. People on the street would cheer him on as he drove along Hochelaga Street, the location of the gym where he worked out on a regular basis, or Bennett Street, where the Nomads had a building.

TOP: Dany Kane (second from left) outside the funeral home where the Hells Angels held a wake for slain Nomads chapter member Normand (Biff) Hamel.
(John Mahoney, *The Montreal Gazette*)

BOTTOM: Jean Richard Larivière (right) works security at the April 2000 funeral for Normand (Biff) Hamel along with fellow Rockers Vincent Lamer (middle) and David Lefebvre (left).

Meanwhile, the biker war continued, and the rival gang, the Rock Machine, scored their biggest hit when they killed Normand Hamel, a founding member of the Nomads and Boucher's friend for many years. He was gunned down in a Laval parking lot on April 17, 2000, after he and his wife and child had visited a doctor's office. Boucher drove up to the scene of the shooting in a Volkswagen as homicide investigators searched the parking lot for evidence. Within an hour of Hamel's shooting, the police listened in through a wiretap as two members of the Rockers discussed the death of a man they had been expected to protect at all times. Dany St-Pierre, of the Rockers told his fellow gangmate, Ronald (Popo) Paulin to put all of the Rockers on standby.

Later that night, a man who would later become a member of the Nomads chapter, Normand Bélanger, talked with a friend as the police listened in. Bélanger called Hamel's murder "part of the game we play," but he also considered it "pretty disgusting" because it had happened while Hamel was with his wife and child.

On May 12, 2000, the Hells Angels responded to Hamel's slaying with an attack on two members of the Rock Machine. Shots were fired at Tony Duguay and Denis Boucher as they drove through Saint Laurent, a suburb of Montreal. Both survived the attempt on their lives, though Duguay suffered bullet wounds to his arms, right hand and thigh. He was wearing a ring with the inscription "death before dishonor" on it. Three years later, the Hells Angels' suspicions would be confirmed when Duguay would be charged with killing Hamel.

Boucher's newfound celebrity appeared to stir something in him; he seemed to want to toy with his notoriety. On April 14, 2000, René Charlebois, one of Boucher's best drug dealers with the Rockers, graduated to the status of full-patch member in the Nomads chapter. About four months later, Charlebois got married at a church near the Hells Angels' bunker in Sorel. It was the reception on Boucher's estate in Contrecouer that would grab headlines. The Hells Angels had managed to hire popular singers Ginette Reno and Jean-Pierre Ferland to sing at the reception. Reno, a beloved singer with a matronly image to most Quebecers, belted out "My May" for the bikers, and later posed for photos with Boucher as a photographer he had invited from the crime tabloid *Allô Police* clicked away. The published photos caused a small scandal, prompting an embarrassed Reno to issue a public apology.

On October 8, 2000, Boucher would again put on a public display, staging a dinner at a restaurant in downtown Montreal called Bleu Marin, where members of the Rock Machine and the Hells Angels actually dined together. The two gangs had been discussing a truce, and the dinner apparently finalized it. Again, *Allô Police* was invited to photograph the gathering. Boucher put on a show, hugging longtime enemies like Paul Porter and shaking hands with other Rock Machine leaders like Frederic Faucher, the driving force behind the gang's merging with the Bandidos.

Representing the Hells Angels were Nomads Michel Rose, Richard (Dick) Mayrand and Normand Robitaille. When he walked out of the restaurant, Robitaille approached two police officers who were outside watching making notes of who was present at the dinner, and joked that with the war over the police would be seeing their budgets cut. After dining, the group of gangsters then moved on to the Super Sexe, a strip bar in downtown Montreal on Sainte-Catherine Street where they kept the party going.

The "truce" was used as a chance for the Nomads to make a new ultimatum. Later in 2000, the Nomads offered Rock Machine members the opportunity to defect to their side, keeping the same status they had in their old gang. But it was a limited-time offer.

Boucher had managed to grab national headlines this time with his public stunt. But he would have to watch the fallout from the truce from behind bars. Two days after the dinner at Bleu

Marin, the Quebec Court of Appeal quashed Boucher's acquittal on the prison guard murders, taking issue in particular with Justice Boilard's instructions to the jury. A new trial was ordered.

While awaiting trial, Boucher filed a $30 million lawsuit against the Quebec government through lawyer Robert Lemieux. Lemieux had defended members of the Front de Libération du Québec, a terrorist organization responsible for kidnapping and murder, during the October Crisis in 1970. The lawsuit alleged Boucher was being held illegally while he awaited his second trial and that the province was persecuting an innocent man. But the lawsuit also claimed Boucher worked as a cook, and included several factual and spelling errors. The suit was eventually dropped.

The second time around, the jury was convinced Boucher had enough power to effect the murder of the prison guards and convicted him on May 5, 2002. The first-degree murder convictions came with an automatic life sentence with no chance at parole for 25 years. Nonetheless, even while behind bars, Boucher would still have people trying to kill him.

Maurice (Mom) Boucher Behind Bars

On August 13, 2002, around 8:30 p.m. at the Special Handling Unit in Sainte-Anne-des-Plaines, a group of inmates were being moved into a common area. Gary Brent Huska, a Saskatchewan man serving a life sentence for murdering his girlfriend with a steak knife, was in the common area. He approached and attacked Boucher as the Hells Angel was going through a revolving door. According to procedures at the unit, inmates entered the common area one by one. The weapon was a shiv, hidden in Huska's pants, made out of plastic, measuring about 10 inches long and one inch wide and very sharp. Huska had entered the common area just before Boucher, and he placed himself next to a table near the door.

Boucher no longer had his underlings around to protect him,

but when he was attacked, several other inmates jumped in to protect him. Boucher took a few steps back and watched as the others piled in and started attacking Huska. A prison guard called his colleagues and as they arrived, they could see six or seven inmates piled on top of Huska. The guards ordered them to stop and eventually most did. One guard used a gas spray to clear the area. But inmate Jean Roch Lefrançois continued the attack, pushing Huska to a shower stall while someone shouted "Kill him!" A guard entered the shower area and put an end to the assault on Huska. By now Huska was lying on the shower floor. He had been stabbed several times. Lefrançois was ordered to strip down and was searched. Prison guards put on special equipment to prevent them from coming in contact with Huska's blood, and they approached him in the shower. By now, the unit's nurse had arrived. Almost ten minutes after the attack, Huska was taken to the infirmary, where it was determined that his injuries were serious enough for him to be transferred to a hospital.

The common area was shut down and treated as a crime scene. Some inmates resisted the order to return to their cells and a special intervention team was called in to restore order. The inmates weren't cleared out of the common area until 10:30 p.m., approximately two hours after the attack. They had played cards and watched television while waiting for the prison officials to sort things out. In the interim, the Sûreté du Québec was called in to investigate. All the main players in the attack were placed in isolation, including Boucher.

Huska was released from the hospital weeks later and was never charged with attempting to kill Boucher even though Huska had a history of such attacks. While at the Saskatchewan Penitentiary, he had used a knife on another inmate, and he had openly admitted that his intention was to kill the man because he had committed sexual assault. One theory to emerge from the attack on Boucher was that Huska wanted to kill him because of his conviction for the 1984 sexual assault. Lefrançois was also not charged for his attack on Huska.

Less than a month after the incident with Huska, someone else tried to get rid of Boucher. As in the first attempt, Boucher was attacked as he exited the revolving door that lead to the common area. This time, at around 11 a.m., Boucher was heading in for lunch. The weapon was a homemade firearm concocted of materials that were accessible, even to an inmate at the Special Handling Unit: a rolled up newspaper, straps from curtains and electrical wire with a standard switch. Boucher was knocked off his feet by the blast. A guard asked if he was all right and Boucher said he was.

The RCMP were called in to investigate this time but could find no clear motive for the attempt on Boucher's life. The inmate alleged to be behind the second attack was Ryan Starr, a Manitoba aboriginal who was serving a life sentence for killing someone while robbing a grocery store. Like Huska, Starr was not charged with attempting to kill Boucher. These unpunished attempts were a sign that it was open season on Boucher, and, without many Hells Angels at the Special Handling Unit, he was an easy target.

But signs emerged that the Hells Angels no longer cared about their once-feared leader. The clearest indication came in the form of an article published in the crime tabloid *Allô Police*. The article contained an interview with Normand Bélanger, a man who was brought into the fold of Hells Angels because he was familiar with the drug ecstasy before many people in Quebec had even heard of it. He was also described as a close friend of Boucher. He had entered the gang's hierarchy as a member of the Rockers, and in little over a year he had graduated to being a prospect in the Nomads chapter. Bélanger was eventually made a full-patch member in the Nomads chapter but for some reason he was stripped of his patch while behind bars and awaiting trial in the Project Rush investigation.

Normand Belanger (left)
walks with Dany St. Pierre,
a member of the Rockers.
(John Mahoney,
The Montreal Gazette)

Bélanger would become gravely ill with several diseases during one of the megatrials, and doctors gave him only months to live.

Before his death he talked to an *Allô Police* reporter who happened to meet him at a doctor's office. When asked what he thought of his old friend, Bélanger said Boucher had been a greedy man, adding that if it hadn't been for him, everybody arrested in Operation Springtime 2001 would then be quietly going about their business as free men.

3

It was dubbed Operation Springtime, but the weather on March 28, 2001, felt like anything but. Spread out across Quebec and Ontario, police officers prepared to give many Hells Angels

Arrests en Masse

and their underlings a rude awakening, while in and around Montreal Island the temperature hovered at a few degrees below zero. A light snow fell steadily.

It was a police operation like no other before in Canada. It involved nearly 2,000 police officers and civilians, and its influence ranged from the RCMP, to the Sûreté du Québec, the Montreal Urban Community Police and 23 other municipal police forces. At least 20 buildings, including luxury houses, were seized, along with 28 vehicles, 70 firearms and more than $8 million Canadian in cash. The fact that the police also seized 120 kilograms of hashish and 10 kilograms of cocaine was practically an afterthought, once the goal of the operation was made clear. This wasn't about a one-time bust. It was about an investigation that had begun in 1998, and most of the principal targets had already been selected at that point.

Of the 42 Hells Angels or Rockers named in the warrants connected to Project Rush, 14 were already behind bars when it was carried out. About another half dozen could not be immediately located, but most were found eventually. The charges in the warrants included 13 of the more than 160 murders that had been committed during the biker war. All of the gang members were charged with drug trafficking and with doing it for the benefit of an organized crime gang, which was relatively new legislation intended specifically for the Hells Angels in Quebec. There were also two charges that the Hells Angels had conspired in two failed attempts to kill many of their rivals at once with massive bombs.

The officers armed with search warrants had specific instructions to look for anything that suggested the occupant of the home belonged to the Hells Angels or the Rockers. In some cases, that would involve judgement calls on the part of the officers involved. For example, were photos of gang members grouped together or simply sporting their gang colors enough? In other homes, like that of Luc (Bordel) Bordeleau in Contrecoeur near Boucher's estate, many of the items to be seized were obvious proof of his membership.

Luc (Bordel) Bordeleau and his Rocket Launcher

Bordeleau was one of the 14 already behind bars when the operation was carried out. He was serving a sentence for a weapons offence. Inside his home on Marie Victorin Street, the police found proof that he was involved in collecting information on informants and on the leaders of the Alliance. That included copies of written statements to the police from informant Normand Tremblay, a man police believed was the possible intended target of the 1995 explosion that killed 11-year-old Daniel Desrochers. Bordeleau also had a copy of the contract of a police informant and a former associate of the Alliance named Denis Bouthillette, who had become an informant around the same time as Tremblay. Another document seized at Bordeleau's home concerned Harold Pelletier, the brother of Sylvain Pelletier, whose 1994 death was widely considered to be the starting point of the biker war.

The fact that the Hells Angels had the contracts was not that alarming — if any of the informants had testified in a trial, the

Maurice (Mom) Boucher (left) and Luc (Bordel) Bordeleau.

contracts would have been turned over to the lawyers of the accused. What was more disturbing was the small arsenal Bordeleau kept in his garage.

The police seized a handgun, three shotguns, three semiautomatic Cobray machine guns along with various types of ammunition. They also found a grenade launcher which left police wondering what the Hells Angels had planned for the near future. At another residence in Montreal, where Bordeleau lived with a woman, the police found more than $9,000 cash plus more evidence that the man nicknamed Bordel was seriously involved in hunting down rival gang members. They found a piece of paper with Bandidos leader Jean (Le Français) Duquaire's name, social insurance number and home address on it. They also found a remote-control device that a police expert later determined was a twin of one the police had recovered years earlier when the Rock Machine's clubhouse on Huron Street had been damaged by an explosion. Bordeleau was behind bars at the time of the explosion, but the devices were obviously made by the same person.

Bordeleau had been made a prospect in the Nomads chapter in June 2000, around the same time that Louis (Melou) Roy, a founding member of the chapter went missing. The police noticed Bordeleau had made the jump from longtime Rocker to his new status rather quickly, considering he had spent a large chunk of the war serving his sentence at the Leclerc Institute in Laval.

Éric (Pif) Fournier

Also named in the warrants was Éric (Pif) Fournier, a Hells Angels' underling who had served as Melou Roy's bodyguard. Fournier's introduction into the gang apparently began while he was serving a sentence for severely beating a man in his home near Quebec City with two accomplices in 1990. The man suffered several broken bones and the trio also caused $3,000 damage to his house. Fournier pleaded guilty to conspiracy and aggravated assault and was sentenced to four years. While he was out on parole in 1993, he beat up another man and had to serve another three years.

By March 1996, Fournier was identified as part of the Hells Angels' vast underling network. He was by that time charged with carrying out two murders at the request of two Hells Angels. But the case against Fournier was dismissed because the Sûreté du Québec mistakenly destroyed the murder weapons Fournier was alleged to have used. The judge found that Fournier could not possibly have a fair trial unless such important evidence could be presented. Fournier eventually moved to Montreal and was welcomed into the fold of the Rockers in 1998. Eight years previously, a prison psychologist had done an evaluation of Fournier: ". . . experience shows us that an individual integrated in the delinquent world will comfortably place his aggression in the service of his delinquent schemes. He will use force to solve his problems with others or to eliminate the obstacles before him that prevent him from getting what he wants.

"We also have to say that the subject is an individual who does not demonstrate any large sensibility towards others and is very centred on himself. His degree of empathy towards the victims of his offences is practically non-existent."

Richard (Dick) Mayrand — One of the Filthy Few

Searching Richard (Dick) Mayrand's house on Lafrance Street in Longueuil provided the police with clear evidence of how close the Nomads chapter came to achieving its monopoly on Montreal's illicit drug trade. They found a map of Montreal that someone had divided up with a pen. Each section included a designation in handwriting, labeling parts of the city as "Nomad" and "Montreal" and "Trois Rivières," proof that Boucher's chapter was willing to let other Hells Angels' chapters deal drugs in the city. The map also indicated that the only other group the Hells Angels would tolerate were the "Italians," who appeared to have kept a small area in northern Montreal as their own.

Inside Mayrand's house the police also found a pair of night vision goggles, a piece of military equipment believed to be used in nighttime drug smuggling operations. Among the Hells Angels' paraphernalia, they found a belt buckle with the inscription "Mtl Filthy Few AFFA" (AFFA stands for Angels Forever, Forever Angels) and another that read "Dick, Filthy Few Montreal." In a bedroom closet, they found a hockey bag neatly packed and full with more than $300,000 in $20 bills.

Mayrand's weight-training equipment would have been sufficient to run a small private gym. Mayrand's bodybuilding was a source of pride for the Hells Angels. The police had recorded some members on wiretaps talking proudly about Mayrand placing third in the Senior Men's Light-Heavyweight class of the Canadian National Bodybuilding championship held in Edmonton in 1999.

As in Bordeleau's case, Mayrand wasn't home when the search warrants were carried out. He was still serving his sentence from an offence, on February 15, 2001, in which he and other Nomads were caught looking over photos of rival Bandidos in a hotel suite, apparently planning who would be their next targets. Mayrand and Bordeleau had been arrested after leaving the hotel.

Sebastien (Bass) Beauchamp

Unlike Bordeleau and Mayrand, Sebastien Beauchamp was at his home in Mascouche when the police came knocking armed with his search warrant. They didn't find anything resembling the firepower they had seen over at Bordeleau's house. Nor did they find any drugs. Beauchamp had only been a Rocker since October 16, 2000, and his time spent with the gang before then had been rough. While investigating the Rockers, by videotaping their meetings, the police learned that Beauchamp owed money to several members of the Hells Angels. At one point, his debt was estimated at $80,000. Some of the Rockers called for his suspension from the gang, arguing that he wasn't responsible enough to wear their patch.

Six years earlier the National Parole Board had a similarly low opinion of Beauchamp, but for different reasons. "You are an impulsive and immature individual who easily uses violence to solve conflicts imposed by others," a parole commissioner wrote in summarizing a 1993 hearing. At the age of 19, Beauchamp was already serving a federal sentence for drug trafficking and assault. Even at that young age, he was already involved in smuggling. While out on bail in a drug case, Beauchamp beat up a man, emptied his pockets of his keys and credit cards and then proceeded to rob the victim's apartment, where he was caught by police and taken into custody.

While out on bail for his second case Beauchamp had been arrested for assaulting an American tourist inside a Burger King restaurant. Beauchamp had been drunk at the time. He later told the parole board that he was an only child, and that when he was one year old, his mother had moved in with a man Beauchamp eventually considered his father. He had only seen his real father once, when he was 14, but by then he had learned that the man was a heavy drinker who beat his wife. He described his mother as having a "hippie philosophy" and letting him do whatever he wanted. By the age of 11, Beauchamp was already doing drugs. All the while his family kept moving. He once went to five or six high schools within one year and eventually decided to drop out because he found switching too tough.

By the time he was serving his federal sentence, a psychologist determined that he had a severe drug problem. Prison guards learned that he had become a regular supplier of PCP to other inmates and was consuming the drug himself. In 1995, Beauchamp was let out on statutory release but was soon hauled back to a penitentiary after a guard noticed that some of Beauchamp's former fellow inmates who were heavily involved in drugs were receiving repeated phone calls from him. A prison surveillance team eventually learned that he was sneaking drugs into the penitentiary. Beauchamp spent most of the 1990s either behind bars or on probation for assault and weapons offences.

In 1999, he was arrested with other members of the Rockers who were doing guard duty at a hospital in Saint-Jérôme. The armed gang members were assigned to protect Denis Houle's wife, Sandra Gloutney, who had been injured while backing out their driveway in a Corvette that he normally drove. Gloutney lost control of the sports car when someone fired shots at her from a wooded area near their home. The police suspected that the men standing guard at the hospital were armed. Their suspicions were correct; besides Beauchamp, Boucher's son Françis and Stéphane Jarry were also caught carrying firearms. Normand Bélanger and Stéphane Faucher were also arrested but were not armed. Among the firearms seized was a .38-calibre gun that belonged to Beauchamp. He pleaded guilty to carrying the unlicensed weapon and was sentenced to one year in prison with two years probation.

About a month later, the police listened in on a call Beauchamp made from prison to Pierre Provencher, a Rockers' leader and a member since 1994. At the beginning of the conversation they joked about how Bruno Lefebvre, a fellow Rocker, had been paroled after serving only one-sixth of his sentence in a provincial detention centre. "*Ciboire*," Beauchamp said laughing at how easy it was to get parole in Quebec if an inmate was serving a provincial sentence of under two years. "They don't want us inside. Not at all, those guys."

He also complained about being behind bars for what he assumed was going to be only two months for carrying "*un hostie* [fucking] *gun*." He seemed oblivious to the fact he was under three different probation orders prohibiting him from carrying a firearm when he was arrested. He griped about his time behind bars, and before they said goodbye, Provencher felt it necessary to check if he was still loyal to the Rockers and if he was in the gang to stay.

"*Ah, bien oui, c'est sur et certain* [it's sure and certain]," Beauchamp said.

"In our heads and in our hearts you are a real brother," Provencher replied. Beauchamp called Provencher again the day before Christmas 1999. He was apparently feeling philosophical and told Provencher: "I look at the people who get up at seven in the morning and get stuck in traffic for ten dollars per hour and then go home again at night. They are the ones who are crazy. It is us who are a little bit more normal."

What definitely wasn't normal were the binders full of photos the police found at the homes of several members of the Nomads chapter's network when the search warrants were carried out on

March 28, 2001. The binders contained pages of photos of members of the Alliance that came from Sûreté du Québec intelligence files. The Hells Angels had somehow obtained the photos and made color copies of the pages containing mug shots, surveillance photos and intelligence notes on each person's gang status. One of the many Rockers who had one of the binders was Sylvain Moreau who was arrested at his home in Sainte Therese.

Sylvain Moreau — Rocker with a Temper

Moreau had served a three-year sentence in the late 1990s for drug trafficking and possession of a weapon. He admitted only to agreeing to store drugs for a dealer at his house for $500 a month. He said he had agreed to do so to support his three children and because he had serious drug debts to pay.

Moreau did not have the record of a hardened criminal. He had spent most of his adult life trying to pull off ill-fated schemes like passing off bogus cheques at grocery stores. He got caught frequently. In 1993 alone, he pleaded guilty to one count of breaking and entering, 21 counts of fraud, 3 counts of conspiracy, 2 counts of being in possession of the proceeds of crime and 21 counts of forgery. During the autumn months of 1987, Moreau went on an equally remarkable crime spree, breaking into 27 houses in small towns near Joliette within the space of roughly two months. He would sometimes do five houses in one night, stealing things like jewelry, firearms, microwaves, radios and any cash he could get his hands on, including $10 in rolled up quarters. He pleaded guilty to most of the break-ins and was sentenced to an 18-month prison term and two years probation.

He spent all of 1997 behind bars working as a debt collector for Hells Angels who were selling drugs inside his penitentiary. The parole board was not impressed with his association with the gang and decided not to grant Moreau day parole during the summer of 1997 though he had to be let go on statutory release by November 1998. The main condition of his release was that he not associate with known criminals, but Moreau obviously ignored this. He was seen doing guard duty outside a Rockers meeting, and was made a full-patch member of the gang on August 24, 1999. Still he was never arrested for the parole violation.

But Moreau was often at odds with his fellow Rockers. He seemed to have a temper that let his tongue fly. Normand Robitaille, a member of the Nomads chapter, once had to tell Moreau to shut his mouth at a meeting where the Rockers were discussing a botched hit. Moreau was one of the very few Rockers ever recorded talking openly about criminal activity while the police secretly videotaped the gang's meetings. One moment in particular revealed his thoughts on the Rockers and what the patch meant to him. During a discussion concerning plans to split up the gang into two territories in Montreal, maintaining their presence in the city's east end but also making them visible in the west end, he said, "It is then that [the police] will realize the Rockers are really imposing. Because actually they know about the Rockers but they don't know how many and where."

Donald (Pup) Stockford

In Ancaster, Ontario, police arrested Donald Stockford, a long-time member of the Hells Angels and a founding member of the Nomads chapter. Inside his home they found tons of clothing bearing the Hells Angels' Death Head logo. Included among that was a T-shirt printed with a photo of the CN tower with the name Hells Angels Ontario, the gang's logo and the words "the first wave." The police also seized more than $32,000 in American and Canadian bills, and found Stockford's will, which stated that in the event of his death the Hells Angels would take care of his funeral services.

The police had always suspected Stockford played an important role for the Hells Angels in Ontario, and on December 12, 2000, those suspicions were confirmed. Through a wiretap, the police listened in on a conversation between Dick Mayrand and Stockford. It would become apparent that what they had been talking about that day was the patchover of the smaller gangs in Ontario at the Sorel bunker due to occur a few weeks later. The conversation indicated it was Stockford who had the kind of clout in Ontario the Hells Angels needed to sell their idea to members of gangs like the Satan's Choice. Mayrand had just finished taking a boxing lesson when Stockford called him up.

"And?" Mayrand asked.

"Very, very, very positive," Stockford replied.

"Nah," said Mayrand, apparently unable to believe that the patchover he was partly in charge of was going so smoothly. Setting up a chapter in a new province required a vote involving all the other Canadian chapters.

"Yeah."

"Nah."

"Everyone."

"Nah."

"Very, very, very positive. Yeah."

Mayrand couldn't believe what he was hearing. Stockford then told him that the people he had met with were in meetings that very day, discussing the Hells Angels' proposal. The conversation switched to how many new Hells Angels' patches they would need to welcome in their new associates.

"You might need to up the order," Stockford said.

"It's, it's done," Mayrand replied.

"Okay."

"I ordered a hundred sets."

"You might need another hundred," said Stockford, laughing.

Walter (Nurget) Stadnick

A longtime member of the Hells Angels and also a founding member of the Nomads chapter, Stadnick was in Jamaica at the time the police operation was carried out. He was arrested at a resort hotel more than a week later and was eventually brought back to Montreal, where he would insist on being tried in English along with Stockford. Except for Maurice (Mom) Boucher, no one in the Nomads chapter was considered by police to have more influence than Stadnick. By all appearances, he was in charge of expanding the Hells Angels into provinces like Manitoba. In 1995, informer Dany Kane told the RCMP that Stadnick was working to establish a drug pipeline that ran between Thunder Bay and Winnipeg. Stadnick had been seen traveling to Winnipeg pretty frequently during the biker war, and, as Stéphane Sirois, a former Rocker turned undercover agent would later testify, Stadnick was sent to the city in 1996 to attempt to set up a Rockers chapter there.

Stadnick already had drug dealers working for him in Winnipeg and the thinking was that the Rockers should set up shop there officially. Four years later, in 1999, the Hells Angels chose instead to patchover an established gang called Los Bravos. On July 21, 2000, the police watched as Stadnick arrived at the Los Bravos hangout in Winnipeg with a big, white bag. Several biker members also headed inside. When they came out, the Los Bravos members were sporting leather jackets with patches on their backs that made it clear they were now prospects in the Hells Angels. The next day, Stadnick was seen partying at a Winnipeg strip bar with members of the Satan's Choice from Ontario.

Inside his house, the police found something they figured could be used as evidence of gangsterism against Stadnick. Ironically, it came in the form of a Valentine from his ten-year-old niece who wrote to her Uncle Wally, "Are you still the leader of the Hells Angels?" and suggested Stadnick was spending way too much time in Quebec. She added, "I hope you can move the club to Canada and out of Quebec." Above a phone in his house was a sticker that read, "Be careful what you say over this phone."

Despite being part of the Nomads chapter based in Montreal, Ontario was home to Stadnick. He initially was a member of a Hamilton-based gang called the Red Devils until he became a prospect in the Hells Angels' Montreal chapter in 1985. Roughly a decade later, he was a founding member of the Nomads chapter.

Alain Dubois — Like Father, Like Son

By comparison to other members of the gang, Alain Dubois' role in the Hells Angels' drug network appeared insignificant. But he faced many of the same charges Stadnick did in Operation Springtime 2001.

Very few people had ever been granted the status of full-patch Rocker in the way Dubois had. It was a testament to his abilities as a drug dealer in the western sections of Montreal which the Hells Angels were intent on conquering. The Nomads chapter imposed Dubois' instant membership on the Rockers on August 24, 1999. He, along with Pierre Laurin, Stéphane Jarry and Gaetan Matte, were welcomed into the gang at a Verdun pizza restaurant that day. But Dubois did not take well to being a Rocker. On top of running his business he was expected to be at the beck and call of his superiors in the Nomads chapter. Dubois had come to the gang with pedigree in Montreal's drug trafficking world. He was the son of Jean-Guy Dubois, a man who was part of a gang of brothers who once controlled several rackets like loan-sharking and prostitution in Montreal's west end.

When the police came knocking at Alain Dubois' home in Chateauguay, he was home. He was handcuffed and taken away while his wife prepared their children for school. Learning that he was being charged along with the Hells Angels must have come as somewhat of a surprise to Dubois since he had quit the

Rockers several months before. But he still had some of their paraphernalia lying around. There were T-shirts with phrases like "Support 81," the Hells Angels' code for HA, using numbers that match the letters' alphabetical order. Hidden in a bag in Dubois' garage was a Ceska pistol and a revolver. The police also seized a bulletproof vest and a canister of pepper spray.

Dubois had managed to quit the gang "in good standing" after only eight months in April 2000, but now he was charged with being a participant in their war. Dubois' father's gang was already known for being involved in smuggling large quantities of hashish. Ironically, Jean-Guy Dubois and his brothers had already fought a similar war for control of Montreal's west end in the 1970s. Jean-Guy Dubois would spend many years behind bars while his son Alain grew up and followed in his footsteps. That Alain would end up doing things like guard duty while members of the Nomads chapter worked out in a gym, appeared to be insulting.

During one particular Rockers "*messe*" or Mass, as the Rockers and Hells Angels in Quebec referred to their monthly meetings, Dubois let his frustrations show. The police were secretly videotaping the meeting on October 12, 1999. After the meeting ended, Dubois stayed behind to discuss a marijuana deal. As the videotape recorded everything, Pierre Provencher, a leader in the Rockers, informed Dubois and Matte that they would have to start taking over new territory for the gang while one of its members was in prison. During the conversation Dubois lost his cool and said that in the future he wanted everything laid out more clearly. He then stated that when he joined the gang he was promised Chateauguay, the city where he lived, as his private turf. Now, he said, Provencher was telling him someone from the Jokers, a Hells Angels' puppet gang, was thinking of moving in.

"I have all of that, Chateauguay," Dubois said in his deep

voice. It was one of the few times the Rockers were recorded discussing business in such an obvious way.

He was displaying the same temper that had sometimes compromised him during his earlier years as a criminal. On December 28, 1984, he and a cousin robbed a Canadian Tire store in Lasalle, a Montreal suburb. The crime was a relatively minor one and Dubois ended up only receiving a sentence of two years' probation. But, because of his temper, he also managed to get some prison time out of it. While his cousin was on trial for the robbery, Dubois had shown up for a pretrial hearing and listened to a police officer testify. During a break in the hearing, on March 27, 1985, he walked up to the investigator in the courthouse corridor and made a veiled threat, saying, "You're doing okay with the police, be careful of that." He later made a more overt threat to the same investigator, saying, "inside [the courthouse] everything is okay. Outside it is not the same."

Later that same year, on June 12, he approached the same investigator at the courthouse, again during a break in the court case. The investigator was using a public phone when Dubois grabbed it out of his hand and said: "You're a liar. You swore on the bible. It's not even true. You're too often with the police. Watch yourself. The world is small and we might meet one day on a sidewalk." So, while he only received a probationary sentence in the robbery, Dubois was also ordered to serve 90 days in a provincial detention center because of his inability to control himself at the courthouse.

Dubois' father Jean-Guy, the third-eldest of nine brothers, was himself behind bars when his son was jailed for threatening a cop. On June 2, 1977, Jean-Guy Dubois had been sentenced to life in prison for beating up a man and then tossing him into the Lachine canal. The man drowned in the canal, and the beating was found to have contributed to the drowning. Two Montreal police constables investigating a stolen car parked near the canal had seen

Dubois and an accomplice dump the body in the canal. When he was arrested, Dubois claimed he had been urinating in the canal and did not know the man who was in the canal near him.

By July 1991, Jean-Guy Dubois had been paroled for the Lachine canal homicide, but within a matter of months he was back behind bars for conspiring to traffic 100 kilograms of hashish. While preparing for parole the second time, in 1993, Jean-Guy Dubois told a psychologist that he had grown up amid misery in the St-Henri district. "Only his close family seems to bring him stability and a source of pride," the psychologist wrote in a report to the board.

During that second federal prison term, Dubois appeared to be a changed man. He was polite to the personnel and had become the penitentiary ombudsman, busy helping other inmates get parole. He would later tell the parole board in 1994 that, at the age of 60, he was finding prison life very tough. A psychiatrist concurred and informed the board that it seemed to have a devastating effect on the man. Little did Dubois know that in a matter of years he would sit in a courtroom and watch as his son was sent to a penitentiary.

4

Pierre (Ti-Bum) Beauchamp

The Hits

It was December 20, 1996, four shopping days before Christmas, and Pierre (Ti-Bum) Beauchamp had to find a parking space in one of the busiest sections of downtown Montreal. Despite the busy shopping period, he managed to find a spot near the corner of Sainte-Catherine Street West and Metcalfe Street. There he sat and waited, watching the many shoppers walk by, and apparently growing impatient as he tried to page someone three times. Inside his Ford Explorer, he had with him $60,000.

The past two months had not been pleasant for Beauchamp. The 46-year-old was a drug dealer who dealt with members of the Rock Machine in southwest Montreal. Beauchamp had learned the Hells Angels had put out a contract on him. But he didn't react the way a member of the Rock Machine would have, especially at that point in the biker war, which would have been to seek revenge. Instead, Beauchamp went to the police and informed them of the threat on his life. He also told his brother. Word of Beauchamp's concern got out, and he managed to arrange a meeting with Maurice (Mom) Boucher at a restaurant in Longueuil. What actually came of the meeting is not known.

But now, Beauchamp was sitting in his Explorer with $60,000 in cash, almost half of it in marked bills. An RCMP undercover cop had used the marked bills to buy drugs on December 18, two days earlier. Where the drug money was destined to go is unknown, but the number Beauchamp paged three times belonged to Michel

Sylvestre, Boucher's former brother-in-law and a close associate of the Hells Angels.

In less than a year, Sylvestre would be among the first six Quebecers ever to be charged with violating federal anti-gang legislation. The arrests followed a lengthy RCMP investigation that uncovered a plot to smuggle 600 kilograms of cocaine and a conspiracy that saw several million dollars in contraband cigarettes shipped to the U.S. only to be smuggled back into Canada and sold under

From left to right: Bruno Lefebvre, Pierre Provencher and Gregory Wooley.

the table — allegedly to maintain product recognition after the federal government had placed higher taxes on cigarettes. A few of the men pleaded guilty to being part of the smuggling conspiracies, but Sylvestre saw the charges against him withdrawn.

As Beauchamp sat waiting for Sylvestre to answer his page, someone walked up to the driver's side window of his Explorer and fired several shots. One bullet struck and killed Beauchamp. The shooter was spotted running for a Dodge Caravan parked nearby with a getaway driver waiting inside. The minivan sped off down Metcalfe Street and was eventually found abandoned near the entrance of the Bonaventure métro station, part of Montreal's elaborate subway system. The Caravan had been stolen a few days earlier as had the new licence plate affixed to the back. The trick would be used in several Hells Angels' hits — drivers often don't notice their licence plate is missing, so placing a stolen plate on a stolen vehicle buys some time when the police run a random check.

All that was found inside the Caravan was the screwdriver used to start it. An employee of the métro station found a gun and a hat inside the Bonaventure station hours later. The gun turned out to be the one used to shoot Beauchamp, and inside the hat the police found DNA that they would later match to Gregory Wooley, who was just 24 years old at the time of the murder and yet to have any status in the Rockers. About four weeks after Beauchamp's slaying, Wooley was named a hangaround in the Hells Angels' underling gang. Stéphane Sirois, a man who later turned against the Rockers and worked as an undercover agent for the police, testified that Wooley walked into a bar where the gang hung out only a few hours after Beauchamp was killed and bragged that he had "got one." From their conversation that night, Sirois also learned that René Charlebois helped out on the hit and that Boucher had given Wooley strict orders to leave the money inside Beauchamp's Ford Explorer because he didn't want the hit to look like a drug deal gone wrong.

Beauchamp's murder would be among the 23 charges filed in connection with Project Rush. All 42 of the Hells Angels or Rockers named in the indictment were accused of conspiring to kill members of the Alliance, the Dark Circle, the Rock Machine or the Bandidos between January 15, 1995, and March 27, 2001. They were also accused of drug trafficking and conspiring to traffic drugs during that period. Gangsterism charges were attached to the conspiracy and drug trafficking charges. For example, all of those charged were accused of participating in a gang, knowing that its members had committed criminal acts within the five previous years. Several of the 42 charged were also accused of conspiring on two occasions to commit the mass murder of Rock Machine members. Both attempts involved large quantities of explosives that never went off but could have easily killed innocent people if they had.

When it came down to the Beauchamp's murder and 12 others like it, the Crown singled out Hells Angels or Rockers who were active in the gang and not in jail when the homicides were committed. Prosecutors would later argue that the 13 murders shared a pattern — all the victims had ties to the Alliance and after they were killed, the weapons and vehicles used in most cases were either dumped or destroyed by fire.

"Each of these victims presented an obstacle to the complete objective that was favored by each and every [gang] member who adhered to the values and adhered equally to the plan that was previously established, that is to say to become the sole organization able to control and sell drugs in the territory of Montreal," said Crown prosecutor André Vincent when he made his opening remarks to the jury on October 21, 2002, during one of the megatrials to come out of Project Rush. "You won't see a witness come here and say, 'I heard a bawling out between the victim and his assailant.' In every case you will see people who will tell you, 'The assailant headed directly [toward the victim], without saying a word, shot in his direction and left immediately.' That is what I call the characteristics of a settling of accounts. It is not about someone squabbling with another, saying 'you took my parking space.' There were no words exchanged. . . . And I would even go further," Vincent said. "In hearing the evidence you will learn how in almost every case the victim did not even see his assailant."

Wooley was tried twice for the murder of Beauchamp after his case was separated from the rest of the group arrested in Project Rush. Both times he was acquitted of first-degree murder by a jury despite a seemingly solid case against him. The Crown had DNA evidence and testimony from Stéphane Sirois who said he heard Wooley brag that he "got one" after Beauchamp was killed.

But the defense created enough doubt in the minds of the

jurors when it revealed there was a hole in the chain of possession of the DNA evidence. The Montreal police were unable to identify where the evidence had been stored for a period of time, allowing for the possibility that the hair found in the tuque was planted.

Wooley, who had already developed a reputation for being lucky when it came to court cases, was able to plead guilty to lesser charges. On June 27, 2005 he was sentenced to 13 years for his role in the biker-gang war. He admitted to conspiring to kill rival gang members, drug trafficking and participating in gang activity. Because of the time he spent behind bars awaiting the outcome of his case, he is eligible for parole in 2007.

Marc Belhumeur

Marc Belhumeur likely didn't see the man who came to shoot him. Belhumeur, a former prospect in the Rock Machine, was talking on a pay phone inside the Le Chalutier brasserie in Montreal's east end when a masked man opened fire on him. At around the same time Beauchamp had learned the Hells Angels had a contract out on his head, Belhumeur, who was out on bail on drug trafficking charges, began to notice he was being followed. He too assumed his days were numbered and he asked that his life insurance be increased. He also started telling his relatives what kind of funeral he'd like. One sign that the Hells Angels were after him came while the Sûreté du Québec was executing a search warrant at the Hells Angels' bunker in Trois Rivières — they noticed Belhumeur's photo on a bulletin board.

A little over a month after the Beauchamp murder, around 1 p.m. on January 24, 1997, Belhumeur was shot with a 9-mm Smith & Wesson firearm. He dropped the phone and tried to flee but was gunned down, on the day of his 25th birthday, near the entrance to the brasserie's kitchen. The shooter fled out the back door, as if he already knew the layout of the bar very well. It was a sign of a well-planned hit. The shooter left no fingerprints, but Sirois would later testify that René Charlebois boasted of carrying out the perfect hit in killing Belhumeur.

Yvon (Mon Mon) Roy

A few months after Belhumeur's murder, Yvon (Mon Mon) Roy, another member of the Alliance, had been cleared of charges involving the plot to kill Maurice (Mom) Boucher. According to Harold Pelletier, the hit man who had turned informant, Roy had attended the meeting where the plot to kill Boucher with a truck bomb had been hatched, but there was no proof that he took action after the meeting was held. Of course, that didn't take Roy off the Hells Angels' hit list. He was well known as a dealer for the Pelletier Clan and was apparently doing business in Montreal's contested east end.

More than a year after being cleared in the murder conspiracy, Roy was shot to death in front of his home in Repentigny. The 57-year-old drug dealer was mowing his lawn at around 10 a.m. on July 30, 1998, when two gunmen opened fire on him, emptying their weapons, a .38-calibre revolver and a Cobray automatic pistol equipped with a silencer. Roy was struck in the head, neck, left arm and forearm. After he fell to the ground one of the gunmen dropped the Cobray near his driveway. Stunned neighbors watched as the two gunmen fled in a purple Chevrolet Cavalier. The revolver was tossed out the car's window.

As the police investigated the murder, they tried to track down the getaway car. They soon learned that a Cavalier fitting the description had been rented by someone using a false name the day before the shooting. After doing a little digging, investigators learned the car had been rented by a man named Stéphane (Archie) Hilareguy. Two months after the Roy murder, on October 1, 1998, Hilareguy (who with his red curly hair actually did resemble Archie, the comic book character he was nicknamed after) was made a striker in the Rockers. Hilareguy never returned the Cavalier, but the police learned that he and René Charlebois paid the rental company compensation for the lost vehicle. Thanks to the evidence linking the Rockers to the hit on Roy, his murder was one of the 13 included among the Project Rush charges.

Richard (Bam Bam) Lagacé

Richard (Bam Bam) Lagacé's murder was not included in the Project Rush charges, although it appeared that his murder was timed to coincide with Roy's. About an hour before Roy was killed, Lagacé, a member of the Rock Machine, was shot as he left a workout gym in a small town north of Montreal called Saint-Lin. In that case as well, two shooters were involved, but they were unprepared and had to storm into a woman's house and threaten her with a firearm in order to steal a getaway car. It was later found abandoned in a cemetery. It was apparent that Lagacé had been a drug dealer for years. In 1994, he had been arrested at this home in Saint-Lin where the police seized cocaine, hashish and PCP. They also found several firearms and a tazer.

Lagacé had been the target of a Hells Angels' murder plot before, and he had been arrested in Quebec City after the police broke up a meeting in a posh restaurant where the Rock Machine dined with George Wegers, then the U.S. national vice-president of the Bandidos. Wegers had entered the country illegally and was shipped back to the U.S. but the meeting turned out to be the first clear sign the Bandidos were interested in taking over the Rock Machine, something the Hells Angels in Quebec would not tolerate.

Johnny Plescio

A little over a month after Roy and Lagacé were murdered, Johnny Plescio, a founding member of the Rock Machine, was watching television in his Laval home when the cable suddenly shut off. Plescio got up from his chair to find out what had happened and as he neared the television, which was next to a window at the back of his house, he was greeted by a hailstorm of bullets. At least two men were believed to have carried out the hit on Plescio, on September 8, 1998. One had placed a lawnchair underneath the window and climbed up on it. Another cut Plescio's television cable. Twenty-seven shots were fired at Plescio as he stood near the window. Sixteen of them found their mark.

The gunmen left the scene in a stolen Plymouth Neon that was found abandoned three miles away. It had been doused in gasoline and set on fire. Witnesses watched as the two men headed for a minivan that was parked nearby. The vehicle's engine was already running and the pair jumped in before it sped away. After putting out the blaze, firefighters noticed two firearms inside the Neon. They turned out to be the two Cobray automatics, equipped with silencers, used in Plescio's murder. Plescio's body was discovered in his home hours later.

At his funeral, Plescio was laid out in a shirt with the word "Bandidos" written on it. The international biker gang had also sent floral arrangements, yet another sign that the Bandidos were interested in the Rock Machine. Plescio had been involved in the biker war from the very start. About a year before he was killed, someone had made two attempts to burn down a bar he owned on Bélanger Street in Montreal's east end. The police had information that the bar was being used as a front to sell drugs.

Plescio had spent the 1980s in and out of jail for relatively minor crimes. But in 1983 he had admitted to preparing to blow up a grocery store in Saint-Leonard, near Montreal. He was exposed by an accomplice who confessed and wanted the whole affair to be kept quiet because he was worried his mother would "freak out" if she caught wind of it. The Montreal police had caught Plescio circling the store apparently sizing up his job. At his house, the police had found seven sticks of dynamite and a 12-gauge shotgun. After his arrest, Plescio told the police he had been paid $1,000 by a rival grocer to get rid of his competition.

By 1993, Plescio's name was coming up frequently in police reports as they monitored the Rock Machine's bunker on Huron Street in east Montreal. A police station in the area had made the bunker a priority because investigators knew the gang was selling drugs out of bars in the east end. That same year, Plescio had been charged with uttering death threats to two police officers. During a break one day while his preliminary inquiry was being heard at the Montreal courthouse, Plescio told Serge (Merlin) Cyr that he was going to kill the cop who had just testified against him. What Plescio didn't know was that a plainclothes cop was standing near him as he said this. Some time later, Plescio was charged with uttering threats a second time. Ironically, he was acquitted in the original case but convicted in the second and sentenced to three months in prison.

Jean Rosa

A month before Plescio was killed, residents in another section of Laval began to notice suspicious vehicles parked in their neighborhood, which was normally quiet. From August 8 to September 14, 1998, the Laval police received five phone calls from people who reported seeing the mysterious cars and mini-vans parked in their neighborhood.

On September 1, the police decided to check out one of the vehicles, a minivan parked on Gilbert Street. There was no one in it but the officers who responded to the call noticed that it had two licence plates, one on top of the other. The licence plate on top had been stolen and the one underneath it was the vehicle's proper plate. When they searched the minivan they found a contract from a rental company in Sorel. It had been rented by a man whose wallet was also found in the minivan. The man later reported his wallet stolen.

More than three weeks later, Jean Rosa, a member of the Dark Circle, was shot to death in front of his home just as he got out of his car. The likely motive for the killing was the fact that Rosa had been charged in 1995 with being part of a Dark Circle plot to kill a Hells Angel.

Before joining the Dark Circle, Rosa had worked as a bouncer at a Montreal bar and seemed to enjoy beating up unruly patrons. He once tossed a man out of the bar because he didn't feel the man's boots were appropriate attire. On another occasion, he and three other bouncers were charged with pummeling a patron for clogging the bar's toilet with toilet paper.

The shooter approached Rosa from behind and fired away, causing fatal damage to his skull, liver and a few vertebrae. The gunman then got into a Plymouth Voyageur and fled the scene. The car was found five kilometres away, and as in Plescio's murder, it had been set on fire. The minivan had been reported stolen a month before. As the police began piecing together the homicide, they learned that the Plymouth Voyageur the Laval police had searched on September 1 had already been the subject of a police report earlier that summer. On June 25, the police had pulled it over, possibly during a spot check as the Hells Angels were heading to a party. Driving the van was Daniel Lanthier who had been a Rocker since 1998. Normand Robitaille and Denis Houle were following Lanthier on their motorcycles.

Pierre Bastien

Like Jean Rosa, Pierre Bastien had also been a member of the Dark Circle and had also pleaded guilty to conspiring to kill a Hells Angel early on in the biker war. He was sentenced to a 30-month prison term for attempted murder and was released after serving two-thirds of his sentence in 1997. Bastien's days as a drug dealer dated back as far as 1979, when he was caught selling LSD.

But by May 1998, Bastien was found to be following the strict requirements of his release to the letter by supplying his parole officials with bank statements and a diary of his daily life.

On October 22, 1998, Bastien arrived at his home in Laval at around 8 p.m. His eight-year-old daughter was in the back seat of his car. He parked the vehicle on the street and turned on the dome light to read some papers. Moments later a dark colored Dodge Neon pulled up in front of Bastien's car. There were two men inside and one stepped out from the passenger side. He walked right up to Bastien's driver-side window and opened fire. Bastien was struck several times, but one bullet in particular did a lot of damage to his heart, liver and stomach. Two stray bullets struck a nearby house and one went through a child's bedroom window. Bastien's daughter was not hurt. She cowered in the back seat until the killers left and then she ran to a neighbor's house. The neighbor had heard the shots fired and saw Bastien's daughter run toward his house. He buzzed her in before she even reached the door. Bastien was taken to a hospital quickly but his injuries were too severe, and he died.

The police already knew that Bastien had been targeted by the Hells Angels. In December 1997, when they arrested Stéphane (Godasse) Gagné as a suspect in the murders of two prison guards, they found Bastien's home address among his personal effects. When he turned informant, Gagné told the police he had watched Bastien's house on the orders of André (Toots) Tousignant, a member of the Rockers.

Stéphane Morgan and Daniel Boulet

Gagné told the police that he had done surveillance on Stéphane Morgan as well as on Pierre Bastien. Gagné knew Morgan well from when he was sent to a provincial detention centre and was greeted by him and other Rock Machine members. At the time, Morgan was in the detention center doing a one-year sentence for selling PCP. He had been arrested in 1993 while driving through the east end of the city at 1 a.m. in a rented Chrysler New Yorker with two other men. A patrol officer would later say in court that spotting three young men in a late-model New Yorker driving through a rough part of Montreal at that time of day caught his attention. Morgan was asked for his licence and registration but couldn't find the latter document in the glove compartment. He got out of the car to open the trunk, to find the registration, but at that point the officer had noticed a white bag on the back seat of the car. The police officer later testified that when he asked Morgan, who was wearing a Rock Machine baseball cap, what was in the bag, Morgan had replied: "You know what it is. Do your job." It turned out to be 360 grams of PCP.

In 1994, Dany Kane told his police handlers that Morgan had bragged of wanting to kill Boucher when he got out. Kane also told the RCMP that the Rock Machine member might have sold drugs for the Hells Angels' leader before the biker war ever started.

On November 10, 1998, nearly three weeks after Bastien's murder, Morgan and his friend and fellow drug dealer Daniel Boulet pulled up to a busy intersection in Montreal North and parked the car next to the sidewalk. Boulet was in the driver's seat. Morgan sat in the passenger side, a handgun tucked into the pocket of his pants. Morgan was no stranger to violence and had served a two-year term in the 1980s for attempting to kill a man. But he didn't even have a chance to reach for his gun when a man carrying a Cobray automatic approached the Chevrolet and sprayed it with bullets, leaving 25 spent 9-mm cartridges and an empty magazine on the pavement. Morgan was struck 11 times while Boulet was struck by 13 bullets. Coincidentally, the two 30-year-olds had been born on the same day — they died on the same day, too, within seconds of each other.

In the minutes leading up to the late afternoon shooting, residents in the area had spotted a red Windstar with two occupants, parked on the street. Within minutes of the shooting, the fire department was called in to put out flames in the same vehicle only a few blocks away. Firefighters found the murder weapon inside the van. The Windstar had been stolen the previous May. Its licence plate had been stolen from a vehicle only days before the shooting. When the police searched the car Morgan and Boulet had been killed in, they found enough cocaine to indicate the pair had been summoned to the street corner believing they were about to meet someone for a drug deal.

At the time of his death, Morgan was facing the prospect of a lengthy drug trafficking sentence. He had been arrested during a joint police operation involving the RCMP and police in Kingston, Ontario. The RCMP had been asked to tail an Ontario man when he traveled to Montreal. To do this, the Mounties were advised to monitor the Rock Machine bunker in Montreal and follow anyone with Ontario licence plates. They watched the bunker until the target of their surveillance walked out and got into his car. A man who turned out to be Stéphane Morgan walked out of the bunker with the man, got into his own car and followed the Ontario vehicle to a nearby bar. Morgan went inside the bar and later came out with a brown paper bag. When the police moved in on the Ontario man, they seized more than 8,000 LSD-type pills.

After Morgan's death, the police found a clear sign that he had been actively involved in the hunt for rival gang members. The day after the double murder, the police searched Morgan's house and found his Rock Machine ring, some drugs and a weigh scale, along with a photo of Pierre Toupin, a member of the Rockers.

Richard Parent

Several months before Morgan and Boulet were murdered, Richard Parent had been paroled on a four-year sentence for running his own drug trafficking network for the Rock Machine.

Parent had close ties to the Cazzetta brothers, the founding leaders of the Rock Machine — he was married to their sister. He had told the parole board that he wanted out of the biker war and had plans to move away from Montreal and work as a painter.

But while he was under investigation for drug trafficking a police wiretap recorded Parent talking over the phone about the bunker Hells Angel Scott Steinert was building on the estate he had purchased on Ile-aux-Pruches. The police would later tell the parole board that it sounded like Parent was planning a strike on the bunker, but he denied this, saying the police took his conversation out of context. The semantics were apparently lost on the Hells Angels.

On August 5, 1999, Parent arrived at his home on Versailles Street in Montreal's Little Burgundy district at around 12:30 in the morning. He parked his car across the street and headed for his nearby home. Ten minutes earlier, a neighbor had noticed a vehicle that had parked in the darkness. While Parent was walking along the sidewalk in front of his home, a man approached and shot him with a Cobray automatic pistol equipped with a silencer. Parent was struck four times and fell to the ground as the shooter headed for the mysterious car parked in the nearby alley. Before he jumped into the car, he dumped the firearm in the laneway where it was later discovered by the police. It was a clean hit in which the shooter left very little evidence behind.

Serge Hervieux

The next homicide to take place during the biker war, one of the 13 murders included in the charges filed in Project Rush, was a disaster for the Hells Angels from beginning to end. Unlike in the Parent murder and some of the others before it, key evidence was left at the murder scene.

Another mistake was that Hervieux was not the target. Married and a father of two, Hervieux had the misfortune of working at the same location and sharing the same first name with Serge Bruneau, a member of the Dark Circle. Like Bastien and Rosa, Bruneau had done a 30-month sentence after pleading guilty to conspiring to murder a Hells Angel. After serving two-thirds of his sentence, Bruneau was released. Besides being a drug dealer, Bruneau had invested his money in real estate and legitimate businesses like a car rental agency.

Three weeks after Parent was murdered, two hooded men walked into the car rental agency that Bruneau owned and where Hervieux worked. Witnesses would later recall that it was a picture-perfect summer day in Saint-Leonard when Hervieux was shot. The car rental agency was located on one of the busier streets in the area but surrounded by rows of tidy duplexes, which are common in Saint-Leonard. One of the masked men called out for "Serge" and Hervieux responded. Mistaking him for their target, one of the men fired off six shots toward Hervieux with a .357 Magnum Colt Python revolver. Hervieux was struck by four bullets and died quickly. Both his lungs were damaged and one bullet severed a pulmonary vein. Hearing the gunshots, Bruneau hid under his desk in his office.

The two hooded men walked out of the rental agency's garage, the shooter dropping his revolver on the floor. They escaped in a stolen black Chrysler Intrepid. They abandoned the car a few streets away and, as with many of the other murders, they prepared to set the getaway vehicle on fire. But in this case the gas didn't burn very well and by the time the police located the vehicle, the flames had petered out.

But more important to homicide investigators was the rare find laid out on the car's seats: undamaged evidence from a Hells Angels' hit. Crime scene technicians managed to find two balaclavas, a pair of running shoes, two baseball caps and two pairs of gloves. They also found three sheets of paper folded together that made it clear that Bruneau was the intended target of the shooting. Among the papers were photos of Bruneau and intelligence on other members of the Alliance. These sheets of paper also gave the police a remarkable lead. Fingerprints found on them were later matched to Jean-Richard (Race) Larivière, who months earlier had been made a full-patch member of the Rockers. Another set of fingerprints was matched to Éric (Pif) Fournier who would receive his patch three months after the Hervieux murder. Becoming full-patch members of the Rockers automatically made them targets of the Project Rush investigation. The police also found DNA evidence in one of the balaclavas. The same DNA turned up in a pair of gloves but the police were unable to make a match.

Despite the obvious screw up, witnesses testified that the two masked men appeared to know exactly where they were going, as if they had studied the layout of the rental agency. They walked in through an open garage door and strode right past a mechanic.

Bruneau, who had known Hervieux for seven years, would later be called to testify in one of the trials to come out of Project Rush, heard before Justice Réjean Paul. He appeared uneasy and never looked toward the 13 men sitting in the specially designed, bulletproof prisoners' dock. The courthouse had been specifically built to try the Hells Angels' Nomads chapter. Construction began shortly after Operation Springtime 2001 was carried out. It was built on land near the Bordeaux detention center to facilitate the transfer of the many gang members. The new courthouse, which cost taxpayers $16.5 million, featured state-of-the-art equipment. Testimony could be recorded digitally, and lawyers sitting at each table could watch video evidence on computer screens. The dock could seat several of the accused for one trial. Bruneau stood several feet away from the accused as he described himself as a car dealer. Prosecutor Éric Marcoux asked him about what he remembered from Hervieux's murder.

"I heard shots and I hid," Bruneau told the jury. "I waited for things to calm down. I saw Serge Hervieux and I called the police."

"What did you think then?" Marcoux asked.

"I heard [the first] shot and a window break and I hid under the desk. I knew it was gunfire and I hid." Bruneau's testimony confirmed how badly the Hells Angels had botched the hit on him. Some of the photos that were found inside the getaway car were surveillance shots taken at a funeral he had attended but the photos were not of him. Whoever had supplied them to the shooters had written in pen "Serge Bruno" with an arrow pointing toward an unknown man.

"Did you think you were the target?" Eric Marcoux asked. Bruneau paused for a long moment and his face gave away his anxiety. He rubbed his hand across his face. "Yes," he replied, while admitting to the jury that he had a criminal record that included drug trafficking. "I was sure it was that. I thought it was because I was involved in drug trafficking."

"Who did you deal with?" Marcoux asked. Bruneau fidgeted and appeared deeply miserable. The defense lawyers objected strenuously to Marcoux's questions. But Bruneau was eventually able to say that he was associated with Jean Rosa and Pierre Bastien.

Despite a botched hit and the killing of an innocent man, the Hells Angels killed again only a little over a month later.

Tony Plescio

It would seem that the Hells Angels' hits on rival gang members were becoming increasingly sloppy. On October 1, 1999, Johnny Plescio's brother Tony was murdered in the parking lot of a McDonald's restaurant in Montreal North. Plescio had just taken his family to a children's party at the restaurant. While Johnny Plescio's murder appeared to be well planned — he was drawn to his window after the killer sliced his cable — Tony's was reckless.

Plescio was shot six times in the head and neck at point blank range in the parking lot. But a stray bullet struck Plescio's wife, who was getting some diapers from the trunk of their car. The bullet wounded her foot, but she managed to make sure the couple's child was safe in the car once she realized Plescio had fallen to the ground fatally wounded. Other people in the parking lot scattered; some were young mothers, terrified that their children were about to be killed. The shooter escaped in a car that sped away from the restaurant. As the shooter and a getaway driver crossed a bridge heading for Laval, the shooter apparently tried to toss the firearm into the Rivière-des-Prairies. Instead, the .357 Magnum fell to the pavement of an underpass below where it was later recovered by the police.

Like his brother Johnny, Tony Plescio was a member of the Rock Machine. In 1990, he had been caught selling quarter-grams of cocaine for $30 out of the same bar on Bélanger Street owned by Johnny that someone had tried to torch twice during the biker war. At the time of his death, Plescio was waiting to be sentenced in a drug and weapons case.

But Plescio had already made headlines years before the biker war ever started. He was arrested in 1985 in a strange incident that also involved Alex Hilton, one of several boxing brothers who came to prominence during the 1980s. By 1984 Alex and his brother Davey were both Canadian champions in their respective weight categories, and younger brother Matthew had a promising career ahead of him. But the Hilton name soon became as synonymous with crime as much as it was with boxing. The family was tied to Mafia leader Frank Cotroni, but the brothers' crimes were, for the most part, tied to drinking. Alex Hilton in particular had been arrested several times for alcohol-induced mischief.

On February 11, 1985, Plescio and Alex Hilton left the Action Disco Club, a bar on a service road of the Trans-Canada Highway that runs through eastern Montreal, after a heavy night of drinking.

While in the parking lot, Hilton reached into the trunk of his car and pulled out a .22 calibre rifle. A witness, fellow boxer Serge Cusson, later said that Hilton merely fired into the air and then Plescio grabbed the rifle and did the same. No one was injured in the shooting, but one of the shots did go through a window of a nearby building. The police were also told there had been an altercation inside the bar just before the shots were fired. Plescio was only fined and handed a probationary sentence for the offence.

Patrick Turcotte

On May 1, 2000, Patrick Turcotte was shot dead just after leaving a video rental store. Turcotte was a drug dealer who worked with the Rock Machine. Turcotte was crossing the street late in the afternoon when someone got out of a blue van and shot him in the back several times. The shooter then got into the van on the passenger side and it sped away. The gun used to kill Turcotte, a Beretta automatic pistol equipped with a custom-made silencer, was found lying under a white car, near where the van had been waiting. Two bystanders tried to help Turcotte and attempted to resuscitate him. When they loosened his belt, a gun fell to the ground. It had been stuck inside the back of his pants. His pager was left lying a few feet away.

Ten minutes after the shooting, the blue van used in the murder exploded a few blocks away. It had been stolen earlier that day in Brossard. Witnesses saw two men run from it just before the loud blast. Police recovered two pairs of gloves on the ground nearby, and they were able to find DNA samples in both pairs. The DNA was later matched to Pierre (Peanut) Laurin and Paul (Schtroumpf) Brisebois. Both were Rockers at the time of Turcotte's murder, but, on December 11, 2000, each was promoted to the status of prospect in the Hells Angels.

In February 2003, while evidence in Turcotte's murder was being heard in the trial before Justice Réjean Paul, Brisebois' lawyer Real Charbonneau was rude to the judge after he cut off his cross-examination of a police witness. Paul ordered Charbonneau out of the courtroom and suspended the trial for the day. Charbonneau was charged with contempt, but was later acquitted. In the interim, Brisebois had his trial severed from the 12 other gang members. Months afterward, the entire trial came to an end when some of the accused reached plea bargain agreements.

Brisebois and Laurin were not offered plea bargains, however, because of the solid evidence against them. But they did later agree to plead guilty to second-degree murder in the Turcotte case. In exchange, they were sentenced to life with a chance to apply for parole after serving ten years. The three years they spent behind bars awaiting the outcome of their case was not counted as double, as it usually is, so they would have to wait at least seven years before applying for parole. The pair also pleaded guilty to conspiracy to commit murder, drug trafficking and gangsterism.

François Gagnon

François Gagnon's murder would be just as sloppy as the Turcotte and Hervieux murders. But the homicide also indicated that either the Hells Angels were running out of targets or the Rock Machine were running out of capable people to deal their drugs: Gagnon was a drug dealer, but he was also mentally unstable.

The early part of his criminal record indicates that Gagnon made a career out of drug dealing. On June 4, 1977, he was arrested with 27 grams of hashish and 7 grams of marijuana. Two years later he was charged with trafficking in cocaine. During the summer of 1980, he was caught selling small quantities of cocaine. In 1986, he was caught with 25 grams of hashish.

Then in 1987, he was caught trying to smuggle 42 grams of hashish into the Bordeaux detention center. Gagnon had been out on a weekend pass and the guards suspected that he was smuggling drugs into the prison. They placed him in a special 72-hour cell, equipped with a modified toilet that didn't flush, because they suspected Gagnon was smuggling hashish in through his stomach. They didn't have to wait 72 hours. After one night, the guards came to check on Gagnon and found him sitting at the edge of the bed, balloons full of hashish near him. When he saw the guards he grabbed the balloons and threw them in the toilet.

During the early 1990s, there were still signs that Gagnon was a very active drug dealer. But sometime after 1995, the criminal cases brought against him were of a very different nature. In 1997, he was charged with threatening the life of a Montreal police officer and his family. He was also charged with making threats against then Prime Minister Jean Chrétien. A judge asked for a psychiatric evaluation, and the case was eventually dropped after Gagnon promised to take medication. But the following year, he was charged with a series of strange crimes, including damaging a woman's lawn furniture. On July 22, 1998, he sent a package to *Journal de Montréal* reporter Michel Auger that spooked security guards at the newspaper. Again, a judge asked that Gagnon undergo a psychiatric evaluation.

On September 22, 1998, Gagnon was arrested for making threats to Montreal Urban Community Police officers. Again, a judge asked for him to be evaluated by a psychiatrist. But Gagnon resisted. The psychiatrist ended up sending a letter to the judge in the case citing reasons for his inability to examine the accused. He wrote that Gagnon "would only come to an external clinic to have his welfare certificate renewed and to get benzodiazepine." The psychiatrist also noted that the 350-pound Gagnon showed up for examinations intoxicated and that when he didn't get benzodiazapine, a tranquilizer, he became aggressive and threatened the staff.

So, after years of eliminating rival gang members, some of whom were millionaires, the Hells Angels decided to go after Gagnon, a man dependent on psychiatric medication to function.

Gagnon was sitting in the kitchen of his Montreal North apartment while either one or two men quietly walked up the outside stairs at the back of his building. Gagnon was shot through the patio door that led to his kitchen. Three shots were fired from a .357 Magnum Smith & Wesson revolver, and three were fired from a .38 calibre revolver. Four of the shots struck Gagnon and he died quickly. The shooter or shooters left the scene in a blue Dodge Caravan. It was later spotted making an abrupt stop in the middle of the street a few blocks away. Three men were seen jumping out of the van. They all then jumped a nearby fence and disappeared into an alley.

Four members of the Rockers during better days. From left to right: Gregory Wooley, Jean-Guy Bourgoin, Stéphane (Archie) Hilareguy and Daniel Lanthier.

Back at the murder scene, the police recovered the gun used to shoot Gagnon. Inside the van they found the other firearm used in the murder, as well as a .357 Ruger revolver. They also found a fuel can with gasoline still in it and a box of flares. It appeared Gagnon's assailants had tried to destroy the evidence but failed miserably. Police also recovered two pairs of running shoes. In a garbage can near where the van was abandoned, the police found two pairs of gloves. The fingerprints found on the flare box matched those of Stéphane (Archie) Hilareguy, a Rocker implicated in the murder of Yvon (Mon Mon) Roy, and his DNA was found in one of the pairs of running shoes. Inside the other pair the police found a DNA sample that would later be matched to Rocker Éric (Pif) Fournier. Inside one of the gloves found in the garbage can was a DNA sample that matched the unidentified sample recovered after the Hervieux murder.

The fingerprints on the flare indicated that Hilareguy was in charge of destroying the evidence in the Gagnon hit, but he had apparently failed. His name was now tied to at least two Hells Angels' hits and it appeared the Hells Angels could no longer tolerate the attention he had attracted. On June 16, 2000, less than two weeks after the Gagnon murder, Hileraguy's young child was found standing outside his home in St-Roch while it burned. After the flames were extinguished the police found a body inside. It turned out to be Hileraguy's 30-year-old girlfriend Natacha Desbiens. She had been shot to death before the house was set on fire. Several months later, Hilareguy's remains were discovered in Potton, a small municipality in the Eastern Townships.

5

An Ocean of Cash

On October 20, 2004, Stéphane Plouffe, a longtime member of the Hells Angels' Montreal chapter, walked into the Montreal courthouse and surrendered himself to the Sûreté du Québec as had been arranged beforehand. Within hours, he was ushered into a courtroom where he pleaded guilty to drug trafficking. Plouffe had been in hiding for more than three years and his surrender put an end to one of the most successful criminal cases ever brought to a Quebec court.

Project Ocean was an unexpected bonus for the police investigators who had spent years gathering evidence for what would lead to Operation Springtime 2001. It virtually landed in their laps, yet netted more full-patch members of the Hells Angels than any other investigation had in many years (with the exception of Project Rush the parallel investigation that led to Operation Springtime 2001). Project Ocean also helped the Sûreté du Québec settle an old score with Gerald Matticks, a man whose influence in the Port of Montreal made him a key asset to Boucher and the Hells Angels.

On the same day Plouffe surrendered, he was sentenced to three years in prison. The police had little knowledge of how he had managed to avoid capture since 2001. Ironically, as he was preparing to do his time behind bars, some of the people who had almost immediately pleaded guilty to charges related to Project Ocean, and were serving much longer sentences than Plouffe's, were just being released on parole.

The Nomads Bank

Of the 51 people charged in connection with Project Ocean, 50 were eventually sentenced, including 36 who received federal sentences averaging about four years. Only one person, a Hells Angel named Guy Dubé, would see his charges dropped because the evidence against him was very thin. Faced with the mounds of evidence the police had gathered in only six months, almost everyone charged in connection with Project Ocean pleaded guilty within months of being arrested. They were people from all walks of life, ranging from full-patch members of the Hells Angels to people who claimed they were only vaguely aware they were working for the gang.

The focus of investigation was a collection of apartments the Nomads chapter had used to conduct the accounting of what had become a vast drug empire that stretched across Canada. The system, with its vaults, counting machines and detailed accounting, would be referred to in court as the Nomads Bank since it handled more money in some weeks than some branches of Canada's chartered banks. The Hells Angels employed people they knew had no criminal records to run their bank with the hope they would never draw police attention to the place where the gang's millions flowed. According to one investigator, some in the organization were 60 years old, others upwards of 80.

"They have no criminal records. You don't use known criminals to transport sums like this because they are more investigated by the police," the officer would later say in court.

But in September 2000, police tailing Jean-Richard (Race) Larivière, a member of the Rockers who was about to graduate to the level of prospect in the Nomads chapter, noticed that Larivière made frequent visits to an apartment building on Beaubien Street in Montreal. The surveillance opened a crack into the Hells Angels' finances that soon produced a flood of evidence against the 50 people who ended up convicted. They ranged from a grandmother with expensive tastes who buzzed money couriers into her apartment building, to full-patch Hells Angels from across Quebec who were either making large cash deposits or, as was more often the case, withdrawals for their respective chapters. While making sentencing arguments before Judge Réjean Paul on September 23, 2003, prosecutor André Vincent made his assessment of what the Nomads Bank represented.

"When you talk of legal businesses in Quebec, these are figures that correspond to something much higher than a medium-sized business can hope to have. The sales for the 39-day period are in the order of $18,104,000. That amount corresponds to the sale of 452 kilos of cocaine and 115 kilos of hashish." It was during the April 9, 2001, bail hearing of Jean Adam and Dominic Tremblay, both minor players in the Nomads Bank, that all the details began to spill out. Canada now had an open window on what the biker war was truly about: millions in drug money.

Richard Despaties, a Sûreté du Québec officer, testified during the hearing.

"How did this investigation get initiated. During what period?" prosecutor Valerie Tremblay asked him.

"First of all, it started around July 25 [2000], in another case, there was an informant named Dany Kane, who we called IN3683," Despaties said, referring to the member of the Rockers who had been feeding information to the police since the beginning of the war. "Dany Kane was a member of the Rockers and served as the chauffeur for Normand Robitaille who is a Nomad. And, from what I know, Normand Robitaille had asked Dany Kane to watch his leather briefcase and Dany Kane searched [it]. He found certain documents, photocopied them and turned them over to his controllers."

During the summer of 2000, Robitaille had decided to try Kane out as a chauffeur and someone to run his errands. It was a position of trust. The fact Kane was still working for both the police and the Hells Angels was incredible at that point. He had started working as an informant for the police in October 1994, after contacting RCMP Sgt. Jean-Pierre Lévesque through a call he placed to Interpol. Sgt. Lévesque set up a meeting. On October 18, 1994, he met at a Best Western in Dorval at 6 p.m. with Lévesque and Sgt. Pierre Verdon. To prove his worth, Kane told the officers several things about the Hells Angels and one of their puppet gangs, the Evil Ones.

"The source has remarkable potential," Verdon would write in his notes of that meeting, which began a working relationship that ended in 1997 when Kane was arrested for a murder in Nova Scotia. Kane's trial for the homicide ended up being tossed out of court, and he slowly worked his way back into the Rockers. The fact that he was so close to key members of the Hells Angels was what kept the police interested in him, despite the fact that when he agreed to work as an informant the second time around he confessed to having murdered for the gang.

About two years after being arrested for the Nova Scotia murder, Kane was working for new police handlers in the Regional Integrated Squad in September 1999. He started out working like he had for the RCMP, providing information and being paid each time he did so. By March 2000, he had signed a contract that meant he was officially working for the police as a double agent and expected to eventually testify in court. Before signing the contract, Kane admitted to all of his crimes, including a murder he had committed while working as a tipster for the RCMP and had tried to pin on someone else through the information he was feeding the police.

The financial compensation called for in the contract was indicative of Kane's value as an informant. He was required to collaborate with the Sûreté du Québec and would be paid three installments of more than $500,000 each after Operation Springtime 2001 was carried out and as the Project Rush investigation made its way through the courts where he was expected to testify. The contract also called on the Sûreté to cover several of Kane's expenses like his mortgage, $587 per month for his motorcycle and the rental of a Neon and two Plymouth Voyageur vans. The police gave Kane $600 for new clothing because Normand Robitaille once asked him to dress more stylishly; he was given $1,000 to buy a gift for René Charlebois' wedding; he was given money to cover his contribution to the Rockers' ten percent fund. All of this put the police in a strange position where they were financially supporting the gang.

But in the end Kane never spent a day on the witness stand. Instead, he took his own life for reasons that are not known. He was found dead inside the garage of his home in Saint-Luc on August 7, 2000. He had died of carbon monoxide poisoning after starting up a luxury car, opening the sunroof and the windows and letting the garage fill with the deadly fumes.

Knowing that he was under constant police surveillance, Robitaille once asked Kane to drop him off at a métro station and handed his underling the briefcase for safekeeping. Kane received the briefcase around 5 p.m. He raced to meet his controllers and they photocopied the documents inside. Within three hours, Kane had the briefcase back with all the originals and was ready to pick up Robitaille as planned at another métro station several kilometres from the one where he had dropped him off. The investigators instantly recognized the names of five men tied to the Rock Machine among the documents Robitaille was carrying. That Robitaille would be interested in personal information on his rivals came as no surprise. But the investigators struggled to make sense of coded accounting ledgers that were also inside the briefcase.

The Vault Opens

"They were on 8.5 by 14 pages with all kinds of names, names we did not know, with money figures next to them," Despaties said at the bail hearing, offering several copies of the documents to the lawyers involved. "At the office, we looked at these documents but we couldn't understand them because the names on the documents are not the surnames of bikers that we knew. Because we knew the bikers by very specific surnames, we looked at it and we said we didn't understand, except that we knew it was an accounting sheet for drugs." Despaties explained that the figures next to the names appeared with dates as well. In one column, figures were accompanied by the initials BL, and in another, BR. Despaties said he immediately took them to be abbreviations of the French words *blanc* and *brun*. He said that in his six years of experience in narcotics, he came to know the word *blanc*, French for white, was commonly used as a code word for cocaine, and *brun*, French for brown, meant hashish.

Despaties said that at the moment of this finding the police were heavily involved in Project Rush, which was within months of coming to an end. Kane's discovery was set aside and initially not considered a high priority.

"The documents were placed into exhibit. There wasn't a prolonged investigation except that Dany Kane, the informant in the case, was doing drug deals with certain members," Despaties said. "If he wanted to buy a kilo of cocaine, he had to go through Jean-Richard Larivière, who was a member of the Rockers as well. By the month of September 2000, we started to follow Jean-Richard Larivière. On the first days we were following

Jean-Richard (Race) Larivière, a prospect in the Nomads chapter.

145

him," Despaties elaborated, "Mr. Larivière went to a condo situated at 7415 Beaubien in Montreal. What we found curious about Mr. Larivière was that it was a building with an entrance on Beaubien and an underground parking lot on the east side of the building. Mr. Larivière entered the building by what I would call a panic door, but it required a key. According to the people following him, Mr. Larivière had the key. It caught our attention, but nothing more than that. We thought that maybe he was visiting a member of his family. We didn't know. However, shortly after, Mr. Larivière returned to this building twice. That's when we decided there must be something going on inside. We started to do surveillance for weeks at the building to see what was going on."

Despaties said that during their surveillance, the police noticed that a known drug dealer named Paul Gaudreau visited apartment 504 inside the building several times. They checked with Hydro-Québec, the provincial utility, and were told that there was very little electricity being consumed inside the apartment. They also noticed that during nighttime hours lights were rarely used inside the apartment. As the interest grew, investigators dug up a months' old intelligence report that made mention of the Beaubien Street building. The report detailed how, on August 31, 2000, a police surveillance team had tailed Sylvain Laplante, a member of the Rockers as he left his hometown of Valleyfield, an eastern Quebec city near the Ontario border, in a red Ford Taurus. Hours later he showed up at the Beaubien Street apartment building in a Buick Century. He entered the building with a briefcase.

Despaties said the information was enough to get a search warrant. "We went inside the apartment. It was an apartment that did not have much furniture. What was peculiar was that there was very little clothing and the refrigerator was empty. It led us to believe that no one actually lived in the apartment." What they did learn was that the apartment was being rented by a retired member of the Canadian military who was actually living in Hull at the time. The police listened in on a conversation the man had had with Richard Gemme, the accountant behind the Nomads Bank. Gemme joked that it was a good thing the military man had retired because if the police ever found out he was lending his name to rent apartments for the Hells Angels it would likely ignite a large-scale investigation.

The police got a warrant to place a listening device and video camera in the apartment on October 16, 2000. Despaties said that during surveillance they saw other people show up at the address. The first to catch their attention was Jacques Nepveu, a former member of the Rowdy Crew, a Hells Angels' underling gang based in Lavaltrie, a town east of Montreal. Despite having left the Rowdy Crew, Nepveu was still known to be close to the Hells Angels' Montreal chapter. The police watched as Nepveu arrived at 7415 Beaubien Street on October 3, 2000. He was carrying a bag. But when he left, he had no bag.

Six days after spotting Nepveu, Sgt. Pierre Boucher of the Sûreté du Québec managed to make his first surreptitious entry into the apartment. According to Despaties, "When we installed the camera and the audio in the apartment, we noticed that people would show up on Tuesdays, mostly on Tuesdays, but also on Thursdays, from 8 in the morning to 4 in the afternoon, and the person who took care of the apartment was a man named Robert Gauthier. He did not live at the address but somewhere else in Montreal.

"Most of the time it would happen like this: people would show up at [apartment] 504, enter inside the apartment and hand over a bag to Mr. Gauthier. After that the clients would leave. What was very particular to Mr. Gauthier in his methods of operation was that after the clients would leave he was very vigilant. He would look through the peephole, he would look out the patio doors. Once the clients had driven away, we would see him leave 504 for a minute or two and return to 504. We realized that there was certainly another apartment that Mr. Gauthier was going to because he would always leave with the bags."

"And when he came back?" Tremblay asked.

"His hands were empty," Despaties said, adding that as they continued their investigation, the police found that Gauthier was traveling down one floor to apartment 403. Inside apartment 504, meanwhile, the television would play all the time. Whenever someone showed up with a bag of money, a radio would be turned up loud. Despaties said they could hear almost no conversations on their wiretaps.

In order to more fully monitor Gauthier, the police got a warrant on October 24 that enabled them to do electronic surveillance inside apartment 403. It turned out to be a sparsely furnished four-and-a-half rooms with a safe inside a bedroom cabinet. A bill for the safe was found in a kitchen cupboard. There were no clothes in the closets and no food in the fridge or cupboards.

"It was just like apartment 504 except that there were a lot of gym bags," Despaties said. "There were all kinds of them, all kind of brands. They were empty and piled inside a closet." Another investigator later remarked that the pile of gym bags was stacked about five feet high.

"We noticed that Gauthier was bringing the bags from 504 to 403 and returning to 504 to wait for clients. Except that when Mr. Gauthier would bring the bags to 403, we entered after he left. We had a key and we counted how much money was in the bags and looked at the notes that were inside the bags," Despaties said. "The smallest amount we found was around $5,000. The biggest was $600,000." Inside the bags, investigators always found little notes with codes on them. Despaties said that as the investigation progressed investigators began to sort out who the drug dealers were behind the codes.

What the police would later learn was that couriers who were bringing the money to the apartment had very specific instructions. Carl Ouellette, a man who was making deliveries for the

Quebec City chapter and one of the people arrested in Project Ocean, would later reveal an important detail the police had not learned during their investigation. Ouellette said that on the days he made deliveries he was instructed to send out a coded message on a pager when he was at least an hour from the apartment building. The message would include what time he wanted to make the delivery. Then he would wait for a coded reply on the pager giving him the green light to make the delivery. Investigators soon noticed that a man they later identified as Stéphane Chagnon would enter apartment 403 and take control of the bags, check the money and then record the amounts on a computer. On October 25, the police entered apartment 403 and made copies of a ledger, a diskette and the hard drive on a laptop computer. Cracking the passwords for the computer files proved absurdly easy as they were all "0000."

"From the beginning of November 2000 we had a surveillance team outside the building. All of the clients who brought money were filmed. Most of the time, their licence plate and car were filmed at the same time," Despaties said. Chagnon would transfer the money to another apartment building, 8101 Place Montoire, in Anjou and just a short trip west of the Beaubien Street address. Through their surveillance, police learned he would always head for apartment 309, rented by a 64-year-old woman named Lise Gelinas.

"What was curious in this part of the investigation was that Lise Gelinas was renting apartment 308 on Place Montoir and a Lise Germain Gelinas was renting apartment 309. We found that curious," said Despaties, who also reported that the police had obtained a warrant and entered apartment 309. "At that location, what we found were money-counting machines, elastic bands, everything needed to count money. Three counting machines if I'm not mistaken and a large safe [with a digital combination]. No sign of life though, and no clothing."

The police got a warrant to place an audio wire in the apartment. Despaties said that what the police learned next amazed them.

"They were counting [money] every morning. We thought it was a bank. It went from eight in the morning to between 10 or noon. There was counting all the time. We heard nothing but the counting machines." The police also learned Gelinas was buzzing people in to the apartment building from her residence across the hall from the counting room. They also noticed that Gelinas and Monique Gauthier, a frequent visitor to apartment 309, were often engaged in conversation. It turned out that Monique Gauthier was the one counting the money. It also turned out that she was the ex-wife of Michel Rose, a member of the Nomads chapter. The police would also later learn she was sister of Robert Gauthier, the man running the Beaubien Street apartments for the Hells Angels. Of all the members of the Nomads chapter, it was Rose and André Chouinard who appeared to have clear ties to the banking system. Whenever Larivière would show up at the Beaubien Street apartment, it was often after meeting with Rose.

The apartment across from Gelinas' was not only used to store money but to pay off large-scale suppliers to the Nomads chapter drug network. "For example," Despaties explained, "*Usine* [French for "factory" and the code name for] a supplier of cocaine. So, *Usine*, when we did copies of their accounting we noticed there was a new client that was on the account sheet. Instead of being a client/buyer he was a client/supplier. We noticed that when people went to Place Montoir and left with boxes, the total of the accounts went down."

Clients and Suppliers

Investigators also noticed that when a man they eventually realized was a courier for the "Usine" account would leave Place Montoir with a box, the account for Usine was always noted as having been paid around $1.5 million. The account was paid more than $8 million between November 23 and December 15, 2000. Despaties said the police figured the Hells Angels were using two apartment buildings to prevent burns.

"The goal of the investigation was to . . . well it evolved from day to day. We noticed that it was always the same people who showed up, always the same clients, the same codes."

The police soon realized that Chagnon was hiding something in apartment 403. They got a warrant again and found out it was a zip disk. A computer specialist copied the diskette for the police before anyone would notice it was missing. During their surveillance investigators noticed the man they would later realize was the accountant, Richard Gemme, was interacting with Chagnon. Both were childhood friends of André Chouinard.

"Chagnon appeared to be having trouble with his accounting and the diskette. We noticed that Gemme seemed to be more at ease in accounting."

The police eventually seized two documents. One seemed to break down accounting by chapters. They also found a note that appeared to be orders to move to new apartments. They heard this order in their surveillance on bugged rooms as well. After doing what the police referred to as "sneak entries" into the apartments on Beaubien Street several times, the police had begun to pick up on the patterns of the accounting. Investigators were becoming so familiar with the system they weren't caught off guard when the Nomads chapter ordered that their accounting lists be broken down by chapters, instead of by individual Hells Angels. The first column was the Quebec City chapter. The second, dubbed "Granche," was the Montreal chapter and the one labeled "Top" was the Nomads. The accounting program also listed bad accounts and an inventory of what drugs they had in stock and in what amounts. The red column covered what they owed their suppliers.

Despaties said that, most of the time, the accounting was very accurate. There was only a small margin of error between what was brought in and what was accounted for. The police copied Chagnon's zip disk about three times. The last time was on December 19, 2000. What they learned was that the accounting on the computer disc closely resembled the documents Kane had supplied them months earlier, except for the point in November when the Nomads chapter asked it be broken down by chapter. The investigators also realized that Kane had heard right when he was told by David (Wolf) Carroll, a founding member of the Nomads chapter, that each member of the chapter was being paid a fixed salary of about $5,000 a week from the Nomads Bank. While they monitored the apartments, the police noticed that Larivière appeared to deliver money to members of the Nomads chapter in shopping bags, always on Tuesdays and almost always $40,000 in hundred dollar bills.

The accounting software even included detailed breakdowns on large quantities of drugs the Hells Angels had purchased. For example, 50 kilos of cocaine would be broken down by the price they had paid and the profit the Nomads chapter had made off it. When the entire quantity was sold, the profit would be transferred over to the general accounting sheet. Other details included the fact that Stéphane Faucher, who was once a prospect in the Nomads chapter, was not allowed to buy drugs from the network. What the police would later find out was that Faucher had done something to embarrass the gang which had caused Denis Houle, a longtime member of the gang, to advise the others that he was not Hells Angels' material. After his arrest, Faucher would become a Crown witness, supplying prosecutors with additional information to help bolster their case. But when it was his turn to testify in court, he backed out.

Another fact that caught the eyes of investigators examining the accounting system was that the Nomads chapter was charging independent drug dealers the same price for cocaine as they were members of other Hells Angels' chapters. The Nomads were cut-throat business men who wouldn't even give fellow Hells Angels a discount.

It was a cold, businesslike attitude the Nomads chapter took toward their drug empire. December 12, 2000, was the day the account in Louis (Melou) Roy's name was terminated. The account was code-named "Jenny" and tens of thousands of dollars were still in it, even though Roy, a founding member of the Nomads chapter, had disappeared sometime in June. His body had yet to be found but investigators believed he had been purged from the gang. His disappearance coincided with negotiations the Hells Angels were having with the Mafia over what price a kilo of cocaine could be sold for in Montreal. Within days of Roy's disappearance, the police found his luxury car parked on a downtown Montreal street covered in parking tickets. No one outside of the gang could say for sure whether Roy had been killed. But now the police noticed, through the copied accounting computer disk that his drug money was being distributed to members of the Trois Rivières chapter, the one where Roy had started his career as a Hells Angel.

The police monitoring the accounting also noticed the Trois Rivières chapter had purchased, in a six-month period between July 5, 2000, and December 19, 2000, 164 kilos of cocaine along with 105 kilos of hashish from the Nomads chapter. The Nomads chapter's reach extended even to Quebec City.

"The goal of the case, among other things, was to identify the client accounts. There were many who we were able to identify," officer Despaties said, adding investigators were able to identify about ten full-patch Hells Angels who showed up to deliver money. "I just want to say to the court that they did not show up wearing their Hells Angels' colors. During the years we've investigated them we've got to know some well," he said.

But most of the couriers were people the police did not recognize. Dominic Tremblay, the man whose bail hearing Despaties was testifying in, was monitored as he made frequent trips to Montreal for the Trois Rivières chapter. The first time he was seen was on November 2, 2000, at the building on Beaubien Street. He brought $40,000 to the apartment building. Three weeks later, on November 23, 2000, he brought more than $200,000. On November 30, he brought $53,655; on December 5, he brought $125,545; on December 7, he brought $22,445. Then, on December 14, 2000, Tremblay was recorded bringing a bag to Gauthier that contained $253,335.

"Concerning the proof in your investigation, it ended on what date?" Tremblay, the prosecutor, asked.

"You could say the first phase ended on January 30, 2001. We executed three search warrants that night."

On December 11, 2000, they overheard tenant Lise Gelinas telling her sister she could no longer deal with the stress of guarding millions of the Hells Angels' money. During one conversation, Gelinas indicated that the banking system had been in place for four years. Other wiretaps suggested the couriers and the people accepting the money had known each other for as many as six years. Soon after Gelinas talked of quitting, she got her wish — investigators noticed the banking system had changed. The counting machines were moved from the apartment across from Gelinas's to apartment 403 back on Beaubien Street. Robert Gauthier was there regularly now, so it became harder for the police to enter the room surreptitiously.

"We decided that January 30 was a good day to hit those apartments, because we saw money going in but it didn't go out," Despaties said. In apartment 403, the police found $800,000 in a safe. In apartment 504, they didn't find money but they found documentation, the coded amounts each courier had left with the money. These papers were hidden everywhere, in the fridge and in cupboards.

Despaties said the police noticed that another apartment had been designated as a replacement for Place Montoir before they executed their search warrants. It was 3276 De la Pepiniere Street, the residence of a 77-year-old man named Richard Musselle, a man with ties to Louis (Melou) Roy and Normand (Biff) Hamel, and he had worked for Irazu, the importing company owned by Maurice (Mom) Boucher. But the Hells Angels hoped he would never draw the attention of the police. Muselle was being paid $300 a week for his troubles. Musselle had a wife and a child so there was usually someone home, which prevented the police from doing surreptitious entries into the residence.

The order to change the money drop-off point had come directly from the Nomads chapter. On January 11, 2001, the police listened in as Chagnon told Gauthier that they weren't going to have any clients that day. Chagnon left the Beaubien Street building and drove to an Italian restaurant on a highway service road in the north end of Montreal. There he met with Jean-Richard Larivière, who by now was a prospect in the Nomads chapter. Investigators weren't privy to their conversation, but Chagnon returned to the apartment on Beaubien Street and was overheard on a wiretap telling Gauthier: "When those people decide to shut it down, you shut it down. You don't have a word to say."

What the police later learned was that the bank was ordered shut down because the Hells Angels had learned that someone associated with the Trois Rivières chapter who had been delivering money had been scrutinized by the police in that city. When the police searched Musselle's apartment, they found more than $900,000. At Place Montoir in apartment 309, they found $3.8 million still stored in a safe, even though the gang had stopped using it as a place to count their cash. The police seized a total of $5.6 million in U.S. and Canadian funds from the three apartments.

Closing the Bank

Stéphane Chagnon was arrested, questioned and released. The plan was to arrest him again weeks later along with everyone else targeted in Operation Springtime 2001. Richard Musselle was arrested in January as well. When the police picked up Chagnon, he had five cellular phones and three pagers on him. One of his clear ties to the Hells Angels was that he was dating the sister of André Chouinard, a member of the Nomads chapter. While the apartments were under surveillance, he had been careful to never use the phone lines in them. Some people arrested in Project Ocean were carrying more than 20 pagers. When Despaties was asked whether the police had other evidence to support their suspicion that the accounting ledgers belonged to the Nomads chapter, he read from his notebook, "Among other things, Stéphane Chagnon was taking care of the money and was always in contact with Jean-Richard Larivière and had several meetings, or at least two dinners with Michel Rose, a member of the Nomads and the former husband of Monique Gauthier."

Despaties also described how Sylvain Laplante, a member of the Rockers who worked for Gilles (Trooper) Mathieu, a founding member of the Nomads chapter, had a bug in his car for several months during Project Rush, and on November 14, 2000, he was recorded bragging to his wife that the Nomads controlled everything and sold drugs to all the chapters in Quebec except for Sherbrooke, one of richest chapters in all of Canada. In fact, it appeared the Sherbrooke chapter was supplying their brothers in the Nomads chapter. One courier who was suspected of working for the Sherbrooke chapter was eventually arrested with more than $1 million stashed in a Montreal apartment. Laplante was delivering money for Mathieu's account.

Despaties also said that when they raided Donald (Pup) Stockford's home in Hamilton, the police found the number and address of the apartments on Beaubien Street. When asked if it appeared the January seizures had placed a dent in the Nomads chapter's operations, Despaties replied that it didn't appear to make much difference. When Operation Springtime 2001 was carried out two months later, arresting officers found another set of accounting sheets at the home of Johnny Royer, a member of the Trois Rivières chapter. The ledgers indicated the money kept coming in, even though the Nomads chapter had lost more than $5 million. A factor that had frustrated the Project Ocean investigators was that there simply wasn't enough time to fully investigate every person tied to the Nomads Bank, even though extra investigators were called in. The account labeled Usine, for example, belonged to someone who was apparently one of the Nomads chapter's biggest drug suppliers. But who that account belonged to remained a mystery, even years after the investigation ended.

Normand Bonin, the man who picked up boxes of money at the Nomads Bank for the Usine account, was followed to Longueuil where he would transfer the cash to a pickup truck. On November 23, 2000, he picked up $1.3 million. Six days later he picked up $1.4 million. Two days after that, Bonin left with $955,000. On December 6, he left with $1.2 million. The boxes were being delivered to a tool machining shop in Longueuil. Police watched as Bonin transferred the boxes to a pickup truck, then the company's vice-president, Yvon Lacoursiere, would get into the pickup truck and drive home.

Lacoursiere was a go-between for the mystery drug dealer who had made millions in a matter of weeks selling to the Nomads. Yet when they searched Lacoursiere's home and company, they found nothing to tie him to the Hells Angels or any other drug dealer. Lacoursiere reported on his taxes that he made about $50,000 a year. When he was arrested, he confessed right away and insisted that his girlfriend and two daughters had nothing to do with the money. He told the police he received $2,000 per shipment of money but refused to tell the police who he worked for. For his part, Bonin told the police he had met Chagnon at a campground and had been hired to move the boxes. He claimed he was told he was merely transferring $5,000 each time.

At his bail hearing, Lacoursiere testified on his own behalf. He described himself as a businessman and said his company sold forestry equipment in the Maritimes, Quebec, Ontario and in the U.S. He also claimed his company was suffering while he was behind bars. He described his job as vice-president, purchaser and manager. His company, which had about 18 employees, did about $400,000 worth of business in 1984, but he had helped build it to $2 million in sales per year. He went on to explain that he had had open-heart surgery two years prior to his arrest and that he was diabetic, a condition complicated by the fact he wasn't eating well in prison while awaiting a possible trial. Judge Rolande Matte was unmoved and denied bail.

The Nomads Bank had provided the police with a huge new target. When the bank came crumbling down it took with it a lot of people who were drawn in by the promise of easy money, people who had no criminal records, who suddenly found themselves charged with federal anti-gang legislation.

Bankers Behind Bars

Lise Gelinas, the woman who buzzed couriers into her apartment building, was sentenced to four years in prison after pleading guilty to conspiracy, drug trafficking and gangsterism. Gelinas had been caught on wiretaps telling someone that she had worked for the Hells Angels for years. The Hells Angels had supplied her with cell phones, registered under false names like Marco Polo. She was also overheard bragging to a friend that the gang was paying her $7,000 a month for her work, and that the money had already bought her seven fur coats and a luxury camper. During the late 1990s, Gelinas only declared earning

$8,000 annually off a fixed income, but when the police raided her apartment they found $30,000 in a safe.

The enormous risks of her job obviously got to Gelinas. The police heard her tell her sister, on December 6, "I'm quitting this thing because it's too much stress."

Two years after her arrest, at the age of 66, Gelinas was hoping for day parole. She told the board she initially did not know who was using the apartment across from hers but agreed to buzz in the couriers because she needed money to support her son and in-laws. But she also admitted that she agreed to keep doing the work once she realized she was employed by the Hells Angels. The gang even used her apartment for secret meetings. But the parole board found Gelinas to have a low risk of re-offending, and she was granted day parole on December 16, 2003. Life in a federal penitentiary had proven to be very stressful for Gelinas and she expressed regret at losing two years of watching her granddaughter grow up.

Richard Gemme, the accountant who designed the Hells Angels' spreadsheets, had been granted day parole six months earlier. He told the parole board his involvement with the Nomads Bank started when he helped a friend with a software program. Now, with his life in tatters, Gemme told the board he planned to give speeches to criminology students on the dangers of organized crime. While his case was before the courts, Gemme told Judge Jean-Claude Bonin that he was just an underwriter for an insurance company looking to make some money by helping two old friends. At the time of his arrest, he had been doing risk assessments for the insurance company for three years and was taking courses at a Montreal university. His father was ill, in a palliative care unit and he weighed only eighty-five pounds; he was not expected to live. Gemme said he wanted to live with his parents so he could care for his father.

"Mr. Gemme, we learned during the investigation, had grown

up with André Chouinard and Stéphane Chagnon. They were people who knew each other for 20 years. The link of confidence between them had been established for 20 years," said Sgt. Boucher during Gemme's bail hearing. "The investigation also demonstrated that, concerning computers, Mr. Gemme had the responsibility to look after the computer system. Mr. Gemme had considerable talents in computers."

Gemme was also heard on wiretaps explaining to someone that he was not considered a member of the Hells Angels but that he was also friends with Richard Lock, one of the founding members of the Rockers and a close friend of Maurice (Mom) Boucher. From other wiretaps, the police believed he was also buying real estate for gang members using cash, a sign he was helping them launder their money. During the investigation, the police saw Gemme make deliveries, including the Nomads chapter's payroll and a $1.2 million delivery for the Usine account. He was also described on wiretaps as the guy the Hells Angels could go to when they had a computer problem. Chagnon was once overheard telling another person how Gemme had set things up so everything was stored on the zip disk. While he was being recorded, Chagnon joked that if the police ever seized the computer they wouldn't be able find anything. What Chagnon didn't know at the time was that the police were secretly copying the zip disk and reading from it on a regular basis.

After Stéphane Chagnon was first arrested on January 30, 2001, Gemme got a call from André Chouinard and they talked about "Roger," a code name for Chagnon. Chouinard talked in strange parables saying that, sometimes when you play golf you have some bad holes. You put them aside and you try to clean them up later and you can add up your score later. Boucher, the investigator, said he understood Chouinard's strange lecture to mean that Gemme was getting orders to erase any files they had.

Gemme was overheard saying that if the police searched his

place of work and found what he had there, his employer would be embarrassed. So when he was arrested, the police made a point of going to Assurances Gosselin on Fleury Street and seized his laptop computer. On it they found documents that had all the codes for the accounting sheets, but the information was scrambled. Investigator Boucher said it appeared to be the work of someone who really knew computers. The information could only be unscrambled with a password.

But the police also found files on the laptop that helped shed a little more light on how the Hells Angels had discovered the identity of a particular police informant who was subsequently killed. It appeared Gemme had helped the Hells Angels sort through the files of a computer they had stolen from Rick Perrault, an Ontario Provincial Police (OPP) officer whose hotel room had been broken into while he was working in Sherbrooke. In December 1999, the laptop and diskettes were removed from his room while he ate breakfast in the hotel restaurant. Besides the information that helped the Hells Angels identify the informant, there were also transcripts of wiretaps the anti-biker gang squad had done. Even after the Hells Angels were arrested and held in the Bordeaux detention center along with Gemme, it was he they asked for help with the computers they had been supplied with to prepare for their defense.

Robert Gauthier, the caretaker of the apartment on Beaubien Street, was 58 years old when he was granted day parole on October 28, 2004. He had pleaded guilty to conspiracy, drug trafficking and participating in the activities of a gang and was given a seven-year sentence, one of the longer ones handed out in Project Ocean. He told the parole board he had only taken part in helping to run the Nomads Bank for seven months before he was arrested. For his troubles, the Hells Angels paid him $100 a day. The Hells Angels had employed Gauthier because, as a retired city of Montreal employee, living on a $2,400 monthly pension, he would draw little police attention.

While behind bars, Gauthier, who had diabetes and heart trouble, was a model inmate. He also chose not to associate at all with anyone tied to the Hells Angels. While out on day parole he lived at a halfway house and took a computer course to fill as much free time as he could. By April 11, 2005, he was granted full parole.

Gauthier's sister Monique, the ex-wife of Nomads member Michel Rose, also did not associate with the Hells Angels, but that was because she did her time at the women-only Joliette Institution, where Canada's most notorious female inmate, Karla Homolka, was serving out the final years of her 12-year sentence for the sex-slayings of two Ontario teenagers. Monique Gauthier admitted to being a problem gambler and eventually agreed to take part in the institution's rehab programs. She also took courses on dressmaking. She claimed to have been unaware of whose money she was counting as the millions poured in. She noted that Rose hadn't been a Hells Angel when they were married. The parole board didn't buy her claims of being the naïve ex-wife and turned her down for parole. She had to wait until the two-third mark of her four-and-a-half-year sentence until she was released.

For his part, Lacoursiere received a three-year sentence. He qualified for an expedited review of his case before the National Parole Board by April 2002. At the age of 50, this was Lacoursiere's first federal sentence. He had no criminal record and the parole board found his risk of re-offending to be "non-existent." He was released on the condition he supply a regular report on his finances for the duration of his sentence. "The recruitment of people with no criminal records who would not be suspected were frequently part of the strategy used by criminal organizations to launder the fruit of their illegal activities," the parole board noted in its decision to release Lacoursiere. He told the board he had owned his company for 20 years and that he decided to help move the money because the company was in trouble. He found prison difficult because he wasn't a hardened criminal and had been held with some of the toughest gangsters behind bars while awaiting trial.

Bonin, who was in his early sixties, ended up sentenced to nearly four years. He claimed to have only been working as a cash mule for eight months before he was arrested. Bonin said he met some Hells Angels' associates through a campground where he worked, and when they got to know him well enough they hired him, in part because he didn't have a criminal record. He had spent most of his adult life living on the margins, working out of bars under the table while collecting welfare. From the beginning of his sentence, Bonin asked to be separated from the Hells Angels in his penitentiary because he wanted nothing more to do with them. Despite never shedding any light on who was behind the Usine account, Bonin was out on full parole by the spring of 2004.

Not everyone outside the Hells Angels in Project Ocean was as careful as Lacoursiere and Bonin in prison. Tony Capozzi, a man with alleged ties to Montreal's Mafia and a former member of the Canadian Armed Forces, had delivered more than $210,000 to the Nomads Bank using a silver briefcase, making four trips between November 2 and December 14, 2000. Capozzi's money was accounted for in the "independents" column of the Nomads chapter's computerized ledger, but police were unable to determine how much money he brought on five other occasions, between December 21, 2000, and January 30, 2001, after it became more difficult for the police to sneak in to the apartments used by the gang. What they did learn was that Capozzi was able to buy drugs for the same price as any member of the Hells Angels.

When the police searched his home in Ile Bizard they found weapons, including a .38-calibre firearm that was later determined to be part of a shipment of 30 firearms that had been smuggled into Canada illegally and had already been linked to a biker gang. The police also found paperwork that suggested Capozzi controlled a small network that sold 39 kilos of cocaine in six months. They found a laminated card showing all the telephone numbers of the Syndicate, a Rockers affiliate gang. Capozzi was 34 when he was arrested along with everyone else on March 28, 2001, a few months before his scheduled wedding. And while he was serving his six-year sentence related to Project Ocean, Capozzi was hit with more bad news: the Quebec government had seized his luxury home, claiming Capozzi owed them $550,000 in unpaid taxes.

Capozzi was also turned down for parole in November 2004 because he was caught serving contraband food, or "hearty meals" as the National Parole Board phrased it, to two other inmates, both with drug trafficking convictions.

One of the more interesting motives for being a courier for a gang as notorious as the Hells Angels can be seen in the case of Claude Joannette. He was a founding member of the Dark Circle and had been convicted of plotting to kill members of the Hells Angels in 1996. As a way to erase his role in the 1996 murder plot, he agreed to deliver their drug money. While serving a three-and-a-half-year sentence for couriering, Joannette disassociated himself from gang members and asked to be separated from them while behind bars. Because of this, he was granted early parole by November 2003.

Éric Bouffard was one of the full-patch Hells Angels arrested in Project Ocean. He would later be mentioned in a scandal that took on great importance to the average Quebecer. It came after the *Journal de Montréal* published a photo of Montreal Canadiens goaltender José Theodore partying at the bunker belonging to the South chapter of the Hells Angels. The photo was seized at Bouffard's home when he was arrested on March 28, 2001. The police also learned Bouffard had the hockey star's cell phone number. The story came out on the heels of the arrests of several members of Theodore's family who were operating a loan-sharking ring.

Meanwhile, Bouffard had been a member of the South chapter since 1998. While the police were monitoring the apartments used in the Nomads Bank, they saw him make two deposits totaling roughly $1 million.

While serving his three-year sentence Bouffard used the time to complete a college degree in social sciences, but he maintained his allegiance to the Hells Angels.

"I don't see why I should be blamed for all the crimes of the Hells Angels," Bouffard told the parole board on August 21, 2003. "Eventually I plan on leaving the group, but that moment hasn't come yet. I want to do my sentence as a Hells Angel." Because of this devotion, the National Parole Board decided to hold Bouffard until he served the full two-thirds of his sentence. But his statutory release was revoked in April 2004. He had been spotted months earlier on day parole at the same South chapter bunker where Theodore had partied with the gang.

Someone else who had no intention of leaving the Hells Angels was Daniel Gagné, the son of Yves (Flag) Gagné, a long-time member of the Trois Rivières chapter. At the age of 22, Daniel Gagné took one for his dad's team and pleaded guilty in Project Ocean on October 29, 2001, and was handed a three-year sentence. At the time, the police considered him a mere striker in the Rowdy Crew, a Hells Angels' underling gang. He had made two deliveries to the Nomads Bank worth around $400,000 total. While in prison he turned down a transfer to a minimum security penitentiary because he wanted to hang out with the Hells Angels in medium security. According to the police, his loyalty and pedigree were rewarded because, when he had reached the point of statutory release and was let go, he was immediately made a prospect in the Hells Angels' Trois Rivières chapter.

Marc-André Hotte, a full-patch member of the Hells Angels'

Trois Rivières chapter, surrendered himself to the police 14 months after Project Ocean was carried out. He quickly pleaded guilty and was sentenced to more than four years in prison. When he arrived at his penitentiary, other members of the gang welcomed him into their wing. They even cleaned up his cell and helped him carry the personal effects he was allowed to have with him.

When he was up for parole in April 2004, Hotte told the commissioners that he was only interested in the Hells Angels as a motorcycle club. They didn't buy it. His request was rejected because of his obvious devotion to the outlaw biker gang. Other Hells Angels were also finding out that the parole board had apparently decided to take a hard line with them. If they were still members of the Hells Angels and maintained their ties to the gang while behind bars, they would have to wait until their statutory release date.

Dean Moore, a longtime Hells Angel, received a six-year sentence thanks to Project Ocean. Until December 2004, he was considered a model inmate, helping to run a suicide-prevention program and becoming president of an inmates' committee. During the biker war, the police were told by Dany Kane that Moore seemed to show no interest in what Boucher and the other members of the Nomads chapter wanted to accomplish. But according to police intelligence, Moore had also been Godfather to the Evil Ones, a Hells Angels' underling gang.

A couple of weeks before Christmas 2004, Moore, a member of the South chapter, was turned down for parole. To add to his woes, Project Ocean had also made Moore a lightning rod for the provincial taxman. Moore was stuck with an $80,000 bill for taxes on his undeclared revenue.

Another member of the South chapter taken out of commission by Project Ocean was Bertrand Joyal. He claimed to like the motorcycle riding aspect of the Hells Angels. At the age of 48, he told the parole board in September 2004 that if he got out he'd go back to managing a motorcycle store or work on a farm. Again, the parole board could not get past the fact that, like the others, Joyal remained loyal to his gang. He was turned down for parole. He was only released after serving two-thirds of his six-year sentence. On June 8, 2005, the parole board could only place restrictions on him that forbade him from associating with his gang, or other known criminals, for the remaining two years of his sentence. He was also ordered to supply his parole officer with a budget and a record of expenses on a monthly basis.

Despite being a Hells Angel for more than a decade, Jean-Paul Ramsay had never done serious prison time until he ended up as one of the people nabbed in Project Ocean. The long-time member of the Montreal chapter had managed to operate pretty much under the radar until he was noticed making several cash deliveries for an account labeled "Nath." He was given a five-year sentence. While behind bars, Ramsay tried to use the time well and enrolled in school courses. He was considered an excellent student, but

Jean-Paul Ramsay, a longtime member of the Hells Angels' Montreal chapter, arrested in Project Ocean.

snitches in his penitentiary also revealed that he was the head of a drug trafficking ring that operated from May to October 2003.

Ramsay was immediately placed in isolation and sent to a maximum security penitentiary. When it came time for his statutory release on March 10, 2005, the National Parole Board chose instead to keep him in. This is something reserved for the worst federal inmates — only five percent are held after the two-thirds mark of their term. In its explanation for keeping him behind bars, the board declared he was a high risk to sell drugs while still serving his sentence.

It was an indication that many of the Hells Angels in Quebec saw drug trafficking as a way of life.

The Actual Dollars and Cents

Luc Landry, a police investigator and a financial analyst for the Sûreté du Québec, was given the task of sorting out how much money the Hells Angels pocketed from their drug trafficking. While testifying during the trial of Walter (Nurget) Stadnick and Donald (Pup) Stockford, both members of the Nomads chapter, originally from Ontario, he submitted his analysis of the chapter's accounting.

Landry detailed the chapter's $18 million in sales between November 10 and December 19, 2000. During that period, the Hells Angels moved 1,916 kilograms of cocaine for a profit of more than $8 million. They were averaging $4,530 profit on every kilo sold. When it came to hashish, the chapter was not doing too badly either. They moved 838 kilograms of hash and made more than $680,000 profit.

6

Santa Claus aka Gerald Matticks

If there is one thing to emerge from Project Ocean that might define Gerald Matticks, it was the contents of a folder found on his desk of the butcher shop and meat warehouse he owned on the South Shore. The police were monitoring him as he conducted high-level drug deals with Maurice (Mom) Boucher and other Hells Angels, and based on their investigation, they obtained a warrant to search Matticks' office above the butcher shop. Matticks had long been known as a member of the West End Gang, a group of criminals, mostly of Irish descent, who emerged from a poverty-stricken area of western Montreal to become influential thieves and drug traffickers.

Besides his personal items, like the negatives of photos of him celebrating Saint Patrick's Day, the police noticed a folder that contained only two pieces of paper. One was a letter from the Bandidos politely asking Matticks if he wanted to switch sides and supply them, instead of the Hells Angels, with drugs. The document was evidence of Matticks' notoriety in Quebec as a drug trafficker. But in the same folder was a document concerning the details of an Easter party for children. Matticks' meat company was sponsoring it. The documents were indicative of Matticks' dual nature. On the one hand, he was a cunning smuggler who had collected photos of police investigators he believed were tailing him; on the other, he was a generous person to the communities where he lived, and especially kind to children.

Gerald Matticks was considered "the door" to the Port of Montreal.

L'Affaire Matticks

In 1995, he had beaten the system when charges that he was involved in one of the largest seizures of hashish ever in Quebec, were stayed. Matticks and his brother Richard as well as five other men, were arrested in connection with 26.5 tons of hashish that had been seized in containers at the Port of Montreal. But according to investigators, a shipping document collected during the Sûreté du Québec investigation had gone missing, and it was replaced by a copy faxed by Customs Canada to the Sûreté du Québec's offices. A judge determined that what the Sûreté had done was the equivalent of planting evidence. The question remained — had the bill of lading ever actually been seized? The charges were stayed, causing a genuine scandal. "L'Affaire Matticks" became a household phrase in Montreal and leant the West End Gang notoriety. The scandal also opened the door to a probe of the Sûreté du Québec and how it had managed its criminal investigations during the 1990s. The probe was headed by Lawrence Poitras, a former chief justice of the Quebec Superior Court. When the Poitras Commission ended two years after it began, the 1,700-page report depicted the Sûreté du Québec as a backward police force that routinely broke the law during its investigations. The report contained the blunt statement: "A crisis of values has shaken the Sûreté du Québec from the beginning of this decade."

Sidestepping the charges he faced over the hashish seizure merely added to the lore surrounding Gerry Matticks, the youngest of 14 children who emerged from the poverty of

Montreal's Goose Village and, for appearance's sake, lived the life of a gentleman farmer on the South Shore. In 1971, Matticks, along with some of his siblings, had been charged with attempted murder, but they managed to beat the case. In 1977, the police searched his home in St-Hubert and found a small stash of stolen jewelry including 28 women's gold rings and three pairs of earrings. All told, the jewelry was worth nearly $5,000, and it had been stolen from a store during an armed robbery on Montreal's Chabanel Street. But again, Matticks managed to get an acquittal.

One of the few times Matticks was ever sentenced to jail time came in 1990, when he was caught as part of a ring that stole trucks, repainted them and resold them. The police monitored members of the ring while they stole the trucks using a tow truck licensed to Matticks. He served only 24 weekends as his punishment. But a different image of Matticks emerged after his Project Ocean case was brought to court, and he would eventually be sentenced to 12 years in prison.

During Matticks' bail hearing, a parade of honest citizens, including a priest, testified that he was a generous man who deserved some leniency. "Did he come to church every Sunday? No. Did he help out people? Yes. Did he practice his faith? Yes," said Father Marc Mignault. Mignault, the parish priest of a church in Saint-Bruno, testified at Matticks' bail hearing on July 3, 2001. Mignault said that while Matticks certainly was not a churchgoer, he was a decent man with a charitable heart. The priest said he had come to know Matticks from conversations they would have at a restaurant the West End gang member owned.

Mignault said Matticks donated frozen turkeys for Christmas baskets, and once gave enough turkeys to fill an 18-foot freezer. Matticks also donated toys to the church, and, through a trucking company he owned, he would supply cases of food that had been claimed as damaged in insurance claims. Mignault said that when the presbytery roof was leaking, the church had hired four different roofers to fix the complicated problem without any success. "One day when talking to Gerry, he said, 'I'll send someone over. I had a similar problem at home. This guy is excellent. He'll fix it.' He came over. He fixed it. I asked [Gerry] for the bill three times and he said it was lost in the mail."

Even before Mignault testified, others had told Judge Gilbert Morier that Matticks was an honorable businessman and the equivalent of Santa Claus. Max Freid, a 61-year-old livestock broker from Côte St-Luc, an affluent Montreal suburb, said he had known Matticks for 20 years. They had done business together through a company Matticks owned called G.M. Livestock, and he considered him a friend. Freid dealt in up to $25 million a year in cattle. "I know Mr. Matticks but I don't know what the case is about," Freid said, adding that, despite this, he was willing to make a $50,000 deposit to secure Matticks' bail. "To me, I always did business with him and he was honorable." Testifying after Freid was Jean Lepine, a 63-year-old plumber from Greenfield Park who immersed himself in charitable work.

"I call him my Santa Claus," Lepine said of Matticks whom he had known for 20 years. "I knew Mr. Matticks for the good things he has done. I am someone who has done charity work for 30 years. I am surrounded by people like Mr. Matticks and when I need donations, Mr. Matticks is very accessible." Lepine told the story of a Christmas float that Matticks had arranged for a Christmas parade for 15 years. The float was very generous with gifts to children. Matticks would ride on the 45-foot float, accompanied by Santa Claus, distributing gifts and ornaments to poor children.

Lepine had also told of how, during the January 1998 ice storm that damaged Quebec's hydro system so badly thousands of homes went without electricity for weeks, Matticks opened his restaurant and helped out by offering 2,200 free meals to people. During that trying time for many, especially on the South Shore,

Matticks had given out free wood to families, Lepine said, pounding his hand on the witness stand to emphasize his point. "He was very flexible. He did not consider the cost," Lepine said. Matticks' lawyer also produced an affidavit from Steven Olynyk, the former mayor of Greenfield Park and a retired police officer. It described how, on one Christmas, Matticks had donated 100 food baskets to the poor.

But from that bail hearing, another image of Matticks emerged, one that came from the police who saw how Matticks had made the fortune that allowed him to be so generous. Some of the most important members of the Hells Angels were going out of their way to meet with Matticks while they were under investigation in Project Rush. Investigators in the Sûreté du Québec were elated when they learned Maurice (Mom) Boucher and other members of the Nomads chapter had started showing up at Matticks' butcher shop and meat warehouse in St-Hubert.

One of the first meetings between Mom and Matticks was on May 25, 1999. The police were tailing Boucher and his chauffeur Guy Lepage, a former police officer who left the Montreal Urban Community Police in shame and later joined the Rockers. The two ended up at Viandes 3-1. It was a building Matticks co-owned with one of his sons. On the outside of the building was a large shamrock, proof that Matticks was proud of his Irish heritage. A plainclothes cop followed Lepage and Boucher inside, posing as a customer, and noticed they were not at the service counter. But he did notice a stairway that led to an office. Lepage and Boucher spent about 30 minutes in the office. On December 2, 1999, Lepage and Boucher returned to Viandes 3-1 and again stayed for about 30 minutes.

Months later, it appeared that Boucher had delegated the Hells Angels' meetings with Matticks to other members of his gang. At the time, the Quebec Court of Appeal was considering the possibility of a new trial for the murders of two prison guards, which meant Boucher would certainly be held in custody until he was brought before a jury again. One of the first indications that other Hells Angels had taken over for Boucher's dealings with Matticks came from police informant Dany Kane. He told his controllers that in May 2000, a meeting had been held between Michel Rose, Normand Robitaille, André Chouinard and Guillaume Serra at an exotic restaurant in Boucherville. Kane said he stood watch at the restaurant along with Dany St-Pierre. After the meeting the Hells Angels went to Matticks' butcher shop. Boucher was not there, and six months later, in October, he was arrested for the new trial.

By December 7, 2000, investigators had grown very interested in Matticks and his dealings with the Hells Angels. They followed a car he was in to an Italian restaurant on Taschereau Blvd. in La Prairie. Matticks and Louis Elias Lekkas, a man the police knew very little about, were seen going into the restaurant together. Minutes later, a Jeep Cherokee driven by Kenny Bedard, a member of the Rockers, pulled up to the restaurant. Normand Robitaille, who was by then a full-patch member of the Nomads chapter, climbed out of the Jeep carrying a briefcase. He walked into the restaurant and sat down with Lekkas and Matticks. After the meeting, Lekkas and Matticks drove back to Matticks' butcher shop.

On January 10, 2001, the police were tailing Lekkas as he left Viandes 3-1 in a BMW and headed to a pizza restaurant in St-Hubert where he grabbed a table. Again, Kenny Bedard and Normand Robitaille showed up minutes later in a Ford Expedition. After the meeting, Lekkas went back to the butcher shop where he met with Matticks. On January 11, 2001, Lekkas went to the same restaurant to meet with Robitaille and Marc-André Hotte, an important member of the Hells Angels' Trois Rivières chapter and the godfather of their puppet gang, the Jokers.

The police eventually established that Matticks and Lekkas were friends as well as business partners.

"On several occasions they worked in the same location, almost every day at Viandes 3-1," said Michel Girard, a Sûreté du Québec organized crime investigator, during a bail hearing. "They would go to get haircuts together. They'd go to sex boutiques together, do errands together, go to the casino. They were like two good friends."

Girard had been called as a reinforcement to help in Project Ocean as the police tried to determine who were the mysterious figures behind the coded entries that camouflaged who was supplying the Hells Angels' drug network in such large quantities. Girard's task was to find out whose names belonged to the codes "Beef" and "Beef 2" on the Nomads chapter's accounting ledger. As they began seeing Lekkas leave the Nomads Bank with huge sums of money, they would soon learn the codes were for Matticks and Lekkas.

Lekkas had been working at Viandes 3-1 since 1995. On October 10, 2000, before they knew who Matticks was, the police tailed Lekkas as he drove away from one of the Nomads Bank apartment buildings with Donald Driver, a man who had long-established ties to the Matticks brothers. Lekkas picked up two large cardboard boxes full of money and headed to the Longueuil courthouse where he was facing a possible trial for stealing a truckload of chicken breasts. The pair went to the small, dingy snack bar inside the courthouse. Lekkas and Driver left the courthouse around 4:30 p.m. and headed for Viandes 3-1, presumably with the money. After a while, a man Girard described as elderly walked out of the butcher's shop. He headed for a Chevrolet and Lekkas accompanied him. The man got into the car, which was registered in Matticks' name. On that day, the surveillance team was not able to identify Matticks. But now the police realized there was a chance that the smuggler who had escaped prosecution in their most embarrassing moment was involved in drug deals with the Nomads chapter. The police followed the car as it traveled to a farm in La Prairie, another town in the South Shore. The police were already familiar with the farm, as Matticks had lived there for a while with a woman named Katherine Harris and his 12-year-old son. The farmhouse on the land was far off the access road. The police also noticed Matticks had installed surveillance cameras everywhere.

On November 16, 2000, the police followed Lekkas again after he left one of the Montreal apartment buildings used for the Nomads Bank. He was carrying a grey Brooks sports bag with him, which he placed in the trunk of his BMW. Just moments before, Sûreté investigator Pierre Boucher had sneaked briefly into the apartment to try to determine who it was for. He spotted a note in the grey bag that read, "For Young Italian $500,000, Beef." Lekkas was handed the bag by Robert Gauthier, the man running the day-to-day operations of the Nomads Bank. Lekkas drove to Matticks' farm in La Prairie. Matticks' black Chevrolet was there, too. After leaving the farm, Lekkas headed for a house in Carignan. It was owned by Matticks and, he would later tell the police, it was where his mistress, Cindy Wade, lived.

On December 12, 2000, the police watched as Lekkas again left one of the apartments. They tried to follow him but there was a severe blizzard that day and he disappeared into the snowstorm. But by then the police had a good idea of what was going on. Lekkas would often be seen using a pizza restaurant in St-Hubert for his meetings. It was close to Viandes 3-1 and close to a bar named Miss St-Hubert which the police believed was run by some of Matticks' associates and his son Donald.

"Through wiretaps we heard several conversations that showed that Mr. Matticks has a control over things like repairs at Miss St-Hubert," Girard said during the bail hearing.

On paper, Donald Matticks seemed to be a mere employee of the bar. In tax declarations, he claimed to have worked there between 1994 and 1999, making a mere $14,000 annually. Girard said the building that housed Viandes 3-1 was owned by Gerald Matticks and Donald Matticks through a numbered company. Through wiretaps, the police learned that Gerald Matticks ran and controlled Viandes 3-1. The police overheard him complaining about an order of chickens. They also overheard him authorizing orders for a children's party. But the clincher was when they overheard Katherine Harris call and ask for "Gerry." She was passed on to the wrong person and to make herself clear she said that she wanted to speak to "the president." It would become significant information when one of Matticks' lawyers would later claim he was just an employee there.

Other evidence came up suggesting that Matticks had his drug money tied up in other legitimate businesses. When the police raided Matticks' office on March 28, 2001, they found a lease signed by Matticks and Lekkas for a tanning salon on Grande Allée in St-Hubert. They also found a security video monitor that had four screens in one showing what was going on in each room in Viandes 3-1. In his office, Matticks kept police scanners and a list of all the principal channels of the municipal police forces in the area. The scanners were the same ones the police had seized from him in 1994, after the large hashish seizure. They were returned to Matticks after the case was tossed out of court — they even still had the Sûreté's old evidence tags on them. There were also two money-counting machines. Inside a refrigerator the police found a small piece of paper. On it were the words "Guy" and "Mom" with two phone numbers. One was the cell number of Guy Lepage, Mom Boucher's chauffeur; the other number was for a pager in Guy Lepage's name. The police also found an electronic scale that could weigh up to 1,200 grams, and they found about six grams of hashish in one of Matticks' desks.

But during his bail hearing, the police acknowledged that it had been tough gathering evidence on Matticks. They described him as a cautious man who seemed to assume he was under constant police surveillance.

An example of how cautious Matticks and Lekkas were came from a bug that had been placed in Lekkas' car. Over one three-and-a-half-month period, the pair had only one conversation that was of any interest to the investigation. Lekkas and Matticks often talked on walkie-talkies instead of using cellular phones, which thwarted any attempts to pick up their conversations through wiretaps. One time, as the police listened in through a telephone wiretap, they overheard Katherine Harris complain about hearing the phone make a strange sound. Matticks, who was on the other end, immediately figured correctly that the phone was bugged. He told her to hang up and call back again. He asked if she heard a delay on the line. She said she did. He said that meant the police were listening in.

On Lekkas' car bug, the police overheard him constantly saying that he felt he was being followed. He once asked Matticks if there was something they could buy that could detect if they were being followed. It appeared that Matticks was successful in that search. When they searched his house, the police found a device that could detect radio frequencies. It would vibrate if it picked up frequencies coming from police surveillance equipment.

While the police did not have a mountain of evidence, they did have enough to link Matticks to the Nomads Bank. If they could prove Matticks and Lekkas were behind the Beef and Beef 2 accounts, the men would likely face a sentence of anywhere between four and eight years. But as Matticks was preparing to be freed on bail, months after his arrest, a surprise announcement was made. "Mr. Lekkas is not present your honor, the reason being that Mr. Lekkas, for the second time, has tried to commit suicide," defense lawyer Loris Cavaliere told Justice Morier on July 16, 2001.

Louis Elias Lekkas

The following day, the defense revealed another shocker. "The minister's office has informed me this morning that my former client Elias Lekkas has decided to become an [informant]," Matticks' lawyer said.

A Crown prosecutor then informed Judge Morier that Lekkas had indeed met with the police the night before, while he was recovering from a suicide attempt. The Crown said she could add new evidence to the bail hearing because of what Lekkas was leaking to the police. It would later be revealed that by agreeing to testify against Matticks, Lekkas would get a sentencing recommendation of seven years on top of what he had already served. But Lekkas didn't end up testifying against Matticks. Faced with the prospect of having his business partner testify against him, Matticks pleaded guilty in what would be his most serious conviction in a criminal career that had spanned three decades.

More than two years after he agreed to become an informant, Lekkas found himself on the witness stand anyway, testifying against members of the Hells Angels and Rockers being tried in the megatrial heard before Justice Pierre Beliveau. Lekkas' day in court began with him watching a video. He was asked by a prosecutor if he recognized himself. He said he did. The video was of Lekkas taking money from the apartment building on Beaubien Street. Lekkas said he normally took $500,000 from the apartment at a time.

"I was a drug importer and wholesaler with my partner Gerald Matticks. We had sold several hundred kilos of hash to Norm Robitaille and 65 kilos of cocaine. That is where we would pick up the money," he said. "We imported seven different importations." When asked about Gerald Matticks, Lekkas said they were equal partners in a business that saw them smuggle in drugs through the Port of Montreal and take a percentage of the cargo as payment. "I had met Gerry in 1995 after he got out of jail [in the Matticks Affair]. And he owned the building that had a meat wholesale company underneath. I was working downstairs in the meat wholesale plant. Gerry had an office upstairs in the building and working every day together, we got close. At that time we had stolen a container, a container of Tommy Hilfiger clothing. After that we had bought a load of stolen chicken and during that time business for Gerry wasn't . . ." Gerry controlled . . ." Lekkas said with some hesitation before blurting out what the police had known about Matticks for years. "He was the door of the Port of Montreal for containers to come in . . . Some people had approached him to bring in some product. From those meetings I went down to Colombia to establish contact with the owner of the merchandise. From that trip [came] the first importation that we did of 2,000 plus kilos of hashish."

"When you're talking about product you're not talking about coconuts," the prosecutor asked.

"No."

During his sentencing hearing, Matticks' own lawyer would acknowledge his client had the ability to get drugs through the Port of Montreal, most times without hassle. His influence in the Port of Montreal, in particular with the people responsible for unloading the cargo ships, was crucial in getting drugs through. That influence allowed him to demand a cut of the product being brought in.

"From the different series of importations, we would . . . take a percentage of the product. The first one was 33 percent. That is what we would charge to bring in the merchandise for either ourselves or the people who owned it," Lekkas said, adding he and Matticks would go on to sell the drugs for profit. What they did not have was a distribution network. So Matticks and Lekkas moved their product in bulk. "We had different people that we sold to. Namely, one was Norm Robitaille," he said. "He was a Hells Angel."

Lekkas was then shown a series of surveillance photos. He was able to identify Kenny Bedard, whom he said was always working as Robitaille's bodyguard when they met. Lekkas was then asked if the sales were limited to hashish.

"No, we had sold several hundred kilos of hashish but we sold 65 kilos of cocaine as well. But actually, two of those kilos were wood, so it turn out to be 63 kilos. . . . We were paid in cash. We would give the product and then after that we would have a meeting. Soon after [Matticks] would say 'okay, go to Beaubien, apartment 504,' and we would pick up the cash." Lekkas said the Hells Angels would only pay for the drugs they bought in $500,000 installments. He believed he visited the Nomads Bank about five times to pick up money, and he acknowledged that Donald Driver went with him once. "We would take the money back to Gerry's house in La Prairie and that is where we would count it and see if everything was okay." Lekkas described the transactions as careful business ventures. He said that before they dipped into the cash, he and Matticks would make sure their expenses for a shipment were covered.

Dealing with the Hells Angels had been so profitable for Matticks and Lekkas they were ultimately able to purchase their own drugs and smuggle them into the port. Lekkas said that, through their partnership, he and Matticks accumulated $22 million in merchandise, after expenses. Lekkas described how even though they sometimes had spectacular failures, the profit margin was still good. In December 1999, Matticks and Lekkas managed to bring in 2,363 kilos of hashish through the Port of Montreal. A month later, they tried to bring in 10,000 kilos of hashish but it was seized by the police. In April 2000, they helped to import 260 kilos of cocaine from Panama. Matticks and Lekkas sold their 25 percent cut, 65 kilos, to the Nomads chapter. This transaction was found in the spreadsheets the police had been handed by Dany Kane.

Later that same year, the partners brought in 4,037 kilos of hashish. Matticks was given a percentage of the drugs but was also paid in cash. Several people were arrested in connection with this shipment, so Matticks was not paid in full. Instead, he was given half of a 3,000 kilogram shipment of hashish that came through the port later. He sold the 1,500 kilos to the Nomads chapter.

Their sixth smuggling operation, in October 2000, brought in 5,000 kilos of hash. Matticks was to get 25 percent of the drugs, but it was seized by the Montreal Urban Community Police. This time, the police made a big deal out of the seizure by calling a press conference to announce it. At the time, they had arrested no one, but they attributed the smuggling effort to the West End Gang and accused port employees of helping to get drugs through. In turn, the Montreal longshoremen's union called a press conference of their own and threatened to sue the Montreal Urban Community Police. Lekkas and Matticks' last smuggling operation was in February 2001, a shipment of 9,000 kilos of hashish. They had done seven major smuggling operations together.

Their success appeared to intrigue Maurice (Mom) Boucher. Lekkas said that after he and Matticks worked out the deal to take a 65 kilogram cut from the cocaine shipment they helped smuggle in from Panama, Boucher paid a visit to Viandes 3-1. He was intent on finding out who the owner of the rest of the cocaine was. Lekkas said Boucher often referred to Matticks as "Beef" in their conversations. The meeting was a chilling detail considering Boucher's lust for a monopoly over Montreal's cocaine market and how the Nomads chapter was going about obtaining that monopoly. The Crown prosecutor did not miss the opportunity to highlight this to the jury. He asked Lekkas if he was there for that meeting, and Lekkas replied yes but that Boucher was told they didn't know who the actual owner of the cocaine was.

During his six-year partnership with Matticks, Lekkas had come to learn much about the world of narcotics. He had flown to Colombia to meet with members of the powerful Cali Cartel. These contacts would later help in smuggling other shipments and, ultimately, the deal he and Matticks financed on their own.

In a relatively short period of time, Lekkas had gone from making roughly $24,000 at Viandes 3-1 to living the life of a millionaire. In 1997 and 1998, he reported making $24,000 annually and then getting a significant raise in 1999 to $30,000. In 1992, Lekkas had purchased a modest house for $120,000. But he was later able to renovate it to the tune of $70,000, including a $10,000 renovation to his kitchen. He also held stocks worth between $20,000 and $40,000 and was able to rent a BMW for $12,000 a year. In February 2001, he took a trip to Cancun worth more than $4,000. He also sent his family to Florida, purchased a boat and was looking into buying a BMW M5.

Turning Informant

But that all came crashing down on March 28, 2001. "I was arrested for drug trafficking, conspiracy and gangsterism. I was arrested in La Prairie," Lekkas said when describing how his life took a serious turn for the worse. He told the jury that while he was awaiting trial in the Montreal detention center he initially thought that the proof the Crown had against himself and Matticks was weak. He said he decided to become an informant "under some unfortunate circumstances." He was asked what those circumstances were and the defense lawyers objected strenuously to this. Lekkas was instructed to explain his decision to turn informant in very general terms.

"I had problems with my partner Gerry. And that was the only way . . . I tried to take my life at one time. So, in that game I was finished," Lekkas said, adding Matticks apparently believed he was an informant before he actually became one.

While he testified before the jury, Lekkas was shown his witness contract, which said the Crown would pay him $400 a week for the next two years. Lekkas talked about how he had to admit to all of his crimes. He attested to the seven smuggling operations and received his sentence. At that point, he did not have a criminal record but was still facing charges for the load of stolen chickens. That robbery dated back to 1999 and, while it might sound like petty theft, it involved a large tractor-trailer filled with 1,000 cases of frozen chicken that had been stolen from a Montreal suburb. At his sentencing hearing on July 11, 2002, the case of the stolen chicken was transferred from Longueuil court to Montreal so all of Lekkas's legal woes could be wrapped into one neat package.

"When I say chicken breasts it is a large, large, large amount of chicken breasts. I think it is a value of $57,000. He is charged with possession because this big van in which these chickens were stolen was brought to St-Hubert," the Crown prosecutor said, adding the chicken breasts went straight to Matticks' store. Somehow, the real owner of the breasts suspected they could be found at Viandes 3-1 and sent the police there.

"Mr. Matticks was himself in constant conspiracy with other people. Mr. Lekkas has been described to me as being a kind of coordinator of the activities of Mr. Matticks," the Crown prosecutor said. He recommended a seven-and-a-half-year sentence on top of the sixteen months Lekkas had already spent behind bars leading up to his guilty plea.

Ironically, it was Matticks' mistrust after their arrest that turned Lekkas into an informant. It was also not the only time this would happen within the context of Operation Springtime 2001. Serge Boutin, a very important drug dealer for the Rockers, said he decided to become an informant primarily because Normand Robitaille apparently assumed he was one. Boutin's logic was that he was better off as a living, breathing real informant than dead thanks to Robitaille's misplaced suspicions.

Matticks' paranoia became an issue at his bail hearing. The

issue was raised by his lawyer Claude Girouard. The defense lawyer asked a Sûreté du Québec investigator if the provincial police held any animosity toward the Matticks brothers because of the embarrassing revelations that had come out of the Poitras Commission. The lawyer revealed that the Sûreté du Québec seemed to delight in referring to Matticks as being paranoid in their surveillance reports.

Matticks likely assumed he was a huge target for the police after the charges against him in the Matticks Affair had been stayed in 1995. His high-level drug dealing also meant he worked with people who could never be trusted fully. When the police searched his farmhouse, they found an elaborate security system with video cameras. Inside a huge library they uncovered more than $6,200 U.S. and $41,000 Canadian. They also found an accounting sheet inside a book in the library. The accounting ledger supported Lekkas' testimony that they had dealt in $22 million worth of merchandise. At the house in Carignan, the police found a half-pound of hashish. Matticks' mistress Cindy Wade would claim it was hers and plead guilty to possession in court. Inside one of Matticks' cars, they found a police scanner and a device that could pick up conversations from a long distance. They also found a tazer. At trial, testifying officers also mentioned the two letters found in the folder on his desk, including the one inviting him to extend to the Bandidos his services as a door to the Port of Montreal. Matticks' lawyer tried to suggest the letter was intended for Gerald's brother Richard Matticks, who already had known ties to the Rock Machine and Salvatore Cazzetta.

The police revealed that, while they were monitoring Matticks, he went into a panic when someone was shot and killed near a garage he owned in Montreal. The police listened in as he asked his contacts if his brother "Richie" could be located. When he was interrogated after his arrest, one of the first questions

Matticks had for the police was whether his brother Richard had also been arrested. When he was placed under arrest, Matticks claimed to have no links to organized crime, yet he showed the arresting officers where he kept photos of investigators who had done surveillance on him. While Matticks was interrogated at the RCMP's Montreal headquarters, the conversation turned to Maurice (Mom) Boucher. Matticks said he had merely loaned money to Boucher, and he claimed he had documents to prove the loan.

But Lekkas had given up too much information on Matticks. His statements pertaining to other smuggling operations implicated several other people, including Matticks' son Donald and Donald Driver. Both would be arrested later on and, ultimately, they each got an eight-year prison sentence.

Matticks' Plea

Gerry Matticks agreed to a plea bargain that ensured he would never be called as a witness to testify in the United States, which had been a possibility as some of the drugs he smuggled into Quebec were destined for Newark, New Jersey.

"Mr. Matticks is not a member of a biker gang, but he did do business with them," prosecutor Robert Rouleau said as he detailed the plea agreement the Crown had agreed to. Rouleau said that besides the tons of hashish, the police knew of at least 700 kilos of cocaine being sold to the Hells Angels by Gerald Matticks. Matticks' plea bargain had saved the prosecution a lot of time. His Project Ocean trial was expected to last four months, and another trial for new charges based on Lekkas' statements could have dragged on for another four months.

Lekkas' confessions to the police shook up Matticks' gang. One of the men arrested when Lekkas turned informant was John Mclean, a longtime member of the West End Gang. He, too, would decide to clean up his act while he and the others were awaiting trial. He pleaded guilty in 2003 and received an eight-year sentence in exchange for testifying against Matticks' son, Donald Driver and the others. Donald Matticks, Driver and a few other men tied to the West End Gang pleaded guilty when faced with the prospect of a trial that would feature at least two informants. Once he had turned against Gerald Matticks, his partner in crime for 20 years, John Mclean feared for his life. In December 2004, the National Parole Board turned down his chance at day parole because it felt no halfway house in Montreal could be considered safe if Mclean were staying there, since he was still in Matticks' bad books.

In spite of all his charity and good deeds, Matticks was left with a bad reputation after all.

7

Project Rush: Guilty Pleas and Surprises

Only one of the so-called megatrials to emerge out of Project Rush ever actually made it all the way to a jury verdict. As the months clicked by following March 2001, the bikers began to be separated into groups for different trials. The groupings were based on their suspected level of participation in the biker war. One group was assembled together based on language. Hells Angels like Donald (Pup) Stockford and Walter (Nurget) Stadnick demanded to be tried in English, requiring the translation of hundreds of documents and wiretap transcripts.

By September 2001, Justice Réjean Paul realized he would have a logistical nightmare on his hands if there was indeed one megatrial. Prosecutors were pushing to have 36 of the 42 gangsters arrested in Project Rush tried together, but Justice Paul was against this. During some of the pretrial hearings, he stated that it was too much to expect of a jury and one judge — he dreaded the delays caused by 36 defense lawyers cross-examining a witness.

Two months later, Paul agreed that 14 of the Hells Angels and Rockers, selected because their suspected involvement in the 13 murders, could be tried as a group. Initially, Maurice (Mom) Boucher was expected to be among the 14, but he was still tied up with his second trial for the 1997 murders of two prison guards. By April 2002, a trial that grouped together 17 other gang members began before a jury and a different judge, Justice Jean-Guy Boilard.

The first accused to become an informant was Stéphane (Blond) Faucher, a young drug dealer who was believed to have been introduced into the Hells Angels' network through Maurice (Mom) Boucher's friend Normand Bélanger. Faucher had been Bélanger's runner, helping him to move the drug ecstasy before either of them had joined the Rockers. After joining the Rockers at the entry-level position of a "hangaround" on October 13, 1998, Faucher began dealing drugs with Serge Boutin, another Rocker who would eventually turn informant. Boutin and Faucher formed a successful team, generating cocaine sales that impressed the Nomads chapter. Faucher was more willing to deal with the violent end of operating a drug business and was rewarded for it when he was made a prospect in the Nomads chapter in December 2000.

The promotions came even though Faucher had apparently made some mistakes as a Rocker. He had ordered a hit that did not go very well, which caused a heated argument during one of the Rockers *messes*. He had been ordered to set off bombs at five Montreal Urban Community Police stations, but they failed to go off because of faulty detonators.

Perhaps because of this botched bombing, Faucher's promotion was only temporary. At least one Nomads chapter member, Denis Houle, had serious reservations with Faucher being named a prospect in the Hells Angels, and eventually Faucher was told to return to the Rockers. After this demotion, Faucher apparently quit the gang altogether. The police noticed from the gang's accounting sheets that he was even barred from buying from the Nomads chapter.

The insult occurred within weeks of Operation Springtime 2001 being carried out. A few days after his arrest, Faucher asked for a transfer out of the Hells Angels' wing at the Bordeaux detention center and asked for police protection. He told the police where they could find a weapons cache, and about how the Nomads basically controlled the flow of drugs to other Hells Angels' chapters in Quebec, except for Sherbrooke, which remained independent of Boucher's monopolistic ways. He also gave incriminating evidence against Serge Boutin that set off a chain reaction that caused Boutin to turn informant. But several months later, Crown prosecutor André Vincent had to admit in court that he was having problems with Faucher, his supposed star witness — the snitch wanted to back out of his deal. He refused to plead guilty to conspiring to murder members of the Alliance during the biker war, or to a gangsterism charge that would have doubled any sentence he received. Vincent said Faucher would have to testify either way, and that if he had to be called as a hostile witness, it would be done. This set up the scene for one of the more bizarre moments of the trial heard before Justice Pierre Beliveau. Faucher ultimately ended up pleading guilty to the charges anyway in October 2002 and received a 12-year sentence. But the question was still up in the air about what kind of witness he would be.

To say that the moment Faucher took the witness stand was bizarre would be an understatement. When Crown prosecutor François Briere asked the simplest of questions, like Faucher's age and where he had been born, the former Rocker stammered and mumbled things that were barely audible. Briere then asked Faucher what neighborhood he was from. Faucher didn't answer, but, sounding nervous, he turned to Judge Beliveau and started to spit out half sentences that made little sense. "They arrested me. The police got me on the street," he said tossing in some French swear words for good measure. "All of this is a frame-up by two pigs." He then named two of the lead investigators in Project Rush. These names were barely out of Faucher's mouth when near pandemonium took over the courtroom. Lawyers jumped out of their chairs to object, and Beliveau tried to call for order. He shouted, "*une instant!*" several times, each one louder than the last. When calm was restored, Faucher was told he could only continue testifying by answering Briere's questions. But he continued his rambling speech. "When the birds arrived, they did their little story, their little song. Always the same two guys," Faucher said claiming that he never intended to talk to the police and that he felt he had been burned by them.

"And now I find myself here. I refuse to testify. It's as simple as that."

Briere asked Faucher if he was currently detained.

"I'm not answering anymore."

At that point, defense lawyer Pierre Panaccio cut in. "Let me speak, I have something to say. I represent someone on trial here!" Panaccio shouted. He was referring to Richard (Dick) Mayrand, one of the more important gangsters on trial in the case. Again Beliveau called for order. But Panaccio bellowed that Faucher was willing to talk about an "exceptional situation" concerning the police investigation. He claimed that Faucher was willing to answer certain questions critical to his client's defense. Faucher listened quietly as Beliveau and Panaccio argued. He then continued again to sputter out half sentences. "Me, my gun, they did a ballistic on it simply because I obliged them to do it!" he blurted out.

"In April —" he began, but was interrupted. "Let me speak a minute! In April, I was brought . . . I asked them, 'Christ, where is the gun? There is no gun.' All of a sudden they talk on the telephone and pretend they are doing ballistics." Faucher sounded like a desperate man. He turned toward the judge and said that he wanted to talk to him in private. Beliveau excused the jury so the lawyers could sort out what to do next. After much discussion, Briere was allowed to try again with Faucher. The prosecutor again asked Faucher what neighborhood he came from.

"I'm sorry about before. But anyway. Even when they arrested me . . . when they brought me to Parthenais [detention center], there weren't any cameras. There were all kinds of those things happening . . ."

"Excuse me. That is not the question," Beliveau said cutting in. "What I want to know from you is are you going to answer the questions that are asked of you?" Faucher refused, and eventually he was sent back to his cell. He was later charged and convicted of contempt of court and saw another two years tacked on to the 12 years he was already serving.

Beliveau managed to keep the trial on the rails despite Faucher's outbursts. A remarkably patient man, Beliveau was not supposed to be in the judge's seat in that trial. He had been called in to pick up the pieces after Justice Jean-Guy Boilard dropped a bomb on the first trial to emerge out of Project Rush. On July 22, after 113 witnesses had testified and 1,114 exhibits had been entered into the record, Superior Court judge Boilard suddenly announced he was removing himself from the trial. He cited a letter from the Canadian Judicial Council that criticized him for remarks he had made to a defense lawyer during the unrelated bail hearing of a biker several months before the megatrial had started. The letter brought up similar past incidents where Boilard had verbally ripped into lawyers, and it further stated that he undermined the image of the magistrature as a whole. The letter had been leaked to a CBC reporter.

"I feel I no longer have the moral authority, and perhaps the required aptitude, to continue my role as arbitrator in this trial. The parties and their lawyers, as well as a reasonable observer, will always be justified in doubting the accuracy of my decisions or the aptness of my interventions, considering the comments of the Canadian Judicial Council," Boilard said before leaving the stunned courtroom. His announcement left serious doubt as to what would happen to the already lengthy and costly trial.

But the provincial government took quick action and, within a week, Beliveau was named to replace his Quebec Superior Court colleague and was given the responsibility of deciding how to proceed. On August 7, 2002, after taking a week to assess the situation, Beliveau saw no other option but to end the trial and start from the beginning with a new jury. Before making his decision, Beliveau listened to the jurors, some of whom were openly bitter about Boilard's departure and especially the duration of the trial. At that point, the jury was already down to ten members due to illness.

Meanwhile, Boilard's decision to step down was questioned by Quebec's Auditor General, who took the rare step of asking the same council that had sent him the damning letter in the first place to investigate his actions in response to it. Such a request had only been made four times previous in the then 30-year history of the Canadian Judicial Council. Months later, the board would find that while Boilard had acted improperly, his actions were not grounds for removing him from the bench.

"Clearly, the judge's conduct was not that of a judge concerned with the due administration of justice and the image of detachment and calm which the judiciary should project to the public," the council wrote in its final decision. "In view of all these circumstances, we consider that the conduct complained of did not make him incapacitated or disabled from the due execution of his office . . . and for these reasons we do not recommend the removal of Justice Jean-Guy Boilard."

The wait for a new trial would be long, giving some of the accused time to rethink their strategy.

Plea Bargains

On November 18, 2002, the trial that once featured 17 Hells Angels and Rockers was whittled down to those 9 who had not accepted plea bargains. Crown prosecutor Madeleine Giauque stood before Justice Beliveau and gave the condensed version of the case as she explained the guilty pleas.

"For more than five years, police forces were faced with a war between gangs for control of the sale of drugs throughout the entire province but principally on the streets of Montreal," Giauque said. She then outlined in broad strokes the methods the police had used to conduct their investigation.

"The investigation demonstrated that the Hells Angels' Nomads were at the head of a highly structured organization, suppliers of drugs on a scale without precedent. In effect, drugs, principally cocaine and hashish, but without excluding ecstasy et cetera, were distributed by the other clubs of the Hells Angels throughout the province in all regions of Quebec, with the exception of Sherbrooke." The prosecutor detailed the analysis done by Sûreté du Québec investigator Luc Landry, who estimated the Nomads chapter's average net profit on a kilo of cocaine to be $4,500, and $817 for each kilo of hashish.

"This same expertise demonstrates that during a period of 39 days, at the end of the year 2000, 115 kilos of hashish and 452 kilos of cocaine were sold for an average of 11.5 kilos of cocaine and three kilos of hash per day. That shows the importance of the organization. . . . To grow and maintain their selling territory," Giauque summarized, "the Hells Angels decided to eliminate their competition by any means necessary, be it pacifist, through assimilation or by using violence like intimidation and/or murder. . . . All people who decided to approach the organization had to have common values and share a common agreement — maintaining and expanding drug dealing territory by all means necessary," Giauque stated.

"The Rockers, even if they weren't the actual authors of murders, participated in the war effort as a resource. Be it through the gathering of information on the rival clan, the protection of the Hells Angels' Nomads, the possession of firearms, the distribution of drugs, the payment of an obligatory contribution of ten percent of all their revenues that came from their criminal acts, which served to purchase firearms and stolen cars, to the prison cantines of jailed members, payments to lawyers in case of arrests and to members of the organization."

Because they were pleading guilty to gangsterism charges, the six who pleaded guilty that day would have to serve at least half their sentences before being eligible for parole. Prosecutor Giauque then proceeded to do a breakdown of the participation of each. The sentences would appear light when compared with later cases, but Giauque admitted that among the six before Beliveau that day, the Crown had no evidence of direct participation in a murder.

Kenny Bedard, a full-patch member of the Rockers, pleaded guilty to conspiracy to commit murder, drug trafficking and participating in the criminal activities of a gang. He had joined the Rockers as a hangaround in April 1997 and only a few months later was arrested in possession of an assassination kit: a Luger pistol, a mask and documents with personal information on several members of the Rock Machine, including Peter Paradis, Simon Lambert and Nelson Fernandez. He was a cog in the Hells Angels' extremely violent expansion into western parts of Montreal Island like Verdun and Lasalle. By March 1998, he had impressed his bosses enough to be made a full-patch member of the Rockers.

Prosecutor Giauque also noted that Bedard was one of the eight gangsters arrested on February 15, 2001, when some of the members of the Rockers and Nomads were caught looking over photos of members of the Alliance. Bedard was carrying a loaded .357 Magnum while standing guard at the hotel. Based on a joint recommendation on sentencing, Bedard was ordered to serve ten-and-a-half years in prison on top of what he had already served since March 2001.

Maurice (Mom) Boucher's son, Françis, pleaded guilty to the same charges as Bedard. He had become a striker on September 28, 1998, and a full-patch member of the Rockers on March 26, 1999. Giauque said that Boucher's son had participated in the conspiracy to kill members of the Alliance, and she noted that the police had found photo albums of rival gang members at his home. Françis Boucher would be ordered to serve a sentence of ten years starting from the day of his guilty plea.

"Mr. Brunnetti's is a case that is a bit distinctive," Giauque said in an understatement. Salvatore Brunnetti had managed to sidestep anything resembling a murder charge and pleaded guilty only to drug trafficking and gangsterism. The police could find no proof that he had participated in a murder conspiracy, Giauque said.

Brunnetti had been a member of the Dark Circle until December 2000 when he decided to be one of the first Alliance members to jump ship and join the Hells Angels after their leaders made a "patch-for-patch" limited-time offer. Brunnetti had been with the Nomads chapter for only a few months when Operation Springtime 2001 was carried out.

"It is evident that Mr. Brunnetti did not conspire to kill, himself, and he was not involved in drug trafficking between 1995 and 1997 because he was in the other group," Giauque said, adding that Brunnetti joined the Hells Angels during a cease-fire in the war.

But there was evidence that Salvatore Brunnetti quickly benefited from being in the Nomads chapter. He had an account in the Nomads Bank, and, while carrying out a search warrant on January 30, 2001, the police linked Brunnetti to $70,000 that had gone through the gang's accounting system. At his home, the police found $3,000 U.S. and more than $10,000 Canadian in a safe, along with a loaded .38-calibre gun. Because of his limited involvement in the biker war, however, Brunnetti was sentenced to only three years on top of the time he had already served.

Brunnetti's defection to the Hells Angels was remarkable because only five years earlier the police had information that the Nomads chapter considered him high on their hit list, if not number one. He was believed to have been the leading force at one point among the Alliance. He had been arrested in 1994, along with a dozen other people, including some tied to the Rock Machine, in a major drug trafficking and counterfeit conspiracy, but the charges against Brunnetti were withdrawn. By the fall of 2004, Brunnetti had already reached his statutory release date after having served two-thirds of the sentence he received in the Project Rush case. The parole board had no choice but to release him, even though corrections officials saw no change in his attitudes toward organized crime while behind bars. For the last year of his sentence, Brunnetti was forbidden from hanging out with known criminals and from using things like pagers or cellular phones. He was the first person arrested in Project Rush to walk out of a penitentiary.

Like Brunnetti, Stephan Jarry had not been with the Rockers long. He had been recruited into the Rockers and made a full-patch member instantly on August 24, 1999, when the Hells Angels welcomed five experienced drug dealers into their network to help them expand into western Montreal.

Before joining the Rockers, the most serious time Jarry had done was three years for a series of armed robberies he had committed in the early 1980s using a fake gun. Prosecutor Giauque said there was evidence Jarry had participated in the murder conspiracies, and was one of the people caught, on March 28, 2001, possessing a binder full of the Sûreté du Québec's intelligence photos of Alliance members.

Although there was some feeling among the Rockers that Jarry had been imposed on them, he was at one point made the gang's treasurer. Also, Faucher gave the police a statement alleging Jarry had purchased a semiautomatic for the Rockers using money from its ten percent fund. The police also had information that Jarry was able to move ten kilos of cocaine a month.

But Jarry had helped incriminate himself as well. During the Project Rush investigation, a bug planted in a car recorded him complaining about the way the Hells Angels cut his cocaine. During a Rockers meeting, he was also recorded comparing the gang's pursuit of Rock Machine members to a hunt for animals. Jarry pleaded guilty to the same charges as Brunnetti, but the best he could get out of a plea bargain was 11 years, not including the time he had already served.

Vincent Lamer, one of the six to plead guilty before Beliveau, had been arrested several times as a member of the Rowdy Crew. He had become so blasé about being arrested that he once asked a police officer to take a new mug shot of him because he didn't like the ones that were being run in the newspapers.

He left that Hells Angels' underling gang the Rowdy Crew to join the Rockers. He had become a striker on March 2, 2000, but somehow earned his full-patch in less than two weeks. He was even president of a Rockers chapter for a month. By December 2000, he graduated to the level of prospect in the Nomads chapter, but for some reason he was demoted back to the Rockers the following month. Because of his heavy involvement in the Rockers, Giauque wanted a heavy sentence for Lamer. She noted that when the police searched his home, they found two video cassettes that contained evidence the Hells Angels were planning a hit on Sun Chin Kwon, a member of the Rock Machine and a martial arts expert. Lamer was sentenced to a ten-and-a-half-year term starting from the day of his guilty plea.

Pierre Toupin had been involved with the Rockers since April 1997 and was made a full-patch member on March 20, 1998. He was suspended from the gang on December 16, 1999, but returned on April 3, 2000. Prosecutor Giauque said that besides doing guard duty and participating in *messes*, Toupin primarily sold cocaine for the Rockers. During the investigation, the police had overheard him on wiretaps bragging about buying a speedboat and building a new house in Sorel. He was sentenced to 11 years.

While they were the first group of gangsters in Project Rush to plead guilty, they were not the last.

Sentencing the Profiteers

While the trial carried on for several months before a jury and Justice Réjean Paul, the judge originally chosen to preside over the entire Project Rush case, the lawyers involved in the case were holding closed-door meetings at the specially built courthouse, working out plea bargains. For several weeks the judge and lawyers involved would meet, sometimes after a full day in court.

The trial came to a halt when some of the accused were allowed to enter guilty pleas on the condition that the murder charges against them be dropped. On September 23, 2003, Crown prosecutor André Vincent informed Paul of the sentences that everyone had agreed to. Vincent was seeking sentences of 20 years for full-patch members of the Nomads chapter, 18 for prospects and 15 years for Rockers.

"You have to look also before 1995, that is to say before the biker war, and after 2001. What was the situation in Quebec? I don't think that we can say the arrests of the accused put the brakes on the sale of drugs in Quebec and more particularly in Montreal," Vincent said. "Before 1994 it was known that there were several groups or dealers that I would describe as being independent or tied to certain people to sell drugs."

The prosecutor then went on to say that by the end of the war, the only groups tolerated in Montreal by the Nomads chapter were Hells Angels from other chapters and the Mafia. To help convince Judge Paul to accept the joint recommendations on sentencing, he brought up other conspiracies that the Hells

Angels or the Rockers were involved in, which the jury would have had to hear if the trial continued. He mentioned how the Hells Angels got information on their enemies by buying off two people who had access to Quebec's automobile insurance bureau. The gang would supply the pair with names and they in turn would find out the licence plates and addresses of Alliance members. The same methods were used to get information on *Journal de Montréal* journalist Michel Auger before he was shot in the newspaper's parking lot.

One of the Rockers being sentenced that day, Jean-Guy Bourgoin, was the man connected to the people who were leaking the information. Vincent said the police had gathered two elements of proof that Bourgoin was buying the information the first being that informant Stéphane Sirois testified that he had overheard Bourgoin telling another person that he could easily get a person's address if he had a licence number.

"The other element came from the investigation after the arrests of Ginette Martineau and Raymond Turgeon. Ginette Martineau was an employee of the SAAQ [Société de l'assurance automobile du Québec] and Raymond Turgeon, her boyfriend, related information to Mrs. Martineau who was in charge of finding the people she was asked to." Martineau was paid $200 for each piece of information.

Turgeon was sentenced to five years in prison and Martineau was sentenced to a little more than two years for selling information to the Hells Angels that likely helped the gang kill several rivals.

"The only *raison d'être* of these groups was to take part in the trafficking of drugs," Vincent said, making reference to things like the Hells Angels' "church," or *messes*, and how the discovery of the Nomads Bank had opened the door to Project Ocean. "It permitted [the police] to discover, I wouldn't even call it a small business. I would call it a business involved in very large volumes." To make the point of how sophisticated the Hells Angels were, Vincent noted that even though Project Ocean was highly successful in turning up drug money, as well as the gang's customers and suppliers, none of the drug caches indicated on their accounting ledgers were ever recovered.

"The criminal organization was structured so that the compartments were detached between the different operations. We know from information obtained that a person who wanted to order drugs had to contact someone and it was never a member of the organization who delivered or transported the drugs," Vincent said. "When you talk of legal businesses in Quebec, these are figures that correspond to something much higher than a medium-sized business can hope to have. The sales for the 39-day period are in the order of $18,104,000. That amount corresponds to the sale of 452 kilos of cocaine and 115 kilos of hashish."

It was during the sentencing hearing that Vincent brought up an interesting detail concerning Normand Robitaille and the Montreal Mafia. Vincent went over the details of a meeting the Rockers had with Robitaille at a restaurant on July 4, 2000. Robitaille told his underlings that there were new territories available to be taken over. He also mentioned that the going rate for a kilo of cocaine was now $50,000. Vincent noted that Robitaille made these announcements shortly after the police spotted him meeting with Vito Rizzuto at a Montreal restaurant called Onyx.

"A young dealer who decides to take part in illegal activities today, who places himself at the corner of Sainte-Catherine and Saint-Laurent to say 'it should be worth it to sell drugs. I'll start selling drugs.' How long could he stay on the corner? The answer, according to the witnesses who have turned [informant], 'if you do ten minutes it will be great,'" Vincent said.

"The Rockers were formed in 1992. Mr. Maurice Boucher, who was a member of the Hells Angels' Montreal chapter, located in Sorel, started the Rockers club in Montreal. In 1995, certain members from Montreal and Trois Rivières, formed the Nomads chapter, Hells Angels' Nomads. After that you have an explosion, in the literal sense of the term and figurative sense, in the number of people who will gravitate to the organization."

Being part of the organization required loyalty, and Crown Prosecutor André Vincent had no better proof than René Charlebois' wedding video. During his wedding reception, Charlebois told his guests that his "heart and his blood" were pledged to the Hells Angels.

"The organization went before everything and anything," Vincent reiterated, "and if the organization needed or sensed the need to physically eliminate an individual, the person who participated in that physical elimination received benefits."

The prosecutor said this was made clear during a *messe* meeting the Rockers held in April 2000, where Vincent Lamer announced there were new rules concerning what it took to advance beyond being a hangaround in the Rockers. What Lamer said indicated that if someone eliminated an enemy, they would not have to go through the eight-month probation to move up in the network's hierarchy. Vincent also noted that Daniel Lanthier, another Rocker who was being sentenced that day and the owner of a small pager company, was able to find out the pager numbers of the Hells Angels' enemies. It was believed that the Hells Angels used that know-how to lure unsuspecting dealers to their deaths.

The Involvement of René Charlebois

As the trials took their course, one name other than besides Maurice (Mom) Boucher's that seemed to come up in every major conspiracy discussed was that of René Charlebois. He appeared to have been involved in everything, including Boucher's plot to kill prison guards, the conspiracy to blow up a Rock Machine hangout in Verdun and several murders.

According to one informant, Charlebois got his start as a drug dealer while delivering pizzas, submarines and cocaine out of a restaurant in the Hochelaga Maisonneuve district just before the biker war started. By April 1997, Charlebois was a Rocker, but he had already been around the gang for a long time. Other underlings in the gang took note of the fact that Charlebois was willing to pay into the ten percent fund even though, as a striker, he wasn't expected to. Stéphane (Godasse) Gagné, who became an informant late in 1997, claimed that Charlebois had asked him to take photos of Martin Dupont and later had offered Gagné $10,000 to kill him. Early on in the war, Dupont and a few other men had been arrested in connection with some stolen dynamite that was tied to the Rock Machine. Dupont was eventually killed in Montreal.

In January 1999, about five months before Charlebois was

From left to right: Gregory Wooley, Pierre Provencher, Sylvain Laplante, René Charlebois, Guillaume (Mimo) Serra, Jean-Guy Bourgoin, Ronald (Popo) Paulin and Daniel Lanthier.

made a prospect in the Nomads chapter, Charlebois was himself the target of an attempted hit. It happened while he was in his car, parked behind a bar where the Rockers had been known to hang out. He was not seriously hurt but told one of the Hells Angels' lawyers that he had no plans to make a statement to the police.

By the time of his wedding on August 5, 2000, Charlebois was a full-patch member of the Nomads chapter. His wedding caused a major stir in Quebec as the Hells Angels had managed to hire popular singers Ginette Reno and Jean-Pierre Ferland to perform at the reception. By then, Charlebois had come a long way from his days delivering pizzas and cocaine. Informants would say that he was an important drug dealer for the Hells Angels in the Hochelaga Maisonneuve district, the area where Boucher began his dreams of a monopoly.

They also said Charlebois was partners with Robitaille, Paul (Fon Fon) Fontaine and Robert Johnson, a member of the Rockers who avoided being investigated in Project Rush only because he was behind bars for its duration. Early on in the biker war, Johnson and Stéphane Blaquiere, another man tied to the Rockers, had been caught making a deal for 350 kilograms of cocaine. When the police searched Johnson's home, they found more than a kilogram of an explosive called Syntex and 15 detonators.

The trial heard before Réjean Paul was bogged down by several delays, including one caused by Charlebois' teeth. During the trial, he had to ask for a recess because his dental implants were causing him severe pain. Visibly frustrated by the delays, Paul asked Charlebois to be patient while they tried to find a dentist who was willing to travel to the Bordeaux detention center to treat him. Paul even tried to offer the Hells Angel some advice saying: "There is nothing like 600 milligrams of Motrin."

A Rush of Plea Bargains

One of the Rockers to accept a plea bargain before Justice Réjean Paul was Sylvain Laplante. Before joining the Rockers, Laplante had been vice-president of a gang called the Pirates based in Valleyfield, a small city west of Montreal, near the Ontario border. The Pirates were run by Gilles (Trooper) Mathieu who jumped from the Hells Angels' Montreal chapter to the Nomads chapter in 1995. Laplante followed Mathieu and became a Rocker on August 25, 1995. Before joining the Rockers, Laplante already had several arrests under his belt for selling drugs out of bars in Valleyfield.

Pierre Provencher, was in his late forties by the time he joined the Rockers in 1994. His age seemed to give him a fatherly influence among the twenty-somethings in the Rockers. He was once recorded telling someone aspiring to graduate to the Hells Angels that doing so required a 24-hour commitment for three years. He was the one they called from prison when they wanted

From left to right: Andre Couture, Normand Robitaille, Pierre Provencher and Bruno Lefebvre.

updates on what was going on with the gang. During those conversations, Provencher seemed friendly and supportive, a contrast to the smoking skull he had tattooed on his left arm.

Before joining the Rockers, Provencher had already been involved in drug trafficking. In 1982, he had been sentenced to six years in prison for drug possession. Provencher's family was well aware of the life he was living. Through wiretaps, the police listened as Provencher's wife discussed biker gang hits with the wives or girlfriends of other Rockers. On one wiretap, recorded on March 29, 2000, Provencher's wife could be heard discussing the preparations being made for their son for his first communion. She said the priest asked their 11-year-old boy if he believed in the word of God and he responded by saying that he believed in the word of the Rockers. Provencher's wife also mentioned that her son planned to set up a Rockers chapter in his school. When the man on the other end of the line jokingly asked if the boy had a Rockers jacket, Provencher's wife said her plan was to not raise him to be a criminal.

Based on information from one informant in the Project Rush investigation, Provencher was making about $60,000 a year selling drugs for the Hells Angels in Verdun. He remained a Rocker throughout the biker war as several other younger men passed him by on the hierarchy. In wiretap conversations, the police could hear other members of the Rockers wonder why Provencher never moved higher than a Rocker. But Provencher seemed content with his lot in life. He purchased a maple syrup farm near Montreal and used it to host parties for the gang. He also seemed to have Boucher's respect.

Another person who had Boucher's respect was Guillaume (Mimo) Serra. Informants said his membership was imposed on the Rockers in July 1995. Two months earlier, Serra had beaten the rap on a cocaine trafficking charge despite being caught red-handed dealing on Saint-Laurent Blvd. A patrol officer was looking into why Serra was double-parked on the busy street and saw Serra and the man to whom he was selling freeze up. When the police searched the car they found 42 grams of cocaine. Serra was described as a key cocaine supplier to the Hells Angels and was suspected of establishing international drug routes for them. Shortly after Serra was imposed on the Rockers, Dany Kane told the RCMP that Serra appeared to have close ties to the Mafia and had purchased, in the Laurentians, the luxury house of a very influential member of the Rizzuto family.

According to Dany Kane, Serra once asked Maurice (Mom) Boucher about the possibility of selling heroin for the Rockers. Kane told his police handlers that Boucher pointed out that the Hells Angels have a strict rule that states, "All contact with or use of heroin is forbidden." But Boucher also advised Serra that he didn't have to know everything he did.

Even though Serra had been a prospect in the Nomads chapter for only a few months before his 2001 arrest, Crown Prosecutor Vincent wanted him to serve 18 years.

"The principal motive of the [Minister of Justice's] position is not at all the time Mr. Serra was part of the Hells Angels under the title of prospect but how he came to acquire that title. It is not a vocation, to become a member of this organization. You are chosen for the qualities a person possesses to be part of the organization." Vincent noted that one informant claimed that Serra could move 80 kilos of cocaine per month for the Hells Angels. He was considered a model for other Rockers to follow.

Serra's lawyer, Gerald Souliere, felt his client was getting a raw deal, in particular because he had only been a prospect for a few months and during that time the Hells Angels had agreed to a truce with the Bandidos.

"He is an individual who was born in 1965. He is today 38 years old. He was 30 years old when he joined the Rockers. He is not the youngest person being sentenced but he is among the youngest," the defense lawyer said. Serra's lawyer said that if his client received a sentence of more than ten years, he would likely have to serve it in Donnacona, a maximum-security penitentiary near Quebec City, which would cut him off from his family. Paul agreed with some of Souliere's arguments and sentenced Serra to 15 years, the same sentence members of the Rockers received. Meanwhile Paul agreed that full-patch members of the Nomads chapter should be punished more harshly. He sentenced Hells Angels like Robitaille, Charlebois, Houle and Mathieu to 20 years.

But the authorities weren't done with some of the bikers who pleaded guilty that day. For a few there was still the question of the assets seized after their arrest.

Trial Far from Over

In Normand Robitaille's case, the province was especially interested in his plans to become a real estate mogul with his drug money. Evidence of his plans fell into police hands on June 27, 1998, when they recovered a suitcase belonging to Robitaille at a brasserie in Greenfield Park. Inside the suitcase, police found three documents titled Real Estate Action Plan. The documents contained details on the potential construction of buildings and the purchase of buildings through Cogesma, a company Robitaille was using to launder his money. Through the documents, the police learned Robitaille planned to buy $1.5 million worth of real estate with equity totaling between $200,000 and $300,000.

Before he was murdered by the Hells Angels, informant Claude De Serres told his police handlers that Robitaille was gathering real estate using other people as fronts for the purchases. De Serres said he himself was used to buy an apartment building in Longueuil and a commercial building on Sainte-Catherine Street East in Montreal. Robitaille was also suspected of using the mother of Patrick Pepin, a hangaround in the

Rockers, as a front to buy property worth nearly $200,000. Pepin had been a member of the Scorpions before Maurice (Mom) Boucher's son, Françis, personally vouched for him to become a Rocker. The police also had evidence Pepin worked as a runner for Robitaille. But unlike most of the other Hells Angels and Rockers who had assets seized in Project Rush, Robitaille wasn't about to give up his mini-empire without a fight. Most of the gangsters agreed to out-of-court settlements, but Robitaille challenged the government's claims in a court battle that dragged on for months.

In the end, Judge Paul decided the government had a fair claim to $500,000 worth of Robitaille's assets. In a judgement he rendered on March 24, 2005, the Superior Court judge said it was obvious Cogesma Inc. was used as a front to pay Robitaille a salary, so he could file his taxes, and as a way to launder his dirty money. Paul ordered the confiscation of $199,980 which police had found in a blue sports bag in one of Robitaille's residences, as well as money found in various bank accounts.

But Paul also ordered that the government could not touch a house in La Prairie where Robitaille had lived with his wife Annie-Sophie Bedard, who was also a defense lawyer. Paul said that while the intentions behind the 1995 transfer of the house from Robitaille's name to his wife's were dubious, there was not enough evidence to justify taking it from Bedard.

The government also could not confiscate some of the properties Robitaille was suspected of purchasing through underlings like De Serres. On top of what was confiscated, Robitaille was ordered to pay a $49,000 fine for the more than $200,000 in assets the government could not locate, including Robitaille's Harley-Davidson, estimated to be worth more than $26,000. Paul also tacked on an additional year to Robitaille's 20-year sentence. When Paul finished reading his decision, Robitaille had a smile on his face that nearly stretched from ear to ear. Losing half a million while behind bars seemed to be no skin off his nose. From the prisoners' dock, he raised his handcuffed hands and congratulated his lawyers for their work.

8

Stéphane Sirois: A Man Inside

"The war was always about expanding the drug network. That is why there were murders and settling of accounts. They had to show that they weren't going to let things be. A Hells Angel can never lose face."
— Stéphane Sirois in a statement he gave to the police after turning informant.

On June 15, 1998, Stéphane Sirois was approached by the police out of the blue. They had done their homework on Sirois and knew he had made a tough choice. He had been told by the Rockers he couldn't be a member if he stayed with his girlfriend — whose previous lover had been an informant. He chose the woman. The cops thought there was a chance Sirois would turn on the gang because his departure from the Rockers had not been a smooth one. If he did decide to turn, he would be a valuable part of the investigation because he knew intimate details regarding how the Rockers functioned overall as a gang. Sirois told the cops he wasn't interested in their offer. But for some reason, he kept the business card that had been handed to him by officer Robert Pigeon, an investigator with the elite Wolverine squad.

Sirois married the woman and they went on a honeymoon, but the relationship was doomed. Just minutes before he headed for the church to get married, the Rockers were hassling him for

$5,000 they felt he owed them. Within months of the marriage, Sirois and his wife were planning their divorce. Sirois fell into a depression and became hopeless. He wasn't sure what to do to rectify the situation when he remembered detective Pigeon's business card. Only months after their first meeting, on March 12, 1999, Sirois called Pigeon and told him he was now interested in becoming an informant.

The Rockers' Godfather

For starters, Sirois gave the police a series of statements about what he knew of the biker war. He confirmed what other informants had said about the starting point of the war being Maurice Lavoie's murder. Lavoie had decided to buy drugs from the Hells Angels instead of the Pelletier Clan. Soon after, he was dead, and the Hells Angels took the murder as a direct threat to their authority.

"Anyway, it seemed to me that the war was inevitable. The Rock Machine and the Alliance would have had to join the Hells Angels [to avoid a war]," Sirois told the police.

Nonetheless, it was the information Sirois had concerning the day-to-day operations of the Rockers, plus his relative good standing in the gang, that would be invaluable to the Project Rush investigation. The police were trying to build a gangsterism case against the Hells Angels and the Rockers. Now they had a former secretary of the Rockers on their side. The position Sirois had held in the gang meant he had recorded all the minutes of Rockers' meetings. Because of this, he knew what each member contributed to the ten percent fund, which, in turn, meant he could estimate how much each Rocker had made in drug sales.

Sirois said the ten percent was paid on good faith, but members were expected to pay a minimum of $300. He said part of the money was reinvested in the gang while, during the early years of the biker war, another chunk went directly to Maurice

(Mom) Boucher. At one point in Sirois' stint with the Rockers, Boucher was making $500 on every kilo of cocaine the Rockers sold. If Sirois' figures were right, Guillaume (Mimo) Serra was by far the Rockers' best drug dealer. On a monthly basis Serra led the pack by paying $3,000 to the ten percent fund. Longtime Rockers like Richard (Sugar) Lock, Paul (Fon Fon) Fontaine and Robert Johnson were paying $2,000, while Sirois' drug dealing allowed him to contribute $1,000.

Sirois also said the Hells Angels supplied the Rockers with the services of two accountants who provided the gang members with bogus income statements to create the illusion, on paper at least, that they held down steady jobs.

Sirois told his police handlers that in their earlier days the Rockers had to be unanimous on who could become a striker in the gang. But he also noted that Boucher eventually started imposing decisions on his underling gang. He said that was the case when Serra and Stephan (Sandman) Falls joined the gang.

"Every affiliated group has a godfather," Sirois told the cops in describing how Hells Angels' puppet gangs like the Rockers, the Jokers and the Rowdy Crew worked.

"With the Rockers it is Maurice (Mom) Boucher. They were created so the Hells Angels would have a presence in Montreal. What's more, the Rockers are the *groupe de frappe* for the Nomads. The Rockers are different from affiliated groups. It is the Rockers that do most of the work and we are respected, even in western Canada. If you were to say what the Rockers represented, it would be the image that Maurice Mom Boucher projected. We are the pride of Mom."

To display that pride, Boucher selected a patch for the Rockers that featured a logo just as menacing as the Hells Angels' winged skull. It was the front profile of a skull with the barrels of two guns pointing out from behind it.

"I don't know why the Rockers or the Hells Angels used that

symbol on their patches. But then a drawing or an acronym of death represents fear. It's more threatening for the public to see a symbol of a Death Head than to have two doves on a bikers patch. That is a bit why you've chosen to have a Wolverine for your squad," Sirois told his police handlers, adding that both gangs had a rule that, if anyone outside their membership wore the patch on their backs, it had to be burned.

After taking several of his statements, the next step for the police was to get Sirois to infiltrate the Rockers by joining the group again. It would be no easy task.

A Foot in the Rockers' Door

While Sirois would be vague later on the details when testifying in the megatrials, his decision to marry was not supported at all by the Rockers. The woman in question had previously been with a man the Hells Angels believed to be an informant. The man was eventually murdered, but the Hells Angels still didn't

The Rockers celebrate a key moment for them in the biker war in 1999. Normand Robitaille (top left) welcomes in the new underlings.

like the idea of someone in the Rockers marrying a woman who was once so close to a suspected snitch. Sirois said ultimately the choice of whether to marry her or stay with the Rockers was imposed on him by Boucher. Sirois quit and turned over his drug business to the Rockers.

Now he had to get back in, but he had very little credibility among the gang's members. His contract with the police called on him to take notes and gather information on specific members of the Rockers and the Hells Angels. Sirois signed on with the police on June 23, 1999. In exchange for his life-threatening work, he was promised police protection after he testified. Crown Prosecutor Madeleine Giauque at one point revealed that Sirois was paid about $100,000 for his work. That included a $50,000 payment when the arrests in Operation Springtime 2001 were carried out. Sirois' contract also called for him to be paid an additional $20,000 at the end of the preliminary inquiry and another $30,000 after he was done testifying in the trials.

To ensure his security, the Sûreté du Québec agreed to shell out $6,500 so he could pay off some debts with utility companies and a credit union. The police promised to change his identity and supply him with anything he needed after working for them. According to Sirois' contract, that included housing, moving expenses, psychological assistance and financial planning. To continue receiving this help after testifying, Sirois agreed to "change his lifestyle and live like a person who was prudent, reasonable and respectful of the law." But first, he had to be bad enough to get back into the Hells Angels.

Initially, infiltrating the gang would appear to be easy because Sirois' former business partner Marc Sigman actually called on him, looking to see if they could start doing business together again. His police handlers told Sirois to ignore Sigman because he wasn't among the people targeted in the investigation at that point. The investigators in Project Rush wanted the heads of the network — the members of the Nomads chapter were their priority. The lowest ranking gangsters targeted in Project Rush were full-patch members of the Rockers. Pursuing anyone below that mark threatened to widen the focus of the investigation too much. So Sirois started calling his closest connections in the Rockers.

He started with Stephen (Sandman) Falls, but Falls wouldn't return Sirois' calls. Sirois tried André Chouinard, who was, by then, a full-patch member of the Nomads chapter. Chouinard returned Sirois' calls and suddenly the new double agent found a crack in the door that might get him back in.

He began by inquiring about getting his patch back. Slowly, Sirois infiltrated the Rockers in a way only Dany Kane had done before. He began taking notes on his every interaction with the Rockers and agreed to wear a wire from time to time. Within weeks, he had already gathered some very damaging evidence. But he was pulled out of service when Claude De Serres, another informer, was found out and murdered. What Sirois had gathered on the Rockers did not become public information for more than two years. It came out during the trial of the 17 gang members.

In July 2002, Sirois took the stand and faced his former fellow gangsters for the first time in years.

"Mr. Sirois, you were part of the Rockers at a certain part in your life," prosecutor Roger Carrière asked.

"That's exactly right."

"At what moment were you associated with that club?"

"In 1994."

"And before that period, before 1994, what where you doing?"

"I was selling drugs, but I was independent."

"You trafficked in drugs, but you were independent?"

"Yes."

"Did you have some associates at that time?"

"Not at that time. I had contacts but not associates." Sirois then gave a little background on himself. He said he had started dealing drugs from the age of either 17 or 18, when he was already working in bars.

"At what moment did you become close to the Rockers?" Carrière asked.

"In 1994, I was close to the Rockers because there was a group of people who wanted to leave a gang known as the Chiefs. I knew those people."

"Who were those people?"

Sirois rattled off the names of several members of the Chiefs, including Jean-Guy Bourgoin and André Chouinard. He said Boucher was involved in a decision that saw the Chiefs fold as a gang. Members were offered the opportunity to join the Rockers because Boucher could not tolerate the presence of another gang on the same turf as his.

"When did you decide to live this kind of life?"

"It was at what we called a bike show. It was proposed to me a bit more seriously. They told me they had striker patches for starters. I didn't know what a striker was, or a full-patch."

"You didn't know what it meant?"

"I didn't know what it meant. They said, 'Look, after [being a striker], you'll become a member.' A member of what, I still wasn't sure. At the first show, I started to get interested. I liked it. It was more a temptation. They tempted me with what it would be like. But after that first show, they took back the patches. They decided they gave them out too fast. They didn't know the people they gave them to."

"And this was during 1994?"

"Yes, this is still during 1994."

"Had you been given a striker patch at that moment?"

"Yes."

Shortly after the Rockers took back the striker patch from

Sirois, on December 5, 1994, a drug dealer named Bruno Bandiera was killed in an explosion as he drove along Taschereau Blvd. in Longueuil. The bomb had been detonated by remote control. Bandiera, who was 28 at the time, was ejected from his car and died instantly of severe head wounds. Sirois said it was Bandiera who had brought him into the Rockers fold and his death had some influence in Sirois wanting to join the Rockers. He joined them for his own protection, but Sirois might have thought twice about his choice had he known what Dany Kane had told the RCMP about Bandiera's death. Kane told his handlers it was the Rockers who had killed Bandiera because he owed them money and had started buying drugs from the Rock Machine to cover his debts. Jean-Guy Bourgoin welcomed Sirois into the gang and proposed to the other Rockers that he be accepted officially.

"I started to get close and after that we became hangarounds," Sirois explained. "Me, Stephen Falls, Robert Johnson and Alain Chevalier, we became hangarounds the same night." Sirois was considered a hangaround until March 1995, when he learned that he had graduated to striker and was given his patch, the bottom part that identifies the gang's territory, at a motorcycle show in Sherbrooke. The Rockers were impressed with how Sirois stuck around after a bomb went off at their Montreal clubhouse on Gilford Street. Most people would have been scared off by the bomb or the police attention that was sure to follow. But Sirois stayed close to the clubhouse making sure no other damage would be done to it.

Sirois said his drug dealing then became more structured and that Bourgoin supplied him with drugs to sell. Sirois in turn would distribute the drugs to a small network of five or six dealers who worked for him.

"And you sold how much drugs per week, per month?"

"At that time, when I was a striker, I couldn't sell as much because I had to take care of the club. I couldn't just sell drugs. So I was selling 250 grams of coke per week and a little bit of hash and marijuana."

"What do you mean when you say you couldn't work full-time?"

"It's because when you are a striker or a hangaround, the club goes before everything else. So you have to have a business that can work without you being there 24 hours a day."

"What other tasks did you do for the club?"

"When a member goes out, you have to be his bodyguard. You have to do the watch during parties. You have to do any task that you can. It could range from going into clubs and assault people or do intimidation if someone asks you to do it. The particular tasks of a hangaround are to make sure the club runs well. The term I should use is the pig jobs, to do the things others don't want to do. It's the only way to get known in the club. It goes from cleaning up the clubhouse to chauffeuring members, even chauffeuring strikers, doing the watch, doing the orders, food and drinks, the dirty jobs."

Sirois became a full-patch member of the Rockers in March 1996, at the gang's anniversary party. He said André Chouinard gave him his patch at the clubhouse on Gilford Street.

"Who decided if someone could be held back or make exceptions to the rule?" Carrière asked.

"At the time, the only person who could propose things or make real decisions was Maurice Boucher."

"Who was he to you?"

"He was the godfather to the Rockers."

"Did you know him?"

"Yes."

"From when?"

"I knew him in 1994."

"When you were an independent?"

"At the moment I became a hangaround, when I joined the club."

"Did you have conversations with him?"

"I had conversations with him. But at that time they were short conversations."

"You couldn't approach him easily?"

"No, he was an approachable guy, but you had to have a good reason to talk to him about something."

"The functions of a striker, your functions as a striker were what?" Carrière asked.

"The functions of a striker are somewhat like that of a hangaround. A striker has to be more responsible, more available, his social life disappears. If the telephone or the pager goes off he has to answer the call right away. He has to follow the members, that means not one particular member. It could mean that a member says, 'Okay, Charles tonight you're with me,' but at 2:30 in the morning another member could call you and you have to follow him and your job is to be his bodyguard."

"What happened with your drug business while you were a striker?"

"You have to be able to multitask. You have to be able to do both. That is what it takes to move up in the club. That's what the members want to see. That's what I wanted to do to become a member. Someone who is able to do what he has to do and able to follow the club, while continuing his business."

"You became a member in March 1996. It changed what in your life to become a member of the Montreal Rockers?"

"A little more free time," he said.

Going to Mass and Playing Baseball for the Rockers

Stéphane Sirois noticed the links between Boucher and the Rockers had changed at some point shortly before he left the Rockers to get married. The change seemed to coincide with the timing of the creation of the Nomads chapter.

"There was a time when, for each kilo of coke that was sold by the Rockers, by anyone in the Rockers, you had to pay $500 to Maurice Boucher," Sirois said. "After that, what happened was that there were two or three members of the Rockers who bought packages of cocaine in bulk. The members would buy it from them."

Sirois said that when one of the Rockers would buy cocaine from a fellow gang member who was buying in bulk, the Nomads chapter's cut was already fixed in the price. Sirois said that Montreal's Hochelega Maisonneuve district was controlled by Paul (Fon Fon) Fontaine, Robert Johnson, Normand Robitaille and René Charlebois. He said the decisions over territory were handled at their meetings, *messes* or "church," as the Quebec Hells Angels and Rockers called them. "The serious things were discussed while taking a walk outside, between the people who wanted to negotiate, who wanted to talk about 'hot' topics. We didn't talk about those things at 'Mass.'"

"When you're talking about big things or hot things, what do you mean?"

"It could be a murder, or a guy that you want to keep an eye on. It could have been someone on their territory. Take, for example, Hochelega Maisonneuve. René Charlebois, Bob Johnson, Normand Robitaille and Paul Fontaine, if there was a [gang] to destroy in Hochelaga Maisonneuve, it didn't affect me, so they would take a walk and talk about what they were going to do that night."

"Did you ever participate in a 'baseball team'?" In the language of the Hells Angels, a "baseball team" is an intimidation squad.

"Yes, at one point in particular."

"On what occasion?"

"I was a member of the Rockers. We went to Saint-Sauveur.

Myself, Paul Fontaine, Bob Johnson, Daniel Lanthier and Kenny Bedard, we went there and put masks on our faces. This was requested by Paul Fontaine who got the request from David [Wolf] Carroll. We met Wolf somewhere and he gave his last instructions to Paul Fontaine. Paul Fontaine gave us the instructions. We went in a Dodge Caravan and arrived at the club, placed the masks over our faces. Paul Fontaine bent the licence plate so no one could read it. Bob Johnson was supposed to find the owner and give him a chance. If he didn't accept, we'd destroy everything with baseball bats. And the club was open and there were clients inside when we arrived."

"What happened?"

"We did exactly what I just described [smashed up the bar and broke bottles], except that Bob Johnson couldn't find the owner. That didn't happen. After that we were gone, and very calmly, like nothing happened."

"What was the reason for doing this at that club?"

"If I remember correctly, the owner did not want drugs in his club, and the territory belonged to David [Wolf] Carroll. It was a way to persuade him to let the drugs enter."

Sirois went on to say he knew that Charlebois, Robitaille and Fontaine participated in "football teams," or murder squads. He said the trio put pressure on him to join them. He said Fontaine in particular asked him to join a football team with Sylvain Moreau but he declined.

While on the stand, Sirois also revealed that he was asked to kill the owners of the Castel Tina, a strip bar on Jean Talon Street in Saint-Leonard. Again he refused. The owners of the strip bar were Paolo Gervasi and his son Salvatore. The father had ties to Vito Rizzuto, but he had sided with the Rock Machine in the biker war, and even had a special table reserved for its members at his strip bar. In April 2000, 31-year-old Salvatore was killed. His body was stuffed into the trunk of his Porsche, which was then parked in front of his father's home. A few months later, someone made an unsuccessful attempt on the father's life. Paolo Gervasi survived but nearly four years later, on January 19, 2004, he was gunned down outside a bakery in Saint-Leonard.

As early as the mid-1990s, the Rockers were aware that the Castel Tina owners were financial supporters of the Rock Machine. But Sirois wasn't interested in killing them, in part because of who was assigned to do the job with him.

"You refused to work with Sylvain Moreau. Why?" Carrière asked.

"At that moment I didn't have confidence in Sylvain for a job like that."

"Did you work with René Charlebois?"

"Yes."

"What kind of work?"

"We sold drugs, and also we took part in what we called 'the hunt,' two or three times, to find Marc Belhumeur and the father and son who owned the Castel Tina." Belhumeur had been gunned down on January 24, 1997, and was one of the 13 victims many of the Hells Angels were accused of murdering. He was considered an associate of the Rock Machine and was shot at a brasserie called Le Chalutier, a place he frequented. René Charlebois would later brag to Sirois that he was the trigger man in what was considered a well-executed hit.

To avoid being monitored by the cops, the time and location of mass would be written down somewhere in the clubhouse. A gang member doing the watch that day would page all of the members and tell them to come immediately to the clubhouse. Each member would travel to the clubhouse to learn the time and place. This was done so no one would ever have to say out loud where meetings would be held. Sirois was named as the gang's secretary, which meant he took notes during "church" meetings.

"The ten percent that you paid, it served what, as far as you knew?"

"The ten percent was to give a cut to Maurice Boucher; it served as the administration of the club, to pay the rent; it served as well to the costs of the club; there was a defense fund; the ten percent also bought weapons."

Sirois said he was able to sell one to two kilos of cocaine per month as well as the same quantity of hash per month while he was a full-patch member of the Rockers. He described the Rockers as being well organized when it came to assigning each member an area where they could sell drugs. He said that members like Daniel Lanthier and Richard St. Armand were assigned the task of finding new turf where the Hells Angels had never sold before. The Rockers were also given permission to sell drugs elsewhere in Quebec as long as someone from another Hells Angels' chapter was not already there. Sirois said that this allowed him to sell drugs as far away as Chicoutimi and Baie-Comeau.

"I had to leave Chicoutimi because I found out it belonged to someone who sent an associate to our club. It belonged to someone in the Sherbrooke Hells Angels. He came to Montreal and met with Maurice — and when I talk about Maurice, I mean Maurice [Mom] Boucher — he called me and told me to get my guys out of Chicoutimi," Sirois said.

Sirois said Boucher also advised him to ask the Hells Angels' Quebec City chapter if it was okay for him to sell drugs in Baie-Comeau.

"Unfortunately I only sold there for a while because it was a long distance to travel when there were problems to take care of there. After a couple of months I left the Baie-Comeau territory alone," Sirois said. Carrière then asked about the war in Montreal. He asked about all the groups that made up the Alliance and why the Hells Angels were interested in eliminating them.

"It was territory to conquer the sale of drugs. They could take it from us or they had to go, or they had to fall," Sirois said.

"What were the methods employed for this?"

"Intimidation that ended with murder."

Sitting at the Ecstasy Table

Carrière then went through the long list of gangsters charged in Operation Springtime 2001 and asked Sirois to comment on what he knew about them. When Sirois was asked about Normand (Pluche) Bélanger, he was able to elaborate at length. He said that before he quit the gang to get married, Bélanger was not a Rocker. He described Bélanger as being close to the club because he was good friends with Boucher and sat at what the gang called the Ecstasy Table.

Sirois said he conspired with Bélanger to kill people who blocked the Hells Angels' way into the ecstasy market. The owner of a Montreal after-hours club called the Playground was targeted. "We decided to take control of the distribution of ecstasy in Montreal. A table was formed. There were members of the Rockers who were part of the table. There were Hells Angels who were part of the table. There was also Normand Bélanger."

"And what does an Ecstasy Table do?"

"It was to manage the distribution, the importation and the distribution of ecstasy for each person."

Sirois said, when he joined, Daniel (Boteau) Lanthier was already a Rocker and he sold Sirois cocaine and ecstasy. He also owned an arcade and a pager company. Sirois didn't elaborate, but he said he chose not to use the pagers that came from Lanthier's company. Sirois said Lanthier got into trouble for dealing drugs on the South Shore for a while. He was ordered out because another Hells Angels' chapter had dealers there. Lanthier was reminded that his patch meant he was supposed to sell mainly in Montreal.

When asked to describe André Chouinard, Sirois said he had

started out as a member of the Rockers in 1994 and quickly climbed the ladder to become a part of the Nomads in 1997. Sirois said that during the time he was in the Rockers and not yet working for the police, he could always go to Chouinard for cocaine. That was why he chose Chouinard to be one of the first people he called when trying to get back in as a double agent.

"The contact went well. Chouinard made small talk at first. After that we got on to important subjects."

"What was that?"

"The important subject, primarily, was still about the person I had married. There were stories she had told certain people in the milieu. I wanted to see how they had been perceived. They told me to forget about it, they were the stories of a slut."

"You asked about that to know if you could continue with your business?"

"I asked André Chouinard questions about that subject in particular for several minutes. I also told him I wanted to go back to work, I wanted to go back to the club. When I married that person, they told me I didn't have the right to work. And now I told him I was divorced, so I wanted the permission to work, which meant, to be able to sell drugs in Montreal."

"What did he say?"

"He gave me the permission and he said he'd put me in contact with someone, because the first point of entry would be to set up a marijuana house. What he said was 'open your marijuana house and after that I'll introduce you to someone who will buy it from you.'" Although Sirois wasn't asked to elaborate on what a "marijuana house" was, he was likely referring to the Rockers common practice of renting homes in Montreal suburbs and using them solely to grow marijuana hydroponically.

Sirois said Chouinard put him in touch with Jean-Guy Bourgoin, and things started happening for him. He took notes of every phone call and every meeting between different people.

All the while, he managed to buy drugs from Bourgoin. He also set up a meeting with Chouinard at a jewelry store. Using a hidden recorder, Sirois recorded the meeting and began to ask questions more pertinent to the violence in the war. He told Chouinard that he wanted to "score points with the Rockers."

"What did you mean by that?" Carrière, the prosecutor, asked.

"To win points, to get me higher [in the gang's hierarchy], to skip steps. André told me it was not impossible and that what would help most would be to get information on the other side."

"What does that mean? What did you understand from that phrase?"

"Personal information on the Rock Machine and their affiliates."

Sirois said that shortly after his conversation with Chouinard he was able to contact Jean-Guy Bourgoin. They set up a meeting at the Pro Gym, the workout center in the Hochelaga Maisonneuve district where the Hells Angels worked out religiously during most of the biker war. Besides pumping iron, they would take boxing and martial arts lessons from professionals.

"The advantage of the Pro Gym," said Sirois, "was that it was right in front of a police station."

"That's an advantage?" Carrière asked.

"It's an advantage when it comes to security."

Sirois said that during his meeting with Bourgoin, he arranged to buy 250 grams of cocaine. The cocaine was delivered by one of Bourgoin's runners while Sirois waited at a pizza restaurant. The runner brought it in a shopping bag, packed into a box of Ritz crackers. Then Sirois reported the transactions to his police controllers, Roch Coté and René Beauchemin. They gave him money so he could keep buying drugs from Bourgoin. At this point, the jury had to endure listening to recordings of conversations that Sirois had made while talking to Bourgoin. The quality was poor but transcripts had been made to help the jurors along as they struggled to make sense of what they were hearing.

Sirois met with Bourgoin again on December 15, 1999, at a tanning salon on Sherbrooke Street East in Montreal's east end. Sirois told Bourgoin that he needed a kilo of hashish. Bourgoin agreed to the deal and told him he could get him Viagra and ecstasy "in industrial quantities." Two days later, Sirois tried to arrange a meeting with Chouinard, but the Hells Angel couldn't attend because his son was involved in a Christmas pageant.

In the next taped conversation presented to the jury, Sirois got Bourgoin to reveal what the Hells Angels were planning in terms of their expansion westward. During a December 23, 1999, conversation that Sirois secretly recorded, he and Bourgoin discussed the province of Ontario. Bourgoin said the Hells Angels considered it virgin territory. Prosecutor Roger Carrière asked Sirois to interpret what Bourgoin meant when he said "there's a damned huge market over there."

"The province of Ontario was a virgin territory and that the drug market was open. First come, first served," Sirois explained.

Days later, Sirois met Bourgoin at a fast-food restaurant and arranged to buy four kilos of hashish from him. Bourgoin appeared to be opening up to Sirois. He asked Sirois if he was interested in renting an apartment for him in Montreal's Plateau district where he could stash and sell drugs. Bourgoin later surprised Sirois by delivering the drugs himself. Sirois began to learn more about the Hells Angels and how their ways of dealing had evolved since he had left.

The Hells Angels now had a tight-knit group that made decisions regarding where they would buy their cocaine. The Hells Angels appeared to be only interested in purchasing large quantities of cocaine and only if they could be assured of its quality.

"I started by saying that I could put my hands on 20 kilos of coke, [asking] if I could bring it to the Table, to sell it to the

Table. Because at the beginning of our conversations, André [Chouinard] told me that the new rule was that everything had to go through the Table. I proposed that I could get 20 kilos of coke and could I sell it to the Table. Excuse me, I told him I could get kilos of cocaine. He asked me how many kilos. I told him about 20. He said it was not enough, the Table was only buying between 100 and 1000 kilos, so my guy would be stuck with his 20 kilos."

Bourgoin informed Sirois that if he wanted to start selling ecstasy in Montreal, he needed the permission of the table that had been formed years earlier with Normand Bélanger, who was, at that point, a member of the Rockers.

The Prices Paid

Jurors were soon treated to some of the more illuminating evidence heard during any of the megatrials. It came during a secretly recorded conversation Bourgoin had with Sirois at a sushi restaurant in downtown Montreal. By now, Bourgoin appeared to fully trust Sirois, but the fact that he was drinking potent sake during the dinner possibly helped loosen his tongue. At the beginning of the recorded conversation, the pair is overheard discussing mundane things like the flavor of the California rolls. Sirois is heard complimenting Bourgoin as an expert on ordering sushi and complaining that he hadn't eaten it in a long time. Then the conversation turned to gang business, doing guard duty or little things like "the watch." While secretly recording what Bourgoin was saying, Sirois assured him that he would never disrespect the Rockers name.

Bourgoin became worried at one point that someone seated near them in the restaurant was a cop. But he soon calmed down enough to start talking about how the Plateau was his territory. Bourgoin also asked about a problem Sirois had had with a member of the Mafia over the rights to sell drugs in a bar. It was around that point that Sirois asked about how he could move up quicker in the gang. Bourgoin then revealed that the Hells Angels had a price list. The gang was willing to pay up to $100,000 for the murder of a full-patch member of the Rock Machine.

"During the same conversation, Jean-Guy [Bourgoin] told me it was $25,000 for a hangaround, $50,000 for a striker and $100,000 for a full-patch member of the Rock Machine. In the same example he said that if you killed two strikers and a member, it was $200,000 in your bank account," Sirois said. Right from the mouth of someone who had served many years as a Rocker had come solid evidence of how far the Hells Angels were willing to go in their war.

Shortly after that bomb was dropped, Sirois' testimony ended, and the defense was left to try to clean up the mess. Defense lawyer François Bordeleau began the cross-examination by asking Sirois about how he had been prepared as a witness. Sirois complained of having to provide "too much" information on how he came to be a Rocker, that his handlers required too much of him. The conversation then turned to Sirois' past. He described how he had started working in bars as a young teenager. As an adult, he continued to work in bars. He was once a busboy at Montreal's infamous Chez Parée strip club, a lightning rod for tourists and gangsters. Sirois' criminal record was actually very light, but he had confessed to several things he had never been arrested for including several robberies and a home invasion.

"During that period, with certain people, we heard news that someone had $70,000 in their home. We decided to go there, to get in the home. We made threats. Unfortunately, yes, the person was a 70-year-old woman. She was tied up. We searched the house and found nothing and left. And while on the road I convinced my partner to pull over to call the police to make sure the woman was okay," Sirois said. Bordeleau continued to grill him.

"And to untie her?"

"To untie her and make sure she was okay. And to this day it was something that bothered me."

"You were trying to find money and you threatened her?"

"We threatened her dog."

"Do you know what a dog represents to a 70-year-old woman?"

"Yes."

"*Voilà*, so then you threatened her."

"I don't deny it."

"*Voilà*."

"I'm 33 now. I was 18 then."

9

Stéphane Gagné: Trigger Man

On the surface, Stéphane (Godasse) Gagné might appear to be a man of little consequence. He speaks with a nasal voice and an accent that immediately gives away the fact he was raised in Hochelaga Maisonneuve, historically one of Canada's poorer areas. His face often seems fixed in a goofy grin giving him the appearance of being dim-witted. Even his nickname, *Godasse*, a French expression for old shoe, suggested he was more of a folksy type than an aggressive street dealer looking to become a millionaire.

But that might also have been his strength for it may have led people to underestimate him. Gagné apparently enjoyed playing that card. He once pretended to be mentally challenged during an examination by a psychologist, while serving a federal sentence during the early 1990s. He had hoped the act would get him an early release, but a corrections official caught on. The corrections official made sure the National Parole Board was aware the psychologist had been tricked.

After he turned informant in 1997, Gagné originally was told he would only be expected to testify in two trials — one against Maurice (Mom) Boucher, involving the murders and attempted murder of prison guards; and another that was supposed to be the trial of the gang members who had attempted to level a Rock Machine hangout in Verdun with a powerful bomb. But Gagné had been a witness to the biker war from the early disputes that in 1993 until his arrest near the end of 1997. Gagné had been a successful independent drug dealer and it was made clear to him that he would have to choose sides. He chose the Hells Angels. He would later admit he liked the idea of joining a gang that offered the chance of climbing a ladder toward prosperity.

When the first murder trial against Boucher ended in an acquittal, however, many observers blamed Gagné, saying it was apparent the jury could not believe the word of a trigger man looking to get a lenient sentence.

Taking the Stand Again

Newspaper editorials began to question the value of using witnesses like Stéphane (Godasse) Gagné. In Boucher's first trial, Justice Jean-Guy Boilard had instructed the jury that they had a very important decision to make. If they didn't believe Gagné, they should acquit Boucher on all three of the charges, which they did. When the Crown appealed the acquittal, part of the prosecutors' argument was that Boilard's instructions were misleading and did not allow the jury the opportunity to assess the merits of the evidence concerning all three charges as required in Canadian law. Investigators had gathered significantly more supporting evidence in one of the prison guard murders, and, the Crown argued, the jury might have given it more weight had Boilard instructed them properly.

By the time Boucher's retrial rolled around, Gagné was a much more polished witness, and this time, elements of his testimony were now backed by other former Rockers, like Serge Boutin, who turned informant after he was charged in connection with Operation Springtime 2001. The former Rockers supported Gagné's testimony by showing how the Nomads chapter functioned as a highly structured drug trafficking network. With other former gang members attesting to the hierarchy's existence, Boucher's motive for murdering the two prison guards in order to destabilize the justice system, especially to keep that multi-million dollar network running, seemed more plausible.

Gagné himself would acknowledge, while testifying during the trial of the nine Rockers and Hells Angels before a jury and Justice Pierre Beliveau, that his previous experience being cross-examined had polished him into a much better witness. He was now testifying for the fifth time in a major trial. He had been schooled by police investigators who practised with him while taking on the roles of aggressive defense lawyers. Gagné had also survived the experience of being grilled twice by Jacques Larochelle, Boucher's lawyer in both murder trials and a man recognized as one of the best defense attorneys in the province. Gagné started testifying in the Beliveau trial in August 2003, detailing how ten years prior, he had been partners with another drug dealer named Tony Jalbert. They were independents, but Gagné said it had been obvious to him who would inevitably win the war. He claimed he could already sense that the Hells Angels would stop at nothing to win.

Gagné had first met Jalbert in 1991, while they were both serving federal prison sentences. At that point, Jalbert was serving two federal terms. In 1985, he had been convicted for armed robbery and sentenced to six years. Then, while out on parole in 1990, he was caught dealing drugs and saw almost six years tacked on to his sentence. Right around the time they met, Jalbert was doing a good job of convincing the National Parole Board he was on the road to rehabilitation.

"It's like he has realized, bit by bit, the pain he has caused as a drug trafficker," a psychologist wrote of Jalbert in 1991.

Gagné met Tony Jalbert again in 1993. By then, Jalbert was out on day parole, having convinced the parole board that he wanted to help handicapped people and even attend university. But according to Gagné, during that same period of time, he and Jalbert were talking of the possibility of dealing drugs on St-

Hubert Street, a diverse roadway that runs north-south for several kilometres through Montreal. One section of St-Hubert is shopping central for brides-to-be looking for wedding dresses, other stretches run through low-income neighborhoods like the one where Jalbert and Gagné discussed dealing their quarter-grams of cocaine. But eventually Gagné told Jalbert he preferred dealing in Hochelaga Maisonneuve. It was where he had grown up and he knew people there. Jalbert agreed, and they became equal partners in a plan that saw them sell cocaine out of apartments rented specifically for that purpose. They would hire small-time dealers to work shifts from noon to midnight while the more serious dealers would handle the tougher late-night hours.

Things were going well until Jalbert was arrested again and Gagné was left to run the business for both of them.

"When Jalbert went in for the second time, the war had just about started. So we had a choice. Go with the Hells Angels or go with the Rock Machine. And the Rock Machine had a lot of guys in groups like the Palmers and the Alliance, things like that. So Tony told me that he had met Mr. Maurice Boucher," Gagné said during the Beliveau trial, explaining how it was Jalbert who had arranged the fateful introduction.

Jalbert's first instinct was to join the Hells Angels' side in the war. He instructed Gagné that they should start buying their drugs from Boucher, and he gave Gagné a contact to set up the meeting. Before that, the pair had been buying from whomever was known to be carrying the best quality cocaine. They dealt with the Mafia, the Hells Angels, the Pelletier Clan and important independent dealers like Jean Duquaire, who would later become a member of the Rock Machine.

The Hells Angels had already demonstrated their power to Gagné. Their underlings in the Rockers robbed one of his apartments, commonly known as a *piquerie* in the milieu, relieving him of about 15 hits of cocaine. That was about the most cocaine the clever dealer would leave in one spot at any given time. Even though Gagné had lost less than three grams of cocaine, it still stung, and he insisted on confronting the thieves, which was easy because the Rockers had let it be known they were behind the heist. Gagné contacted the gang and got his drugs back with an explanation that the Rockers didn't know who was running his drug den. Shortly after meeting one of the Rockers, Gagné paged the contact he was given by Jalbert. He said Boucher called him back within a day and set up a meeting.

The two met in an alley where Gagné boasted that he was able to move three kilos of cocaine a month in Hochelaga Maisonneuve, Boucher's stomping grounds before he became a high-level drug dealer. They arranged a deal where Gagné would pay for a kilo of cocaine with cash and then take a second *sur la bras*, slang among drug dealers for credit. Gagné left Boucher with an address, and shortly afterward, a man carrying what appeared to be a case of beer showed up. Inside the box were the two kilos of cocaine. Gagné said he paid Boucher $34,000 the next day. They continued to deal together, but sometimes Boucher was out of stock. It was then, when Gagné was looking for more cocaine, that it was made clear to him that he had to deal with the Hells Angels exclusively.

"After a while, I wanted more coke, and I went to see Mom, and Mom said, 'Look, you know who is with us' because he didn't have any. He said, 'Get it from a guy who is with us.' I went to see Pierre Quintal because he was getting it from Steven [Bull] Bertrand and Steven Bertrand was a friend of Maurice Boucher. In the Hochelaga Maisonneuve neighborhood, everyone knew each other before the war started. When I said I knew Sylvain Pelletier, it was because I had bought coke from him. Before the war started he was wearing an Alliance ring," Gagné told the jury.

"What was the Alliance?" asked Crown prosecutor François Briere.

"The Alliance was a group that formed at the start of the war with the Pelletier family. They wore rings. They were a part of a group of independents who did not want [to buy drugs] from the Hells Angels," Gagné said, adding he was asked to join the Alliance. "I never wanted to join the Alliance or the Rock Machine because I knew they were going to lose."

"To lose?" Briere asked.

"The war."

"Okay and this was in 1993?"

"Yes."

Gagné said that after they had been dealing together for a while, Boucher seemed impressed by his ability to move cocaine. At around this time, Jalbert was still serving his sentence. Gagné was faithfully forwarding his partner's share of profits from their business to an elderly woman — Jalbert had introduced her to Gagné as his aunt. Perhaps not so coincidentally, the parole board had taken note that Jalbert seemed to spend a lot of his free time, while out on day parole, at an aunt's house. He went there to eat on weekdays and then returned to his halfway house at night. On weekends, he would sleep over at her place.

The business relationship with Jalbert deteriorated when Gagné was caught with a kilo of cocaine after selling a quarter-gram to an undercover cop. He was arrested and, Gagné said, Jalbert was not interested in paying his bail, having just gotten out of prison himself.

Gagné said he later learned that Jalbert had spent his time behind bars getting to know Jean Duquaire and had decided to join the Alliance. With no one else in the milieu to turn to, Gagné said he called Paul (Fon Fon) Fontaine from the Rockers and was told the gang would help him out. But when Jalbert caught wind of this, he rushed to pay off Gagné's bail instead.

Gagné said that when he got out, he and Jalbert had a meeting at a submarine restaurant. Jalbert lay down the law, saying

Gagné was responsible for $40,000 worth of cocaine they had lost in a seizure connected to Gagné's arrest. Jalbert also informed Gagné that they were no longer partners. The meeting grew increasingly tense as Gagné reminded his partner that he had swallowed losses that were Jalbert's fault. Gagné testified that Jalbert had once dumped 200 grams of cocaine because he mistakenly thought the cops were following him. Gagné also reminded Jalbert that he had helped him out while he was in prison by faithfully delivering the profits of their business to the elderly woman believed to be his aunt. The lines were already being drawn, so Gagné bluntly told Jalbert that he was going to buy his drugs from the Hells Angels.

Shortly after the messy meeting, a buddy of Gagné was released from the Bordeaux detention center. He informed Gagné that if he ended up convicted for selling the cocaine to the undercover cop, he should avoid the Bordeaux detention center because Alliance members like Jean Duquaire and Michel Boyer had his photo and were waiting for him.

"What did you do when you got that information?" prosecutor Briere asked.

"Well, then I called Tony Jalbert and I said, 'Hey, your buddies are waiting for me at Bordeaux?' and he said 'No, no, no, no.' I said, '*Hostie*, it's the photo of you and me and a Harley, so it's you who supplied it to them. They didn't get that from a box of Cracker Jacks.' He finally admitted that it was him," Gagné said. At that point, Jalbert asked Gagné again if they were partners. Gagné replied that they were still partners until he paid Jalbert what he owed for the seized cocaine, but after that he was going to buy from the Hells Angels.

It would later become evident that Jalbert had completely switched over to the Alliance. In the years that followed, he became a member of the Rock Machine and was part of the gang when it was patched over by the Bandidos, an international gang with chapters all over the world. Jalbert would end up being arrested again, late in the biker war, serving a five-year term for growing marijuana, drug trafficking and weapons possession. He was released from prison in late 2004 and corrections officials still believed him to be a Bandido.

But as their partnership was falling apart in 1994, Gagné pleaded guilty to selling the quarter-gram to the undercover cop and, as if determined by fate, was sent to the Bordeaux detention center where Jalbert had set him up. He was placed in the C wing, reserved for repeat offenders, and was quickly welcomed as he had been warned. Three members of the Alliance, Stéphane Morgan, Michel Boyer and Jean Duquaire, served as the welcome wagon. Gagné said the trio insisted on knowing which side of the war he was on. He lied and told them he wanted nothing to do with the war, that he just wanted to sell drugs.

"Duquaire [Le Français] took out a photo of Maurice Boucher, threw it to the ground and told me to piss on it. I didn't piss on it, so they beat me up," Gagné said. Gagné said he responded, a little later, by storming into Duquaire's cell with a homemade pick and stabbing him several times, intent on killing him. Duquaire was sent to the hospital, while Gagné was bounced around detention centers all over Quebec, including one in Sorel, where he met up with Boucher again.

A Fateful Decision

Boucher appeared to be very interested in having Gagné as part of his network. Whether it was Gagné's ability to move cocaine or the loyalty he had so violently demonstrated at Bordeaux, Boucher took a liking to Gagné and told him he'd look after him while he was in prison and that Gagné should look him up once he got out. Boucher put Gagné in contact with his son, Françis, who would make sure Gagné's prison cantine was well stocked with his favorite foods. Inmates are allowed to have a certain amount of food kept at their detention center if they can afford it. Having a well-stocked cantine gives an inmate certain bargaining chips behind bars. It also breaks up the monotony of only eating prison food.

While they did time together, Gagné carried out the little tasks Boucher asked of him. One such task was mounting an inmates' protest when Boucher declared they were being fed shepherd's pie far too often. He requested a transfer to Boucher's wing but was refused. The pair would meet only when they were placed in the detention center's general population for exercise.

Andre Chouinard, a member of the Hells Angels' Nomads chapter.

After being bounced around to various detention centers, Gagné was released after serving more than two-thirds of his sentence. He testified that he was able to set up a meeting with Boucher almost immediately after his release. He paged Boucher's son and set up a face-to-face. The next day, François Boucher merely asked Gagné for his pager number and told him to wait.

Mom Boucher contacted Gagné soon after and said they should meet at the building on Bennett Street that the Nomads chapter had turned into their hangout. Gagné recalled there was a used car dealership inside as well as a jewelry store. He said André Chouinard, who was one of Boucher's drug couriers at the time, Gilles Mathieu and Richard (Sugar) Lock used the building for their offices. Gagné also recalled that Chouinard would answer the phone with "Gestion Wow," a company that Maurice Boucher owned.

Stéphane Gagné said that after hanging around the Bennett Street building for a while, he, Chouinard and Boucher went to a restaurant in the Plateau.

"It was there that Maurice Boucher said that he had big things for me. And he didn't say much more than that," Gagné said. It was the "big things" that the prosecution wanted Gagné to tell the jury. What Gagné brought to the Beliveau trial was evidence of how the gang functioned, particularly when members of the Nomads chapter, and especially Boucher, plotted to eliminate their rivals.

After eating at the restaurant, Boucher and Gagné headed back to the Nomad hangout on Bennett Street. It was there that Gagné was first introduced to André (Toots) Tousignant. Gagné had known him as an independent drug dealer before the biker war started. Now, Tousignant was a Rocker and one of Boucher's most trusted lieutenants. They spent most of the day at the Bennett Street hangout, and then Tousignant, Gagné and Boucher drove to a location in the South Shore region across from Montreal Island. They left their pagers in their car, and Boucher and Tousignant went for a short walk while Gagné waited behind.

When the pair returned, Boucher used a hand gesture to ask Gagné if he had a gun. Gagné said he didn't. Boucher replied that there were some stored in the Bennett Street building, and told Gagné to stay close by because they might need him soon.

Gagné stayed with his parents and waited a few days until Boucher and Tousignant showed up. The trio packed into a car and headed for Verdun where Gagné finally learned of one of the "big things" Boucher had planned. Their first stop was at a garage in Verdun that Gagné would later learn was close to a Rock Machine hangout on Lesage Street. Boucher had kept mostly quiet during the car ride, but now, as they passed the garage he turned to Tousignant and said, "You are going to be there." Boucher then asked Gagné and Tousignant to hide so they wouldn't be seen by the men outside the red-brick building who were doing guard duty for the Rock Machine that day as he drove past.

The trio then drove on to Lachine, a municipality next to

Verdun, where Gagné was told his part of the plan was simply to place a bomb underneath an empty car and blow it up. Boucher figured that the police would arrive after the bomb detonated and that the commotion would draw the attention of the Rock Machine members and cause them to all head inside their hangout. Then another team would detonate a much more powerful bomb with the goal of destroying the Rock Machine hangout and killing everyone inside. This second team was supposed to be paged after the first bomb had gone off.

Gagné said the diversionary bomb was supposed to be set off in a parking lot next to a condominium. He was going to do this with Stephan (Sandman) Falls. The plan was for the pair to wait for a page showing a series of 1s. They would then detonate the bomb using a remote-control device. After agreeing to the plan, Tousignant led Gagné and Falls to a bar on the South Shore to pick up the bomb they were going to use.

"We went inside the office and he showed it to us. It had a remote control," Gagné said.

"This is in the office of the bar?" prosecutor Briere asked.

"Yes. There was a waitress there who kept saying, 'What are you doing there? What are you doing?' Toots said, 'Mind your own business,' and slammed the door." Boucher appeared to have thought of everything. Gagné was coached on how to detonate the explosives. Boucher also had Gagné and Tousignant repeatedly go over the routes they were supposed to use, insisting that they drive the speed limit and make all of the proper stops.

The day they were supposed to blow up the Rock Machine hangout, Gagné said he was waiting in an apartment for the message to give him the go-ahead on the diversionary explosion. But Tousignant showed up and said he couldn't start the car the second team was supposed to use. Tousignant asked Gagné if he had booster cables and they headed to the garage Boucher had pointed out earlier.

"When we got to the garage, Mr. Tousignant asked me to close my eyes. So I closed my eyes. The door opened and when it closed I could hear voices. The voices were familiar. One was Jean Damien Perron, a Hells Angel from Trois Rivières. At the time, he was a hangaround and I had done two months in prison with him, so I recognized his voice," Gagné said. Tousignant insisted that Gagné keep his eyes closed and ordered the two other men from the second team to hide in a bathroom. It was obvious the Hells Angels didn't want one team to know who was involved in the other. It was apparently an effort to reduce the number of arrests if anyone later turned informant. Only Tousignant was trusted enough to know who was on both teams.

Gagné said there was a Ford car parked in the garage and he couldn't help but notice the huge bomb inside it that the Hells Angels planned to use to level the Rock Machine hangout. The dashboard of the Ford was open and it was immediately apparent to Gagné that the vehicle had been stolen. The experienced car thief said he realized what the problem was right away. He explained to Tousignant that GM vehicles that are stolen by jamming a screwdriver into the ignition start differently from Fords. He said he used a special trick on the Ford and it started right away. Tousignant then drove Gagné back to the apartment where Steven (Sandman) Falls was still waiting. They hid out in the apartment and waited for the signal.

"We were waiting for the ones [to appear on his pager]," Gagné said, adding they waited for about two hours and that they were under a lot of stress. One hour could feel like three in that situation, he said. But Tousignant arrived after a while and informed Gagné and Falls that the plan was scrubbed because, somehow, the police had shown up at the same building where the second team was lying in wait. The police seemed interested in another section of the building, one other than the garage, Tousignant told Gagné and Falls with no further explanation.

Prosecutor Briere then asked Gagné if the Hells Angels had made other attempts on the Rock Machine hangout.

"Yes, after that we tried another way. This time, we held a meeting, Paul Fontaine, André Tousignant, Sandman and René Charlebois. The plan consisted of placing a vehicle in front of the place," he said. The second part of the plan involved having guys drive by the hangout on motorcycles and fire shots at anyone standing guard for the Rock Machine that day. Charlebois was supposed to drive the truck to the clubhouse and dump it there. The others were supposed to pick up Charlebois and drive to a nearby apartment and detonate the bomb from a distance.

Gagné said that the first time they had talked about it was in the park in front of the Montreal Forum, the former home of the Montreal Canadiens. The second time was in a Chinese restaurant near Place Versailles, a shopping center in eastern Montreal and the location of the Montreal Urban Community Police major investigation squads. Someone showed up at the restaurant and delivered two Japanese brand motorcycles that were supposed to be used by the shooters. Charlebois left on one of them.

Gagné said he and Paul Fontaine, who rode the other Japanese motorcycle, left afterward. They headed to a second restaurant and met up with Tousignant, Falls and Charlebois. The small group held another meeting, but not inside the restaurant. Gagné said a waitress agreed to take care of their pagers and cell phones while they all went for a walk outside. "We were scared that our things were bugged. That they were wiretapped," he explained. The five bikers left the restaurant and went to a nearby park. There they discussed who was going to do what for the second attempt on the Rock Machine clubhouse.

"It was supposed to happen because the vehicles were all ready, including one with the bomb inside it," he said. But the gang members hit another roadblock because, when they returned to the restaurant, they noticed an unmarked car parked near the Japanese motorcycles. Inside the car were men who appeared to be trying to hide from view. The bikers figured right away that these were undercover cops doing surveillance on the Rockers. The bikers figured they had been followed to the restaurant and the police now could tie them to the Japanese motorcycles. A decision was made to ditch the plan.

"Did you make a third attempt?" Briere said.

"Yes," Gagné replied.

"Can you tell us how?"

"Yes, in the third attempt, I had to steal trucks that were mouse-grey, like Hydro Quebec's. The color of Hydro Quebec at the time was mouse-grey. A Dodge Caravan, or a Suburban or else a Cherokee."

"So you had to steal that?"

"Yes, it was Paul Fontaine who asked me. Toots said, 'Make sure it is the same grey as Hydro Quebec because one of my buddies will give me their stickers and we will decorate it like a Hydro Quebec truck." Gagné said he found the truck they needed the following day. He had actually considered stealing one from a Hydro Quebec parking lot, but there were surveillance cameras everywhere.

He said that Kenny Bedard, René Charlebois and Steven (Sandman) Falls were at least aware of the third attempt on the clubhouse. He went on to explain that he was with Kenny Bedard when they spotted the grey Dodge Caravan they wanted. It was parked at the Place Versailles shopping center, and they followed the owner as he drove it to a hardware store and then to a building in an industrial park. Gagné said he stole the truck using a screwdriver. He later parked it near the St-Hubert Airport where the Hells Angels kept a garage for their stolen vehicles.

What was key to Gagné's testimony was that he could recall that there were two boxes inside the Caravan; one contained a shirt while the other had two flashlights inside. The items were later found inside the van used in the actual attempt on the Lesage Street building. It was an important detail to remember because Gagné did not take part in the actual bombing attempt. He was somewhere else at the time, namely a provincial detention center.

Gagné's trouble began after he set off to find a second van that would match Hydro Quebec's colors. Fontaine had grown impatient and told Gagné to find anything that was mouse-grey. Gagné said he and Kenny Bedard settled on a Jeep Cherokee in Montreal's north end. It was a high-end vehicle Hydro Quebec employees never used. Gagné stole it anyway and drove off, but soon after that he spotted a cop right next to him at a red light.

"But do you know why you where looking for those trucks?"

"Yes, it was for the project in Verdun."

"And what were you supposed to do with those trucks?"

"What we wanted to do was to put dynamite in the mouse-grey Dodge Caravan." Gagné said that Falls, Fontaine, Tousignant and René Charlebois were in on the plan. He said Charlebois was supposed to drive the Caravan to the front of the clubhouse. Gagné also said he, Falls and Fontaine were going to open fire on anyone in front of the building to draw everyone inside. Tousignant was supposed to drive the second vehicle. But while Gagné was driving the stolen Cherokee, the police officer who had pulled up beside him noticed the broken dashboard. Soon after, another police vehicle was following him as well. Gagné sped away, ditched the Cherokee and ran. But a police officer caught up to him and he was placed under arrest. He spent the night at a police station and was taken to the Montreal courthouse to be arraigned. He did not make bail and was sent to the Parthenais detention center. He was charged with theft of the vehicle, quickly pleaded guilty and was sentenced to six months.

In the meantime, the Hells Angels tried to carry out their risky plot to level the Lesage Street building. On August 23, 1996, Verdun residents who lived near the intersection of Lesage Street and de L'Eglise Ave. were treated to an odd sight. A mouse-grey van with Hydro Quebec logos slowed at the intersection and its driver leapt out. He jumped into another vehicle that had been following behind his. The abandoned truck had been placed in neutral and kept moving forward until it rolled to a stop against a street sign. There it rested until one resident decided to take a peek inside the van. He immediately noticed the 91 kilograms of explosives inside. They were connected to six detonators. Something had happened that caused the Hells Angels to abandon their plan to blow up the Lesage Street hangout. The police would later learn that at the same moment the gang members driving the trucks approached the two-storey building on Lesage Street, several members of the Rock Machine including Renaud Jomphe and the Plescio brothers were standing outside it.

The Hells Angels' underlings abandoned the truck within metres of two gas stations in a mostly residential neighborhood of aging triplexes. RCMP explosives expert Jean-Yves Vermette would later run tests and find that the bomb could have leveled several buildings at the intersection. To conduct his test, Vermette blew up a similar van with a similar bomb at the Valcartier military base; it generated a fireball eight metres in diameter. Shrapnel from the blast was carried as far as 500 metres.

One witness would provide a description of the driver of the van which somewhat resembled Charlebois. The getaway vehicle was found abandoned in eastern Montreal. It had been set on fire to destroy any evidence including any fingerprints or DNA on the six handguns that had been ditched. But the police managed to recover something that proved interesting. Someone had left a pager behind, but not close enough to the flaming van for it to be destroyed. The police were later able to trace it to Steve Boies, a man they already knew to have ties to the Rockers. The police had a solid lead connecting the Hells Angels to the bogus Hydro Quebec truck packed with explosives.

Meanwhile, Gagné kept his mouth shut about the purpose of the stolen Jeep and faithfully did his time for the Hells Angels. He was out by February 1997, eager to resume working with the Rockers. He said that the same night he got out, he headed to the Rockers bunker. There he met Falls and Pierre Provencher. They asked if he wanted to join the Rockers football team.

"What does a football team do for the Rockers?" Briere asked.

"The football team is a team of killers."

"They kill who?"

"They kill members of the Rock Machine."

"Did you agree to be part of this football team?"

"Yes."

Gagné said his first task on the football team was to head out to Verdun with Gregory Wooley to locate a particular Pontiac Bonneville. They were given an address in Verdun and found the truck easily. Gagné wasn't told who the target was, only that the vehicle's owner was tied to the Rock Machine. They were to do surveillance work on the Hells Angels' next target in the biker war.

But Gagné became concerned when he realized how brazen the Rockers had become, especially in their attitude toward conquering Verdun. He said he heard Pierre Provencher tell a Verdun drug dealer that for every 500 grams of cocaine he sold he was to pay ten percent to Gagné. The drug dealer asked why and Provencher informed him that "Godasse is going to open some doors" for the Rockers in Verdun. The drug dealer was still puzzled, so Provencher laid it out in plain French. He said that Gagné was going to kill anyone not selling for the Hells Angels in the dealer's territory.

Gagné said he was completely caught off guard by the statement. He said he didn't know the drug dealer and didn't like the situation Provencher was placing him in. The way he saw it, his name was being mentioned to every drug dealer the Hells Angels were friendly with in Verdun. "Who are these people?" he thought to himself, and what was to stop them from informing on him if they ever got into serious trouble with the police? Gagné said he headed straight to Bennett Street to talk to Boucher, but instead ran into Fontaine and Tousignant. He told them he wanted off the football team. Fontaine said he was glad to hear it because he wanted Gagné to join his newly formed team of drug dealers who were assigned to continue their dominance in Montreal's Gay Village. Serge Boutin, a drug dealer with remarkable business acumen, had already been sent to prison, and the Hells Angels were restructuring their network in the Gay Village, a section of Montreal packed with bars and after-hours clubs.

By his own admission, Gagné said he worked on the Gay Village project from February to March 1997. He said his partners were Fontaine, Danny Decelles and two men who would later play a major role in his decision to turn informant: Steve Boies, the man whose pager had been recovered after the botched bomb attempt in Verdun, and Christian Bellemare.

He said that Fontaine had told him to set up apartments, or *piqueries*, in the Gay Village where they could sell drugs 24 hours a day. He said the majority of the clients were prostitutes. "A *piquerie* is a place where someone goes to by a quarter (gram), consumes it there and then goes out to do more prostitution or petty thieves, people like that," Gagné said.

When Boutin got out, Fontaine made the decision to keep the team together. Boutin was assigned to do the accounting. Decelles and Boies were in charge of the *piqueries* and two municipal parks. Jean Roch Lussier was going to be in charge of PCP. Gagné said Decelles was supplying pot and cocaine to dealers in the parks.

"Me and Paul [Fontaine], we had the same job. The same job was to kill people for the Hells Angels organization and the Rockers."

"You were being paid how much at that moment?" Briere asked.

"I was paid about $1,000 per week. Sometimes it was more. Sometimes it was less." Gagné said he and other gang members began doing close surveillance on two brothers who were dealing on St-Hubert Street. He said the Hells Angels began taking photos of the brothers and "created a file on them."

"You know if you kill the guy who is the head, and you don't know who else is working for him, you don't advance much more," Gagné said. "You have to create a file, take photos, hide cameras inside vehicles." Gagné went on to say the gang used Mazda 323s and Chryslers for their surveillance-camera operations. They used boat accessory batteries to plug in their video cameras so they could run for hours. They would hide the video cameras in a tissue box mounted in the back seat of the vehicle. They would connect the cameras to a videotape machine hidden in the trunk which allowed them to tape for several hours.

Once they got someone on video, the gang wanted photos of their targets as well. For this they used a mid-sized truck. They used tinted windows on the truck but, Gagné said, realizing that a drug dealer might be suspicious of such a vehicle, they had signs made up to make it look like an electrician's vehicle. They even had a fake company registered to match the truck's lettering and assigned a cell phone number and pagers that was to be used only for the phony contractor. The company was registered in the name of Gagné's wife. Gagné said that the phone would always stay inside the truck and that sometimes they would get calls from curious people asking why their truck had been parked on their street such a long time. Sometimes, Gagné said, they would reply that the truck needed to be towed and then they would call a Hells Angel associate who would come over and help them in their subterfuge by towing the truck away. They also had police scanners inside the truck to listen if anyone called in to report a suspicious truck.

Gagné said that he was also asked by André (Toots)

Tousignant to do surveillance on a guy in Laval. It turned out to be a member of the Dark Circle. "To my memory, we did it as well in Montreal North, around Langelier. We did surveillance and even tried to follow the guy. What Paul Fontaine told me was that he was a rock. In the milieu, when we talked about the Rock Machine we called them the Ducks. We didn't call them rocks. A rock in the milieu was an informer for the police, an informant or a police witness," Gagné said. Fontaine told him that killing the informant would be worth $50,000. Gagné said they often followed the man as he drove in his Jeep Cherokee to an industrial park in Rivière-des-Prairies.

"The morning that we decided to do it, we were waiting inside a Dodge Caravan," Gagné said. At this point, prosecutor Briere interrupted Gagné.

"Stop. I'd prefer it if you'd use the term . . . instead of using 'we' talk about who."

"Me and Paul Fontaine. We prepared the getaway because we were always going to this shop. We said we would cut him off on the street before he went in the shop. Paul was going to get out and shoot him and get back in our truck. We were going to dump it and set it on fire, climb into the legal car and drive away. That morning we went to the shop and nothing was happening. We returned to his place and he didn't leave for a week. After a while we said let's forget it, the plan is dead. After the police had arrested me and I took them there and they told me the man had died of a heart attack."

That man turned out to be Domenico Rossi, an informant for the Montreal police's anti-gang squad. As they were checking out Gagné's potential as a credible witness everything he had told them about the planned hit pointed to Rossi being the target.

The Crown prosecutor then asked if Gagné had done surveillance on prison guards. Gagné testified that by the summer of 1997, Maurice (Mom) Boucher had apparently hatched his plan to kill prison guards in a twisted plot to knock the justice system on its back. Gagné said he was told, by Paul Fontaine, to do surveillance on a provincial detention center in Rivière-des-Prairies, on the eastern tip of the Montreal Island and was instructed to follow vehicles that might be carrying three or four guards.

"The first time that I went there I left my truck on St. Jean Baptiste [Street] because one of my aunts lives there. After that I went to the prison on foot," Gagné said. He began his surveillance from a wooded area near the detention center and soon noticed that an employee would cross a railway track nearby to get to work. Gagné thought he might make a good target but he soon realized the man was likely a prison cook because he always dressed in white. There was little progress to report. He had done about eight or nine days worth of surveillance when suddenly plans changed.

"At the beginning, when Paul Fontaine asked me to do surveillance on the prison guards at Rivière-des-Prairies, a few days later André Tousignant paged me and asked me to meet him on Bennett Street. He said we were going to take a walk, so I left my pager behind. He took me by the ear and he said, 'We have a screw to do at Bordeaux and I thought of you.' In our milieu, 'a screw' is a prison guard. Why do we use the term screw? It's because they lock and unlock the door on our cells like turning a screw," Gagné said.

"From there, I said I'd have to talk to Paul because I was occupied with something. Toots said he would take care of it. At one point I was at Fontaine's because Tousignant paged me. When I got to Paul Fontaine's, André Tousignant was already there. Toots asked Paul Fontaine if he wanted to go in with him and Paul said 'No, no.' So Toots said 'I'm going to do it with Godasse.'"

Gagné and Tousignant held several meetings to discuss possible ways of murdering a prison guard. They decided on a plan in which they would leave their getaway car in the parking lot of a

Laval shopping center. Tousignant then decided they would do the hit while both rode on a stolen Japanese motorcycle, a Katana Suzuki. But the first one they tried had mechanical problems and Tousignant considered scrapping the Japanese motorcycle idea all together.

Diane Lavigne

On June 26, 1997, Gagné was paged by Tousignant and told to meet him at a pizzeria. They parked their getaway car, a Ford Escort, in the Laval shopping center parking lot as planned. They then headed to a garage on St-André Street in Montreal where another Japanese motorcycle was waiting. The pair left on the motorcycle with Tousignant driving and Gagné riding on back. When they got near the Bordeaux prison, they quickly spotted a Jeep Cherokee which had several prison guards inside. They followed, it but quit the chase as soon as they realized the Jeep wasn't heading in a path that would easily let them get to their getaway car. So, they waited near the prison for another potential target.

Diane Lavigne had just finished her shift at the prison, and she drove past them in her Plymouth Caravan. Tousignant spotted the guard insignia on her uniform. They followed her to the highway on the motorcycle and accelerated once she was on it. Tousignant brought the motorcycle to the driver's side of the Caravan and Gagné opened fire on the tinted window. He would later claim he had no idea his target was a woman.

Danielle Leclerc, another prison guard, was following close behind Lavigne's car and noticed Tousignant and Gagné on the motorcycle. She watched as they made the dangerous maneuver next to Lavigne's minivan and heard the shots fired, but she assumed the pair had left something on the highway that had caused Lavigne's tires to blow. Tousignant hit the gas and Gagné tossed his firearm away. They rode to the shopping center where they had left their Ford Escort. They took off the clothes they had been wearing during the hit, and Gagné dumped them in the back of their getaway car. They returned to Montreal where Gagné collected all of the clothes and the helmet and burned them at another location.

Gagné said he got his orders for the murder from Tousignant. He said that Fontaine and Tousignant were by then hangarounds in the Hells Angels, which made them his bosses. Briere asked if he had received compensation for the event. Gagné said he was in the hospital in July because of an accident, but that he received his striker patch in the Rockers in August as a reward for what he had done. He also said that the day after the murder he received congratulations from Mom Boucher.

"The morning after, Paul Fontaine came to pick me up. He said we should stick together," Gagné said. The pair drove to the Bennett Street hangout where the Nomads chapter members did business.

"Mom was there with Trooper. Mom asked me to go to a florist with him and Trooper."

"Who is Trooper again?" Briere asked.

"[Gilles] Mathieu. I always knew him as Trooper, but afterwards, the police told me that Trooper was Mathieu," Gagné explained. "After that we went to the florist. We waited while Mom Boucher bought two or three bouquets. He put them in his truck, and we went for a walk. I was looking around because I had on a kangaroo [a jogging jacket with a pouch] and I had my hands in my kangaroo for my piece."

Gagné was jittery about the police rushing in on him at any moment for killing the prison guard. He said that he, Fontaine, Boucher and Mathieu walked to an alley to talk and they were whispering into each other's ears. Gagné said that he whispered to Fontaine that it was he and Toots who had murdered Lavigne. Fontaine then went over to Mom Boucher to whisper it into his ear. "I continued to walk towards them, between Mr. Boucher and Trooper. Mom told me, 'It's good, my Godasse, it doesn't matter if she had tits.'"

Gagné said Boucher went on to warn him, because whoever talked to the police would likely end up getting 25 years, even if they came forward as an informant. He also said that if the death penalty existed in Canada the murderer would get that instead. Gagné said that Mathieu appeared to approve of Lavigne's murder as well.

After that, everyone headed to Chez Parée, one of Montreal's oldest strip clubs, for lunch. Gagné said he didn't ask many questions after the murder. He said he knew it was the best way to get up in the Hells Angels — do a job, do it as fast as possible and don't talk about it afterwards. Gagné said he knew murdering prison guards would be strongly approved by the Hells Angels and that he was ready to do anything to move up in the hierarchy. Tousignant was already on his way.

On June 30, 1997, Gagné was injured in a motorcycle accident caused by a member of the Rock Machine. As he lay in his hospital bed recovering, he was visited by Tousignant and Robitaille. Tousignant then informed Gagné that he had received his bottom patch in the Nomads chapter, giving the underling something to aspire to. After recovering from the accident, Gagné was quickly placed back on duty, continuing the surveillance of the Rivière-des-Prairies prison that Fontaine had asked him to do before Lavigne's murder. After a few days, Gagné told Fontaine about how most of the prison guards heading home would turn right as they exited the detention center's parking lot. They would often end up jammed at a busy intersection. Gagné described how there was a pedestrian button that could be used to change the traffic light at the intersection.

Fontaine decided that it would likely be there that they would carry out the next hit. Fontaine and Gagné put a plan in place that involved using motorcycles and a bicycle path to help in their getaway. But Gagné said that when they were ready to do the next hit on a guard, Fontaine called it off at the last minute. It was the first indication that Fontaine was worried about the fact they were killing innocent people.

"Paul said it didn't feel right, that the getaway wasn't good and all that. I said, 'Yeah, but we have to do it.' He said, 'Yeah we have to do it, but you're not ready to do 25 years for a prison guard who has done nothing. Rock Machine guys don't bother me because they're trying to kill us and we're trying to kill them,'" Gagné recounted. Fontaine decided that they should wait for another chance.

At this point they selected a Mazda B2000 pickup as their legitimate vehicle, to be used after they torched the vehicle used in the shooting. They also had a green Dodge Caravan ready for the hit. Gagné prepared that vehicle by wiping it down with gas to get rid of fingerprints. He also put on fake licence plates. He said he took down the licence plate number from the same model of vehicle and then made a copy of that plate by using a blank plate and some paint.

"If a cop was following us and checked the plates, he would think it was not stolen," Gagné said. The pair set off on another day, prepared to do the shooting. By now, Fontaine had selected a bus used to transfer inmates on trial to the courthouse. He noticed that it always had two prison guards in it. Gagné was positioned near the detention center waiting for the vehicle while Fontaine was waiting near the intersection where it would have to stop. But the bus didn't show up that day.

Robert Corriveau and Pierre Rondeau

On the day of the actual hit, September 8, 1997, Gagné and Fontaine went to Pointe-aux-Trembles, on the eastern tip of the Montreal Island, and picked up the stolen Caravan that had been prepared for the job. Gagné drove that vehicle and Fontaine followed in a Mazda 323 as they headed to the Rivière-des-Prairies detention center.

They got to their designated spot near the prison around 6 a.m. and waited in a bus shelter for the prison bus to arrive. At around 6:10 a.m., Robert Corriveau and Pierre Rondeau pulled out of the underground garage of the Montreal courthouse and headed for the prison to pick up inmates who had cases in court that day. They were alone on the bus. The passenger seat was positioned perpendicular to the driver seat, and as they drove along the two men chatted. They had no idea what was waiting for them.

"Paul Fontaine asked me if I felt okay. I said, 'Yes' and asked him how he was doing, he said, 'Yes.' I said, 'Hey, there's two guards in there and one of them is armed, one of the two guards.' He said, 'You'll get out with me and when they make their stop we will open fire, both of us.' He was going to take the driver and I was going to take the other [guard]. When they arrived at the stop, Paul took the lead. He took out his piece and I took out mine. He opened fire and I opened fire."

Gagné had said in earlier trials that Fontaine carried a .357 Magnum. He opened fire on Rondeau, who was driving the bus. Gagné testified he fired one or two shots with his semiautomatic in the direction of the passenger, Robert Corriveau. He said Fontaine continued to fire and climbed onto the hood of the bus to get a better angle. Gagné said that at this point, his 9-mm semiautomatic jammed on him. "During the time that I unjammed the firearm I could hear shots fired. When I unjammed it Paul Fontaine was already running away. I went to the side [of the bus] and continued to shoot," Gagné said. A ballistics expert who showed up at the crime scene afterward gathered evidence that would later confirm Gagné's story about his weapon jamming. But Gagné had still managed to unload a full clip on the bus and the victims.

Rondeau was declared dead almost two hours later at the Maisonneuve Rosemont Hospital. Despite the hail of bullets, he had been struck by only two shots. One came from a .357 and that one delivered the fatal wound; the other came from Gagné's 9-mm. Corriveau managed to survive.

After emptying his weapon on the unsuspecting guards, Gagné followed Fontaine to the stolen Caravan, which was parked about 100 to 150 feet from where the shooting occurred. Gagné did the driving.

"When I got into the truck I closed the door and started to count: 1st Street, 2nd Street, 3rd Street and I turned right because between 1st and 2nd Street there is a light on Notre-Dame, so if I took those two streets I might end up at a light. I wanted to avoid that."

Gagné said the pair headed for their legitimate car, the Mazda 323, on a quiet street near tall evergreens with the hope they wouldn't be noticed making the transfer from the Caravan. Fontaine bolted for the Mazda 323. It was Gagné's duty to torch the Caravan and destroy any remnants of evidence. He emptied a five-gallon container of gasoline and set to igniting it.

"I placed the matches in the truck but there were fumes everywhere because I had sprayed it with gas. When I lit the match the flames leaped out. I burned a bit of my face. When I walked away there was a girl at a bus shelter. I had a baseball cap and a mask. I walked in a way so she could not see me. I got in the 323 and we got to Montreal."

The teenaged girl who was waiting for a bus at the intersection of Demontigny Street and 47th Ave. turned out to be an important witness. She testified during Boucher's first murder trial that she saw the Caravan parked on 47th Ave. She was able to give the police enough information about Gagné that they were able to produce a composite sketch. Once he had walked past her, Gagné panicked when he realized the girl might have seen his face and realized he couldn't be seen driving around in the Mazda. He had to switch to another vehicle and burn all the other evidence like their clothes.

Boucher apparently thought the young woman was an important witness as well. After he was acquitted in the first trial, Boucher paid a visit to a furniture store where she worked and walked toward her. Without saying a word he circled around her, staring in her eyes the whole time. Then he left. When Boucher's second trial rolled around, she was too terrified to testify a second time.

"Erase and Start Over Again"

Gagné said Fontaine headed immediately for a hospital to do "the watch," or guard duty, on Louis (Melou) Roy, who had been shot in the parking lot of his father's motel in Jonquière and was recovering. Gagné headed straight for the garage in St-Hubert, bringing all of the clothes that were used in the shooting. He tossed them in a bag and put it and a five-gallon container of gas into the Mazda B2000 and drove it to Mont St-Bruno. He then torched everything "to get rid of the evidence."

The day after the murder, Normand Robitaille paid a visit to Stéphane Gagné, handed him $5,000 and advised him to take a vacation in western Canada. But later that same day, Fontaine advised him to take his family to the Dominican Republic to create a cover story about his burned face. If anyone asked, Gagné could claim it was from a sunburn. When he returned from the vacation, Gagné and Fontaine headed for the Pro Gym to see Boucher who was busy with his regular training routine. They left their pagers and cell phones with Normand Robitaille who followed them in his car from a distance. At that time Robitaille was just months shy of getting his prospect patch in the Nomads chapter.

At first, they all made small talk. Gagné recalled that Boucher joked about the fact he had brought his wife along for the vacation. But then things got serious. Boucher said, "You know, my man, we erase and we start over again." He was likely referring to Gagné's screw-up of getting burnt. Boucher then said they had to be subtle when they talked because the ears of the police were everywhere. Gagné said it was then that Boucher explained that he was having prison guards killed by particular people in part to assure that his closest associates would never become informants. Boucher figured that no one in law enforcement would want to deal with men who had killed prison guards. Boucher repeated that if the death penalty existed in Canada, Gagné would be executed for what he had done. To emphasize his point, Boucher mimicked a person hanging from a gallows pole.

By now, Boucher had learned how far Quebec's criminal justice system was willing to go to get at the members of the Nomads chapter. A career criminal named Serge Quesnel had turned informant, and there was a wave of followers who had been nabbed for serious crimes like murder and were looking to get lenient sentences. Gagné noted that Quesnel had been given only 12 years for the five murders he had admitted to carrying out for Louis (Melou) Roy and other Hells Angels. Boucher figured cops and prosecutors cared little if an informant had racked up a body count of drug dealers, but they would never accept dealing with someone cold-blooded enough to pull the trigger on one of their own.

At this point in Gagné's testimony, Crown prosecutor François Briere asked if there were other targets discussed. Gagné said that Boucher once told him that they were "going to do other screws." Gagné said he pointed out to Boucher that prison guards were now being escorted home by members of the Sûreté du Québec. Boucher scoffed at it and said that, if need be, they'd start killing police officers, judges and prosecutors.

By now, paranoia had set in within the highest levels of the

Hells Angels. Normand Robitaille ordered that all the people working under him supply personal information like social insurance numbers and lists of relatives on the assumption that this would ensure their loyalty if they were ever arrested. Gagné complied with the order.

"In the days that followed [the Rondeau murder] I was paged by André Tousignant. He asked me if I was occupied. He asked me to join him at the Imprevu Bar on Sainte-Catherine and Pie-IX," Gagné said. (In previous testimony, Gagné had said Tousignant asked this of him on the same day as the Rondeau murder, despite the fact his face was burned.) Tousignant asked him to buy a large quantity of bolts and gave him $100. Gagné said he went shopping at a big-box home renovation store and brought along his wife and three-year-old son. He brought the bolts to Tousignant who took a look at the package and quickly said there weren't enough. Gagné said Tousignant gave him another $100 and sent him to do the same chore. Gagné went to a different renovation store the second time, he said, to avoid arousing attention. Again he brought his wife and kid.

While testifying at the Beliveau trial, Stéphane Gagné was shown security tape images of him, his wife and kids, in one of the hardware stores and he agreed that it was indeed him. He said he paid cash, both times using the "browns," $100 bills, that Tousignant had supplied him with. The hardware was to be used as shrapnel in a powerful bomb the Hells Angels hoped to use on several members of the Rock Machine.

The Hells Angels had somehow learned that lawyer Gilles Thibault had been renting a conference room in his office building to members of the Rock Machine. On October 30, 1997, Thibault asked his secretary to move some boxes out of the conference room because he was going to use it for an interview with a French-language television network. While she was moving the boxes, the secretary got the surprise of her life. She had stumbled upon a bomb with 130 sticks of dynamite that weighed about 20 kilograms. It contained a battery-operated detonator that could be activated by a pager. The police also found the nine kilos of hardware Gagné had purchased, along with the receipt that someone had left among the bolts.

The left-behind receipt was an expensive error because it eventually led the police to Gagné as they investigated the origins of the unexploded bomb. They tracked down the store from which it had originated. Another convenient detail from the receipt was the date and time when Gagné had purchased the hardware. When they went to the store, the police discovered it still had the security tapes from the day Gagné had made the purchase.

The Crown asked Gagné if he was ever asked about the receipt he had been given when he purchased some of the nails. "After a while," Gagné responded, "about two or three weeks later, André Tousignant told me it was possible that I would be arrested by the police because they had found the receipt. It was inside the office of a lawyer with dynamite and the bolts."

Despite the heat that was now on Gagné, the Lavigne murder had put him square on a path toward membership in the Rockers.

Early on in his testimony, Gagné was asked if he knew what the Rockers were. The question prompted one of the many time-wasting objections from the defense that marred the trial throughout. It was François Taddeo who made the objection, saying Gagné was not considered an expert on the Rockers. Judge Beliveau quickly dismissed the objection saying that even if he was not an expert on Place Ville Marie he had been inside the building and could talk about it. Beliveau, who had been remarkably patient with the defense throughout the trial, asked Gagné to continue.

"I was part of the organization. I was a striker in the Rockers, and before that I was a hangaround in the Rockers. It is a biker gang that is affiliated with the Hells Angels' Nomads [chapter],"

Gagné said, adding later that he was made a hangaround in May 1997. On August 21, 1997, he got his patch making him a striker in the Rockers. He was handed a leather jacket that had a patch with the word Montreal written on it. But the Rockers' menacing logo was absent. Only full-fledged members get those.

"It happened at the Shogun [restaurant] in the South Shore. It was Jean-Guy Bourgoin's birthday. Jean-Guy Bourgoin is the vice-president of the Rockers. In general, we receive our patches during a party for one of our members. So that was it. We were partying that night. It was Boteau — that is Daniel Lanthier, the president of the club, the Rockers — it was him who asked if I was willing to do something special for them. I said I was ready to do anything to become a member. They said, 'You will have something special, you have become a striker.' That night I could have a drink because generally when you go out, you're not a member and you can't drink. Members can drink and you are there to do surveillance." Gagné rattled off a list of who was also there that night. Kenny Bedard was present and was a striker at

Ronald (Popo) Paulin (seated, far left) with other members of the Rockers.

that point. Richard (Sugar) Lock was the gang's secretary treasurer, and René Charlebois was sergeant at arms. Guillaume Serra and Ronald Paulin (one of the Rockers on trial in the Beliveau case) were at the restaurant as well, and Paul Fontaine joined them later on.

Briere asked questions about specific people in the Hells Angels' organization whom Gagné had dealt with. In particular, Gagné was asked about Normand Robitaille. The question opened a door that made the trial almost surreal. Gagné began to talk about how the Hells Angels allegedly plotted to kill lawyer Pierre Panaccio who was at that very moment representing Richard (Dick) Mayrand, the highest ranking member of the gang in the Beliveau trial. Gagné said that shortly before he himself was arrested, he was at Robitaille's home when someone in the gang talked of "doing Pinocchio," the nickname the gang used for Panaccio.

Gagné testified that the following morning he and Robitaille went to Panaccio's office. Robitaille explained to Gagné that the issue was money. Panaccio had defended Pierre Provencher and Stephen Falls in a case, but they didn't want his services anymore and had asked Leo René Maranda to represent them instead. Panaccio wanted to keep the $15,000 he had been paid up front, but the Rockers felt he should get only part of it. Gagné said Robitaille had already gone to the office with Boucher, but they did not hear the answer they wanted. After that, they decided to kill him.

Gagné started to talk about the visit he and Robitaille paid to Panaccio's office. At this point, Panaccio objected, and Beliveau asked the Crown what the pertinence of the event was to the trial. Briere argued it had the same weight as the prison guards. Although the defendants in the Beliveau case weren't charged with killing the guards, Gagné could testify about the murders because it was pertinent to proving gangsterism charges.

"That they could kill me or not, what pertinence does it have here?" said Panaccio, uttering a question no defense lawyer would ever dream of having to ask in court. Judge Beliveau agreed and cautioned prosecutor Briere that it seemed "very far" from the testimony given earlier that day — and he said it was disagreeable for everyone involved.

Gagné was only able to tell the jury that he didn't know what happened with the plans to kill Panaccio because he was arrested early on in the conspiracy. To wrap up Gagné's testimony, Briere asked him why he had decided to become an informant. His arrest, Gagné replied, had come at the end of a very busy day.

The Big Party

Considering that December 5, 1997, was the 20th anniversary of the Hells Angels' Montreal chapter, the one Boucher began his career as a biker in, it is ironic to look back and see that Gagné's arrest on that day would begin Mom's downfall.

The Hells Angels had a huge party planned in Sorel where dozens of members were expected to attend. Gagné began the morning preparing things for the party at the Rockers' hangout on Gilford Street in Montreal. He had fallen asleep and was awoken by a phone call from Boucher at around 6 a.m. Boucher told him, "Yeah, come meet me at our place in Sorel."

Gagné told Boucher he had already been ordered by someone else to go to the airport to pick up Hells Angels from outside Quebec as they arrived for the party by plane. Boucher responded by ordering Gagné to find a replacement for his airport duties and then come to his house on the South Shore with Tousignant. After the conversation, Gagné and Tousignant headed to Boucher's home in Contrécoeur. At Boucher's home, Gagné and Tousignant were told they would be handling security at the Sorel bunker. They were supposed to ride in a helicopter looking out for any signs that the Rock Machine intended to attack the building packed with Hells Angels. There was a snowstorm that day and the helicopter was grounded, so Gagné's assignment was canceled again. While they were in Sorel, Gagné was riding with Boucher in a Dodge Ram. The police presence was heavy around the bunker and many vehicles carrying Hells Angels were being pulled over so the police could identify them.

Gagné would testify in Boucher's first trial that Boucher had made reference to the authorities being on to Gagné for the prison guard murders. But Boucher added that it wasn't serious because he had something "dirty" prepared for the cops. He also advised Gagné to be careful, saying, "Pay attention if those guys . . . they are following you because they could try to kill you, you know."

What Boucher apparently did not know is that the police already had a plan in the works. After leaving the party in Sorel, Gagné headed to his mother-in-law's to pick up his kid. He was with his wife when the police arrested them both at around 10 p.m. that day.

"I was arrested on December 5. They accused me of attempted murder. But before that, when I was arrested, they said, 'Don't move'; they put my hands behind my back and said I was arrested for the attempted murder of Christian Bellemare. They brought me to a police station in Joliette. At the police station in Joliette, when they were transferring me to Parthenais, the SQ [headquarters] in Montreal, one of the two guys in the vehicle said, 'There are two other things coming and you know what we're talking about.'"

"And that guy was?" Briere asked.

"I imagine he was an investigator because he was a police officer. He was in plain clothes. So I knew he was talking about the murder of the two prison guards. I said nothing. I got into the car. We got to Parthenais and there was an investigator who showed up. He said 'We know each other, you and I. We already did business together.' I said I never did business with the police. I didn't know it then, but it was the double agent I had sold powder to in 1994. It was Robert Pigeon [a Sûreté Du Québec investigator]. He accused me of attempted murder on Christian Bellemare. He asked me questions and I said I had nothing to say, things like that. Sometimes he would change the subject and I would say silly things as answers. It lasted a while until at one point he said that Steve Boies had become an informant. He went out and then came back in and told me I was accused of the murder of the two prison guards. So I asked to speak to my lawyers. I had already spoken to them, but now I wanted to tell them I was accused of murder."

"You're talking about the murder of who now?"

"The murders of the two prison guards. I tried to reach the lawyers. I called and told the secretary to have Benoît Cliche call me. He didn't call me because he had come in late. After that I tried to call Gilbert Frigon. Those were the lawyers working for the Hells Angels, for us. He didn't call me. He didn't call me. I knew that Steve Boies had become an informant and there were other things that had happened before."

Gagné said that at that point in his interrogation he remembered several things that made him feel cornered. His wife was being detained in the same building. This was yet another bargaining chip the police had. She had been arrested with Gagné, and one of the officers who had put them in cuffs had said that she was an accomplice in the attempt to murder Bellemare. Gagné said he worried about her security and that of his son. Gagné said that, as far as he was concerned, his wife was not an accomplice — but then he recalled that she had rented him a motel room while he was on the run after he tried to kill Bellemare.

Gagné went on to explain that Fontaine was supposed to do the murder of Lavigne with Tousignant, but Fontaine had refused, apparently bringing him down several notches in Boucher's opinion. Fontaine was frustrated afterward and he let Gagné know it, saying he hadn't got his patch with the Hells

Angels because he hadn't participated in the Lavigne murder.

"After my arrest, when the investigator told me that Steve Boies was an informant, I asked to see the cassette. In effect, Steve Boies was talking about me," Gagné said.

"When I did [Diane] Lavigne, it was Paul Fontaine who was supposed to do it. After that, I was in a motorcycle accident. But just before the bike accident, we went to Saint-Marguerite, me and Paul Fontaine because it was the anniversary of the Trois Rivières chapter, on July 1." Gagné said he and Fontaine were doing guard duty for members of the Hells Angels. They had stopped in Saint-Sauveur to fuel up their motorcycles when Fontaine told Gagné he wanted to go for a walk.

"Paul Fontaine took off his pager and I took off my pager and we went for a walk. He told me he had met Mom Boucher earlier that day and that he was not going to get this [Gagné said, motioning to the lower part of his back]. He was talking about his bottom [patch] as prospect because he didn't [kill Lavigne]." Gagné said that when he got out of the hospital he discussed the situation with André Tousignant. A meeting was called. In attendance were Maurice (Mom) Boucher, Denis Houle, Gilles (Trooper) Mathieu, Normand (Biff) Hamel, Normand Robitaille

From top left to right: Michel Rose, Donald (Pup) Stockford, Gilles (Trooper) Mathieu, Richard (Dick) Mayrand, Denis Houle, David (Wolf) Carroll. From bottom left to right: Walter (Nurget) Stadnick, René Charlebois, Normand Robitaille, Maurice (Mom) Boucher.

and Paul Fontaine. At the meeting, Fontaine admitted to his comments to Gagné. Since he had exposed Fontaine in this way, Gagné figured, Fontaine already had a grudge against him and would likely give him little financial support in fighting two first-degree murder charges.

Gagné said he also started to think that if he didn't turn informant, Fontaine was going to kill him. He said that Boucher had at one point specifically asked who else knew of the murder that Gagné and Fontaine had committed together. "So it was there, when the police were asking me all these questions and I wasn't answering I thought of those events in my head. It was there that I changed sides, that I became an informant."

Switching Sides — Not So Simple

Gagné would be cross-examined by some of the defense lawyers in the Beliveau trial. They attacked his credibility but appeared to have little success. In fact, some of the cross-examination only opened new doors for Gagné to provide more incriminating information. Defense lawyer Guy Quirion, who represented Rocker Éric (Pif) Fournier, started the cross-examination by bringing up the history of Gagné's testimony in Boucher's two murder trials as well as his testimony in the trial overseen by Justice Jean-Guy Boilard which was scrapped.

"Does it happen that you make up some details while recalling events?" Quirion asked.

"No."

Quirion brought up a previous statement Gagné had given concerning a truck that was going to be used in one of the aborted attempts to bomb the Rock Machine hangout in Verdun. Gagné had told the police that he had dumped the truck at the Place Versailles shopping center but that Tousignant had forgotten to remove the large quantity of dynamite inside it. Tousignant asked Gagné to go back and get the vehicle but Gagné had refused.

"Well, yeah I refused. It was obvious. I had parked it at Place Versailles and I explained it to Toots. I said, 'Look, I dumped the truck at Place Versailles shopping center around 10 or 11 in the parking lot. The truck was left there and there is dynamite inside. So I'm sure someone has called the police to see why the truck was still parked there.' That is what happens in shopping centers. Leave your car there, and see what happens. You're going to get a call. And there was dynamite. If the police saw that it was a stolen truck they might leave it there and then spot me when I get into it, with that dynamite, and they would arrest me," Gagné said.

Quirion brought this up to make the point that underlings could refuse orders from the higher-ups in the gang. He suggested that Gagné conveniently forgot to mention this during a trial where it would challenge the theory of how the gang works. But the question did not faze Gagné in the least. In fact, he appeared to turn it to his favor. He countered that it was only logical to turn down such a ridiculous assignment.

"I'd be better off calling the police and saying, 'Hey I left a truck there. Come arrest me,'" Gagné said, which caused many people in the courtroom to laugh.

But still, Quirion appeared to score small points. He got Gagné to admit he had trouble recalling little details, just like anyone else might. He also got Gagné to admit that when Boucher was plotting to level the Rock Machine hangout he gave strict instructions that no civilians should be hurt, something Gagné had left out of his earlier testimony.

But Quirion's questions also opened a few doors that had not been pursued by the Crown. In responding to one question, Gagné revealed that during the time the Hells Angels were trying to kill prison guards, he was at the Imprevu Bar with René Charlebois and Normand Robitaille. He said someone was asked to turn up the volume on a television to hear a news story about a man who had been shot just as he left a prison in Laval.

Robitaille and Charlebois appeared happy because it appeared that a prison guard had been killed, Gagné said. "But when it turned out that the guy was still alive and was not a prison guard, they were no longer in a good mood." This was in reference to an incident on June 28, 1997. The group leader of an Alcoholics Anonymous meeting was shot as he came out of the Montée St-François Institution in Laval. The police would later learn that the man drove a car very similar to one driven by a prison guard at the federal penitentiary. Charlebois and Robitaille were never charged with the attempted murder.

Quirion asked Gagné about the moment he decided to become an informant. Gagné admitted that he didn't tell the police everything right away. He said that during this first 45 minutes of spilling his guts, he told the police about Lavigne, Rondeau, Christian Bellemare and the escape of Richard Vallée, a member of the Nomads chapter. Vallée had been sprung from a Montreal hospital room on June 5, 1997, while he was under tight guard, awaiting a possible extradition to the U.S. He had been charged in a northern New York court with murdering a man named Lee Carter. On July 29, 1993, Carter was killed after a bomb placed under the driver's seat of his car went off as he started the engine. Carter's death and the possible extradition meant the Sûreté du Québec had to drop drug trafficking charges against Vallée.

Richard Vallée, a founding member of the Nomads chapter.

When Serge Quesnel turned informant, he told the police that Vallée had made comments to him about Carter's death, and he was able to describe the bomb that killed him in detail. Carter had tipped off the New York State Police and the U.S. Customs

Service about a drug smuggling operation he was asked to help out with in 1992. He was willing to testify that Vallée had conspired to smuggle 54 kilograms of cocaine into Canada through the U.S. border, but he was murdered before he could.

After being on the RCMP's most-wanted list for six years, Vallée was arrested in Montreal in April 2003 after having undergone plastic surgery to his face. His brazen escape from the hospital six years earlier was still a mystery to the police but Gagné had managed to give the police some clues as to who was involved. Quirion pointed out that it took Gagné a while to tell the police what he knew about Vallée's escape and tried to portray him as a liar.

But the experienced witness didn't take the bait. Gagné openly admitted to lying throughout his life, something any juror could understand was part of the life of being a career criminal. Gagné said gangsters lie about everything, and added that by the age of 13 he was already a frequent liar. He admitted to lying to get welfare and about cutting down cocaine that he sold to make $2,000 more off a $32,000 kilo of coke. The day ended with the defense failing to score any major blows, and the jury headed home for the weekend, their heads full of days worth of Crown testimony from Gagné.

With a fresh start the following Monday, Quirion took a new approach. He brought up a statement Gagné had made to the effect that criminals don't lie to each other, that there is honor among thieves. The defense lawyer then asked why if there is such honor, Gagné would have turned so harshly on his former partner Tony Jalbert to the point of wanting to see him dead — he had given Jalbert's address and licence number to Maurice (Mom) Boucher.

Quirion's questions began to sound familiar to Gagné. He had answered several of them before. Quirion brought up the fact that Gagné had told the provincial parole board in 1994 that he wanted out of the criminal world because he wanted to take care of his family. He also told the parole board that he dealt drugs because his wife was pregnant.

"I wasn't going to say, 'I want to sell drugs and become a Hells Angel and make lots of money dealing in drugs.' [The parole board] would have said, 'Well, you go back to prison,'" Gagné explained. "When I started to sell drugs and I saw that it was profitable, my goal was to become a big boss in drugs." At this point, Gagné realized where his déjà vu was coming from and turned the tables on Quirion, accusing him of merely repeating the same questions asked by Jacques Larochelle, one of Québec's best defense attorneys, during Boucher's two murder trials. Gagné's allegation that Quirion was liberally borrowing from Larochelle's work drew a few laughs in the courtroom.

An Experienced Criminal

Unfazed, Quirion dug in his heels and started asking tougher questions and brought up Gagné's violent past. If he couldn't make him look like a liar on the stand, he could at least show how Gagné was a violent thug. Quirion brought up details like how he had beaten a prostitute because she had stolen from a dealer of his who had fallen asleep. After soundly beating the woman, Gagné dragged her around by her hair.

"Look," Gagné replied, "in the milieu, if you let that kind of thing go, all the druggie girls are going to steal from you. They'll think, 'there's no problem with it.'"

Quirion also scored points when he got Gagné to admit he lied to penitentiary officials to get into a medium-security penitentiary in the early 1990s because he wanted to avoid doing time with possible snitches. Gagné had learned from others that dealing drugs in a minimum-security penitentiary is difficult because that is where so many snitches end up.

"Ah, because your intention was to sell drugs, even though you were in prison?" Quirion asked.

"Yes," Gagné replied. Gagné had also lied about the number of cars he had stolen in his life, to ensure he got into medium security. But it came back to slap him in the face and corrections officials grilled him on it. So, to cover that up, he made up a story that a police officer had advised him to lie to get into medium security.

But Gagné also made it clear that life in the penitentiary system is another world, where inmates lie frequently to manipulate the quality of their lives. He recounted how he once got himself tossed in "the hole" in order to meet up with someone who was smuggling drugs for him inside his body. Gagné said that to accomplish this he started screaming at a guard, accusing him of incest and sleeping with his children. The trick worked. Gagné admitted to acting like a mentally challenged person because he wanted to appear "like a guy who wasn't too bright." But his parole officer noticed the psychologist's test in Gagné's file afterward and made sure to point out to the parole board that the results did not jibe with what he knew of Gagné.

Quirion also tried to bring up a new motive for the prison guard murders and asked questions that suggested Gagné hated prison guards long before he joined the Rockers. Gagné admitted to having once thrown a homemade bomb at a prison guard; he seemed even a little proud of his creation. "Yes. It was with a battery. You take a battery, you take out all of the inside. You take matches and crush them until they become nothing but powder. You mix this together and you wrap it in Saran Wrap. You stick a rolling paper in it and put your powder inside. Then you light it. Sometimes it will go *pssst* . . . Or sometimes it'll go POW! Like a gunshot." Gagné also admitted to hitting a female guard who had grabbed him by the throat during a cell search.

Then Quirion brought up another infamous detail that had come from a previous trial. Gagné called it the shit-pen. He said he came up with the idea when members of the Rock Machine were being walked right past his cell and those of other inmates who sided with the Hells Angels in the war. Gagné said that at the time, inmates could purchase large bottles of shampoo from the prison cantine. At first, Gagné just used water to spray the Rock Machine inmates who passed by. He said that he and other inmates then decided to urinate and defecate into a tobacco can. They left the mess to ferment in the can for a week and then transferred the liquid into the shampoo bottle. Gagné said he sprayed Rock Machine members with it and ended up splattering the guards as well. Again, instead of being ashamed of his actions, Gagné laughed as he told the story.

Prepared for the Stand

Defense lawyer Quirion then zeroed in on a moment in the trial that had seen Boucher acquitted of the prison guard murders. Larochelle had gotten Gagné to agree that he had no scruples and lied often to get what he wanted. Gagné told the jury in the Beliveau trial that he had been referring to his life before he had been arrested in 1997. He was better prepared to answer the question this time around. That brought Quirion to his next line of questioning. He got Gagné to openly discuss how he had been prepared as a Crown witness.

"What we do is the police officers act like defense lawyers. They ask me questions," Gagné said.

"This was where?"

"It was in a room. There was a desk. What we would do was the intercom was the judge or jury. There was a little intercom. The police officers acted like defense lawyers. They took notes, they talked."

"Am I right in saying that one acted as a Crown and another as the defense?"

"No, both acted as the defense."

"Both were the defense?"

"Yes, and they would say things like [clearing his throat in an exaggerated manner], 'Is it not true that after . . .' and they would ask me all kinds of questions. I would answer." His imitation of the police acting as defense lawyers drew laughter in the courtroom. Gagné said the preparation took place over at least a few days. He was given a book. It was from a police-training course and had been written by a Crown prosecutor. The book warned that defense lawyers will ask suggestive questions, and it is dangerous to answer them. Quirion then asked if Gagné was coached on how to address contradictions in his testimony. At this point, Gagné got a little frustrated.

"You want to know who taught me how to testify? It was Jacques Larochelle [in the Boucher trials] during my testimony. He's really good," Gagné said. By now, he was drawing howls of laughter in the courtroom.

Quirion tried a different tack, asking if Gagné was coached by the police to bring up the contract on Panaccio during this trial. He claimed that he wasn't. Well, said Quirion, had Gagné helped the Hells Angels plot to kill other lawyers? Gagné admitted that he once did surveillance on Gilles Daudelin, an attorney who had represented several bikers. He said Fontaine later told him that any plans the Hells Angels had for Daudelin had been called off.

The defense lawyer found it curious that Gagné could remember things that suddenly applied to the trial he was about to testify in and accused him of having a selective memory. Gagné said that it was difficult for him to consider all the conspiracies he was privy to or all the crimes he had been part of.

"Look, even Michel Auger is included in that," Gagné said in reference to *Journal de Montréal* crime reporter Michel Auger, a veteran journalist who broke many stories about the biker war. Auger was shot in September 2000 while he was in the newspaper's parking lot. The attack came shortly after he had written a group of stories shedding new light on recent developments in the biker war, in particular the loan-sharking scene. He survived the attempt on his life and eventually returned to writing for the newspaper, continuing to follow organized crime, including the Hells Angels.

The man who manufactured the firearm used in the attempt on Auger had ties to the Hells Angels. Later on, two people tied to Quebec's licence bureau were arrested for selling information to Jean-Guy Bourgoin, a longtime member of the Rockers. Included among the list of people Bourgoin had requested information on were several members of the Rock Machine and Auger. Now Gagné was providing even more information that pointed toward the Hells Angels having a role in the shooting.

"What? Michel Auger?" Quirion asked, seeming surprised.

"Yes."

"You have knowledge of this?"

"Yes, I even called Michel Auger to tell him we were supposed to kill him." This was something Gagné had done after he turned informant.

"You knew this?"

"Yes."

At that moment, Judge Beliveau called for a break. When the jury returned, Crown prosecutor Briere used the opportunity to make a few things clear to them. He pointed out that Gagné had mentioned the plots on the lawyers' lives in his previous statements to the police. Beliveau also told the jury that it was normal for any good lawyer to prepare a witness to testify. After a while, Gagné's cross-examination testimony touched again on what the Hells Angels had planned for journalist Michel Auger.

"We were at the courthouse the first time we talked about it. [Auger] had come out of a courtroom. So then André Chouinard said, 'Do you know Auger?' I said, 'No . . .' I looked at his face. [Chouinard] said, 'It's possible that we're going to do him.' Paul Fontaine also told me that once we had Auger's address, we were going to do him."

Perhaps realizing that he had opened a door that wasn't help-ing his clients, defense lawyer Quirion then switched to Gagné's attempt to kill drug dealer Christian Bellemare, the crime that actually led to Gagné becoming an informant. Gagné said the Hells Angels had no problem with Bellemare being killed because he had started to owe people money so he had started buying drugs from the Rock Machine to get out of debt. Gagné said he also learned that Bellemare had cloned the Rockers' cell phones, which he would use while the gang paid the bills.

"I told Paul [Fontaine] to get rid of him because I didn't need him to open *piqueries*. I was capable of opening them. Whether it is in the Gay Village or Hochelaga Maisonneuve it doesn't take long to do it. It is not very hard. You rent a place and you put in a drug dealer. After that you ride around Ontario Street or in the Gay Village and when you see the prostitutes on the sidewalk you stop and you give them the address and you say, 'go to this place.' In the milieu we called it doing PR. The girls go and they see that the drugs are good. It's certain she will return and tell her friend and that friend will tell another."

It was during the cross-examination that Gagné brought up more chilling details of the plot to kill Bellemare. He had met Bellemare at a restaurant and told him the Rockers were interested in setting up hydroponic equipment in a house to grow marijuana. Bellemare agreed to make the trip up north with Gagné and Steven Boies. Gagné said he drove Bellemare and Boies up north at a careful speed because there was a heavy snowfall that day. He even managed to stop to fuel up and change his windshield wipers, although he was a little concerned that Bellemare was about to bolt from the car. Gagné's testimony suggested that Bellemare knew he was doomed.

"When we got to Des Hauteurs Road I asked Steve Boies to lower the heat because it was too hot. Bellemare said, 'I'm a lot hotter than you guys.'" When they stopped where Gagné had claimed the marijuana-growing operation would be set up, Bellemare got out of the car and ran. Gagné said he and Boies opened fire on Bellemare and he fell to the snow-covered ground. They walked up to Bellemare and Gagné could see their target was bleeding from at least two bullet wounds. Boies then put a revolver to the back of Bellemare's head and fired. The shot, strangely, was not fatal.

As Bellemare lay on the ground bleeding from his wounds, he asked Gagné why they had shot him. Gagné said he replied by strangling Bellemare. While Gagné strangled the wounded man, Boies proceeded to kick Bellemare. They then heard Bellemare gasp and assumed he was dead. They were wrong. Bellemare regained conciousness. Somehow, he was able to find help and was willing to talk to the police.

After the attempted hit on Bellemare, Gagné burned the clothes they used that day in his fireplace. He then took the firearm he had used and dumped it in a river. He sent someone to Bellemare's house to collect any money that was there. He and Boies went into hiding, but were back on the streets in a matter of weeks.

Quirion then asked about the murder of Diane Lavigne. He asked Gagné to repeat if he knew whether she was a woman at the time of the murder. Gagné repeated that he did not know. He said the windows of the vehicle were tinted.

"Concerning this murder, do you have any remorse?" Quirion asked.

"Now? Yes."

"Since when?"

"It's been some time now with the psychologist and all that. With all the murders and all the things I did. If I could start my life again. At the age of 13, I wouldn't sell drugs. I would finish my studies and . . . it wouldn't be the same," Gagné said, adding that in 1999, a psychologist found that Gagné did indeed feel remorse but had a long way to go.

The question of an informant's remorse in any case before a jury inevitably brings up his contract with the police. Gagne was asked about the list of demands that he prepared for the controller committee who handled his contract. Gagné had asked to do his time in a provincial prison like other informants. He wanted to be able to have family visits in a mobile home during weekends. Gagné said he asked to be paid $500 per week while he was in prison because it was the same amount Serge Quesnel had received after turning informant. He had also asked that his wife and son have their identities changed and he negotiated for $400 a week for his family, which they received until his wife left him. On top of his salary, Gagné said he was getting $140 per month for his cantine. Authorities had agreed to change his appearance upon his release from prison. Following release, he is also supposed to be paid $400 a week for two years.

"They told me, 'You are going to get a life sentence, 25 years, murder in the first degree.' So I said, 'What do I get out of being an informant?' [Crown prosecutor André Vincent] said, 'Well look, we'll withdraw one of the charges because the law had changed,'" Gagné said. Vincent had been referring to Canada's "faint-hope clause," where people convicted of murder could have their cases reviewed after serving 15 years and see a chance of parole. Those with two first-degree murders on their hands do not get this opportunity.

Quirion asked Gagné whether he had asked to receive the $100,000 reward for information that led to the arrest of a suspect in the prison guard murders.

"You have to do it like that," Gagné explained. "I knew that Steve Boies had already asked about it. When I was asking for things like $500 a week, they were saying you're not going to get this and you're not going to get that. So I said, 'If you're not going to pay me the $500 per week like you did with Quesnel, give me the $100,000.' They said, 'We're not going to give you the $100,000.

You were the murderer.'"

"What was their reaction? They must have laughed in your face. You were asking for $100,000 for a murder you had committed. There must have been an explosion of laughter from the controller committee when you said that," Quirion said. Gagné replied that they didn't laugh but rather explained why they couldn't pay it.

"You didn't reflect a little bit in your head? It was before the events of September 11th in the United States. Was it not like if [Osama] Bin Laden showed up in the States and said, 'Do you want to give me the $25 million you promised?'"

"There is a huge difference between me and Bin Laden," Gagné stated.

"A difference between $100,000 and $25 million, eh? That's the difference to you," Quirion said in a tone that did nothing to conceal his contempt. Gagné replied that he didn't consider himself a terrorist. "When you sign a contract, at the base of it all, you really haven't repented. You're still a criminal," Gagné said.

"It takes time, to change mentality and a way of thinking," Quirion prompted.

"Well look. It had been 18 days since I had been arrested," Gagné pointed out. "Not even 18 days. I was arrested on [December 5, 1997]. From the 6th to the 18th is not a long time."

"So your mentality hasn't changed?"

"I still have things to work on. It is evident. When you go as far as committing murder . . . you have to consider . . . Like my psychologist said, I will have to work on me for the rest of my life. It is very evident, and I am very conscious of that. I made efforts and I have efforts to make to change."

Gagné was also cross-examined by other lawyers but with little consequence. For the most part, the other defense lawyers let Gagné portray himself as a victim who was ultimately not getting a sweet deal out of testifying in all the Hells Angels' trials.

Gagné said he assumed it won't be easy to get parole, even after he has served 15 years under the faint-hope clause. He said he lives his life in constant stress because he worries about possible attacks where he would have to defend himself. Gagné said that once, through an error, he was stuck with another inmate, and it was lucky the inmate didn't have a shiv or he would have had to defend himself. To press his point, Gagné brought up what happened to Aimé Simard.

Aimé Simard, an associate of the Rockers who turned informant.

Simard, a former associate of the Rockers, had turned informant in 1996 and admitted to being a hit man for the gang. His most important trial as a witness ended in the acquittal of five members of the Rockers, and Simard went on to become a public thorn in the side for the authorities. His contract was revoked in 1999 after he threatened another inmate and Simard was left to fend for himself in the federal penitentiary system. Despite this, he had a contract to testify in the Nova Scotia trial of a man tied to the Hells Angels, which was scheduled to begin sometime in 2004. Simard never got to testify. He was stabbed more than 100 times his cell in Saskatchewan Penitentiary and died in July 2003.

During his cross-examination by François Bordeleau, Gagné talked of how he was getting sick of testifying in trials. He said he protested when he learned he was expected to testify in the megatrials but was told that he had a contract he had to honor. "I'm fed up with this. It doesn't do me any good to be here. Journalists talk about me and my picture appears in the papers," Gagné said, sounding tired. "And because my photo is in the papers, guys I don't even know throw shit in my wing and tell me they are going to kill me."

10

Serge Boutin: Nowhere to Go But Out

Although he was named in the arrest warrants, Serge Boutin wasn't picked up at home when the police carried out Operation Springtime 2001. He was already in a provincial detention center staring down the possibility of serving a life sentence for helping the Hells Angels kill a police informant. The full-patch Rocker had already spent more than a year waiting for a trial, and now his problems were piling higher. Despite spending the past year in custody, he was named in several of the charges filed in Operation Springtime 2001.

For years, Boutin had dealt drugs in places like the Gay Village and the Hochelaga Maisonneuve district, but he had only once been picked up for a drug-related offence. But in January 1997, he was picked up for more serious charges: he was a suspect in the 1994 plot to kill Maurice (Mom) Boucher with a truck bomb. Not only did he get off on the charge, on May 16, 1997, he managed to become a full-patch member of the Rockers in October 1999. He would later describe his decision to join the Rockers as a part of doing business, devoid of any loyalty to the gang beyond making money as partners.

The Business of Surviving

Becoming an informant seemed to Serge Boutin to be the next

logical step in his life because, at that point, the issue was survival. During February 2000, Boutin helped lure Claude De Serres, a man who was working undercover for the Wolverine squad, to a chalet in the Laurentians. De Serres handled marijuana for Boutin. But the Hells Angels learned that he was working for the police after reading a general description of him contained in a confidential document stored in a laptop stolen from the hotel room of an Ontario Provincial Police investigator. Boutin was not the one who would kill De Serres, but he knew who was involved in the murder plot. Months after his fellow gang members were rounded up, Boutin began to feel like a target. So the same survival instincts that had convinced him to join the Rockers were now telling him to leave.

As his testimony would reveal, Boutin was first and foremost a businessman, so his loyalty to the Rockers was as easy to drop as a used tissue. Joining the Rockers was all about money for Boutin, but now there was none to be made, so the smart move was to turn his back on them and become an informant. His first test as a witness was at Boucher's second trial for the murder of the prison guards, the one that saw the gang leader convicted.

On September 17, 2003, he took the stand in the trial overseen by Judge Beliveau. Prosecutor Madeleine Giauque decided to start off his testimony by letting the jury know Boutin was no angel.

"Why were you arrested on February 16, 2000?" Giauque asked early on in Boutin's testimony.

"Murder. Murder of an *agent source* [double agent]."

"And the name of that *agent source*?"

"Claude De Serres." Boutin went on to explain how he was behind bars on March 28, 2001, when Operation Springtime 2001 was carried out. He decided to become an informant less than two months later, on May 5, 2001, and by September 27 of that same year, he signed informant contract PB1070. As part of his agreement with the police he managed to plead guilty, on October 22,

2001, to conspiracy to commit murder and manslaughter in De Serres' death, avoiding the first-degree murder charge he had faced before. Boutin still received a life sentence but would be eligible for day parole by 2004 and full parole by 2007.

Despite the fact that he had been a drug dealer most of his adult life and had sold countless kilos of cocaine for the Hells Angels, he did not have to plead guilty to those charges. When Boutin testified in the Beliveau trial, he talked about selling cocaine the way a proud car salesman might.

By the age of 23, Boutin had become heavily involved in drug trafficking. "I don't know if I should say whether I was good, not good or extremely good, but let's say I was in it for ten years and the only case against me is one where they convicted me for selling a gram or two. I never sold a gram in my life. I dealt in kilos. So I think you could say I wasn't bad," Boutin boasted. Playing along with Boutin's braggart manner, Giauque asked if he was able to deal in kilos right from the start. Boutin described his quick ascent up the drug dealer food chain after only six months of dealing on the streets.

"I started out by buying a three-and-a-half ball. Three and a half, that's three and a half grams. I moved up to seven grams, doubled that to fourteen grams, to 112 [grams], up to the point mathematically where I reached a kilogram."

Giauque then asked where he got his drugs from early on in his career.

"At that time, when I was 23, there wasn't a biker war. It was pretty much independent. Everyone knew each other and everybody bought from each other. We bought from whoever had the best price and whoever could supply it," he said. Boutin went on to explain that almost right away he understood the key to making money dealing in cocaine at the street level was in how carefully you "cut it" or dilute the drug in order to increase the quantity. He considered it his specialty.

"Did you sell it pure?" Giauque asked.

"It depends on the place where it is sold. There are clients where it has to be more pure than with others. If your client is a tavern or an after-hours [bar] then it can be more cut. I started at 23. What placed me in the criminal world was my first after hours [bar]. It was well known." Boutin said that at the height of his years as a coke dealer, he had about 100 employees working for him, but he only spoke directly to about six or seven close associates. "I think that most of the people knew I was the boss," he said, adding he had only one true partner before the biker war and that they were buying from Richard Pelletier, a member of the Pelletier Clan. Boutin said he bought cocaine from Pelletier without any major hassles for 18 months.

"[Then] the biker war started," he said. Giauque asked if the Pelletier Clan was implicated in the biker war.

"Yes. The head, Sylvain Pelletier was killed October 28, 1994."

Boutin's testimony ended on that note that day. He returned on the next day and Giauque picked up right where she ended, asking if Pelletier's death had changed things. Boutin said that before the biker war, the Pelletiers had told him they were actually on the Hells Angels' side. But, Boutin said, Sylvain Pelletier and Maurice Boucher had a serious falling out. Suddenly, everyone was confused about whose side the Pelletiers were on.

Within months of the war starting, Boutin was approached by the Hells Angels and was offered a chance to join their side.

"When you are involved in drugs . . . when you start to become a big fish, from the financial perspective in the drug world, there is always a bigger fish who wants to say, 'Hey you're on my turf,'" Boutin said of his reasons for choosing to join the gang. He said that in 1995, he started buying cocaine from the Rockers through members like Richard (Sugar) Lock and André Chouinard. "After a few months, I became partners with Paul Fontaine who was a guy from the same group," Boutin said.

Giauque asked Boutin if he and Fontaine did the same job at the time.

"No, my qualities were more as a seller of drugs, we call it 'a business guy.' I was more of the decisional guy when it came to drugs, when it came to my team," he said. Boutin then went on to explain how Stéphane (Godasse) Gagné had also been part of that team. He described Fontaine as handling the muscle end of it, and he said that if he couldn't reach agreements with other dealers, Fontaine was sent in to take care of it. He added that some people in the Rockers network were being paid $500 a week just to beat up people. "Let's say, if you had a problem with a guy who was from a big clique of Italians or someone else, it could degenerate into a big conflict. [Fontaine] would be sent in. Or if it was someone who played with guns. My qualities were more in dealing," Boutin said. "There was a biker war and we were trying to expand in our neighborhood as much as we could."

Boutin dealt primarily in the Hochelaga Maisonneuve district, keeping the Hells Angels very happy. He said that between 1995 and 1997, he never sold less than a kilo a week. Impressed with his abilities, the Hells Angels assigned him to be the business end of a team assigned to move the Rock Machine's drug dealers out of the Gay Village.

But as the expansion was taking hold, Boutin was arrested with several people and charged in the plot to kill Boucher that had taken place more than two years before. The charges against Boutin would not stand up in court, and by now the Hells Angels trusted him. Despite being charged with attempting to kill the Hells Angels' leader, he was able to conduct business from behind bars through people who visited him.

When Boutin was released four months later, in May 1997, he learned that Fontaine had replaced him with three other people. They were Steve Boies, Danny Decelles and the newcomer Stéphane (Godasse) Gagné. Fontaine proposed that they all

287

become partners. But Boutin said he found the others had left his business in a mess and he was not impressed. "Things were bad from A to Z. When I got out we owed money," Boutin said. The team assigned to take over the Gay Village was in debt to the tune of $40,000. Boutin said that within a matter of months he was able to turn things around and put the partnership back in the black.

At that point, Boutin estimated he was making $5,000 a week selling cocaine for the Hells Angels. He told the jury that Fontaine was making the same amount as his muscle. Gagné was making about $3,000 while taking orders from Fontaine (Gagné would testify that he made only $1,000). Boutin noted that in 1997, he was merely an associate of the gang and had no status in the Rockers, while Fontaine had graduated from being a Rocker to being a prospect in the Hells Angels.

"The decisions on where the group could go in terms of territory, it was Paul Fontaine who made those decisions. Number one. The person who made money decisions and business decisions was me. I was number one."

As the business grew, Boutin continued to be supplied with cocaine through Chouinard. The pair developed a series of hand signals to conduct business.

"We didn't speak. When we talked about drugs we knew we were being followed by the police all day long. If we wrote anything on paper we burned it right away. Like in my office, I had a business office, if it was in my office or in my truck I had one of those things where you can make a drawing and erase it right away. It doesn't leave a trace. When we talked about things more serious we talked into each other's ears."

Boutin said in all the time they did business together, Chouinard never handed him cocaine in person.

"Mr. Chouinard had a system of runners and I had a system of runners. Runners are people who bring things from point A to point B. A guy like me who is tied to the bikers is generally followed by the police all the time. The runner is a guy who is not followed. Often we take someone who has no file, who isn't known. It could be someone old, a woman, someone who does not have the look of being in a criminal business."

"What do you call these people?" Giauque asked.

"A citizen."

"How did the transactions happen?"

"I'd give [Chouinard] a little address on paper. It could be a place I had rented somewhere. And his runner would take the kilo and would bring it to the address." Boutin said that within months of his start in drug dealing he trained himself to never come in contact with the drugs because he worked on the assumption that he was always being followed by the cops, and he said he used his own runners to pay Chouinard the money.

Life Divided in Three

Boutin said he became a striker in the Rockers in October 1998, after Fontaine had disappeared to dodge the murder and attempted murder charges against him in the death of prison guard Pierre Rondeau. He said that as a striker he was required to do "the watch" only on occasion. He revealed to the jury that, often, the person doing guard duty at the door of a bunker or gang clubhouse would not carry a firearm because the Rockers figured he was an easy target for the police to arrest on a weapons charge. To counter this, the Rockers often had someone sitting in a car nearby with guns on the floor of the vehicle. Fontaine had asked him to join the Rockers earlier but he resisted. He said he had decided to join after Normand Robitaille asked him to — René Charlebois had been pushing for it too. At that point, Robitaille was a prospect in the Hells Angels. Boutin said that in terms of business it changed nothing for him. Giauque asked how it changed his life, if at all.

"[When you join the Rockers] life is divided in three. It's an expression we use often. You have the family side with kids and you have to put all your time into it like everyone else. You have the business side and you have to watch your business. And you have the club side. It is not necessarily . . . it is more of a . . . it is not business. The club is about power. It is about power," Boutin said. "I can say that when we joined . . . when we put a leather jacket on a guy's back, even if he isn't known, he can enter a restaurant and everyone is scared. That is power."

Shortly after Fontaine disappeared in December 1997, Boutin said he was pulled aside by Robitaille and discreetly told to find a new business partner. But Robitaille also informed Boutin that he had to pay $1,000 a month to Fontaine's family.

Fontaine was like a ghost to almost everyone in the gang, and to the police who were looking for him. Some in the police assumed he was dead because Tousignant's charred body had been found on February 27, 1998, in Bromont, a town in the Eastern Townships. When Tousignant's body was discovered near the side of a road, it was still on fire. A Sûreté du Québec officer named Gilles Cimon put out the flames, but an autopsy later revealed Tousignant had already died of gunshots to the head and chest. To investigators probing the homicide, it appeared that Tousignant had been killed elsewhere and then brought to the area where he was set on fire. There were signs that two people had carried the corpse ten metres from the side of the road and then set it on fire.

But Boutin was part of the chosen few trusted enough to be let in on the gang's well-kept secret: Fontaine was alive. Two years after Fontaine disappeared, Boutin received a risky assignment right around the Christmas holidays in 1999.

"He wanted to see his kids, and he asked to see me too," Boutin said of the trip he had to make with Fontaine's family. A big snowstorm that day only added to Boutin's woes. "We made a lot of detours because, at the time, Paul Fontaine was one of the most sought-after men in North America. So we made detours, we used the métro [subway], we had parked a car at a location. But the windshield was broken so we didn't use it [because it would draw attention and increase the potential of being pulled over by the police]. So we took detours through the métro. I was with Fontaine's wife and his two children. There was also a prospect from the Hells Angels' Trois Rivières chapter. He was in contact by cellular with Paul Fontaine."

After zigzagging through Montreal's extensive subway system, the small group arranged for a taxi to take them to Quebec City. As the group rode along toward the provincial capital, the snowstorm got worse and the taxi driver's wipers broke off. They pulled over at a repair garage. Someone in the group called for another taxi and asked the new driver to take them to the Chateau Frontenac in Quebec City, one of the ritziest hotels in Canada. The group had now told an outsider their destination, the precise location of one of the most wanted men in Canada. Boutin began to wonder if that was a great idea. "I was seated in front," Boutin recalled. "Paul Fontaine's wife was seated in the back with the two children. We gave him the address. The guy who picked me up saw that I was a guy with a woman and two children and he thought we were a couple heading to the Chateau Frontenac. So he says, 'Where are you from?' and I say, 'From Montreal.' I didn't say I was from Rosemont. He said, 'Oh yeah? I was a cop for 25 years in Rosemont.'"

The fact that a retired cop was taking them to see Fontaine alarmed Boutin. He began acting like he and Fontaine's wife were married. But the driver seemed to pay them no special attention, and he left them off at the Chateau Frontenac without incident. Fontaine was able to dine with his family at the Chateau Frontenac and then they headed for a chalet in nearby Stoneham. Although he didn't mention it during the Beliveau trial, Boutin said that Fontaine did not look like the man he knew before. He described him as a wreck and figured being on the run and away from his family had totally destroyed him.

Once Boutin lost Fontaine as a partner, he was paired up with Stéphane Faucher, who did not yet have status in the gang beyond working for longtime drug dealer Normand (Pluche) Bélanger. "At the start, [Bélanger] did not have a status either. He was an intimate friend of Mr. Boucher and Normand Robitaille," Boutin said.

Boutin said he himself was made a striker at around the same time as other people who would go on to play significant roles in the Hells Angels' expansion in western Montreal, including Dany St-Pierre. Boutin also identified Eric (Pif) Fournier and Bruno Lefebvre, two of the nine accused in the Beliveau trial, as being made strikers around the same time as he was.

The Scorpions

The independent-minded Boutin preferred doing his own thing. Instead of relying on people the Rockers imposed on him for protection or acting himself as the muscle, he chose to create his own gang of drug dealers with Stéphane Faucher and called them the Scorpions. Faucher had them dealing on Montreal streets like Sainte-Catherine and St-Hubert. One day, while the police were investigating the Scorpions, they noticed at least 20 of their dealers peddling in the Berri-UQAM métro station, one of the busiest in Montreal. (UQAM stands for Université du Québec à Montréal.)

While Normand Robitaille and Boucher had no problem with the Scorpions, they could not allow Boutin to wear two patches at once, a violation of the Hells Angels' own rules. He was told he'd have to quit the Rockers if he wanted to run the Scorpions with the Nomads chapter's blessing. Boutin had no problem with leaving the Rockers because he was more concerned with someone in the Scorpions stealing his trafficking network. It had to be clear who was running the show, and Boutin believed that doing it from the fringes of the Rockers' network was the wrong way to go about it.

In terms of his drug business, nothing changed, Boutin said. His boss at the time was Robitaille, who was rising remarkably fast in the Nomads chapter. Robitaille gave Boutin instructions to start buying directly from Normand Bélanger. At the same time, Boutin was able to continue buying cocaine from Chouinard. He needed a steady supply of cocaine to feed his network of Scorpions who were now moving two or three kilos per week. The money coming in impressed the Hells Angels, and Boutin began to hear talk of the Scorpions being turned into a puppet gang much like the Rockers. He said Robitaille told him the Hells Angels were thinking of patching the gang over after a probationary period.

"But Normand [Robitaille] made it clear that there were certain guys in the Scorpions who were really not ready to wear a patch on their backs. They were not ready. They lacked discipline. It takes more discipline to be a full member of the Rockers than it does in the Scorpions because you have obligations, like a meeting in Vancouver. You can't say 'I'm not going.' You are obliged to go. It's more like obligations like that. The club comes before a lot of things. Sometimes you have to leave your business aside, your family aside and not everybody wants to do that. The higher you go in the hierarchy, the less you can make mistakes," Boutin said. After taking a closer look at the Scorpions, the Hells Angels realized they were only interested in two members becoming Rockers. Giauque then asked Boutin about Masses, the meetings the Rockers held.

"There are not many big subjects or delicate things discussed at Mass. We had like a . . . we wouldn't say things like 'we have to kill that guy.' We practically never talked about the Rock Machine during a Mass. We were not allowed. If anyone ever heard, it could implicate the big guys who were there." Mass was generally reserved to discuss club business, including paying into the ten percent fund. "The ten percent serves the guys in prison, paying lawyers to take care of their case," Boutin said.

He said that if they had a surplus they would sometimes use the money to buy dinner. Often it was used to cover hotels when they went on a ride, as the Hells Angels are required to do as a motorcycle club. Boutin also said it was used to buy weapons, a touchy issue for the defense lawyers because that aspect of the fund solidly supported the prosecution's gangsterism case. References to the ten percent fund being used to purchase weapons were rare and the defense would contend that informants had been coached to bring the subject up.

Boutin said Mass was not optional. You had to show up and sometimes a member of the Nomads chapter would sit in. Boutin said he knew the Hells Angels in the Nomads held Mass, too, but he never was allowed to attend one. When Robitaille went to one, Boutin was not allowed to call him for two or three hours. He also was never told what happened during Nomads' Masses. But he knew from some of the other Rockers that stuff did leak out of the meetings, like news about who had become a member.

Boutin eventually decided to rejoin the Rockers and was made a full-patch member on October 12, 1999. After that, Boutin said, he had no free time. He was ordered to do menial tasks like buy tickets to a boxing match or go to Trois Rivières to pick up something that needed to be brought back to Montreal. He found the situation occasionally ridiculous. He once had to cancel a $10,000 drug transaction so he could attend a Rockers' Mass where they talked about nothing.

One thing that was made clear to him, Boutin said, was that the Hells Angels in the Nomads chapter were his bosses and his job in the gang was to expand their drug dealing territory.

"If there were dealers who were not with us, we would go to

see them. We would ask them if they wanted to be supplied by us. If they were on our territory, they would have to get off. We always tried to get an amicable agreement from our side. We tried to cover as much territory as possible."

He said that if he considered a rival drug dealer to be small-time, the Rockers would simply send in someone to beat him up. If Boutin felt the dealer was backed by the Mafia or the Rock Machine, they would call in Paul Fontaine. After Fontaine disappeared, Robitaille made the decisions about how to handle the muscle end of the business partnership. Sometimes Stéphane Faucher would be sent in to settle things. Boutin said he had to ask Robitaille for permission if he wanted to buy drugs from someone other than the Nomads. But the benefit to him as a dealer was that he could tell Fontaine or Robitaille whenever there was a Rock Machine drug dealer on his turf. He said the problem was always taken care of.

Giauque asked if the Rockers had a specific territory.

"I could say that Hochelaga Maisonneuve and the Gay Village had been conquered," he said. "When I say conquered I mean all of the streets, from A to Z, every little dealer was selling for a Rocker in Montreal. That's what I mean by conquered. For us, the Rockers of Montreal, it is on our backs. On our patches there was a Montreal. So, we worked on the island of Montreal."

Boutin said he worked Saint-Laurent Blvd. as well and rattled off a list of Rockers who participated in selling on the street for the Hells Angels, including Pierre Provencher, Gregory Wooley, Paul Brisebois and Bruno Lefebvre. He said he knew of several Rockers who were involved in the gang's expansion in Montreal's southwest, including Provencher, Alain Dubois, Stéphane Jarry, Pierre Laurin and Gaetan Matte.

Maurice (Mom) Boucher's old chapter, the Hells Angels' Montreal chapter, were dealing drugs in Montreal's Plateau district as well as Rockers like Jean-Guy Bourgoin, Boutin said. Rosemont was also being handled by the Hells Angels' Montreal chapter and Jean-Guy Bourgoin controlled part of it. In Montreal North, Boutin said, there were only a few drug dealers working for them, and as far as he knew, the West Island, traditionally an anglophone area of the Montreal island, was not monopolized by the Hells Angels. Boutin said the Ruff Ryders, a gang that emerged out of a low-income neighborhood in the West Island, had just started selling drugs for the Rockers through Gregory Wooley in 1999.

Giauque asked what membership in the Rockers had meant to Boutin's way of life. He said it made him feel obligated to the gang. Meanwhile, the territory he had worked so hard to establish in Hochelaga Maisonneuve took a hard financial hit while he had to focus his attentions elsewhere. He said several Rockers took it over. Charlebois was one. Robert Johnson, Dany St-Pierre and Pierre Toupin were also called in to help.

Boutin then began to think back to how his nickname in the gang had changed. He had been called Pacha, a name he didn't seem to mind. But he had a serious weight problem and the Rockers took to referring to him as "Le Gros." While awaiting what he assumed was going to be his first-degree murder trial in the De Serres case, Boutin dropped a lot of the weight. Months after his arrest, he appeared at a bail hearing in Montreal and could actually be described as thin. It was obvious the anxiety of the pending murder trial had gotten to him. It was the mention of his time behind bars that brought Giauque back to questioning Boutin about the De Serres murder.

The Murder of Claude De Serres

Boutin said that months before double agent De Serres was killed René Charlebois had told him that he would soon be asked to bring the man to a specific location. Boutin then elaborated on how the Hells Angels had discovered De Serres was working for the police.

Hells Angels from across Canada had gathered in Sherbrooke on Saturday, December 4, 1999, to celebrate the 15th anniversary of the chapter there. More than 120 bikers from places like Vancouver and Winnipeg were packed into a reception hall located on a hillside in Sherbrooke.

While staying in Sherbrooke, some of the Hells Angels from Montreal had noticed that Sgt. Guy Ouellette, from the Sûreté du Québec, was staying at the same hotel. Seeing him there was not unusual, Boutin said. Ouellette would often end up taking the same flights and staying at the same hotels as the Hells Angels. He was often assigned to monitor their parties and funerals and did so openly and with a level of professionalism that many of the Hells Angels respected.

Boutin said gang members noticed that Ouellette and an Ontario Provincial Police officer named Rick Perrault were carrying briefcases. Some among the gang members staying at the hotel said they'd always wondered what information Ouellette had on them. When the two police officers left their rooms to have breakfast at the hotel's restaurant, two Scorpions were ordered to break in and steal a briefcase. "The Nomads were happy about [the laptop being stolen]. So were the Rockers. Everybody was happy."

Well, not everybody.

Ouellette testified in the Beliveau trial on December 15, 2003, and he made it clear the police weren't happy. He recalled that after working all night identifying the gang members who had attended the party he headed back to the hotel and noticed that members of the Rockers and the Nomads chapter were staying there. He spotted Boutin first, along with Patrick Pepin, who was a hangaround at the time and was not wearing his colors. Ouellette said he put his bags in his hotel room and then he and Officer Perrault left to park their cars at the Sûreté du Québec's Sherbrooke headquarters, just a short distance across the street from the hotel. "After parking the cars, we returned to the hotel and when we returned to the hotel there were more bikers there than when we made our first visit," Ouellette said, adding that he had then noticed René Charlebois, who was a prospect in the Nomads at that point, near the hotel's reception desk.

The hotel seemed to be crawling with gangsters. In the lobby was Stéphane Faucher wearing his colors. Boutin was there as well and so was Paul Brisebois, Daniel Jarry, Pierre Laurin and Normand Bélanger. Ouellette said he and Perrault went to their rooms. But they decided to check out the bar to see if they could spot more bikers. By then it had closed. The two cops called it a night.

The next morning, Ouellette said, he was standing in front of the door to Perrault's room waiting for his Ontario colleague to join him for breakfast. As he knocked on Perrault's door, Ouellette noticed Pierre Laurin, a Rocker, coming out of the elevator. He said Laurin headed straight for his own room, 209, but took a good look at rooms 202 and 204, where the two cops were staying.

Ouellette got into the elevator with Perrault and inside were Normand Bélanger and Maurice (Mom) Boucher. Ouellette said he made small talk with Boucher, asking him how he had enjoyed a production of the popular musical *Notre Dame de Paris*. Ouellette said he and Perrault went to the hotel restaurant where they spotted Gilles (Trooper) Mathieu, a longtime Hells Angel and a founding member of the Nomads chapter. He was seated at a table alone. Ouellette said he knew Mathieu had gone to South Africa a week earlier for an international Hells Angels' event, so he discussed that with him.

"We ate breakfast. We were there for a total of 20 minutes in the dining room. The service was very fast. What was unusual was that there were a lot of individuals showing up while we ate. The first was Pierre Provencher who showed up for a glass of water to take his pills. The second to enter the room was André Chouinard. At the time, Mr. Chouinard was a member of the Nomads chapter and had his colors on. He greeted us, said, '*Salut, salut, bonjour, bonjour*', and then he went and whispered into the ear of Mr. Mathieu and left again," Ouellette told the jury.

With his incredible ability to remember detail, Ouellette described the breakfast as if it were going on right before his eyes. He also tried to make it clear that it became evident to him afterwards that the gang members were checking to make sure Ouellette and Perrault were still in the restaurant while someone was stealing the computer. Ouellette said Laurin showed up as well and started reading a newspaper. "And then I was a little surprised because Mr. Laurin [a unilingual francophone] took the comics page from *The Gazette*. There was the *Journal de Montréal*, *La Presse* and all sorts of other newspapers but he took the comics page in English of *The Gazette*. I did not find that normal," he said suggesting Laurin wasn't reading the newspaper at all but making sure the cops didn't head back to their rooms before the job could be done. Sylvain Demers, a member of the Scorpions, walked in and asked for a pitcher of water and left. Mathieu got up from his table and made small talk with Ouellette and Perrault again, joking that the cops would make good overtime that weekend.

When Ouellette and Perrault left they noticed Boucher and Faucher in the lobby. Ouellette said what he found curious was that Boucher changed his position to watch the cops walk by. Ouellette said Perrault had forgotten the key to his room and went down to the reception to get a copy. Minutes later, Perrault came knocking on Ouellete's door. He seemed disturbed. He told Ouellette that several personal items had been stolen from his room, including his personal computer and diskettes. Ouellette said he and Perrault asked a cleaning lady if she had seen anything. He said the cleaning lady was very nervous and said she did not know anything.

Ouellette went back down to the lobby and spotted Maurice Boucher who was now conversing with Gilles Mathieu. "I mentioned to Mr. Boucher that one of his guys, from 209, had entered Mr. Perrault's room and had taken something from Mr. Perrault and that he should bring it back. Mr. Boucher turned towards me and said it was not one of his guys, and he looked me in the eyes and said, 'I'm not the police.'" Ouellette said he and Perrault headed to the Sûreté du Québec station and called their bosses to report what had been stolen and the circumstances behind it. The computer was long gone and the Sûreté had to sort out what might come of it.

In his testimony, Boutin said that even though the two Scorpions who stole the laptop worked for him they had done it at the request of André Chouinard. (One of the Scorpions suspected of taking part in stealing the laptop was shot to death in Montreal on November 26, 2004. He was still dealing drugs for an organized street gang that had originally been created through the Nomads chapter.) Boutin was curious to find out what was on the laptop computer but the Scorpions had orders from higher up in the network, namely a member of the Nomads chapter, to turn it over to the Hells Angels. Boutin said that several days later Charlebois paged him and asked that they meet at a Dunkin' Donuts. The plot to kill De Serres was about to unfold.

When the pair met at the doughnut shop, Charlebois suggested that they go for a walk, without their pagers or cell phones. They headed for a métro station where Charlebois whispered into Boutin's ear what his assignment would be.

Days after the theft of the laptop, the Hells Angels managed to open the documents contained on it. The police believe that Richard Gemme, the computer whiz who helped the Hells Angels with their accounting software, helped the gang sort through Perrault's computer and software. When Gemme was arrested, they found police documents on his computer. They found

Perrault's laptop at one of the Beaubien Street apartments used for the Nomads' bank system. De Serres' full name was not mentioned in the documents. He was identified by his first name and as a numbered source. But the documents contained summaries of the information he was feeding to the police. The documents also contained information that identified him as someone who handled marijuana for Boutin, which made it very easy to identify De Serres through a process of elimination. Boutin said that when Charlebois asked him about this, he realized right away who the snitch in his network was.

While the Hells Angels set up the hit on De Serres, Boutin was instructed on how to lure him up north. Boutin told De Serres that he wanted to introduce him to someone who was growing pot and asked him to check out the quality. Boutin testified that he was only told part of the plan, but that Mario Barriault, a Hells Angels' underling who had already done time for things like loan-sharking, assault and drug trafficking, was brought in to help out. Earlier on, Boutin had asked Charlebois about what might happen if things got heavy. He said he told Charlebois he considered himself a businessman and was unprepared to deal with what might happen. Charlebois told him it was fine if he didn't want to get his hands dirty, he could use Guillaume Serra if necessary.

In the hours before De Serres was killed, Boutin and Barriault met at a McDonald's. They had told De Serres to meet them there. As they waited for him to show up Boutin noticed something out of the ordinary.

"I saw two suspect cars that I was persuaded were police cars. At that point I turned to Barriault and I said, 'We're going to arrive at this meeting and there is all this surveillance.' He said, 'No, no, no. Maybe you're not used to these murder jobs. Maybe you're nervous. There's no problem. All is well.' So I thought, 'Okay, maybe I'm paranoid.' Maybe it was the adrenaline. I had felt the adrenaline before but in drug deals it is different."

Boutin should not have been so dismissive about the cars. In fact, there was a surveillance team following De Serres that day. De Serres met up with Boutin and Barriault at the restaurant. To make sure he wouldn't worry, De Serres was told he could follow the pair in his car for the trip up north. The surveillance team followed the cars but soon lost track of their informant as he headed up north with Boutin and Barriault. When they got to a point where it would be difficult for De Serres to turn back, Barriault motioned for him to pull over.

"Mr. Barriault said, 'Leave your car there,' in Lanoraie. When De Serres got out, I told him to leave his pager and cellular in his car," Boutin said. With De Serres in the car, Barriault made sure they weren't being followed by driving the wrong way down one-way streets and using other maneuvers. Boutin said that when they arrived at the chalet, there was snow everywhere. He noticed two trucks parked nearby and knew someone was lying in wait inside the chalet. The trio trudged through the snow toward the chalet with Barriault in front of De Serres and Boutin in back.

Boutin testified that as far as he knew De Serres had no idea what was about to happen to him. Barriault and De Serres opened the door. It led to the chalet's basement. Boutin said that as he walked down the stairs he realized De Serres was already on the ground and that someone had a revolver pointed at him. "Our job was to bring him there. So we left," Boutin said.

As the pair drove back south, Barriault seemed agitated and complained about how slow Boutin was driving. After leaving Barriault off, Boutin headed for his home in a small rural village near Montreal. By now, the cops had realized their informant had disappeared and their only reference point was that he had had a meeting with Boutin earlier that day.

Boutin said that by the time he got home he realized that he was being followed by the police. It looked like one of the cops tailing him was very nervous. He said he realized at that point that something was seriously wrong. When he stepped inside his house, he started to consider the huge mistake he had made. When he looked out a window, he could see what he believed were police cars parked on a road a short distance from his house. The morning after De Serres was killed, Boutin noticed an Intrepid was following him wherever he went. If it was the police, they didn't seem to care that Boutin knew they were there. At one point, Boutin slowed his car to well below the speed limit and the Intrepid did the same. That was enough to convince Boutin he was in serious trouble and the message he was getting was that the police were going to pick him up eventually.

Despite knowing that De Serres had been working for the police, the Hells Angels who shot him execution style did not search his body afterward. A truck driver spotted the body on February 4, 2000, lying on top of a snowbank on the side of Highway 125 in Notre-Dame-de-la-Merci, a town well north of Montreal. A bag had been placed over his head and his feet were bound. But most important the police found that De Serres' body-pack, a tape recorder and transmitter, were still taped to his back.

A little over a week later, the television network TQS broke the story about how De Serres had been an informant for the Wolverine squad. A news team had spotted the body-pack on De Serres' body when the police were examining him on the snow-bank. Boutin was at a restaurant when Faucher told him the news.

"Robitaille whispered into my ear that it was all a pack of lies, that if it was the truth everyone would have been arrested by now," Boutin said.

The Business Man Behind Bars

When the story aired, the anti-biker gang squad was sent scrambling and had to make arrests sooner than they had planned. Stéphane Sirois, a valued informant who had infiltrated the

Rockers, had to be pulled out of service. Boutin and Barriault were rounded up quickly — at that point, they were the only leads the police had. In his testimony in court, Crown prosecutor Madeleine Giauque wanted Boutin to touch on how he had become an informant. "Why did you make this decision?" she asked.

"I had been in prison for about 15 months. I never thought I would be an informant. That was the last place I wanted to go. But within the space of two days, it all exploded. First my wife . . . I have ten children and she was totally depressed knowing I would spend up to 25 years in prison. The best friend I ever had in my life was Mr. Robitaille and he was the same. I don't know if he saw me as a danger, that I'd one day end up here, but he was paranoid."

Meanwhile, the people handling the prosecution of the bikers rounded up in Operation Springtime 2001 were disclosing their evidence to the defense. Boutin learned that Faucher had turned informant. The drug dealer who had helped Boutin form the Scorpions was now providing incriminating evidence against him. Boutin said he asked to have his murder trial dealt with right away, before more people decided to turn informant, including people who might have been involved in De Serres' death.

Boutin said he had been waiting 15 months for his preliminary hearing in the murder case and now his defense lawyer was telling him the Hells Angels were thinking of holding it off another 15 to see what the police were going to do with Charlebois regarding his role in the informant's murder.

"It all exploded," Boutin said. "I was risking 25 years for a murder that, in my book . . . it was not me who had decided to kill that person. Yes, in the sense of the law, I am as guilty as anyone." At this point, Justice Pierre Beliveau confirmed to the jury that, if his story was true, Boutin could have been found guilty of first-degree murder even though he only brought De Serres to the chalet.

Boutin said he wasn't sure who was paying for his lawyer's bills but Robitaille had been taking care of him in prison before he himself was arrested. Charlebois had been doing the same for Barriault.

A Kind of Truce

To Boutin, the situation seemed to solve itself. He was pushed into a corner and the only logical way out was to turn informant and let the police know everything he had done in the biker war.

Prosecutor Giauque asked Boutin if the biker war was an ongoing thing, whether the Hells Angels were consistently fighting for territory. Boutin said he was made aware of the truce the Hells Angels had negotiated during the fall of 2000 while he was in jail. But he soon realized that it did not last long. Maurice (Mom) Boucher held two meetings during that autumn with leaders of the Rock Machine. The truce was negotiated, but the Rock Machine would later learn this was done primarily so the Hells Angels could put an offer on the table for their members to join them. The offer was a full-patch member of the Rock Machine could defect and have the same status in the Hells Angels. Even prospects were made similar offers.

Giauque then asked if the biker war had carried into Quebec's prisons.

"In no matter what prison in Quebec, even if you don't have anything to do with the bikers . . . Take for example at Rivière-des-Prairies. It doesn't matter who you are, they [correction officers] take you to a counter and ask you what side you are on, Hells Angels or Rock Machine. Even if you stole a bicycle. For your security, they ask you to choose a Hells Angels' wing or a Rock Machine wing," he said.

Regarding the truce, Giauque asked how it changed things in prison. Boutin said it was Faucher and Robitaille who informed him that a truce was coming. "I was the person with the highest rank in the Hells Angels in prison, or in Rivière-des-Prairies," Boutin said in reference to the detention center where he was held at the time.

"So I asked for the thoughts of my superiors, Mr. Charlebois and Normand Robitaille, what I should do if I met one. They sent me the message."

"By who?"

"By the defense lawyers. [They said] there are individuals, there were six, but there were four that they were sure would be on our side. They said I should take the steps with the authorities in prison so that they be transferred to [the Hells Angels] sector. I took the steps," Boutin said, adding he went to the vice-warden to tell him about the defections. "I said, 'Listen there are four guys known on the Rock Machine side who should come to my wing.' He laughed and said that I was crazy and that he wouldn't do it."

Boutin insisted, so the vice-warden called meetings with other prison staff at Rivière-des-Prairies. Boutin said the Montreal Regional Integrated Squad was called to verify if this could be true. The vice-warden told Boutin that he had a hard time believing what he was hearing and that he was concerned that even if it were true, there would be dire consequences if the truce suddenly ended. Boutin said he told the vice-warden to consider what would happen if he didn't make the transfers and the four men ended up killed in the Rock Machine wing.

"He was stuck in the middle," Boutin said.

Within hours a decision was made to transfer the four to the Hells Angels' sector but not the same wing as Boutin. The four men were Éric (Beluga) Leclerc, Jimmy Larivée, Gaetan Coe and Stéphane Veilleux. Because they were not yet full-patch members of the Rock Machine, they were made prospects in the Hells Angels. Meanwhile, outside prison, Salvatore Brunnetti and Nelson Fernandez, two influential members of the Alliance, were made instant members of the Hells Angels' Nomads chapter.

Another former member of the Rock Machine to cross over was Stéphane Trudel, a man suspected of being behind several of the biker war's murders in Montreal and Laval early on in the conflict. He was considered an expert in explosives. But he had spent most of the biker war behind bars serving a six-and-a-half-year sentence for an attempted murder, passing his time in incarceration serving as vice-president of the inmates committee. He was also suspected of selling drugs in his penitentiary in 1998, and, at around the same time, Trudel lost his status as a full-fledged member of the Rock Machine. Because of this, when he crossed over to the Hells Angels it was only as a prospect. He later moved on to an Ontario chapter and in 2004 was wanted on an arrest warrant alleging he was part of a stolen car ring along with Paul Porter.

Following Trudel to the Ontario-based gang was Daniel Leclerc, the former right-hand man of a full-patch Rock Machine member named Peter Paradis. Leclerc joined the Hells Angels while still awaiting the outcome of the first gangsterism trial in Quebec. While trying for parole on his two years and nine months sentence, Leclerc denied joining the Hells Angels, but police intelligence said otherwise, as did the group photos found in his cell of Leclerc with 13 other Hells Angels.

The police had listened in when Boutin was informed that he was expected to handle the transfer of people who had chosen to defect. They had wiretapped Stéphane Faucher's home in Longueuil. It sounded like any ordinary conversation at first. A baby could be heard crying in the background. Boutin was calling from his detention center and Faucher asked him if he had some paper to write the names down. Boutin asked if that was really necessary and Faucher insisted.

The gang members who had defected were still on trial in a Rock Machine–related case at that point and Faucher and Boutin saw little hope of their being acquitted. Faucher said the transfer had to be done before they were convicted because after that then things might get very confusing. Boutin's huge ego was evident during the conversation. He said had he already spoken to a prison official and was initially told there was a "1 in 10,000" chance of the transfers taking place. "Me, here, I have the power to talk to the assistant-director of the prison," Boutin said in the recorded conversation.

"Okay," Faucher replied.

"When trouble happens here, it's me that they come see."

The police also learned that Boutin in particular did not think much of the guys he was being asked to help transfer. He described Jimmy Larivée as being a "*tête folle*," meaning crazy, and that some of the defectors were "not the cream" of the Rock Machine. "The Rock Machine [guys] were a lot more weak than us in prison," Boutin said during his testimony.

Business Continues

Before Operation Springtime 2001 was carried out, Boutin's business was being maintained by Stéphane Faucher and Paul Cossette, a former member of the Scorpions and by then a striker in the Rockers. Boutin said he was receiving money from Faucher and Cossette. Part of that money, he said, was being paid back to the Rockers, whose members were all paying money into a fund for a new bunker. This was on top of their usual ten percent.

During the trial, Giauque asked that excerpts from a videotape the police secretly made of a meeting the Rockers held on December 16, 1999, be played for the jury. The video captured the Rockers discussing a problem in very vague terms. After watching the tape Boutin explained it was in reference to a meeting he had been summoned to in the South Shore. They were discussing a hit ordered on Michel Bertrand, a founding member of the Palmers, one of the gangs that was part of the Alliance. Bertrand

had a big axe to grind, considering the Hells
Angels had murdered his twin brother
Daniel early on in the biker war. Stéphane
Faucher had ordered the hit on Michel
Bertrand, Boutin said, but it didn't go very
well.

Turning her sights on Alain Dubois, one
of the accused in her trial, Giauque asked
Boutin if he knew why Dubois and other
Rockers members Pierre Laurin, Gaetan
Matte and Stéphane Jarry were brought into
the gang automatically, with no probationary period. Dubois and the others were not

Michel Bertrand, a found-
ing member of the
Palmers.

required to be hangarounds or strikers. During a party at a pizzeria, the Rockers were informed of the rare development.

"They were guys who were respected. They were involved in
drugs for years. They were well respected. It was a good strategic
move for the southwest [of Montreal]," Boutin said.

This was the last key point Giauque wanted to make to the
jury before leaving Boutin to be cross-examined by the defense.
Because he had only been with the Rockers a short time, evidence
against Dubois was scarce compared to what the prosecution had
against the others.

Guy Quirion, Éric (Pif) Fournier's lawyer, started off on the
offensive, and suggesting Boutin had only turned informant so
he'd only serve the equivalent of about a dozen years of his life
sentence.

"All of my problems were turning on me. My wife was very
depressed. Inside, some guys were getting paranoid on me,"
Boutin said explaining that his intentions had more to do with
survival. Quirion then asked Boutin if he had mentioned to his
controller committee that a lenient sentence should be part of
his deal.

"Listen, a contract, it's like in hockey or baseball or whatever else. You make comparisons with whatever," Boutin explained. Quirion then made reference to a letter Boutin had sent to Robitaille before he became an informant. In the letter Boutin wrote, "They want me to implicate you. But I know you had nothing to do with it." The letter was in reference to the Claude De Serres murder and it contrasted significantly with what Boutin had just told the jury. "When I was arrested, I went through an interrogation that lasted many hours. I was in a room with a camera. Then I was taken to another room. . . . When we found ourselves in prison, me and Mr. Barriault, we were isolated, in a corner. We asked why we were being isolated and they said: 'There is a contract on your head. You will be shot by your own gun.' So they isolated us. Even Mr. Barriault, my co-accused, said they were going to kill us. We knew too much," Boutin said in explaining that the letter was an attempt to save his own life.

If any lawyer actually damaged Boutin's credibility in the jurors' eyes, it might have been Pierre Panaccio. During his cross-examination, he made it clear Boutin was ultimately a cold, calculating businessman who prized money above all else. In the lead-up to a question, Panaccio revealed that while De Serres was being driven to the chalet, all Boutin could think about was how much money he owed him. Boutin had said as much in a statement to the police.

"What you're telling me is that, while knowing that you are bringing an individual to the slaughterhouse, your interest was to protect your money? To get as much information out of him to protect your money?"

"It's in my statement," Boutin said in a cold tone.

"No, not in your statement, now." The two continued to verbally joust until Panaccio collected himself and asked again about the statement. "I had problems when I saw that. You're bringing him. You know he is going to be killed. And you coldly ask him about your interests . . ."

"I was not certain that he was going to be killed."

"Oh, so you weren't certain?" Panaccio said sounding very sarcastic.

"I knew he was going to be interrogated because the guys knew, after reading the laptop, that he was an informant. They had a good idea that he was an informant," Boutin said while continuing to insist he was never certain that De Serres was going to be killed. After René Charlebois pleaded guilty to several of the charges filed against him in Operation Springtime 2001, he was also charged with De Serres' murder. Before the case ever went to trial he pleaded guilty to the homicide.

Like Boutin, Barriault was able to plead guilty to a lesser charge than first-degree murder. He was sentenced to two years for complicity after the fact. By the time of his first parole board hearing in June 2002, he was classified by the police as being a hangaround in the Rockers. He was released in September 2002, after having served two-thirds of his sentence.

11

The Colombian Connection

Petite and dressed in a power suit, Sandra Antelo fit the image of a calculating person who had successfully managed to smuggle large quantities of cocaine undetected for more than a decade. But dealing with the Hells Angels made her a target in more ways than one.

It would attract the attention of the police who were constantly monitoring the gang during Project Rush, and it would show her just how greedy the Nomads chapter was. Antelo was 52 when she took the witness stand on November 24, 2003, in the Beliveau trial. And as she would tell the jury, she was lucky to be there.

Antelo and her husband Raymond Craig, who was about ten years her senior, had been cocaine traffickers for years. Her husband was well known to the police and had been charged with attempted murder in the early 1990s. But Antelo managed to keep out of jail and out of trouble until she began dealing with the Hells Angels. She had never done business with any of the nine bikers on trial in the Beliveau case. But her story supported the Crown theory that the gang was all about using violence to gain a monopoly, especially when their leader Mom Boucher got involved.

To begin her testimony, prosecutor Madeleine Giauque showed Antelo a surveillance video of herself and André Chouinard, a member of the Rockers from 1994 until he was made a hang-around in the Hells Angels' Nomads chapter on June 24, 1996.

Antelo's children were visible in the video as well. Through a Spanish interpreter, Antelo, who was born in Colombia, explained that she recognized the video as having been shot after having a business lunch meeting with Chouinard at Place Ville Marie. Giauque asked what she and Chouinard had discussed.

"Everything that we talked about, all of our business was about drugs," she said.

"What kind of drugs?"

"Cocaine."

Antelo had been introduced to Chouinard by Michel Rose. Antelo met Rose in 1997, after telling a lawyer friend that she was interested in meeting someone who could help her move lots of cocaine through the U.S. and into Canada. She and Craig had recently separated and Antelo needed someone willing to move the cocaine, she had become so adept at sneaking across the Canadian border. "I had a meeting with [Rose] in the lawyer's office," Antelo said, careful not to identify the lawyer by name. She described the attorney only as "a friend."

At that point, Rose was not yet a member of the Nomads chapter. In fact, he wasn't even a Rocker. He is believed to have suddenly been made a prospect of the Nomads chapter on October 5, 1998. His connections to the gang were somewhat mysterious as he was the first person able to crack the chapter's ranks, after it was chartered in 1995, without having to go through the training of being a Rocker. Antelo said her first meeting with Rose was inside the lawyer's office and that they kept things very simple, agreeing only to meet at another location where they could speak more openly. They met again four months later.

By late 1997, the pair agreed to try to smuggle in 200 kilos of cocaine. Antelo arranged for the cocaine to be bought in Colombia and have it shipped by her intermediary there. The first shipment went well. Antelo said she and Rose agreed to do more business, and they continued to meet frequently. Then at some point, André Chouinard stepped into the picture. On the surface, Chouinard appeared to be clean-cut and athletic but he had been a member of the Rockers since 1994 and had impressed Boucher enough that he was considered a close associate at one time. Antelo didn't like the idea of a stranger entering into her dealings with Rose. It was then that Rose revealed a bit about himself.

"We had the idea of transporting drugs directly from Colombia by maritime transport. That was after the first meeting with Michel Rose. After we had more confidence in each other he told me that he did not work for the Italians or as an independent. At that moment he said he was entering a group that was bigger, more organized and that it would be more interesting for us to work with. A group that was well organized," Antelo said. "It was at that point that he mentioned the Hells Angels or some other groups. For me it was a surprise. I didn't know he was part of this group." Rose began insisting that Antelo meet with more of his associates, including Chouinard.

"For my own security I didn't want to deal with anyone else but [Rose]. But he said it was important because André Chouinard handled everything that had to do with the importation of cocaine and that his [own] role was hashish," she said. Antelo eventually relented and agreed to deal with Chouinard, but on one condition.

"I told them that even if he wasn't the one who took care of cocaine, the one I had trust in was Michel. That is the reason that Michel was always at the meetings."

With Chouinard now in the picture, more plans to smuggle in cocaine were drawn up. Antelo said there were five batches of cocaine of a few hundred kilos each brought in before they ventured into risking bigger shipments. Giauque asked her about how things went as they continued doing business in 1998. To help Antelo along, Giauque deposited a six-page document the Colombian woman had turned over to the authorities before turning informant. Antelo recognized the documents right away as being six pages of detailed accounting on the quantities of cocaine being shipped from Colombia and how much the Colombians were being paid for them through contacts in Miami.

Antelo said she got the documents from a Colombian man named Victor Mejia Múnera, one of two brothers tied to powerful Colombian drug cartels. She described Mejia Múnera as the owner of the organization in charge of her shipments from Colombia. He was in charge of her account. The document listed things like quantities, price and expenses. For example, one showed that on December 4, 1997, 100 kilos of cocaine was shipped at a value of $1.7 million. A later shipment of 100 kilos was smuggled into the U.S. at $1.8 million. The difference in price, Antelo explained, had to do with who was assuming the greater risk, the Colombians, or herself and the Hells Angels in Canada.

On March 10, 1998, another 300 kilos was sent to Miami. A month later, another 372 kilos of the white powder was sent. These were test shipments that the partners used to see if their routes were secure. Antelo's goal was to bring in much larger loads.

Contract Six

Her first large shipment with the Hells Angels did not go as smoothly as the others. "Contract six," as Antelo described it, covered an agreement to bring in 2,400 kilos of cocaine.

The cocaine was held up in Colombia, requiring Antelo to hold several meetings with Rose and Chouinard. The plan was for the cocaine to be brought into Montreal via Miami and New York. Antelo said she was never physically in either city. She described herself as an organizer. The same shipment ran into another problem as it arrived by ship in Canada. A man brought in to courier part of the shipment was spotted by police in the Gaspé region hauling 400 kilos in the back of his luxury sport-utility vehicle.

The drug mule was a man named Anthony Tomasino. He ended up getting a ten-year sentence for transporting the cocaine. Despite two previous drug-related convictions, the judge who sentenced him did not see any reason to place restrictions on his sentence and he was out on full parole by February 2002.

The rest of the cocaine made it through to the Hells Angels. Giauque asked Antelo if she had negotiated the 2,400 kilo deal on her own with Rose and Chouinard.

"No, all of it was negotiated between Mr. Rose, Mr. Chouinard, my husband and myself," she said.

"When did your husband join in the, if I might use the expression, *affaire*?" Antelo said Raymond Craig got involved with her drug trafficking while she was working on bringing in the 2,400 kilo shipment. Craig was already quite experienced in smuggling via large containers brought in by ship. Antelo had earlier described him as a legitimate businessman, but that was a lie. Craig had been dealing in drugs with organized crime groups like the Mafia for about 30 years.

Antelo had met Craig in 1984. During their relationship, she imported legitimate items like furniture and leather jackets. But her principal source of revenue while she and Craig were married came from drug trafficking. An import company they operated during the mid-1980s did business through countries like Korea and China. After they married, she passed on all of her Colombian contacts to her husband and the couple quietly smuggled cocaine into Canada from 1985 to 1993. By her own account they only smuggled about once a year in quantities that varied between 5 and 50 kilos.

Like his wife, Craig had managed to keep a low profile as a drug dealer in Canada. However his criminal record was highlighted by some strange arrests. In 1977, he was sentenced to one year in prison after pleading guilty to extortion. He had forced a woman to give him $500. To get her address, Craig beat the information out of another man using a miniature baseball bat. During the late 1970s, he was also arrested for beating up a man while stealing a bag of Chinese food, but the charges were eventually dropped. He was arrested for drug trafficking in 1980 but he managed to have the charges withdrawn. Also in 1980, Craig got into trouble after his girlfriend, a stripper, brought home a co-worker who turned out to be 14 years old. Craig and his girlfriend used the runaway in threesomes for two weeks until the police picked up the teenager who turned out to be a runaway from a youth protection center. Craig was charged with gross indecency but got off in that case as well.

Even after his marriage to Antelo, Craig was no stranger to trouble. In 1993, he was sought in connection with an attempted murder and fled the country. He came back in 1996 and pleaded the case down to a lesser charge, agreeing to pay $25,000 restitution to the victim. He and Antelo separated, but Craig was still interested in knowing with whom she was dealing. Initially, he had no idea her new partners were Hells Angels. When he found out, he was not happy.

According to Antelo, Rose and Chouinard were not happy Craig was in the picture either.

"But there was no option. Either they accept to do it with us or not. There was a moment when they accepted my husband as being part of this transaction," she said. "My husband did not want to work with the Hells Angels. He had never worked with them before and he never wanted to. He was very much against the idea of working with this group. But I had no other alternative because I had already started with them. From the start my husband thought it was a bad idea, for both him and I to work with them. He knew. I was not a francophone or a Quebecer. But my husband knew how these people worked. He said from the beginning that it was not the kind of group he wanted to work with. At the same time he knew that if he didn't join in, if I didn't do the deal, I'd have a problem with this group. On several occasions he told me this and was very clear."

Antelo began to cry at this point, recalling the moment when she made a choice in her life that would end up costing her dearly.

A Dangerous Stalemate

Antelo's next deal with the Hells Angels was plagued with problems.

"We couldn't come to an agreement because my husband was part of the discussions," Antelo said. She then paused for a while as emotion overcame her. When she pulled herself together, she said that she had an agreement with Rose and Chouinard to split 50/50 the costs involved in bring their next shipment of cocaine into Canada. But the two sides began squabbling over things like the costs involved for the smuggling operation. She recalled one meeting at a golf course in Boucherville where Rose and Chouinard could not agree with Craig on the price the Hells Angels were going to end up paying for the cocaine they brought in. Giauque asked Antelo how risk affected price.

"When you use the word risk, it's about the transport of cocaine from the United States to Canada. The risk applicable to transport is evident," Antelo said, adding she wanted to assume the least risk possible. The two sides were at a stalemate. Craig was playing hardball with the Hells Angels and now with a stalemate on their hands he demanded to see Maurice (Mom) Boucher.

"The first meeting with Mr. Mom Boucher was in the food court of [Montreal's central train] station. There was André, my husband, myself and Mom Boucher," Antelo said. "It was a meeting where my husband wanted Mom Boucher to participate because he was, in principle, the head of the group. We were not in agreement with the prices written down on paper. Mom Boucher discussed prices with my husband that they could agree on. It was understood by my husband that there was an agreement that had been accepted and we had completed the deal.

"Mr. Boucher was in agreement with everything my husband had proposed. The meeting ended with an agreement on the prices and that the prices would be respected. But the next day I had a meeting with André to see if everything was okay. André said, 'No.' He said that everything would follow what we had agreed on before because Mr. Boucher would not respect anything he had agreed on with my husband." Antelo said at that point Chouinard basically spelled it all out for her. The Hells Angels were going to pay whatever they wanted for the cocaine.

Business the Hells Angels' Way

But it now appears the Hells Angels had decided they no longer needed Antelo or her husband Craig. They had a man spending significant time in Colombia to oversee their investments. Sometime in 1997, Guy Lepage, a former Montreal cop whom Boucher had befriended, was dispatched to Bogota, Colombia, to work for the Hells Angels from there. Lepage remained in Colombia for six weeks during one visit in 1997 and spent about two months in Colombia during the following summer.

Before spending all that time in Colombia, Lepage had helped them branch out in British Columbia in the mid-1990s. He did jail time in the western province for laundering the proceeds of crime. When he was president of the Rockers, Lepage would become the center of a small political scandal after it was revealed that Canada's Federal Business Development Bank had mortgaged the Rockers' bunker in Montreal. It was Lepage who took out the mortgage. He had quit the Montreal Urban Community Police during the 1970s while he was under investigation for fraud.

After being dispatched to Colombia, Lepage became heavily involved in the negotiations over the Hells Angels' cocaine purchases and stayed at the home of a Colombian drug trafficker while he was there. In 1998, the American government seized $2.5 million U.S. in Florida that was bound for a Colombian cartel. A man named Sylvain Roy was arrested at a Holiday Inn in Miami with the $2.5 million that, in fact, belonged to Antelo and the Hells Angels. The Montrealer had been dispatched to Florida to oversee the shipment of money. The U.S. authorities would later learn that Roy had entered the States 15 times in 1998 and 1999.

Whenever the cocaine was successfully smuggled in to Florida, the Hells Angels had truck drivers pick it up at secret locations. The same truck drivers would often bring the money for the cocaine to Florida as well. When Lepage wasn't living in Colombia making sure things went smoothly for the Hells Angels there, he was spotted several times in Quebec meeting with Boucher and other members of the Nomads chapter. In 1999, Lepage was frequently seen chauffeuring Boucher to the Pro Gym where the president liked to work out.

Lepage returned to Bogota in July 2000 and stayed until September of that same year, helping the Hells Angels ship more cocaine. But by then Antelo had decided to turn informant. She knew who Lepage was.

When he returned from an extensive trip to Mexico in December 2001, Lepage was forced to undergo a thorough search at customs. He brazenly told the customs agents he would be headed back to Mexico within days and would be back for another thorough search in April 2002. But within weeks, Lepage found his name on a piece of paper signed by U.S. Secretary of State Colin Powell. It was an extradition request from the U.S. government asking that he be tried on drug trafficking charges in Florida. When he was indicted in Florida, Lepage's name would appear with that of Victor and Miguel Mejia Múnera, the twin brothers whom the Drug Enforcement Administration (DEA) had already tagged in 1998 as up-and-coming cocaine traffickers with ties to the North Valle and Cali cartels. They were also Antelo's contacts.

Lepage did little to challenge the extradition and by September had reached a plea bargain that saw him sentenced to ten years after pleading guilty to conspiracy. As part of his deal, Lepage was allowed to serve most of his time in Canada. Shortly after he was transferred to Canada, Lepage got a chance to tell his side of the story for the first time on public record. On October 26, 2005, Lepage appeared before the National Parole Board for an expedited review, a chance to be released after serving only two-thirds of his sentence.

During his nearly three-hour hearing, Lepage revealed much more about his relationship to Antelo than she did during her testimony in the Beliveau trial. He said Antelo had lived on the same street as his brother and that he knew her well before she was introduced to either Michel Rose or André Chouinard. Lepage said he would sometimes go jogging with Antelo.

He also said it was Antelo who asked him to go to Colombia the first time. "I wasn't a dealer. I was an insurance policy," he explained. Antelo asked him to stay with her Colombian contacts for six weeks while they awaited payment on one of the large shipments of cocaine. During the 1990s, it was common for Colombian drug cartels to insist that a member of a criminal organization they were dealing with stay with them while they awaited payment.

To act as such a guarantor meant putting his life at risk. "I did it for the money. It was the money that attracted me," Lepage said when one of the commissioners asked him why he put his life on the line. Though something went wrong with that deal, he managed to return home safely but claimed he was never paid a cent for that trip.

He returned to Colombia when the relationship between Antelo, the Hells Angels and the Colombians was disintegrating over a loss of $1.8 million. One of the Columbians Lepage had met during his first stay called him and said that Antelo was claiming the Hells Angels were holding out on her. Lepage reported this problem to Maurice (Mom) Boucher, figuring the Hells Angel would want to maintain the contact in Colombia. Boucher said it was Michel Rose's deal and he wanted nothing to do with it.

Lepage ended up going to Colombia merely to introduce Michel Rose, André Chouinard and Normand Robitaille to the Colombians. The bikers took over from there.

"You know how it is. When you're a Hells Angel you are treated like a king by [other criminals]," Lepage said. "I never sat at the Hells Angels' table [where they discussed their drug deals]. That was sacred."

Lepage told the parole board that he got to know Maurice Boucher in 1988 when Lepage owned a discotheque in Sorel, the city where Boucher's Montreal chapter was then based. Boucher soon asked Lepage to rent a building for him that was eventually used as a clubhouse for an underling gang.

The two became friends but Lepage insisted he never was Boucher's "right hand man" as he had been described by the police and in media reports. He said he worked on Boucher's estate in Contrécoeur in 1996, renovating his horse stables, garage and house. He admitted to being a member of the Rockers from November 1993 to April 1994 but denied ever being the president of the gang. Because he once wore a police badge, he could not join the Hells Angels. The gang has a rule that forbids former cops from joining them.

While Antelo did not explain how she knew Lepage, she did mention his name when she told the jury about when she started feeling the walls closing in.

It began after she traveled to Colombia and returned on June 10, 2000. Her intention was to discuss things again with Chouinard. While in Colombia, she had made arrangements for her deal with the Hells Angels but also made plans for another shipment that just she and her husband would be involved in.

Antelo said that after returning from Colombia, she had another meeting with Chouinard, but things did not go very well at all. Despite this, she and Chouinard agreed to meet the following Monday. Chouinard called her later and told her they had to push back the meeting to Tuesday. Antelo didn't think twice about the reason for the change. As far as she knew, the Hells Angels were still interested.

"The meeting on Tuesday was supposed to be at ten in the morning. I called them to let them know I was on the way to the meeting." At this point in her testimony, Antelo took a long pause and became very emotional. Her voice broke down.

"It was at that moment that they tried to kill me," she said with difficulty. "At the entrance to the highway near my house. I was in my car and I was about to get on Highway 15. All of a sudden I saw a car, that was driving fast, pass me." Antelo said she made a maneuver to avoid the car and, in doing so dropped her cell phone, which might have saved her life. As she leaned sideways to get her phone off the floor of her car, she heard shots.

"I didn't want to stop out of fear that they would continue to shoot," Antelo said.

Despite the fact this testimony obviously suggested that Chouinard and the Hells Angels were behind the attempt to murder her, the defense waited until this point to object and ask that the jury be excused. The lawyers then argued over whether Antelo could testify further about either the attempt to kill her or the subsequent murder of her husband. Judge Beliveau determined that it was okay for the jury to hear Antelo talk about what she knew of the attempt to kill her but ordered that she could not mention Craig's murder. The jury was called back in and Madeleine Giauque asked her what she had done after the attack. Antelo said that immediately afterward, she called Chouinard. She said he merely listened to what she had to say and then hung up on her.

She told the jury that, "thanks to God," she was not hurt but had to be treated for cuts to her face. She later moved to an apartment her husband kept in Montreal. After a while, she decided to collect her kids and leave Montreal. By September, she was meeting with the U.S. Drug Enforcement Administration at an office in the American Embassy in Ottawa. In exchange for her statements and all the documentation she had on the Hells Angels and the Colombian brothers she was dealing with, Antelo was given a promise she would not be prosecuted in the U.S. The American authorities also agreed to protect her and her children. What Antelo was not able to tell the jury was that about two months after the attempt was made on her life, her husband, Raymond Craig, who was just weeks away from his 60th birthday, was gunned down outside the Chantadel bar in Sainte-Adele, a town in the Laurentians. He was killed on August 20, 2000. The defense was dead set against the jury hearing about this.

Their strategy in cross-examining Antelo was to suggest that she might well have had any number of enemies other than Chouinard and the Hells Angels. Letting the jury know about Craig's death would only support the idea it was the Hells Angels who wanted to get rid of the couple.

The first defense lawyer to question Antelo was Lucie Joncas. She got Antelo to discuss her past as a drug smuggler, highlighting the fact that she had been doing it for decades. Antelo admitted that she had done business with cocaine traffickers in Bolivia from 1977 until the end of the 1980s. She had done jail time in California in 1983 for drugs. Remarkably, it was her only conviction in her long career as a drug trafficker.

It was during cross-examination by another defense lawyer that the jury almost learned of Craig's murder. Another defense lawyer asked Antelo about a period in 1991 and 1992 when she and Craig lived in Spain. Defense lawyer Roland Roy asked if that was because Craig had been fleeing from the arrest warrant that charged him with the attempted murder near Montreal.

"Excuse me, but that is not pertinent!" Judge Beliveau interrupted.

After a brief discussion with the jury excused, the lawyer was allowed to proceed with the line of questioning. But Antelo was provided a poor translation of a question. Instead of asking Antelo about the attempted murder accusation against her husband, the translator asked about the murder of her husband.

As she began to answer, some of the lawyers on the defense team who understood Spanish shouted and leaped out of their seats. Beliveau was forced to excuse the jury again and argued with the lawyers about the effect the blunder might have had. Antelo's answer had not been translated into French yet, but the defense lawyers argued that some members of the jury likely understood Spanish. Beliveau told Antelo again to not speak of her husband's murder. He then recalled the jury and instructed them to ignore any references to Craig's death.

"In 1993, my husband was outside of the country. After the attempted murder, he went to Colombia for two years. He stayed in Colombia until 1996. He returned in March or February, 1996," Antelo continued. She said that when he returned the couple agreed to separate but did not get a divorce. "During this period, we did not work together. That is the reason I sought out Michel Rose," Antelo said.

Antelo ended the day's testimony on that note. She was brought back the following morning and a new translator was brought in. A defense lawyer asked Antelo about her deal with the U.S. authorities. He asked her how she had managed to reach a deal that saw her do no time in jail. Antelo advised the judge that her answer might touch on what she was ordered not to say before the jury. Beliveau excused the jury and asked what she would say. "It was for my security," Antelo said. She made it clear that Craig's murder convinced her to see the DEA.

"They were saying that they wanted to end things with me. The reason why I brought myself to the North American authorities, is one that you didn't want to hear. So you should not ask the question," Antelo told defense lawyer Roy. She mentioned that she had learned the Hells Angels were looking for her, and Guy Lepage's name was mentioned in particular.

The cross-examination continued with one defense lawyer making the mistake of trying to suggest the Colombians would have wanted her dead. He asked about the $2.5 million that had been seized during the summer of 1999 from Sylvain Roy in Miami. All the question accomplished was to reveal that the Hells Angels had other issues with Antelo. She said the money belonged to her, Rose and Chouinard. It was supposed to be used to pay the Colombians. She was asked who had to absorb such heavy losses.

"It was a discussion that went down to the last minute with André, Mom Boucher and Michel Rose. We were supposed to assume the losses together," she said. "There was no agreement among the people who represented the Hells Angels. There was an agreement among the Colombians, that they would assume half the debt. . . . The Colombians whom I was dealing with were not debutantes in this business. The Colombians who work in large scales like them, they are not used to it, but they know that these losses arrive often."

The defense was having little luck creating other potential enemies for Antelo, so they switched gears and attacked her credibility. They got her to discuss how she was renting a luxury home in Hampstead, a toney suburb of Montreal, while she and her husband were separated. The defence also got her to reveal that she and Craig had lived in a spacious house in Candiac, a South Shore suburb, during most of their marriage, bought on the proceeds of their drug dealing. When Craig was killed, Antelo owned the house and she was able to sell it for $280,000, which was expensive in Candiac.

Defense lawyer Guy Quirion then attacked Antelo on her qualities as a mother. He brought out a surveillance photo. It showed her coming out of a lunch meeting with a drug dealer, her young children at her side. Quirion asked if those were indeed her children. Antelo began to break up. She questioned Quirion's ethics and suggested he was putting her children's lives in danger by showing the photo to the courtroom. Quirion didn't even wait for the translation of what she said — he seemed to understand her Spanish.

"You don't think you put your children's lives in danger by getting them mixed up in your drug dealing?" he asked. Antelo didn't answer.

Pierre Panaccio was the next to ask questions. He queried Sandra Antelo on her legitimate import businesses. She said that, for the most part, she imported furniture into Canada from Korea. Panaccio asked if she ever filed income reports on these companies. She said she believed her husband did file tax returns. Panaccio then asked if Antelo had other kids from another father. Prosecutor Giauque quickly protested that the question was irrelevant. But Beliveau allowed it. Antelo responded that she had children who were between 20 and 30 years old. Panaccio touched a nerve when he asked Antelo how she explained her income to her adult children.

"For that reason, I had several companies to make a screen for my children. My children are now professionals who have graduated from McGill and Concordia. They are not out on the street. They are not criminals. They grew up in a family atmosphere with respect and education. Despite the fact that my husband and I took part in another business, my children were raised through a different system. My children grew up outside of what we were doing," Antelo said. Panaccio asked if that meant she was living a lie when it came to her children.

"What I want to know, sir, is if you explain to your children that you defend criminals. That is your work, no?" Antelo said in a cold tone.

Panaccio understood the question before it was translated into French and did not want the jury to hear it. He exploded. Beliveau allowed the jury to hear what Antelo had said, but did not seem pleased when he heard the translation. He reminded the jury that being a defense lawyer was honorable work.

12

The View From the Other Side

As things slowly sorted out in Operation Springtime 2001 and preparations were made to bring gang members to trial, the prosecution realized they had a unique situation on their hands. Through informants, they could not only provide a detailed image of what life in the Hells Angels' drug network was like, but they could also show the flip side of the coin — what it was like to be hunted by the Hells Angels. For example, long before the Hells Angels in question were arrested, Peter Paradis, a full-patch member of the Rock Machine had turned on his own underlings and testified against them in a drug trafficking case. Just weeks before Operation Springtime 2001 was carried out, four of Paradis' former associates were dinged with some of the first sentences rendered under the anti-gang legislation the federal government had adopted in 1997. People who had helped move cocaine for Paradis were sentenced to 45 months, and saw an additional 45 tacked on because they did it to support the Rock Machine. During that trial, Paradis was asked to testify about life in the Rock Machine and how the gang profited from drug trafficking. Now he was being asked to focus on what life was like looking over his shoulder, knowing he was the Rock Machine's principal man in Verdun, turf the Hells Angels wanted as theirs.

Technically, at 12 years, Paradis' sentence was much stiffer than the people in the Rock Machine he had turned on. But by the time he sat in the witness box at the trial overseen by Jean-Guy Boilard, on July 10, 2002, he had already been out on parole for several weeks. He had benefited from a condition that stipulated he serve his time in a provincial prison, which meant he wasn't subject to federal sentencing laws. He was out after serving roughly one-sixth of his sentence.

"I was a full-fledged member of the Rock Machine," Paradis said when Crown prosecutor François Briere asked him about his role in the biker war. "During the period that I was a full-fledged member, the Rock Machine was in a transition. . . . Several people affiliated together were not in a bike club until the end of 1999. We become an official club of a biker gang, hang-arounds in the Bandidos. It's an international club." Paradis went on to detail how he had joined the Rock Machine in 1994. Before that, he had spent the better part of the previous decade dealing cocaine as an independent, concentrating mostly on Verdun.

"In practical terms, as an independent drug dealer, what does that mean?" Briere asked.

"It's someone who is not obliged to anyone. He can work in an organization but . . . it's difficult to explain. Independent means you don't belong to anyone. You have the right to buy from where you want, you can take from where you want." Paradis described his drug dealing in Verdun as being relatively uneventful up until 1994. He had grown up in Verdun and many of the independent drug dealers in the area respected each other's turf.

"Can you tell us under what circumstances, Mr. Paradis, in 1994, you left your status as an independent and joined the organization, the Rock Machine?" Briere asked.

"I saw an occasion to get a business, near the end of 1993. I was concerned because my business had fallen. I had left Verdun because business had turned quiet. I no longer had interest in doing business seriously." So, at a time when his future as a drug dealer was looking bleak, Paradis was invited to a meeting in a boutique. There he met Renaud Jomphe, a man who would play a significant role in the Rock Machine. Jomphe gave Paradis his phone number and told him he had a proposition for him. It would be an offer to let Paradis move large amounts of cocaine for Jomphe and the Rock Machine.

After years of struggling to make it in Verdun, Paradis saw Jomphe's offer as a way to start making serious money. "It gave me a chance to put myself on the map. I was tired of living like I was. Evidently Renaud was a guy who made a lot of money, with the type of life he had, and Ti-Bum [Pierre Beauchamp] as well, evidently. I said, why not me?"

Paradis' first assignment was to develop a network of clients or small-time dealers who would regularly buy cocaine from him. The issue of loyalty would become more important as the rival gang, the Rockers, made it apparent they were interested in moving into Verdun, even before the biker war started. Paradis said that in 1993 a client of his asked if he had heard that independents were becoming a thing of the past. He said the client suggested Paradis meet Patrick Lock, who was then the president of the Rockers. Paradis said he realized right away he didn't want anything to do with Lock.

"Did you speak to this guy, Pat?"

"The only thing he said to me, after I told him I didn't want to hear anything, was 'you're no longer independent. You have 24 hours to answer me.' I said I could do better than that, that I could answer him right away and I told him to leave. I closed the door and that was the end of that."

Lock, the son of Mom Boucher's friend Richard (Sugar) Lock, would end up spending most of the biker war sitting on the benches. In 1995, he was exposed by Jean Dubé, a man who turned informant after he was arrested in a plot to kill someone on Lock's orders. Lock was enraged after the police had been tipped off to a stash of drugs, explosives and weapons on 25th Ave. Lock wasn't arrested right away. He wanted a man named Marcel Picard dead because he figured he was the rat, when, in fact, it was Dubé who was operating as a tipster for the police.

Lock was arrested and sentenced to more than five years in prison. While behind bars, he dealt drugs and collected on debts for other dealers while remaining loyal to the Rockers. The National Parole had to release him in 2000 because he had reached the two-thirds mark of his sentence, his statutory release date. But Lock was arrested only months later for breaking the conditions of the release.

He had been spotted at a bar, giving instructions to other men. As he left the bar, he realized he was being followed by the police and pointed an object that appeared to be a gun at them. When the police searched his car, they didn't find a gun but did find the business cards of several Rockers, an indication that Lock was back in business. His parole was officially revoked in March 2001, just as his fellow Rockers were being rounded up. However, the parole board was required to release him again the following October.

Lock's confrontation with Paradis and the fact that he was storing weapons in Lasalle, a Montreal suburb near Verdun, suggested Boucher and the Hells Angels were very interested in expanding to areas west of the Hochelaga Maisonneuve district, even before the war started. By recruiting people like Paradis, the Rock Machine were attempting to stem that expansion.

"It was Renaud [Jomphe] who got us started," said Paradis. "We started, I think, with a little ounce of coke. Slowly, within about a month it turned into a quarter pound. That is 112 grams of coke. But while the business grew, that meant that the word got out fast, too. Ear-to-mouth goes very, very fast especially on the streets. At the same time, I was doing propaganda for the Rock Machine, because I was doing work for them."

Paradis said Jomphe was making $100 on every ounce the Rock Machine moved for him. Paradis soon started to see the benefits of working for a large organization. Within months of being in the Rock Machine he was trusted to handle larger quantities of cocaine.

"We had gotten to about a pound, and I didn't want to drive around with a pound of coke in my car."

"Why?"

"I didn't want to get arrested with it."

Paradis said Rock Machine members would drive around almost exclusively in sport-utility vehicles because they had bigger consoles, which they would have customized so they could hide their drugs inside. These custom jobs were sophisticated to the point of being entirely electronic and requiring a code to open. For example, opening the console on Paradis' vehicle required that it be in neutral and that one fiddle with buttons on the heater. The gang also hid large quantities of drugs in the houses of people they knew who did not have criminal records. Paradis started with a woman who worked in a local hospital. The gang also set about taking control of places like Verdun in the same way the Rockers were doing for the Hells Angels in Hochelaga Maisonneuve.

"It progressed slowly. Sometimes, for example, the Rock Machine, we'd make the tour of bars to demonstrate that 'it's us who now sell here.' But the other side was doing the same thing," Paradis said.

"And how do you go about going into bars and saying 'It's us who are going to sell here?'" Briere asked.

"You collect five or six, eight guys. Sometimes a dozen, sometimes less. [We'd put] Rock Machine shirts on their backs and install ourselves in the club. But usually when you go in a club it's because you know someone there, be it the manager or be it a dancer, a waiter. It could be anybody."

Paradis was then asked about the origins of the war, and, like other informants before and after him, he said that for him, the starting point was when Sylvain Pelletier was killed in 1994.

"And it was a war that took what type of form? I'm not talking about incidents, but the war took what form on the ground?" Briere asked.

"That isn't hard," Paradis responded. "If you worked for one side, you didn't work for the other. The war came about because of that. From my perspective, the Rock Machine wanted to keep what we had, and the Rockers, the Hells Angels, wanted to take it away."

"And what you had was?"

"For me it was my territory. But it was the same for all the full-fledged members. Not just in Verdun, but everywhere."

Briere then asked Paradis if he had ever had to replace people who worked for him.

"One thing that happened right away was Jean-Marc Caissy. He was a runner for me. A guy who delivered drugs and collected money. And he was killed."

"And what did you do from that moment on? Did you replace him?"

"I was obliged to replace him so that my business would continue to roll."

"Were there others like Jean-Marc Caissy who you were obliged to replace, in the same circumstances?"

"None come to my memory right now."

"Besides a death, were there other reasons why you had to replace a runner or a dealer?"

"There were some who changed sides, or simply abandoned it. They didn't want to be in the middle of it."

Things changed quickly for Paradis after deciding to sell for the Rock Machine. He was advised to always carry a firearm and he recruited bodyguards to work for him. He told the jury that he always needed to have someone with him when he went outside his home. Two of the men he recruited, Simon (Chiki) Lambert and Éric (Beluga) Leclerc, would later end up being among the people Paradis turned on when he was arrested and charged with drug trafficking and gangsterism.

By May 1994, Paradis had proven himself as a drug dealer to the Rock Machine and was officially made a hangaround in the gang, a move that proved they had adopted the same hierarchy system as the Hells Angels. He was also given an Alliance ring — an A surrounded by diamonds. "The Alliance was formed just before I arrived, I think, or around the time I arrived. When they gave me the Alliance ring they said, 'Take this, you are a part of the Alliance.' But they said at the same time that I was also a hangaround."

Paradis said the ring was handed to him at a restaurant during a meeting with other gang members. He said it came as a surprise and that it was Jomphe who had given him the promotion. It meant Paradis had access to Rock Machine meetings where they made key decisions in their turf war.

"Now, Mr. Paradis, within the frame of what you call the war, were you personally the victim of an attack?"

"Yes."

"Can you tell the members of the jury, this is during what time, what date?"

"The month of August. August 10, 1998."

"On August 10, 1998, what was your status in the Rock Machine?"

"Full-fledged member."

Paradis went on to say that at that point in the war he was aware that the Rockers had recruited well-known drug dealers like Bruno Lefebvre and Pierre Provencher to take control of Verdun. Paradis said he was accompanied by his bodyguard Daniel (Poutine) Leclerc that day and both were prepared for trouble. The pair had only made a trip to the butcher shop, but Paradis was wearing a bulletproof vest anyway. "Guys were falling from one side to the other. It was in my interest to have one on my back," Paradis said, but quickly added that as he started to near his home he felt safer and removed the vest.

He then noticed a car was following them and he told Leclerc to get a gun ready. Paradis watched as the black Toyota Corolla he had been keeping an eye on pulled up next to his GMC Jimmy. They were both now stopped at a red light. The passenger side window began to open and someone opened fire on Paradis' vehicle. His window shattered and he felt something strike his chest.

Paradis was struck four times in all but, he told the jury, he recalled keeping his foot on the brake of his Jimmy because before the shooting started he had noticed women and children crossing the intersection. The incident put Paradis in the hospital for eight days.

Paradis said he figured everyone in Verdun in the drug milieu knew what his vehicle looked like, so it was not hard for the Hells Angels to line him up as a target. By that point the Rock Machine had basically abandoned Verdun because of the war and had they left him on his own to defend it. Jomphe, his mentor and the Rock Machine's key man in Verdun, was killed on October 18, 1996, along with another member of the Alliance. They had been shot while dining at a Chinese restaurant in Verdun.

"When Renaud was killed it really touched at the morale, it really messed up the Rock Machine, and this is not my personal opinion, this is how it was. There was no one left. The full-fledged members said, 'Look, Verdun, we'll leave it to you.' There was no one else to take it over. It is not up to a prospect to take over the job of a full-patch member, when there are 10 or 12 full-patch members who can do it. It was their job to do it. They didn't do it. I think they had their reasons."

The police would later learn, through Hells Angels' informant

Dany Kane, that the hit on Jomphe was likely carried out by three Hells Angels' underlings in the Evil Ones biker gang, all of whom would eventually become full-patch members of the Montreal and South chapters. Kane's claim was supported by another source who said one of the three men named by Kane had bought black jogging pants and a black T-shirt before Jomphe's murder. The man who survived the hit in the Chinese restaurant, Raymond Lareau, told the police that the shooter was dressed in black.

Jomphe was apparently not afraid of the Hells Angels. When 11-year-old Daniel Desrochers was killed in the botched bombing in 1995, Jomphe went public and told the *Journal de Montréal* that the Rock Machine had nothing to do with it. He publicly blamed the Hells Angels, calling them "real hoods."

During the trial, Paradis was asked by Crown prosecutor François Briere to describe how the Rock Machine approached the war, in Verdun particularly.

"We had teams," Paradis said. "Some were made for killing, some were made for burning, another was for placing dynamite, others were to go into selling points that belonged, not necessarily to the Rockers, but everything that belonged to the Hells Angels."

One of Paradis' targets was the Champlain Bar in Ville-Émard. He admitted to blowing it up because he believed that a Rock Machine associate had double-crossed the gang and set up Jomphe for the hit in the Chinese restaurant.

"I had information from the street and I had information personally that [the turncoat] was holding meetings with Mom Boucher on the second floor of the Champlain Bar," Paradis said.

"After getting that information what did you do?" Briere asked. Paradis said he felt he needed permission from the Dubois family to blow up the bar. He said another member of the Rock Machine got the blessing through Alain Dubois, who was not yet a member of the Rockers. Paradis said he also tried to blow up an Italian restaurant where, he had heard, the Rockers held regular meetings, but the dynamite didn't go off. It was right across the street from a private club owned by Pierre Beauchamp, one of the Hells Angels' early victims in the biker war.

Paradis' next assignment was to blow up another bar. "It was in Robert Leger's neighborhood. He said the Italians there had connections, and that the Rockers wanted the club, and the Italians didn't want to be associated with anyone. So Robert Leger asked me if I could do anything about it. So I blew it up, too."

Paradis told the jury how he also blew up a bar on Saint-Laurent Blvd. because the Rock Machine believed it was controlled by Normand (Biff) Hamel and Denis Houle, both members of the Nomads chapter. Paradis said this was done on the orders of André (Frisé) Sauvageau, a Rock Machine member who had long been targeted by the Hells Angels. An informant once told the police that Maurice Boucher and Scott Steinert had once chased Sauvageau down a stretch of the Trans-Canada Highway that runs through Montreal. They had to give up the chase after spotting a Sûreté du Québec patrol car.

When Paradis discovered that a tanning salon in Verdun belonged to the man he believed had sold out Jomphe, he decided to not to blow it up but to burn it down.

"It was in a neighborhood that I knew well. There was a lady who lived above it. So I said it should be burned, not blown up. To use a Molotov cocktail," he said at trial. Briere showed Paradis a photo album that had been seized at Richard (Dick) Mayrand's house. The photo album contained the photos of practically any-one associated with the Alliance. While going over the photos, Paradis noted that some people who gravitated to the Rock Machine were basically flakes who appeared to only be interested in the violence of the war.

"What was the war to you? Why were you involved?" Briere asked.

"That's a good question. But at the beginning . . ."

"What was the goal of being implicated in a war as a [member of the] Rock Machine?"

"What happened was . . . it was more or less like . . . well, how can I explain it? It started by selling to make money. And then we were obliged to protect ourselves. It took several steps. You're protecting yourself, and then you involve yourself more."

"At the beginning of what you call the war, Mr. Paradis, what territory were you defending?"

"Verdun," Paradis said, adding that by the time of the arrest that led to him becoming an informant the Rock Machine no longer controlled the turf.

"Who owned it, then?"

"It wasn't us, so it had to be the other side."

Peter Paradis' younger brother Robert was also a target in the biker war. The two had been close growing up, and Robert followed Peter into the Rock Machine. Someone had made an attempt on Robert's life in 1999 but failed. Remarkably, despite having a brother who turned informant, Robert Paradis was made a full-patch member of the Bandidos biker gang in 2001.

In 2002, he was rounded up, along with several other Bandidos. But he ended up with one of the lighter sentences of the investigation, two years and fours months for conspiracy to traffick and illegal possession of a .45-calibre firearm. He was denied both day and full parole during the spring of 2004 because he remained loyal to the biker gang.

Patrick Henault

Another witness to give a view from the other side of the war was Patrick Henault. Like Paradis, Henault had become disillusioned with the Bandidos and the people who he'd known previously through the Alliance. In 1998, at the age of 20, Henault was already a member of the Palmers and serving a two-year sentence for drug trafficking and possession of an unregistered firearm. Once, while he was preparing for a parole hearing, he told a corrections official, "I'll be killed if I'm placed in a halfway house here [in Montreal]." As they continued to deny him parole during his sentence, the National Parole Board commissioners who heard his case noted they were getting reports that Henault seemed very intelligent and was a crafty manipulator.

A drug-sniffing dog became excited when a woman showed up to visit Henault in December 1998. She refused to be searched, which added to the guards' suspicions that Henault was dealing drugs behind bars. A search of his cell turned up contraband tobacco which Henault claimed to have collected for a hockey pool he'd started. He also appeared to be very familiar with firearms, something Henault attributed to being an Air Cadet when he was an adolescent.

Like Paradis, his decision to turn informant came after being arrested. In Henault's case the decision was made in June 2002 after the police arrested practically anyone tied to the Bandidos' Montreal chapter who wasn't already behind bars. The investigation was dubbed "Operation Amigo."

While awaiting trial, Henault became increasingly worried about how his case was going to play out in the courts. He wanted to get his case over with quickly because the police had videotape evidence of him preparing for a hit on Steven (Bull) Bertrand, Boucher's close friend and a high-volume drug dealer tied to the Hells Angels. Henault decided to turn on the Bandidos. He eventually pleaded guilty to drug trafficking, attempted murder and conspiring to burn down several bars where dealers friendly with the Hells Angels were selling.

Henault signed his informant deal on October 8, 2003, and only a few months later, on January 12, 2004, found himself testifying in the Beliveau trial.

"The fact that I decided to become an informant was because I was fed up with the life I was living. There was pressure from the co-accused who . . . for me, I wanted to settle things. I was fed up. I wanted to transfer to another prison, do my time and not know anything more of bikers. It wasn't part of my image, and I had the pressure from other co-accused to not plead guilty so it would cause delays in the eventual trial of the Bandidos," Henault told the jury. He also said he was not impressed with his lawyer, with while other Bandidos were taking on well-known attorneys. Also, seeing other Bandidos defect and join the Hells Angels had left Henault questioning the gang's worthiness. He had had enough of the life of a gangster.

As the Crown had done with other informant witnesses, Briere asked Henault early on in his testimony about how he got involved in drug trafficking.

"The first time was in 1992. I was 18 years old. It was inside a little bar. I was arrested immediately. I'd say within eight days. It was my first experience. After that, in 1993, I was approached by an independent named Stéphane Deslauriers to sell for him in Hochelaga Maisonneuve, to sell on the streets with a pager. It was from there that I starting selling drugs, around the beginning of 1993." Briere asked Henault what he meant by the term "independent."

"A person who is independent is a person who is not obliged to buy their drugs from someone, be it a biker gang or another criminal organization. So the person buys where they want and sells where they want."

"So at that point you were working for this person Deslauriers?"

"Yes. I worked from 1993 until the start of 1995," Henault said, adding he sold drugs all over the east end of Montreal, including in Rosemont and Hochelaga Maisonneuve. The prosecutor asked him when he had started to make contacts with organized criminals.

"My first contact was during the summer of 1994. I'm not sure when exactly but I'm certain it was the summer. I got a call from someone who wanted to meet in a little club, the White Elephant, on Ontario [Street] at the corner of Amherst. I went there during the afternoon. I asked the barman, who paged me. He said to go downstairs. I went downstairs and there was a group of people there. To my memory there were at least five. Two of those people, who I got to know later, were Paul Fontaine and a guy named D. J. Labonte, asked me to step outside. I went outside with them and they gave me the message that they wanted to talk to my boss, who was Stéphane Deslauriers. They wanted to meet him." Henault said he passed on the message but he didn't know if Deslauriers actually called Fontaine.

Henault said he cashed out of Deslauriers' operation in 1995 and started selling drugs out of a bar for a few months. He said he was selling "indirectly for André Desormeaux and Franco Fondacaro." He also said he knew at the time that they belonged to the Palmers, a gang that was part of the Alliance. Desormeaux had served time for plotting to kill members of the Hells Angels during the mid-1990s. Henault said he'd worked out of the bar until September 1995, when two Molotov cocktails were tossed into the bar. No one was injured but the message had been sent.

"Around September, when I started working directly for Franco Fondacaro and André Desormeaux, I met, at the Brasserie St. Michel, I met . . . it was a guy named Fritz [the nickname of Dark Circle member Jean Jacques Roy]. I forget his first name. And I met Louis Jacques Deschenes, they were members of the Dark Circle."

Then one of the more bizarre events in the biker war led to Henault meeting several more people tied to the Alliance.

At around 1 a.m. on September 21, 1995, four men with ties to the Rock Machine rode in a van to a fortified clubhouse in Saint Luc, a small town several kilometres south of Montreal. The clubhouse belonged to the Jokers, a Hells Angels' puppet gang. Three of them got out of the van and headed for the clubhouse on foot, carrying a very powerful bomb. A 24-year-old man named Stéphane Doucet was guarding the bunker when he noticed the trio. Doucet would later tell the police he fired a single shot from a shotgun towards them, figuring they were Rock Machine members on their way to kill him. The shotgun blast set off the bomb that the three men were planning to plant next to the bunker. Benoit Grignon, 28, Daniel Paul, 26, and Pierre Patry, 27, were killed instantly by the huge blast. The driver of the van, Brett Simmons, was severely injured. Doucet managed to escape prosecution when a prosecutor determined he was acting in self defence.

Simmons was not so lucky. He ended up being charged while still in his hospital bed. The resident of Kingston, Ontario, spent weeks recovering in a hospital, then had to undergo six months of physiotherapy. At that point, he had been a prospect in the Rock Machine, having been introduced to the gang while working as a bouncer at a bar. He was sentenced to eight years in prison for his role in the botched bomb plot. Simmons was eventually released after serving two-thirds of his sentence but was soon hauled back to a penitentiary in Ontario during the spring of 2002, after he was spotted hanging out with biker gang members while out on parole. He wound up defecting to the Hells Angels, joining a chapter in Ontario.

Henault attended the funeral for the three men who died in the blast. It was there, he said, that he started to make several connections with people in the Alliance. Shortly afterward he was fronted some money, which to him meant he was considered a prospect in the Palmers.

Briere was asked what his functions were.

"At the base, my functions were to do errands and be a body-guard."

"For who?"

"For Fondacaro and André Desormeaux."

Henault did this for about 30 days, until Fondacaro was

arrested late in 1995 as a suspect in the failed attempt to kill members of the Hells Angels while they were in a federal penitentiary in Laval. Desormeaux went into hiding and asked Henault to look after his pregnant wife. Fondacaro was arrested at a Montreal restaurant. Desormeaux's wife had the baby in December while the Dark Circle member was hiding out in a chalet the Alliance was renting up north. Desormeaux was eventually arrested, and quickly pleaded guilty to conspiring to kill members of the Hells Angels.

By January 29, 1998, he had served two-thirds of his sentence and was released to live at a halfway house. But he never showed up and was arrested six months later in possession of a firearm. He later told the parole board that he didn't think a halfway house was safe enough for him because he knew he was a walking target. Desormeaux was returned to a federal penitentiary where he was suspected of dealing drugs to other inmates.

Desormeaux was Henault's boss, and as a result, Henault frequently had to work as his bodyguard. When Henault pulled off armed robberies, he was also required to give Desormeaux a percentage of the take.

During that same period in the war, Henault was asked to carry out a variety of tasks for the Alliance. He said he and a man named Jean-François Cyr set up a phony bomb scare at a workout club that belonged to Steven (Bull) Bertrand. Cyr had placed a fake plate on a car in the parking lot and Henault placed the phony call. At another point late in the war, Henault was asked to torch a bar in Montreal's east end. For this, Henault hired out two people, including François Barbeau, who was arrested shortly afterwards. Barbeau was sentenced to six years for tossing a Molotov cocktail into the bar while there were still about fifteen people inside. These six years were tacked on to the federal sentence Barbeau had earned before he tried to torch the bar. Barbeau's previous sentence began in the mid-1990s, 40 months for armed robbery. While out on parole for that sentence, he'd tried to help the Rock Machine spring their explosives expert, Roger Hardy, from the Donnacona maximum-security penitentiary near Quebec City.

Hardy was serving a 32-year sentence that began in 1977 and grew every time he was released on parole. For example, he'd had 14 years added to his existing sentence in 1990 for a series of armed robberies committed shortly after being released. Besides being considered an expert on explosives, Hardy was known to be a master locksmith, and had tried to use his expertise to break out of penitentiaries several times. He is one of a small percentage of inmates who remain behind bars despite having served two-thirds of their sentence.

On March 10, 2005, the National Parole Board decided to make Hardy ineligible for parole. The panel of three commissioners had a hard time looking past several incidents, including the fact Hardy had threatened to kill two prison guards. Just a year earlier, Hardy had told the parole board that his plan, if released, was to either sell drugs or guns. The Rock Machine planned to use the Donnacona's sewer system to free Hardy and at least two other men. The plan was foiled when the Sûreté du Québec, investigating a report that drugs were being smuggled into Donnacona, discovered a manhole cover had been loosened in preparation for the escape attempt. Barbeau had an additional 23 months tacked on to his sentence for that offence.

In February 2005, after turning down his previous attempts at parole, the board had no choice but to release Barbeau for having served two-thirds of what by then amounted to an 11-year sentence. Barbeau was granted the statutory release because he had not been out on parole since the Molotov cocktail arson attempt had been tacked on to his existing sentence. For a variety of reasons, including the fact he appeared to be addicted to heroin, Barbeau was required to stay at a halfway house for the remainder of his sentence, and to take part in a program to deal with his drug problem. By then, Barbeau had severed his ties with his gang, which had become the Bandidos.

"I'm not in nothing and I don't want to be in nothing," Barbeau told corrections officials as they were trying to determine where to place him. He told corrections officials at the time that the gang had treated him like a puppet, something he could not tolerate, so he'd quit. But, according to a parole board report, Barbeau continued to sell drugs while behind bars. His drug dealing started a chain reaction in a federal penitentiary that, by 2003, saw the end of segregation between inmates loyal to either the Hells Angels and Bandidos in Quebec's federal institutions, a clear sign that the war was over.

Henault said that in 1997, he'd carried out a contract given to him by Michel Bertrand, a member of the Palmers. The order was to burn down a tanning salon they believed belonged to the Hells Angels. Henault said Bertrand also gave him the contract to burn down a greasy spoon on Pie ix Blvd. that was tied to the Hells Angels. The jobs gained Henault more respect in the gang and he was soon welcomed into places like the Rock Machine hangout on Lesage Street and the gang's bunker on Huron Street where he started hanging out with Rock Machine members like Yves Murray. This turned Henault into an instant target for the Hells Angels.

"At one point, myself, Yves Murray and Michel Bertrand, who was at the time my boss, we left to go, I can't remember why, to the west [section of Montreal]. We took Ontario Street heading west, and we got to Fullum when Michel Bertrand noticed a car parked in a parking lot and there was someone inside it." Henault said they pulled up to the car and Murray and Bertrand easily recognized the people inside, but he didn't. The vehicle started to follow them. He said he looked back and noticed the windows were open and that the person in the passenger side appeared to be armed.

Henault said Bertrand pressed a button and a hiding place below the dashboard of his vehicle opened up. Inside was a firearm. They drove around, making several turns until they were sure the car was following them. There were three people inside the other vehicle. Bertrand then noticed he was running out of gas and Henault said he was ordered to shoot at the car behind them.

"I lowered the window. I was seated in the back. I took out the gun and fired four times in the direction of the vehicle. I noticed that two hit the ground. I don't know where the other two went. The vehicle stopped. I got down, and then I looked and I saw the passenger take out a revolver and fire towards us once."

Bertrand managed to hide his vehicle in a lane between a Canadian Tire and a rotisserie restaurant, and the chase was over. Henault told a jury he later learned the guys who tried to kill him were Pierre Toupin and Kenny Bedard. But it was not the only time Henault would see gunplay during the biker war. Henault said that he and Yves Murray were once driving around in Montreal's Point St. Charles district when Murray noticed a red pickup truck. Murray turned to Henault, said he had spotted Jean-Marie Fontaine, a relative of Paul Fontaine, inside the truck, and then pulled out his gun.

"He lowered his window and called out to Jean-Marie Fontaine. Jean-Marie Fontaine opened his vehicle and placed his hands on the side of the window and said he wanted to talk to Yves Murray. But Murray didn't want to hear it. Murray said, 'How's it going you *gros chien* [a slang term in French, roughly meaning fat lazy dog]?'"

Henault said he then told Murray to shoot Fontaine. Murray fired one bullet, but by then Fontaine had ducked inside the pickup. He then sped off.

Confrontations weren't limited to Montreal's rougher areas either, Henault said. He recalled how he, Luc Beaupré and Michel

Bertrand went to the Montreal courthouse to watch court proceedings in the case involving Yvon (Mon Mon) Roy and Gilles Lambert, charged in a plot to have Maurice (Mom) Boucher killed. Henault said that when he and his fellow gangsters walked into the courtroom, they noticed that members of the Rockers were already there.

"To my memory, Paul Fontaine was seated in the first chair from the aisle. Next to him was Stéphane Gagné and the third person. Michel Bertrand was sitting directly behind [Fontaine]. I was directly behind Stéphane Gagné, and we saw Paul Fontaine shake his head. He sensed that we were looking at him so he turned. Michel Bertrand said, 'Hi, how's it going?' Just to be specific, Michel Bertrand was accused of conspiring to murder Paul Fontaine in 1995. Fontaine smiled and said, 'Yeah, it's going all right.'"

Henault said Fontaine suddenly got up to leave, and he and Bertrand followed him. Fontaine headed for a pay phone. Bertrand assumed Fontaine was calling for reinforcements in case things got out of hand, and told Henault to call the Rock Machine's bunker to do the same. A few other Rock Machine members, including Stéphane Morgan, showed up quickly, but by then the court hearing the case had adjourned and they found Fontaine in a courthouse corridor talking to lawyer Gilles Daudelin.

"So the game plan had changed. Luc Beaupré looked at me as if to say, 'What do I do?' I said, 'Go ahead,'" Henault told the jury. Beaupré approached Fontaine and threw a punch, but missed and struck the lawyer instead. That's when an all-out brawl broke out. Henault said he jumped on Gagné's back. A huge guy who was with Fontaine and Gagné at the time picked up a granite ashtray and threw it at Beaupré and the others, effectively putting an end to the fight.

Henault revealed that he was also asked to do a lot more than use his fists. He talked about how, during the summer of 1998, he and André Desormeaux were driving in Old Montreal when the latter spotted André Chouinard's Jeep Cherokee. They followed him to a parking lot. Desormeaux then put together a plan in which they would go to an apartment and get prepared for a hit on Chouinard. They also called a man named Yvan Nadeau, someone the gang counted on to supply getaway cars.

"I got dressed. I had a pistol with a silencer. I put that in a back pack and put on glasses," Henault said, explaining his plan to blend in with the tourists in Old Montreal. Henault was assigned to kill Chouinard, but the plan was foiled when a groundskeeper told him to move off the property where he was lying in wait. He said that he and Desormeaux moved into new hiding places but by then Chouinard had left.

"At that time, in the event that we saw someone who was affiliated with the rival clan, if we had the opportunity, we'd kill him. If not, we would call someone who could," he said. Henault said he was also involved in another plot to kill a member of the Hells Angels' network during the summer of 1998. This time the target was Paul Cossette, a member of the Scorpions the Alliance suspected of trying to kill Michel Bertrand, whose twin brother Daniel had already been murdered early on in the biker war. Daniel Bertrand was shot to death at the age of 29 about a week after Sylvain Pelletier was killed, gunned down inside a Montreal bar on Ste. Catherine Street East. One of the bullets that struck him traveled through his left lung, a major vein, and his liver before exiting his body. Henault said the Alliance definitely wanted revenge for the attempt on Michel Bertrand.

The Hells Angels had an associate of the Rockers named Ryan Wolfson try to kill Bertrand. Wolfson used a stolen .357 Magnum to shoot Bertrand, but he did it in a busy park and one of his shots wounded an innocent bystander in the leg. With Bertrand wounded and lying on the ground, Wolfson walked up to him and prepared to shoot him in the head, but he had run out of bullets.

Wolfson had a history of extreme violence. In 1996, he had led police on a high-speed chase where he ended up speeding against the flow of traffic, ramming into a police car when he realized he was trapped. While serving his six-year sentence for attempted murder, Wolfson was found to be addicted to cocaine. He was released on November 10, 2004, having served two-thirds of his sentence, but left his halfway house illegally the same day he arrived. He was arrested just two days later after stealing a car. When his parole was revoked, Wolfson told the board he had been partying and had gotten high after meeting a woman.

Henault had done guard duty while Michel Bertrand recovered from the wounds he suffered at Wolfson's hands. Henault said Franco Fondacaro asked him to kill Paul Cossette, but he initially didn't say why. André Desormeaux and Fondacaro took Henault to the convenience store where Cossette worked to show him what his target looked like. Henault later learned the Alliance suspected Cossette of ordering the hit on Bertrand. The trio then went to a wooded area to try out a .22-calibre gun to see if it would do the job, but the hit was never carried out.

In fact, Henault's testimony revealed that the Alliance's attempts to murder the Hells Angels or the people who worked for them were not very well thought out and, for the most part, consisted of them scraping a plan together whenever they happened to see a potential target.

"During the summer of 2000, I was living downtown on Durocher [Street]. We got a call, André Desormeaux and I, from Jean Duquaire, who was at that moment a [member of the] Rock Machine. Jean Duquaire called us to say he had seen Mom Boucher in the sector of St-Laurent and Sherbrooke. He was at the gas station on the corner. So, me and Desormeaux left from Durocher, which was only a few streets away, and headed to meet Jean Duquaire. Jean Duquaire told us he had seen Mom Boucher in a green Volkswagen Beetle, one street north of Sherbrooke.

Without waiting, me and André Desormeaux headed for the area where Mom Boucher was supposed to be . . . with the goal of killing him. We never saw the vehicle," Henault said.

Bleu Marin

Henault was then shown a series of photos of his former fellow gang members. As he identified them, he made a few mentions of the dinner held at a downtown Montreal restaurant called the Bleu Marin, a meeting between leaders of both the Hells Angels and the Rock Machine where they discussed a truce. Weeks earlier, Mom Boucher and other gang members from both sides had met in a room at the courthouse in Quebec City to discuss the same topic.

While the conversation was supposed to be about peace, both sides were careful to bring a large contingent of bodyguards. Henault said he was on guard duty outside the restaurant. His orders were to eat dinner at a nearby restaurant and wait to be paged to go to the Bleu Marin.

When the truce dinner was over, Henault got a call from his boss André Desormeaux, who invited him to a party at a downtown strip club. Henault said it was there that Desormeaux introduced him to Normand Robitaille and Richard Mayrand, two men Henault would have attempted to kill on the spot before the dinner. Henault said the Hells Angels and the Rock Machine members partied together that night at the strip club. After the celebrations were over, Henault said he was made aware of something that would start him on the road to discarding his loyalty towards the gang.

It came shortly after the truce was announced. He and Desormeaux set up a meeting with Salvatore Brunnetti and Nelson Fernandez at an Italian restaurant owned by a relative of Brunnetti. "We met with them, and it was Brunnetti and Nelson Fernandez who confessed to us that it was not the Hells Angels who had called to ask for a truce, but that in actuality it was the

Rock Machine who had called the Hells Angels," Henault said.

"What kind of reaction did that provoke out of you?" Briere asked.

"Let's say we were surprised, disappointed."

The police later learned the supposed truce had actually developed into an ultimatum from the Hells Angels, who were aware the Bandidos were prepared to patch over the Rock Machine. With both sides agreeing to what amounted to a cease-fire, the Hells Angels made their true intentions more evident. They made an offer whereby certain members of the Alliance could jump ship and enjoy the same status in the Hells Angels. For example, Salvatore Brunnetti, a longtime member of the Dark Circle, became a new member of the Hells Angels. A prospect in the Rock Machine who switched sides would become a prospect in the Hells Angels. But there was a time limit on the offer, and when it ended, hostilities would resume, even months after Operation Springtime 2001 was carried out.

Henault said that after learning Brunnetti and Fernandez were going over to the Hells Angels, he tried to stir up the pot and make sure no one else left. Henault said Guy Langlois, one of the Alliance members who was also quick to join the Hells Angels, tried to convince him to do the same.

"Guy Langlois told me, 'Come over with us. You'll make money. I've never made money like this in my life.' From there, I decided I wasn't a Hells Angel and I wasn't in the Rock Machine. It was the last time that I spoke to him," Henault said.

"What happened that you made the decision, personally, to not join the Hells Angels?" Briere asked.

"I was not interested. I had no confidence in the Hells Angels. They had killed a lot of people I had known. I had no confidence. They are people who purge their own."

The Arrival of the Bandidos

If the Hells Angels had made the truce offer to try to prevent the Bandidos from coming to Quebec, it failed. Henault said Jean Duquaire showed up one day shortly after the truce dinner with the new Bandidos patches. The war was back on. Joining the Bandidos, an international gang much like the Hells Angels with chapters all over the world, was seen as a new level of provocation.

Henault said he watched as his boss, Desormeaux, accepted the new patch. Some time shortly afterward, Henault was given one as well. The Alliance members who'd crossed over to the Hells Angels obviously gave their new partners in crime details about where their old friends could be found and targeted for hits. Brunnetti had been spotted by the police showing up early at the February 15, 2001, meeting where members of the Nomads chapter like Mayrand mulled over who their new targets would be. Also, when police raided the homes of the Hells Angels and Rockers targeted in Operation Springtime 2001, they found updated lists of places where the Bandidos regularly held meetings. Henault was shown the documents and confirmed that he had attended meetings at some of the places mentioned, including the Guy métro station and several shopping mall food courts.

The fact that the entire Nomads chapter was either behind bars or on the lam as a result of Operation Springtime 2001 represented a world of possibilities, Henault said.

"My principal activities [after the arrests] was the sale of drugs, cocaine, pot. In the moments after I received my patch in the Bandidos, it was a question of recovering territory, attempting to recover territory," he said.

When Henault was cross-examined, he was grilled about the most controversial parts of Operation Amigo, the investigation that resulted in a similar roundup of members of the Bandidos, several months after Operation Springtime 2001. The Montreal police had Éric Nadeau, a man tied to the Bandidos, working for them as an informant. The police were monitoring Nadeau, Henault and Desormeaux one day while they prepared for a hit on Steven (Bull) Bertrand, Boucher's close friend. A surveillance videotape leaked to the media shortly after Operation Amigo was carried out showed Henault and the others preparing for the Bertrand hit. It appeared from the video that the Montreal police did little to prevent the hit from happening. Despite watching Henault arm himself inside the apartment on a closed circuit television, a surveillance team showed up only after Bertrand was shot. Henault was arrested only after he'd shot Bertrand several times while the drug trafficker dined at a sushi restaurant in Montreal's trendy Plateau district. It would later be revealed that Bertrand ate there almost routinely, so it had been easy for the Bandidos to find him. Bertrand survived the attempt on his life.

Defense lawyer Guy Quirion began the cross-examination, and asked Henault about what happened that day. Henault had been arrested in the shooting, but was not charged immediately because he had been out illegally at the time and the authorities were able to hold him on that basis without having to disclose evidence in the ongoing Operation Amigo investigation — including the fact that Nadeau was a double agent. Henault had been technically at large for 28 months when he shot Bertrand, and he could be held for a variety of reasons, including the fact he had become a member of the Bandidos. When the arrests in Amigo were carried out months later, the attempted murder charges became public.

"It was after the charges came out in Project Amigo, in June 2002, that I learned that Éric Nadeau was an *agent source*," Henault said.

"What was your reaction, and Mr. Desormeaux's, after you learned he was an agent source. What did you do?" Quirion said.

Henault admitted that he and Desormeaux tried to implicate Nadeau in the attempted murder. They had tried to make it look like Nadeau had first seen Bertrand and had directed Henault to him. Henault said that shortly after the arrests were made, the police showed him the cassette that captured images of him preparing to kill Bertrand. In the video, Nadeau is standing nearby. Henault said he was later told that Nadeau was also wearing a body pack, which could both record and transmit sound. In May 2003, Henault gave the police a statement claiming he had been a victim of police entrapment, and that it had been Nadeau who had actually planned the hit on Bertrand.

But months later, when Henault became an informant himself, he reversed his position and said that it was he and Desormeaux who had planned the hit on Bertrand. Éric Nadeau just happened to be with them at the time, Henault said.

"André Desormeaux and I made the decision to kill Steven Bertrand but Éric Nadeau was not next to us. He was about 12, 15 feet away," Henault said, adding the decision to kill Bertrand was only discussed once. Henault said they had spotted Steven Bertrand by chance.

He and Desormeaux had gone to a restaurant and spotted him seated in the neighboring sushi place.

Within months of his guilty plea, Henault was able to enjoy temporary leaves. Like almost all gangsters who turn informant, he arranged to serve his federal sentence in a provincial detention center, which meant he could get out quicker. By 2004, despite admitting he'd tried to carry out a cold-blooded murder only two years earlier, Henault was out on parole.

13

A Jury Decides

Madeleine Giauque appeared calm for someone waiting to see what a jury would think of the evidence she and a team of prosecutors had worked on for more than three years. After the jury was finally sequestered in February 2004, Justice Pierre Beliveau decided he wanted to meet with lawyers from both sides every morning in the courtroom while the jury members deliberated on the fate of Hells Angel Richard (Dick) Mayrand and the eight other bikers underneath him in the gang's hierarchy. The morning meetings in the large courtroom were informal and friendly. The tension between the defense and the prosecution that had built up over the duration of the trial was subsiding.

The Morning News

Beliveau allowed a number of Montreal newspapers to be made available to the jury as long as all references to the trial and the Hells Angels were removed. Someone from the defense team was always present to verify that any potentially influential articles did not make their way into the jury. One morning there was even a debate over whether an article about the jury hearing the trial of Martha Stewart, the home-decorating mogul on trial for stock fraud in New York, should be cut out.

A courthouse clerk was assigned the duty of removing all the potentially influential articles. Her scissors were very busy on one day in particular when Operation South was carried out. A police operation much smaller in scale and of less significance than Operation Springtime 2001, it still resulted in the roundup of several members of the Hells Angels' South chapter and many more underlings.

Among those arrested on February 26, 2004, was Éric Bouffard, one of the Hells Angels who had been caught delivering money to the Nomads chapter's bank. He had quickly pleaded guilty to the charges brought against him in Project Ocean, and was already out on parole when he was arrested again. The investigation centered on the South chapter, based in Saint-Basile-le-Grand. At the time, the police said the South chapter appeared to have been filling the drug traf-

Eric Bouffard, a member of the Hells Angels arrested in Project Ocean.

ficking void created by the roundup of the Nomads chapter. But the investigation was also heavily focused on loan-sharking. When it was carried out, it made the front pages of all the Montreal newspapers and several pages inside. Some lawyers joked that the jury members were going to be intrigued by the amount of vetting done to their papers that morning.

While waiting for the verdict, Giauque managed to keep her sense of humor as well. While talking to reporters after one of the morning meetings in front of Beliveau, Giauque said that she and other members of the prosecution team killed time waiting for a verdict by watching DVDs. "But there is no way I'm going to watch *Runaway Jury*," Giauque said in reference to a film that had just been released on DVD starring Gene Hackman and John Cusack, portraying two sides engaged in a heated and very illegal battle to sway a jury.

Ladies and Gentlemen of the Jury

It seemed to have taken forever to get to the point where a jury could actually deliberate on the charges filed in Project Rush. The question on many minds was whether the average person could accept that doing things like contributing to a fund, or performing guard duty, or acting as a personal bodyguard facilitated a criminal act and therefore was also a crime. It had taken a long time to get to that point. Jury selection had begun on January 13, 2003. The jury sat for 118 days over a period of a little more than one year. Much more court time was spent without the jury present, as lawyers argued various motions.

The evidence was broken down into 10 stages. The first involved informing the jury of what had been seized at the bikers' homes during Operation Springtime 2001. Rather than allow much of that evidence in without challenge, the defense decided that it had to be scrutinized before the jury. That meant police officers who had seized the items had to be called in to testify. The process created delays that Beliveau would later criticize as being very unnecessary.

The second stage involved showing the jury hours of videotape police surveillance teams had taken of gang members doing things like attending meetings or doing guard duty — "the watch" as the gang called it. Things did not get interesting for the jury until stage three, when they were shown the videotapes police had secretly made of meetings the Rockers held in hotel conference rooms. It was Dany Kane who had tipped off the police as to where the meetings were going to be held. Stage five involved the informant testimony, and stage seven involved much of the evidence gathered on the Nomads Bank.

Giauque was able to begin her final arguments on February 3, 2004. The task before her was to attempt to make sense of all the evidence the jury had heard and seen. In a very thorough multimedia presentation which took four days to complete, Giauque explained the reasons why the jury had watched hours of video-tape and listened to countless wiretapped conversations. She went over the highlights of the Masses, bringing out the importance of some of the comments recorded as they applied to a gangsterism case. For example, in one of the Masses, the gang had discussed where Éric (Pif) Fournier was going to go when the Rockers divided the gang into two chapters, one to remain in the east end of Montreal and the other to give them a presence in the west end.

What became apparent during this Mass was that Fournier was a heavily prized bodyguard to Louis (Melou) Roy. Michel Rose and Roy had discussed the issue, and the possibility of Fournier losing his patch was mentioned. The gang also discussed how difficult it was to protect Roy and that there simply weren't enough guys to act as his bodyguards. Fournier was believed to have committed several murders for the Hells Angels since his introduction to the Hells Angels in 1996.

The police found it interesting that a couple of years after joining the Rockers, Fournier disappeared for several weeks, around the same time as his boss Louis (Melou) Roy. The long-time Hells Angel disappeared off the face of the earth, and was last seen alive some time in June 2000. The police believe Roy was purged from the gang. His name stopped showing up on the gang's membership lists, whereas others like Paul (Fon Fon) Fontaine and Richard Vallée, who turned out to have been in hiding, continued to be noted on lists seized by the police.

Fontaine was found in May 2004, after spending more than six years in hiding. He had been made a full-patch member of the Nomads chapter on June 24, 1998, while on the lam. When the police found him, he had changed his appearance slightly by growing a beard and had gained weight. He was brought back to Montreal to learn he still faced charges for murdering a prison guard as well as the new charges brought against him in Project

Rush. Fontaine's arrest made David (Wolf) Caroll the only member of the Nomads chapter still being sought after Operation Springtime 2001.

Another sign that Roy had been purged was that when police did an analysis of the Nomads' accounting ledgers, investigators noticed Roy's account with the gang was closed and his drug profits split up among the members of his former chapter in Trois Rivières. After Roy and Fournier disappeared, the police originally assumed they had both met the same fate.

But Pif popped up again. He was arrested in Jonquiere, Quebec, much later in 2000, carrying a .357 Magnum and some cash. The cops suspected the cash came from drug sales he had made in a Jonquiere bar. It appeared that Fournier had been ordered to lay low in the aftermath of Roy's disappearance.

During the same Mass, Fournier's membership was debated, the jury got a hint of just how successful the Rockers were as drug traffickers. In the videotape, Normand (Pluche) Bélanger openly complained about always having to collect the ten percent fund during Mass, and that it caused him to carry around a suitcase with a lot of money.

Another meeting Giauque highlighted for the jury was one in which Dany Kane had worn a body pack and given the police a goldmine of evidence. The meeting was held on July 4, 2000, in a restaurant where Robitaille announced the new going price for a kilo of cocaine would be $50,000.

Couture, one of the accused in the Beliveau trial, was at the meeting where the police were able to confirm their suspicions of the high level at which the Nomads chapter was operating in terms of drug trafficking. Robitaille provided an update to his underlings about the state of the Nomads empire. The Rockers present at the meeting informed Robitaille that they were collecting $30,000 a month in the ten percent fund, a clear sign they were making at least $300,000 in profits per month in drug sales.

Paul Brisebois was recorded asking Robitaille about Montreal North, a suburb of Montreal where drug trafficking is normally controlled by street gangs like the Bo-Gars. Robitaille responded by saying the Hells Angels did not want to leave any territory vacant.

Pierre Laurin was also interested in Montreal North, saying the gang could do some "cleaning up" of the potential business in neighborhoods near those controlled by the Mafia. But Robitaille then mentioned that he would have to talk to Mom about Montreal North, saying the Rockers would have to respect the "Italians'" territory. They had right to what was theirs, but they should not be allowed to expand, Robitaille said, adding the Mafia controlled Little Italy and some other parts of the city, but that Montreal North was "wide open" for anyone who wanted to take it. Robitaille also lectured the Rockers on controlling the quality of their cocaine, because the Nomads chapter didn't want it to be too cut by the time it was retailed.

Giauque told the jury that this meeting in particular was clear evidence of a Hells Angel giving orders to the Rockers. But it also reflected a constant theme in Rockers meetings — everyone had a say but the Nomads chapter's authority was undeniable. A key part of the gangsterism charge was whether the Rockers used the ten percent fund to buy weapons. If that had been the case, it would be easier to convince a jury that the gang was paying into a system that murdered people. Giauque pointed out one mass in particular where Rocker Pierre Provencher explained to another gang member that the ten percent fund was used to pay for the clubhouse and "for this," while he made the sign of a gun while the videotape recorder rolled.

Giauque also told the jury the informants who testified were not there to incriminate anyone in particular, but to facilitate a general understanding of the evidence. They were there to explain the hierarchy of the gang, Giauque said, adding that the case could have been prosecuted without the informants. They were there to support evidence, for example that "business" was the gang's euphemism and code word for drug trafficking. The informants were able to explain why gang members were often seen talking into each other's ears when they were captured on video.

"Only certain people, of confidence probably, knew who really committed [a serious] crime. It is an important measure of security, because if someone became an informant they couldn't say this person did this and that other person did that," Giauque explained while describing the whispering as symptomatic. "They were doing it all the time."

The prosecutor acknowledged that informants were criminals who'd only turned when they were put into a corner. "The defense will tell you that they are witnesses who are degenerates and you should not believe them. They have good reason, on one point, they are degenerate witnesses. But here you should believe them. And why? Because they are corroborated by the evidence presented before you. It's certain these are not people you would invite to have supper at your house. None of them. But everything they said here was uncontestable."

She explained her reasons for using Stéphane (Godasse) Gagné while acknowledging that the murder of two prison guards were "*crapeleux*," a French term for villainous that has a better emphasis than the English equivalent. She noted that Gagné was only made a striker in the Rockers for the first murder and was going to be a full-patch member of the gang after the second. It gave the jury something to consider when deciding what it took to eventually graduate to the Nomads chapter.

Gagné was a valuable witness, Giauque told the jury, because he was able to explain the terms the gang often used. For example, when a Rocker said he was "occupied," it was enough to explain to the other Rockers that he had an important job to do for the Nomads chapter and shouldn't be asked questions. Giauque also felt it necessary to explain why witnesses like Peter Paradis had been called.

"His situation was a bit different. He was the enemy, a duck, a bird, a quack-quack, call him what you want," Giauque said drawing a few giggles from the jury. The reference was to the logo featured in the Rock Machine's patches. It was apparently supposed to depict an eagle's head, but it appeared cartoonish and ducklike. According to Giauque, "you probably understood, when you saw his patches, why the Hells Angels call them ducks or quack-quacks. It is very clear when we see the patches."

Giauque also told the jury that despite being a high-profile drug dealer in Verdun, Paradis was left so down and out in his final days as a member of the Rock Machine, he had stooped to stealing food from grocery stores. This was around the same time that Pierre Provencher had declared, during a Rockers Mass, that the east was theirs but that places in western Montreal like Verdun were still to be conquered.

Giauque described Paradis as a regular witness and not an informant. He had already fulfilled his first contract by testifying against his former gangmates. He was out of prison when he agreed to sign the second contract, and placed his life on the line to come out of hiding and testify. Giauque also fully acknowledged that Stéphane Sirois might have been looking for revenge over his failed marriage when he decided to become an informant. The prospect of making $100,000 when he was broke also didn't hurt. "The Sirois aspect is important because it involves real evidence that directly implicates members of the organization," she said.

That "real evidence" included a conversation with André Chouinard in which Sirois asked what it would take to get back into the good graces of the Nomads chapter. Chouinard told Sirois to call Jean-Guy Bourgoin. Chouinard also told Sirois to just keep working, make his own path and get as much information on their rivals as he could.

On December 23, 1999, Sirois set up a meeting with Chouinard where he said he wanted to officially ask to be made a member of the Rockers. Chouinard said it was up to the Rockers and that they were 25 members at that point who all thought differently. He said he even felt he had lost control of them. Giauque brought up the now-infamous sushi dinner where Bourgoin said the Hells Angels had a price list rating the value of each rival gang member who was killed. But Bourgoin also explained that Sirois could climb up in the gang without killing someone, that it would just take longer. Giauque reminded the jury of the evidence they'd heard from Gagné, who testified, among other things, about the plan the Hells Angels had to level the Rock Machine hangout in Verdun.

"It demonstrates that the identity of a person had no importance when they were part of the enemy. It is a clear evidence of the intentions of the gang to eliminate the competition through murder," she said.

Ronald (Popo) Paulin, a member of the Rockers.
(John Mahoney, *The Montreal Gazette*)

Down to the Nitty Gritty

The following day, on February 4, 2004, Giauque continued her final arguments, now narrowing the evidence down to each of the accused. She asked the jury to consider several things. First, she asked them to remember a gathering on Provencher's maple syrup farm, where several Rockers from prison made collect calls to talk to the rest of the gang. During one conversation, Ronald Paulin told Beauchamp that there were 30 members of the Rockers at that point. Beauchamp had replied, "We're a nice clique."

"Don't forget that our theory is to the effect that the Hells Angels' Nomads [chapter] controlled the trafficking of diverse drugs while generating huge profits. The proof shown [earlier in the trial] clearly shows how it was done," Giauque said. "It is evident from the evidence that these are not autonomous drug dealers but an association of people who dealt in drugs in a way that was highly organized." Giauque added that videos proved things like how Beau-champ had done guard duty on Michel Rose, who was importing a lot of cocaine for the Nomads.

She also reminded the jury that at one of Luc Bordeleau's residences the police found several weapons and an agenda that indicated he was doing a lot of intelligence gathering for the Hells Angels, and was going to set up gang members with courses on wiretapping and courthouse research. He also had notes concerning the Café Cosenza, known to be a favourite hangout of Vito Rizzuto's at the time. In his bathroom, underneath the mirror, Bordeleau had kept a stash of money.

When going over André Couture's involvement, Giauque pointed to video evidence that indicated he was heavily involved with Normand Robitaille's drug business. Couture helped do himself in by talking very openly during some of the Masses videotaped by the police.

"Remember that the simple fact of being at a Mass is important, very important. The full-fledged members have to attend or they would be sanctioned or have to face the Nomads. It is a significant presence for

André Courture, a member of the Rockers.

the gang and the pursuit of their activities," Giauque said.

On April 27, 2000, during a gang meeting at a motel, it was Couture who announced that Dubois had quit the gang. Couture was reminded that he owed $3,400 to the ten percent fund. He was videotaped saying he had no problem with paying the money. The money was due from a period when he was in prison, a clear indication that his business was operating even while he was behind bars.

Couture had had his share of run-ins with the law while he was with the Rockers. On November 29, 1997, he was arrested after two officers patrolling the Hochelaga Maisonneuve district noticed Couture driving erratically on Bennett Street, in front of the Nomads chapter's hangout. He had backed up into a pole left over from a former railway crossing. When the officers pulled Couture over, they asked him for his licence and registration. When he opened the glove compartment they couldn't help but notice the chrome-plated revolver inside it.

Couture refused to get out of the car. As the officers prepared to arrest him, they could hear someone inside the Nomads chapter's hangout shout, "If you shoot him, we will shoot you." One of the arresting officers would later say in court that he wanted to get out of there fast because he knew who occupied 2101 Bennett Street.

While Couture was being processed, the police opened a sports bag he had with him. It contained a bunch of papers and a note pad. For some reason, Couture consented to having the pages photocopied by the police. He was able to plead guilty and received a $350 fine with a sentence of just two years probation.

But the papers he allowed to be photocopied would later come back to haunt him. Some of the most damaging evidence against Couture in the megatrial was contained in those papers. His lawyer fought to have the documents excluded, because they were evidence from a previous conviction, but lost. It helped prove that Couture worked for Normand Robitaille, collecting money that dealers owed and keeping an accounts receivable. Among the papers was a to-do list citing things like "debug the vehicle" among Couture's chores.

Stéphane (Godasse) Gagné would later recount how Robitaille was furious with Couture when he learned the police had photocopied the documents. Couture was only supposed to have been in possession of the papers for a short while. Gagné would later explain just how important the documents were to Robitaille and the Nomads chapter, as they contained information on how Robitaille had his cocaine cut and listed some of his major clients, including one of Gagné's brothers. But the documents also contained evidence that Robitaille was in the process of gathering personal information on every member of the Nomads chapter's organization to help prevent people from turning informant. Gagné had testified that Maurice (Mom) Boucher once ordered everyone working with him or under him to hand over all personal information, such as their social insurance numbers. Included among the documents photocopied with Couture's permission were personal details, like the social insurance numbers of Donald (Pup) Stockford and Walter (Nurget) Stadnick, the two Ontario members of the Nomads chapter.

As she continued to make her final arguments, Giauque broke down the evidence the prosecution team had on each of the accused. She mentioned how when the police searched Bruno Lefebvre's house in Sainte-Marthe-sur-le-Lac, west of Montreal, they found paperwork in the kitchen indicating he was ready to sell it for $435,000. He also had a mortgage for $150,000. The police also found a document that claimed he worked for a company, earning $317 net per week. Yet Lefebvre could afford to pay $50,000 cash as a down payment on a house and was sometimes videotaped by the police driving around in a brand new Cadillac. Stéphane Sirois had said Lefebvre was introduced into the

Rockers while dealing drugs for Pierre Provencher in Verdun between 1996 and 1998. In 1997, Lefebvre took one for the team when he was shot while he and a few other Rockers were breaking up a Rock Machine drug den. But the shot didn't come from a Rock Machine gun.

Informant Aimé Simard testified in a trial a few years earlier that it took Lefebvre a few minutes to realize he had been shot by accident by a fellow Rocker while they were shaking down the rival drug dealers, torturing them for information on who ran the drug den. The gang was left to search for a doctor who would remove the bullet, which had lodged in Lefebvre's upper body, without calling the police.

While going over the evidence against Richard (Dick) Mayrand, Giauque focused on his apparent role in the brief truce between the Rock Machine and the Hells Angels. Mayrand had been present at the dinner at the Bleu Marin restaurant where the two gangs had agreed to a ceasefire. "What you have to understand of this is that the people who were present [at the dinner] and represented the two rival gangs had the authority to stop a war that had lasted for years. These were the heads of each organization," Giauque said.

Giauque also used wiretaps to show that Mayrand had apparently been brought into the Nomads chapter as a leader, in particular over diplomatic issues. On November 28, 2000, at around 9 p.m., the police listened in as Mayrand called George Wegers, the U.S. leader of the Bandidos. Wegers lived in the west coast state of Washington. The conversation was brief but polite, considering it was between the leaders of two rival gangs.

"How are you?" Wegers had asked. Mayrand laughed and said that things "could be better" and repeated that he was willing to take a plane to meet with Wegers somewhere "to fix something."

"So Mr. Mayrand was the person designated by the Hells Angels' organization to meet a [member of the] Bandidos at the other end of the country to settle business," Giauque said, adding it was obvious the conversation was related to the biker war. "Does this not give you an idea of Mr. Mayrand's importance in the gang?"

What Giauque was not able to tell the jury was that the police had tracked Mayrand to the eventual meeting with Wegers. Sûreté du Québec Sgt. Guy Ouellette was informed that the meeting was going to take place in British Columbia. Based on past experience, he figured Mayrand and Wegers would meet at the Peace Arch Park, which sits on the spot where Washington Interstate 5 meets with Highway 99 at the Canada/U.S. border. The park is a sort of no man's land where both Mayrand and Wegers could meet without technically having to cross an international border. Both men had criminal records, and could have been arrested crossing into either country. Wegers had already been arrested years earlier for meeting with the Rock Machine in Quebec City.

The meeting was believed to be related to something that had happened at a motorcycle show in Europe a week earlier. Several members of the Rock Machine had attended the show and were shown what their patches as new members of the Bandidos were going to look like. This was while the Hells Angels and the Rock Machine were supposed to be in a truce. Mayrand was recorded calling his former Hells Angel brother in the Montreal chapter, David (Gyrator) Giles, who had moved to B.C. to join a Hells Angels' chapter there, asking him for bodyguards for the meeting. Giles said he would take care of it.

On November 30, 2000, Mayrand met with Wegers in Peace Arch Park while the police watched from a distance. Mayrand had two bodyguards with him, Rick Ciarnello and John Bryce. Wegers also had bodyguards. The two gang leaders talked for a while, with Mayrand appearing to do most of the talking. Wegers listened with no expression on his face. The meeting ended without incident. Judging by what happened almost immediately afterward, it appears that Mayrand let Wegers know that the Hells Angels were going to respond to the fact the Rock Machine was to be patched over by the Bandidos in Quebec and Ontario.

Within days of the meeting with Wegers, it was apparent Mayrand was helping to lead the push to create new Hells Angels' chapters in Ontario. On December 7, 2000, Mayrand and Mathieu were recorded in a phone conversation discussing an order of some 100 new Hells Angels' patches. By December 12, that number had increased to 160, apparently thanks to Donald (Pup) Stockford. Mayrand was recorded talking to Jacques Emond, a longtime member of the Sherbrooke chapter, informing him of the good news. Emond had once lived in British Columbia and apparently still had ties there.

"So it's going to happen in eight days?" Emond said of the eventual patch-over party to be held in Sorel.

"That's it."

"Okay."

"Is that all right?"

"So, I'll alert the west."

"You're going to alert the west and your chapter," Mayrand told Emond before saying goodbye. Giauque pointed to the calls as proof of Mayrand's importance in the Hells Angels.

"The defense might tell you that Mr. Mayrand only joined the Nomads on January 12, 2000, that his actions before that date prove nothing and that they were meetings between friends and that is all. I believe it is impossible to believe this. Could you really believe that Richard Mayrand had been a member of the Hells Angels' Montreal [chapter] for more than 15 years without having anything more than an amicable relationship with them? It is impossible," she said.

When Giauque talked about Sylvain Moreau, she mentioned how his passport showed he had traveled to Barbados on November 4, 2000, and to Cancun in February 2001. Giauque said it was not bad for a guy who claimed to make $511 net for two weeks and $10,915 net annual income for 1999.

Closing Arguments

"All of the manifest acts committed with the goal of eliminating the competition by the co-accused named in the indictment are opposable to each of the accused," Giauque said as she began to wrap up her arguments. Even the objects seized at their homes, which might have seemed somewhat banal at first, could be considered as important.

"We submit that the different objects found are manifestly proof of an agreement between the co-conspirators and can serve as evidence on all three charges. All of these objects can be considered as manifest acts against the accused because they were used in the pursuit of the common goal. Think of the patches on different clothes, the laminated cards [with each member's phone numbers listed on them], the plaques, the trophies, the greeting cards, the photos of friends and of enemies but also the map, the weapons, the money found and the money found in the Nomads Bank. All of those objects had one utility: to assure the cohesion of the gang, its visibility and its supremacy."

The prosecutor also explained the importance of the boring videos the jury had watched of gang members standing in front of restaurants and hotels obviously doing guard duty.

"They showed the importance of the gang and the hierarchy. Think of the watch. Think of the way the Nomads accepted that the Rockers were doing their watch. It was their due," she said. "If there is one [type of] evidence that should be considered as the pursuit of a common goal it is the Masses. In looking at them, you realize immediately that they were only held to assure the proper function of the gang and its diverse activities. There is no other reason for its existence. Presence was obligatory and they were held in secret. Any absence had to be justified. It is impossible to think that we can take part in a Mass by chance. We pass by and see a closed door, we open it and sit right down. It's impossible to think that happened."

The wiretaps the jury listened to also opened a door to life in the Nomads chapter and the Rockers. The calls gang members made from prisons in particular were revealing.

"Even in prison they were combating their enemies. Even if they were detained, the situation did not change. You know that in the case of André Couture and Sylvain Moreau, they continued to pay their ten percent while they were detained," Giauque said. "Prison changed nothing when it came to business. Just because they were detained, that didn't mean they couldn't continue to take part in their gang activities and were still part of the gang. To the contrary, everyone took care of them."

The prosecutor then explained the gangsterism charge the jury was going to have to decide on. "I would submit to you that the evidence demonstrated that all of the members of the gang regularly committed criminal acts punishable by a sentence of five years or more, and that [they did so] with the knowledge of all of them. So, all of them knew that the other members were trafficking in prohibited substances," she said.

"I will repeat again that being part of the Hells Angels is not a crime in itself. But we have surely proven to you that the organization is a gang in the sense of the Criminal Code, and that it is a criminal organization. A criminal organization does not exist on its own. It is the members who compose it that commit the crimes."

When the defense lawyers took their turn, the main theme that ran through their final arguments was that the Crown had presented very little direct incriminating evidence against their clients. Perhaps the most impressive final arguments from the defense side came from Lucie Joncas, the lawyer who represented Sebastien Beauchamp, who said it would take a "contortionist from the Cirque du Soleil" to perform the "intellectual gymnastics"

372

required to convict her client. In an attempt to destroy the credibility of one of the most damaging witnesses against Beau-champ, Joncas portrayed informant Serge Boutin as a man still fuming over an insult made towards his wife.

"If there was one [informant] who wanted to bury my client, it was [Boutin]," Joncas said. She referred the jury to a wiretapped conversation from October 7, 2000, before Boutin had become an informant and was still facing a possible first-degree murder trial in Claude De Serres' death. Boutin was upset because a not yet full-patch member of the Rockers had insulted his wife at a Rockers' party. At the time, Beauchamp was just days away from becoming a full-patch Rocker. Boutin said two or three friends informed him of what was said while he was behind bars. Provencher tried to keep things cool, apparently aware of how potentially explosive the situation was.

"He didn't know she was my wife?" Boutin asked during the conversation.

"You know him, him there," Provencher replied.

"But even if he didn't know it was my wife. You know, even if he didn't know it was my wife."

"That's it."

"You can't . . . you have to pay attention to what you say."

"Yes. Yes."

"To anybody's wife."

"There are times, you know, when you get unglued."

"Yeah, yeah."

"There are times when you don't know what you're saying."

"Hmmm. Hmmm."

"You know, there are times when you drunk, when you don't even remember what you did."

"Ah yes."

"So, you know, the next morning he apologized and everything."

Joncas argued that the apology wasn't enough, and that when Boutin testified Beauchamp sold drugs for the Hells Angels on Saint Denis Street, he was doing it to get back for the slight to his wife. The proof of that, Joncas said, was in another wiretapped conversation, taped a week later in which Boutin talked to another Rocker and called Beauchamp a nut. He also said he would look into what had happened if he ever got out of prison.

Lawyer Jean-Pierre Sharpe pointed to the most damaging direct evidence against his client Bruno Lefebvre and tried to downplay it. Before his arrest, Lefebvre owned a house in Sainte-Marthe-sur-le-Lac that he was preparing to sell for $435,000. He had made a $50,000 cash down payment when buying the house for $200,000, despite claiming to earn only $370 a week. Sharpe suggested this should not be taken as a sign Lefebvre was a drug dealer. "Some people make a living that way," Sharpe said, alluding to the real-estate deal. "Donald Trump does it. Should we charge Donald Trump with conspiracy for that?"

Guy Quirion, the lawyer who represented Éric (Pif) Fournier, tried to convince the jury that the accused were victims of police planting evidence. He pointed to inconsistencies in how evidence seized at one Hells Angels' home was recorded and accused the police of planting one of the incriminating photo albums containing pictures of most of the members of the Alliance.

Ronald (Popo) Paulin's lawyer, Lise Rochefort, tried to get on the jury's good side by suggesting that everyone involved in the lengthy trial should be given a T-shirt with the phrase "I survived Gouin" written on it, a reference to their time spent in the specially built courthouse in northern Montreal. Rochefort likened her client to a kid who badly wanted to be part of a hockey team but couldn't skate.

"That kid is willing to do menial tasks like fill water bottles and carry pucks but is not part of the team," she said. She pointed out that the jury had heard a wiretapped conversation where one Rocker had said Paulin did nothing but arrange for T-shirts and plaques to be made for the gang.

After Judge Beliveau made his instructions to the jury, they were sequestered and left to assess all that they had heard and seen over the past year. It would take them 12 days to come up with verdicts.

The Verdicts

March 1, 2004, was a spectacular day weather-wise in Montreal. Instead of charging in like a lion, a bright sun ushered in March with a reminder that spring was on its way. In a park less than a kilometre away from the courthouse sat a payloader and other equipment being used to break up ice on the Riviére des Prairies which was overflowing as the weather got warmer that winter. As the trial neared its end, people making their way to the court-house on Gouin Blvd. could see work crews pounding away at huge blocks of ice, hoping to prevent serious flooding in Laval across the river. The announcement that the jury had a verdict came early in the afternoon.

Because of the number of lawyers involved, there was a long delay between the time the jury informed Beliveau that they had verdicts and when they came out to deliver them. As he waited, Éric (Pif) Fournier paced in the enclosed prisoners' dock, look-ing somewhat like a caged predator. His fellow Rocker André Couture paced as well. Richard (Dick) Mayrand appeared to be keeping his cool. He joked with his lawyer through a phone that connected the prisoners' dock with the courtroom. Mayrand shrugged often during the conversation, as if resigned to what-ever fate was about to befall him. After he hung up with his lawyer, Mayrand and Beauchamp shared a joke and laughed.

But as the wait grew longer a sense of tension filled the air. Beliveau felt it necessary to address the situation. He told every-one assembled in the courtroom that if they couldn't take the pressure they should leave. He did not want any outburst reactions to the verdicts.

As the jury entered the courtroom, their eyes were fixed on anything but the accused. Beliveau thanked them for their work and the sacrifice they had made. He also publicly thanked their relatives for putting up with the incredibly long trial. Then juror number eight, a young man, was asked to read out the verdicts.

Following alphabetical order, Beauchamp's verdicts were read first. Some people gasped as they heard the "not guilty" verdict on the first count against him. But Beauchamp had been behind bars for most of the time Project Rush was carried out, so those who had followed the trial closely were not surprised to hear he had been cleared of conspiring to murder members of the Alliance. But he was found guilty of drug trafficking and participating in the activities of a gang. Despite being convicted on the lesser counts, Beauchamp' reaction was not difficult to read. He had a smile that stretched from ear to ear, and he shot a wink towards his lawyer Lucie Joncas that was plainly visible from the back of the courtroom.

All of the remaining eight gangsters were found guilty on all three counts. Luc (Bordel) Bordeleau appeared genuinely stunned as the foreman repeated "*coupable*" three times in his case. Mayrand raised his eyebrows and shook his head in apparent disgust. He then turned towards the section of the courtroom reserved for the audience and stared toward a friend, his face revealing little emotion. Alain Dubois appeared to be furious with the verdicts. His arms were folded tightly across his chest and his face turned crimson red. But he'd obviously expected to be convicted of something. He was the only accused out on bail in the case and had packed a gym bag full of clothes that day. After he was led into the prisoners' dock to sit with his former gangmates, he fumed. One of the Rockers tried to make a joke out of it, but Dubois wanted nothing to do with it. He appeared to tell the others to shut up, or something to that effect. Paulin sat quietly, sometimes shaking his head in apparent disbelief. Before being arrested in Project Rush, the most serious thing Paulin had ever been convicted of was unemployment fraud and neglecting his dog by not feeding it. Now a jury had concluded he was a gangster.

Sentencing Those Who Went the Distance

All that was left to decide was how the convicted would be punished for their crimes. A few weeks after the verdict, the two sides debated what sentences were merited. Because they hadn't plead guilty, like most of the others arrested in Project Rush, it was argued by Giauque that their sentences should be exemplary. Luc (Bordel) Bordeleau slapped his knee and laughed out loud when he heard Giauque say she was seeking a 29-year sentence for Richard (Dick) Mayrand. Bordeleau also laughed when she mentioned, during sentencing arguments of March 22, 2004, that she was seeking 24 years for him. Alain Dubois would be at the low end of the sentencing recommendations. But even though he had only been with the Rockers for a matter of months, Giauque was still asking for a 14-year term.

The sentence recommendations did not seem out of order considering that just two weeks earlier, two members of the Nomads chapter, André Chouinard (who left the Hells Angels just before Operation Springtime 2001 was carried out) and Michel Rose, had pleaded guilty to similar charges and received 20-year sentences. Unlike Mayrand, they had spared the province the cost of a lengthy trial. Other members, like Mathieu and Robitaille, had agreed to plead guilty in exchange for 20-year sentences.

Before the defense lawyers made their sentencing arguments, François Bordeleau made an odd request by seeking a publication ban on the identities of some of the people who might testify as to the good character of his client, Bruno Lefebvre. He said he had witnesses lined up who would testify only if their names wouldn't be mentioned. For example, Bordeleau said, he had the owner of a golf course ready to come in and vouch for Lefebvre, but who did not want his business associated with the Hells Angels. Beliveau said he could understand why someone wouldn't want to be associated with the Hells Angels, but rejected the request.

In Paulin's case, one witness was willing to testify on his behalf. It was the owner of the Montreal embroidery shop where Paulin had ordered all of the Rockers T-shirts over the years. Paulin was so good for business, the owner had hired him as a part-time salesman in 2000, after Paulin decided to retire from the Rockers.

Witnesses portrayed Dubois as a loyal and loving hockey dad who gave a lot of his free time to the Chateauguay Hockey Association. He sometimes coached games and treated the kids to dinners. After his arrest, Dubois limited his work to being a volunteer for hockey tournaments, doing things like selecting the stars of games and serving as a goal judge.

"I don't know one kid who doesn't like him," said one witness. Another witness said she'd known the Dubois family for years. "They have family values," she said as Dubois' father Jean-Guy, a convicted killer, looked on from the audience section of the courtroom.

By April 8, 2004, Beliveau was ready to deliver his sentences. His 69-page judgement was the first real glimpse into what the Superior Court judge truly thought of the Crown's case. He agreed with the Crown arguments that, at least in the cases of Bordeleau, Couture, Fournier, Lefebvre, Mayrand and Moreau, exemplary sentences were appropriate. He noted that it hadn't been proven that Bordeleau and Fournier sold drugs for the network. But it had been proven that all members of the Rockers paid into the ten percent fund, so the pair had to have been doing something to earn their salaries. It had also been proven that

Fournier had done "the watch" on several occasions, and that Bordeleau was an organizer of the guard duty. In doing so they played necessary roles in maintaining the gang's turf.

In Dubois' case, Beliveau took into consideration that he had apparently been a drug dealer for a long time. But he also felt that Dubois' departure from the Rockers after only a few months reflected that he didn't believe "in the values of the organization." It was a value system where Rockers knew that if they became Hells Angels they were joining a lifestyle. In his judgement, Beliveau quoted Sylvain Laplante acknowledging, during one of the Masses the police recorded, that life as a Hells Angel was "24 hours out of 24 hours."

Beliveau rated Paulin's involvement as "medium," because while it was obvious he adhered to the gang's values, there was little proof he participated in their more serious activities. Beliveau didn't see any hope of rehabilitation except in the cases of Dubois and Paulin. He accepted the argument from Paulin's defense lawyer that he was like the kid who didn't have enough talent to make the local hockey team so he was willing to do any minor tasks to fit in and be accepted. But he noted that such an attitude in the context of the Hells Angels presented a real danger for society. He couldn't look the other way on the fact that Paulin had held down regular jobs in his life and chose, well into his adult years, to become a member of the Rockers and remain there for six years, knowing full well what the gang did.

Beliveau also let his opinion be known about how some of the defense lawyers behaved during the trial. When it came to factoring in the time eight of the nine accused had already spent behind bars awaiting the outcome of their case, Beliveau could not look past the irritating delays caused by some of the defense lawyers, calling their refusal to admit certain evidence nothing but a stall tactic. He estimated that without the useless delays, the trial would have lasted about six months, half as long as it actually did.

He also pointed out that during the English-language trial of Donald Stockford and Walter Stadnick, which had just begun at that point, the lawyers involved had agreed to submit 213 admissions which took prosecutor Randall Richmond just four days, and several sips of water, to read before Justice Jerry Zigman.

In Sebastien Beauchamp's case, Beliveau sentenced the Rocker to eight years for his conviction on the drug trafficking charge, and another five to be served consecutively for participating in the activities of a gang.

In Luc Bordeleau's case, Beliveau noted his lengthy criminal record and association with the Hells Angels, right up to the point where he became a prospect in the Nomads chapter. The judge sentenced him to 10 years for conspiracy to murder, 10 years to be served concurrently for drug trafficking and another 10 to be served consecutively for participating in the activities of a gang.

Alain Dubois received only a two-year sentence for conspiring to murder rival gang members but also an eight-year sentence to be served concurrently for drug trafficking. He was also sentenced to two years to be served consecutively for participating in gang activities. Beliveau did not require that Dubois serve at least half of his sentence.

In Richard Mayrand's case, Beliveau took note of the fact he had been a member of the Hells Angels for years. He was sentenced to 10 years for conspiracy to murder, another 10 to be served concurrently for drug trafficking and 12 years to be served consecutively for participating in gang activities. With time served factored in, he would be required to serve 16 years and 9 months, and do at least half of it behind bars.

Beliveau felt that if anyone in the bunch had a chance at rehabilitation it was Paulin. He was sentenced to seven years for conspiracy to commit murder, seven to be served concurrently for drug trafficking and five years to be served consecutively for participating in the activities of a gang. With time served factored in, he had to serve six years and nine months, with the obligation of having to serve two and a half years before being eligible for parole.

While Beliveau's tough stance towards the defense was applauded by some, the Quebec Court of Appeal did not agree with him. In June 2005, more than a year after the sentences were rendered, the appeal court reduced Beauchamp's and Dubois' sentences by nine months each.

In the summary of the judgement Justice Francois Doyon wrote that Beliveau "went too far" in lumping together the eight lawyers as a whole. Beauchamp's lawyer Lucie Joncas in particular had not taken part in the aggressive tactics the others employed. Joncas has fought a clean fight and therefore her client did not deserve to be punished.

The appeal court also determined there was no proof that the bikers knew their lawyers were going to act in an unacceptable manner.

Conclusion

Patrick Turcotte was by no means an important player in the biker gang war. He was a street-level drug dealer trying to do business for the Rock Machine in Verdun, a part of the Montreal Island the gang had for the most part given up on by the time Turcotte was gunned down by Pierre (Peanut) Laurin and Paul Brisebois, two members of the Rockers eager to prove themselves to the Nomads chapter. Turcotte did not have the criminal influence of a Renaud Jomphe or even Peter Paradis, two men who paid dearly for trying to prevent the Hells Angels from taking over Verdun. But details of Turcotte's death will remain with me for a long while for a few reasons.

On May 1, 2000, I went out to cover the murder for *The Gazette* late in the afternoon, grumbling to myself about how inconveniently the assignment came late in my shift, coupled with the dark clouds in the sky threatening rain. By then, things had become so predictable in the biker war that I had suggested to the assigned photographer that he drive around the blocks of Verdun that surrounded the murder scene to look out for any flaming vehicles.

Within minutes, the photographer found the smoldering minivan used in the slaying. It had been doused with an accelerant and torched. A flaming minivan had essentially become a signature for the Hells Angels' hits, like marking a Z for Zorro.

Claiming to know the motive behind a murder before even knowing the identity of the victim might sound like a boast, but it isn't. I refer to Turcotte's murder sometimes when attempting to describe the overall mood in Quebec towards the biker war on the day he was killed. The war had been dragging on for six years at that point. Drug dealers were being murdered in broad daylight on residential streets.

Within an hour of arriving at the scene, a police source was able to confirm that Turcotte was dealing drugs for the Rock Machine and tell me who he was friendly with in the gang. The police who were investigating the biker clearly had good intelligence information.

But what struck me most was how the residents of that Verdun neighborhood reacted to the brutally violent slaying that had just played itself out on their streets. As I stayed on the scene and the afternoon turned to early evening, I walked into a nearby restaurant just outside the investigation's yellow police-tape perimeter. I tried to chat up some people as they munched away on poutine and hot dogs, but they had little to say. Despite the fact a murder had just taken place a few hours earlier on their street, the greasy spoon was packed with diners, some of whom made jokes, saying things like, "No one is going to miss him."

Those closest to the restaurant's window could, for their dining pleasure, watch Turcotte's blood trickle into a nearby sewer as the rain began to fall and wash it away. Lying next to the red puddle was Turcotte's pager, the standard tool of the drug trafficking trade. The blood and the pager sitting next to each other on the Verdun pavement while blocks away a minivan smoldered told the story of what had just happened. The average Montrealer could have seen the images on television that night with the sound off and correctly concluded the news item was about a Hells Angels' hit.

As I rode away from the murder scene in a taxi, the blasé mood in that restaurant disturbed me the more I thought about it. Parts of Verdun have always been rough, but people bringing their children into a restaurant to munch on fries within view of homicide detectives looking for things like discarded firearms was unsettling. Montrealers had become so used to the biker war they were numb to it.

Perhaps that is because Montreal's underworld history is so steeped in violence. To some, the biker gang war likely seemed to be a mere continuation of decades worth of murderous violence in the city.

When Alain Dubois decided to join the Rockers, his father Jean-Guy must have thought back to the 1970s when his gang was engaged in a war that featured remarkable similarities to the current biker war. In that conflict, the leaders, who were fighting over southwest parts of Montreal, had also known each other for years before greed took over and hell broke loose. And just like in the biker war, the conflict between the Dubois brothers and a rival gang was, according to some who were involved, touched off when the Dubois brothers killed a drug dealer who refused to buy from them. Also, at least three of the Hells Angels who were founding members of the Nomads chapter joined the gang during the early 1980s, during or just after the Hells Angels' Montreal chapter had forced the Outlaws, a rival gang that arrived in Quebec in 1977, out of the province entirely in a war that featured the same extreme violence, bombings and murders as the Nomads chapter's war with the Alliance did.

One of the clearest signs the war was over came when inmates from both the Bandidos and the Hells Angels requested in 2003 that they no longer be segregated from each other at the Donnacona penitentiary near Quebec City. In the years since Operation Springtime 2001, only a handful of homicides in Montreal appeared to be tied to biker gang activity. With all of the convictions produced by the Project Rush investigation, the Nomads chapter was "frozen," a term used when a chapter cannot meet the minimum requirements of having six full-patch members who are not behind bars. Most of the members of the Quebec-based Nomads chapter are now part of what the Hells Angels call the Big House Crew, a reference to incarcerated members. All Hells Angels who are behind bars receive a newsletter, informing them of where they can correspond with other jailed gang members.

But the Hells Angels, in Canada especially, have a history of not tolerating competition for long. It is something worth considering as the chapters set up in Ontario by the Quebec-based Hells Angels continue to grow.

After refusing to open a chapter in Ontario for decades, the Hells Angels in Quebec suddenly opened the floodgates in 2000 and set up shop all over the province. According to a 2002 estimate, there were 178 members of the Hells Angels in Ontario, with another 66 waiting in the wings at either the prospect or hang-around level. The members are required to communicate with each other through encrypted email. The Angels' influence is apparently spreading, as the gang set up a new chapter in Hamilton in 2005 and were rumored to be creating more. Evidence has also been presented in court indicating that Hells Angels' members based in Ontario were considering setting up a chapter in New Brunswick.

Quebec's influence over the Ontario chapters is very evident. Several of the members of the Nomads chapter in Ontario were participants on either side of Quebec's biker war. Brett Simmons, the same person who was injured as a getaway driver when the Rock Machine tried to blow up the bunker of a Hells Angels' affiliate club in 1995, was arrested ten years later, in June 2005, on charges that, as a member of Hells Angels in Ontario, he was part of a large-scale drug trafficking ring.

An accidental shooting in North York in April 2004 that left a mother of three paralyzed is a further sign the Hells Angels in Ontario are following the model of the men who brought them into the fold, a collection of some of the worst criminals Canada has ever seen. The charges laid in the shooting indicate two things that bear a striking resemblance to how the Nomads chapter operated in Quebec. One is that they have close ties to other powerful organized crime groups, like the Mafia, and the other is that they are just as reckless as they were in Quebec.

But there is also evidence the Ontario chapters have developed a policy of pursuing other means before settling their problems with violence. The presidents of the Ontario chapters are believed to have gone over this policy at a meeting held in 2002.

Cracks are even beginning to show in the quiet-on-the-surface Sherbrooke chapter, considered one of the biggest (in terms of membership) and richest chapters in all of Canada. The mega-trials in Quebec provided evidence that the Sherbrooke chapter tried its best to stay autonomous from Maurice (Mom) Boucher and his monopolistic plans. For the most part, the Sherbrooke chapter kept a low profile during Quebec's biker war. But at least two of its members are under investigation for allegedly laundering millions of dollars and cheating provinces of even more money through the sale of cars.

During the spring of 2005, RCMP investigators spread out in various parts of the Eastern Townships and elsewhere in Quebec searching businesses the chapter's members had acquired over the years. The RCMP investigation started in London, Ontario, where one of the two Sherbrooke members who were being investigated set up a prospect chapter in 2001.

There are also signs that people won't forget that the Hells Angels in Ontario grew out of Quebec's violent biker war. In March 2005, a prosecutor in Barrie, Ontario, played a police videotape of the December 2000 patch-over ceremony in Sorel as he made his closing arguments in an extortion trial involving two Ontario Hells Angels based in Woodbridge. The prosecutor said he did it to prove the pair were part of a large criminal organization, and not just a couple of "motorcycle-riding enthusiasts," as the Ontario chapters would like the general public to believe.

The trial produced a precedent-setting judgement when, on June 30, 2005, Ontario Superior Court Justice Michele Fuerst determined the Hells Angels to be a criminal organization in Canada. Steven (Tiger) Lindsay, a man who had the words "Hells Angels" tattooed on his chest, and Ray Bonner were found guilty of extortion and committing a crime "in association with" a criminal organization, part of federal anti-gang legislation that allows gang members to be sentenced to an additional 14 years for their crimes. In that case, an expert on organized crime testified that the key test of a criminal organization is its ability to exist beyond the control of one leader.

The Hells Angels have grown worldwide from three chapters in California in 1957 to 227 chapters, with more than 2,500 members, in 29 countries. That includes 118 members in Quebec.

Guy Ouellette, the retired Sûreté du Québec sergeant, testified during the Barrie trial as well, revealing that members of the South, Trois Rivières and Sherbrooke chapters picked up the pieces in Montreal's lucrative drug trade after the Nomads chapter in Montreal was shut down in 2001. Fuerst wrote in her judgement: "It simply defies common sense that a group so deeply involved in crime in Quebec would have any interest in establishing benign counterparts in a neighboring province. It makes little sense that its primary ambassadors would be prolific drug traffickers, if the purpose of expansion was benign. It makes even less sense that if it were expanding for benign reasons, it would choose to do so by assimilating long-established outlaw motorcycle clubs, contrary to its usual cautious approach to acquiring new members. It does make every sense that, at a time when it was under pressure because of events in Quebec, it would expand to strengthen its drug trafficking networks and attempt to shut out its competitor."

Hopefully, no one in Ontario is buying the argument the Hells Angels are simply riding enthusiasts.

Cast of Characters

Sebastien (Bass) Beauchamp — Joined the Rockers as a striker on March 26, 1999, and became a full-patch member on October 16, 2000. He was convicted of drug trafficking and gangsterism but dodged a bullet when a jury also acquitted him of conspiring to murder rival gang members. He was sentenced to serve seven years and nine months beginning from the day he was sentenced, April 8, 2004. The Quebec Court of Appeal later reduced the sentence to seven years.

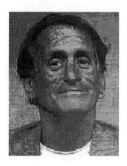

Normand (Pluch) Bélanger — A close friend of Maurice (Mom) Boucher. He was considered an important player in the Hells Angels' expansion into the ecstasy market. He joined the Rockers on March 26, 1998. He became a prospect in the Nomads chapter on October 5, 2000. He was excused from one of the Hells Angels' megatrials because he suffered from cirrhosis caused by hepatitis B, diabetes, hypertension and the after-effects of two heart attacks and was too ill to assist his lawyer. When he was arrested a second time in a loansharking case brought against him and other Hells Angels in February 2004, he had to appear in court in a wheelchair. He died in May 2004.

(John Mahoney, The Montreal Gazette)

Luc (Bordel) Bordeleau — A founding member of the Rockers when the gang was created by Boucher on March 26, 1992. Served a five-year term for the Hells Angels after he was caught scuba diving while looking for a large quantity of cocaine gang members had to toss overboard during the early 1990s. He had close ties to Boucher and lived near his compound. He was made a prospect in the Nomads chapter on its fifth anniversary. When the police searched his house in 2001 they found a grenade launcher among a collection of other weapons. He was convicted in the only Project Rush–related trial to go before a jury. With the time he served awaiting the outcome of his case counting as double, he was sentenced to serve more than 14 years starting from April 8, 2004, his sentencing date. He has to serve at least half that behind bars before he can apply for parole.

Françis (Le Fils) Boucher — The son of Hells Angels' leader Maurice (Mom) Boucher. He was made a member of the Rockers on March 26, 1999. On November 18, 2002, he pleaded guilty to his role in the biker war and was sentenced to serve a 10-year sentence from that date. He is required to serve at least half his sentence before he can apply for parole.

(John Mahoney, The Montreal Gazette)

Maurice (Mom) Boucher — Became a Hells Angel on May 1, 1987. Created a gang of thugs and drug dealers called the Rockers in 1992. Split off from the Montreal chapter and formed his own elite Nomads chapter which was chartered on June 24, 1995. Many informants describe him as the leader behind the Nomads during the biker war and the person who started the conflict. Sentenced to life in prison on two first-degree murder convictions and an attempted murder conviction after he ordered the Rockers to kill prison guards in an effort to destabilize the justice system. He has appealed the verdicts.

(John Mahoney, The Montreal Gazette)

Jean-Guy Bourgoin — A founding member of the Rockers. He remained with the underling gang throughout the biker war and was still a member when he was arrested in 2001. On September 23, 2003, he and a group of fellow Rockers and Hells Angels ended their megatrial by agreeing to a plea bargain that saw first-degree murder charges dropped. Bourgoin was sentenced to 15 years. With time served factored in, he had only 10 years left on the sentence from the day he pleaded guilty.

Serge (Pacha) Boutin — Started out the biker war as a drug dealer for a group called the Alliance which opposed the Hells Angels. Joined the Rockers on October 12, 1999, and decided to turn informant after being charged with helping to kill an informant and several other criminal accusations. He was sentenced to life for the murder of the informant but he managed to plead guilty to manslaughter which meant he would have quicker access to parole.

Paul Brisebois — Was named a member of the Rockers around the same time he and Laurin killed a Verdun drug dealer. He became a prospect in the Nomads chapter on December 11, 2000. His case was severed from one of the megatrials and he later managed to plead guilty to second-degree murder even though his DNA was found at the scene of the murder of drug dealer Patrick Turcotte. As part of his plea bargain he is serving a life sentence but is eligible for parole in 2011.

Salvatore Brunetti — Served time in prison near the beginning of the biker war as a member of the Dark Circle, one of the rival gangs that took on the Hells Angels. When the war ended he was serving a short sentence as a member of the Hells Angels. He defected to the Nomads chapter on December 19, 2000. On November 18, 2002, he agreed to plead guilty to drug trafficking and was sentenced to three years. By late 2004 he was released on parole after reaching the two-thirds mark of his sentence.

David (Wolf) Carroll — Was a founding member of the Hells Angels' Halifax chapter on December 5, 1984. Transferred to the Montreal chapter in 1990 and then joined the Nomads chapter in 1995. Disappeared when a warrant was issued for his arrest in March 2001 and has never been seen since.

René Charlebois — Joined the Rockers in April 1997. Evidence tied him to at least two murders committed during the biker war as well as the slaying of a police informant. Charlebois was apparently rewarded well for his work as a Rocker and was made a full-patch member of the Nomads chapter on April 14, 2000. Originally sentenced to 20 years when he pleaded guilty in his megatrial case on September 23, 2003. He also later agreed to a plea bargain in a case where he was charged with killing an informant. He was sentenced to life after pleading guilty to second-degree murder.

André Chouinard — Joined the Rockers on July 15, 1994. Quickly became a close confidant to Boucher because his clean-cut image and lack of a police record did not draw police attention to the Hells Angels' leader. Four years later he became a full-patch member of the Nomads chapter. He left the gang "in good standing" on July 20, 2000. Despite leaving the Hells Angels he was charged in Project Rush and was in hiding for several months until the police tracked him down. He had been hiding in a house in the Eastern Townships. On March 8, 2004, he pleaded guilty to conspiring to murder rival gang members, drug trafficking and gangsterism. He agreed to a twenty-two-year sentence, one of the harshest given in connection with Project Rush. It is believed he agreed to the sentence because he was also facing the possibility of being extradited to the U.S. to face a trial for drug smuggling which might have produced an even tougher sentence.

Raynald Desjardins — A key member of Montreal's Mafia who spent all of the biker war behind bars. He was doing time for his role in a major drug bust that netted members of the Mafia and the Hells Angels in the early 1990s. During the investigation, Desjardins was seen meeting with Maurice (Mom) Boucher. He was released in 2004 after serving 10 years of a 15-year sentence he received. While behind bars he hung out with members of the Hells Angels.

Alain Dubois — the son of a notorious gangster who himself was part of an organized crime gang. He was made a member of the Rockers on August 24, 1999, but left the gang on April 26, 2000, but was still charged in connection with Project Rush. He was convicted by a jury and was sentenced, on April 8, 2004, to nine years and nine months. The Quebec Court of Appeal later reduced the sentence to nine years.

Paul (Fon Fon) Fontaine — A member of the Rockers early on in the biker war. He was made a prospect in the Nomads chapter on July 1, 1997, and later promoted to full-patch member in 1998, while he was on the lam attempting to avoid being tried for the murder of a provincial prison guard. He would be found by the police in 2004.

Éric (Pif) Fournier — Joined the Rockers on October 24, 1999. He was the bodyguard of Louis (Melou) Roy until Roy disappeared. Fournier got away with murder early on in the biker war after evidence was mistakenly destroyed before his criminal trial could begin. He was convicted of conspiring to murder rival gang members, drug trafficking and gangsterism. On April 8, 2004, he was sentenced to nine years on top of the time he spent behind bars awaiting the outcome of his case. In June 2004 he also pleaded guilty to murdering one of the innocent victims of the biker war and received a life sentence with no chance at parole until he has served 15 years behind bars.

Stéphane (Godasse) Gagné — The trigger man in the murders of two prison guards. Gagné turned informant after he was arrested in 1997. He would become the key witness in the trial that ultimately sent Maurice (Mom) Boucher behind bars.

Normand (Biff) Hamel — A close friend of Boucher who became a Hells Angel on October 5, 1986, only months before Mom did. He was chosen to be a founding member of the Nomads chapter. Was murdered in Laval in April 2000.

Patrick Henault — An aggressive member of the Alliance who turned informant after he was arrested in a botched hit on a friend of Maurice (Mom) Boucher. He would help give details, in the Hells Angels' megatrials, about how the gang war looked from the other side.

Stéphane (Archie) Hilareguy — Was made a member of the Rockers on March 26, 1999. He disappeared about a year later when his name was tied to two murders he helped carry out for the Hells Angels. His remains were later found in the Eastern Townships.

Denis Houle — Became a Hells Angel on October 5, 1982. Was chosen to be among the elite of the Nomads chapter in 1995 even though he had spent several of the previous years behind bars. Survived at least two attempts on his life during the biker war. Pleaded guilty to conspiracy to commit murder and other charges on September 23, 2003, and was sentenced to 15 years on top of the equivalent of 5 he spent behind bars awaiting the outcome of his case.

396

Dany Kane — Part of the Hells Angels' massive underling network for years, he secretly worked with the police for most of the biker war. Near the beginning of the war he worked as a tipster for the RCMP, handing the Mounties information about the Hells Angels for cash. The RCMP dropped him after he was charged with murder in Nova Scotia. He got off in the case and was hired by Quebec's anti–biker gang squad to infiltrate the Hells Angels again. His work was crucial to gathering evidence but he committed suicide before ever having to testify in court.

Daniel (Boteau) Lanthier — A member of the Rockers since April 1994, before the biker war started. He remained an important figure in the underling gang and was part of a committee that ran it. He was part of the group that pleaded guilty on September 23, 2003, and was sentenced to serve 10 years from the day his plea bargain was accepted.

Sylvain Laplante — Joined the Rockers in 1995 after apparently following Gilles (Trooper) Mathieu into the Nomads chapter's vast organization. Before that, Laplante was part of another Hells Angels' puppet gang that operated in western Quebec. He pleaded guilty on September 23, 2003, and was sentenced to serve 10 years from the day his plea bargain was accepted.

Jean-Richard (Race) Larivière — Was made a prospect in the Nomads chapter on December 11, 2000, the same day as Guillaume (Mimo) Serra. Police surveillance on Larivière was one of the keys to unlocking the Nomads chapter's system that managed their millions. In June 2004 he pleaded guilty to conspiracy to commit murder, drug trafficking and gangsterism and received an 18-year sentence.

Pierre (Peanut) Laurin — Joined the Rockers on August 24, 1999, as a drug dealer already well established in Montreal's west end at the time. Was involved in the May 2000 murder of a drug trafficker in Verdun and was made a prospect in the Nomads chapter later that same year. He pleaded guilty to second-degree murder and received a life sentence. He is eligible for parole in 2011.

(Marcos Townsend, The Montreal Gazette)

Bruno Lefebvre — Joined the Rockers in December 1998. Became a prospect in the Nomads chapter on December 11, 2000. He was shot once by accident by a fellow member of the Rockers when they raided a drug den that was controlled by their enemies. He was sentenced, on April 8, 2004, to serve 12 years and 9 months from that date. He has to serve at least half that time before being eligible for parole.

Guy Lepage — A former member of the Montreal Urban Community police who had to resign from the force in the 1970s. He later joined the Rockers and was considered a close associate of Maurice (Mom) Boucher. During the Project Rush investigation the police noticed that Lepage chauffeured Boucher to important meeting with Hells Angels and other drug dealers. He also was making lengthy trips to Colombia which the police later learned were to help arrange cocaine shipments for the Nomads chapter. He was extradited to Florida where he pleaded guilty to drug trafficking and was sentenced to 10 years in September 2002. As part of his plea agreement he was allowed to serve most of his sentence in Canada.

Gilles (Trooper) Mathieu — Became a Hells Angel on December 5, 1980. A constant presence around Boucher when the police were monitoring the gang. He was a founding member of the Nomads chapter in 1995. Was apparently one of the Nomads who decided who among their rivals would be targeted for murder. Mathieu, Mayrand, Houle and a few others were caught looking over photos of their enemies in a hotel suite in 2001. He pleaded guilty on September 23, 2003, and was sentenced to serve 15 years on top of the prison time he already did awaiting the outcome of his trial.

Richard (Dick) Mayrand — Became a member of the Hells Angels on March 1, 1984. Stayed with the gang even though its members killed his brother Michel in an internal purge in 1985. He was not a founding member of the Nomads chapter but joined it later, on January 14, 2000. He was involved in much of the chapter's diplomatic issues as 2000 neared its end. Appeared to be heavily involved in having gangs from Ontario join the Hells Angels en masse and flew to Vancouver apparently just to warn an influential member of the Bandidos from the U.S. that they shouldn't move into Canada. He was convicted of conspiracy to commit murder, drug trafficking and gangsterism in a jury trial. He was sentenced to serve 16 years and 9 months beginning on April 8, 2004. He must serve half that time before being eligible for parole.

Sylvain (Vin Vin) Moreau — Joined the Rockers on August 24, 1999. Before that he was a petty criminal who was often caught trying to pass bad cheques. Before being made a member of the Rockers, he collected drug debts from inmates for the Hells Angels. He was convicted by a jury and sentenced, on April 8, 2004, to 14 years and 9 months. He has to serve at least half the sentence before being eligible for parole.

Peter Paradis — A former member of the Rock Machine who turned informant. He would later testify in the megatrials against the Hells Angels who tried to kill him during the biker war.

Pierre Provencher — A member of the Rockers throughout the biker gang war. As part of his plea bargain he was sentenced to 15 years on September 23, 2003. After factoring in the time he served awaiting the outcome of his case, he had 10 years left to serve.

Normand Robitaille — Joined the Rockers on June 23, 1994. An ambitious young gangster who often paired up with Charlebois in drug trafficking when both were Rockers. Survived at least two attempts on his life during the war. He became a member of the Nomads chapter on October 5, 1998. He pleaded guilty to conspiring to murder rival gang members, drug trafficking and gangsterism on September 23, 2003, and received a 20-year sentence. In March 2005, he saw a year added to the sentence after he was found guilty of hiding the profits of his drug trafficking in real estate.

Michel Rose — Reputed to be an important drug trafficker before he became a prospect in the Nomads chapter on October 5, 1998. He was given his full patch on the chapter's four-year anniversary. On March 8, 2004, he pleaded guilty to a variety of charges and received a 22-year sentence. With the time he served behind bars factored into his sentence, he had 16 years left to serve and will be eligible for parole after serving half of that.

Louis (Melou) Roy — Became a Hells Angel on June 24, 1991. Survived an attempt on his life and beat murder charges after leaving the Trois Rivières chapter and joining the Nomads chapter in 1995. Was last seen alive on June 20, 2000, and is believed to have been purged from the gang.

Guillaume (Mimo) Serra — Was made a prospect in the Nomads chapter on December 11, 2000, just a few months before being arrested in Operation Springtime 2001. Informants would later say Serra brought international savvy to the Nomads chapter and had contacts in foreign countries. He pleaded guilty to conspiracy to commit murder, drug trafficking and gangsterism on September 23, 2003, and was ordered to serve 10 years from that date.

Stéphane Sirois — Joined the Rockers as a drug dealer early on in the biker war. He was forced out of the gang but later returned as an informant. He would secretly record conversations that would be used in the megatrials.

Walter (Nurget) Stadnick — Became a Hells Angel on May 26, 1982. Was once the gang's Canadian national president. He joined Boucher in leaving the Montreal chapter and became a founding member of the Nomads chapter in 1995. An influential figure among the Hells Angels across Canada and described as a key player in helping to spread chapters across Canada. He was convicted by a Quebec Superior Court judge on June 23, 2004. On September 13, 2004, he was sentenced to the equivalent of 20 years — 13 years and 1 month on top of the time he served awaiting the outcome of his trial. Stadnick and his fellow Ontario Hells Angel Donald Stockford were proven to have dealt in more than $11 million worth of cocaine for the gang in a mere matter of months. During that time they were estimated to have made a profit of more than $2 million.

Donald (Pup) Stockford — Became a Hells Angel on May 26, 1993. Like Stadnick, he was a biker from Ontario who was frequently in Montreal during the biker war and joined the Nomads chapter in 1995. He played an important role in convincing Ontario gangs to join the Hells Angels. Worked as a stuntman when he wasn't busy working with the Hells Angels. Like Stadnick, he was convicted by a Quebec Superior Court judge on June 23, 2004. On September 13, 2004, he was sentenced to the equivalent of 20 years — 13 years and 6 months on top of the time he served awaiting the outcome of his trial.

 **André (Toots) Tousignant** — A founding member of the Rockers who was eager to be promoted to the Nomads chapter. He was Maurice (Mom) Boucher's bodyguard and henchman early on in the biker war and took part in the murder of a prison guard in 1997. Tousignant was made a prospect in the Nomads chapter on July 1, 1997. But he disappeared after the Hells Angels learned someone had turned informant in the murder and his body was discovered on February 27, 1998, in the Eastern Townships.